MAKING PEACE WITH THE

BOOKS WRITTEN BY DAVID BURNER

The Politics of Provincialism: The Democratic Party in the 1920s. New York: Knopf, 1967.

A Giant's Strength: America in the 1960s. With Robert Marcus and Thomas R. West. New York: Holt, Rinehart, and Co., 1971.

America: A Portrait in History. With Robert Marcus and Emily Rosenberg. Englewood Cliffs, N.J.: Prentice-Hall, 1974.

A History of Recent America. With Paul K. Conkin. New York: Thomas Y. Crowell, 1974.

Herbert Hoover: A Public Life. New York: Knopf, 1979.

The Torch Is Passed: The Kennedy Brothers and American Liberalism. With Thomas R. West. New York: Atheneum, 1984.

An American Portrait. With Eugene D. Genovese, Forrest McDonald, Pete Seeger, and Thomas R. West. New York: Charles Scribner's Sons, 1987.

Column Right: Conservative Journalists in the Service of Nationalism. With Thomas R. West. New York: New York University Press, 1988.

John F. Kennedy and a New Generation. Boston: Little, Brown, 1989.

Firsthand America: A History of the United States. With Virginia Bernhard, Elizabeth Fox-Genovese, and Stanley I. Kutler. St. James, N.Y.: Brandywine Press, 1991.

BOOKS EDITED BY DAVID BURNER

The Diversity of American Life. New York: Appleton, 1970.

The American Scene. With Robert Marcus. New York: Appleton, 1971.

America since 1945. With Robert Marcus. New York: St. Martin's Press, 1973.

America through the Looking-Glass. With Robert Marcus. Englewood Cliffs, N.J.: Prentice-Hall, 1974.

The American Experience in Education. With John Barnard. New York: New Viewpoints, 1974.

America Personified. With Robert Marcus. New York: St. Martin's Press, 1974.

American Voices. With Robert Marcus. Glenview, Ill.: Scott, Foresman, and Co., 1978.

America Firsthand. With Robert Marcus. New York: St. Martin's Press, 1991.

MAKING PEACE WITH THE

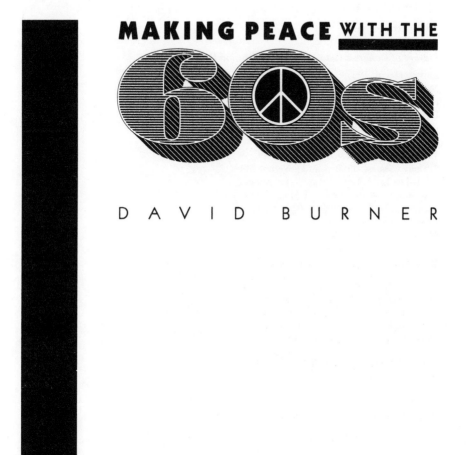

DAVID BURNER

PRINCETON UNIVERSITY PRESS · PRINCETON, NEW JERSEY

Copyright © 1996 by Princeton University Press
Published by Princeton University Press, 41 William Street,
Princeton, New Jersey 08540
In the United Kingdom: Princeton University Press,
Chichester, West Sussex

Library of Congress Cataloging-in-Publication Data
Burner, David, 1937–
Making peace with the 60s / David Burner.
p.   cm.
Includes bibliographical references (p.   ) and index.
ISBN 0-691-02660-2
ISBN 0-691-05953-5 (pbk.)
1. United States—History—1961–1969.
2. United States—Politics and government—
1961–1963.   3. United States—Politics and
government—1963–1969   4. United States—
Social conditions—1960–1980.   I. Title.
E841.B84   1996
973.92—dc20   96-3336

This book has been composed in Sabon

Princeton University Press books are printed
on acid-free paper and meet the guidelines
for permanence and durability of the Committee
on Production Guidelines for Book Longevity
of the Council on Library Resources

Third printing, and first paperback printing,
with corrections, 1998

http://pup.princeton.edu

Printed in the United States of America

10   9   8   7   6   5   4   3

For Thomas R. West

Contents

Introduction

"THE SIXTIES" is among the most evocative of American historical labels. The decimal system cues the public to remember occurrences by the convenience of decades in spite of the obvious truth that events flow with little consideration for the count of ten. But in the case of the 1960s events conspired with that mental habit. President John F. Kennedy was elected in the numerically neat year 1960 and inaugurated in 1961, the first year of the decade. Kennedy's taking of the presidency, along with sit-ins against segregated public accommodations that spread across the South, wheeled the country at a hard angle into a new era. The military frustrations and the moral outcry against President Richard Nixon's invasion of Cambodia in 1970 made clear that the other great issue of the times was going to be resolved: the United States had to get out of Vietnam as expeditiously as possible. From 1961 to 1970 came a ferocity of debate, a challenging of conventions, and a testing of visionary hopes that memory now sums under the phrase "the sixties."

This book examines forces of the era that might have been allies but succeeded in becoming enemies: a civil rights movement that severed into integrationist and black-separatist; a social left and a mainline liberalism that lost a common vocabulary even for arguing with each other; an anti-war activism that divided between advocates of peace and advocates of a totalitarian Hanoi. These were but a few of the rupturings. A period with any life and energy, of course, is going to breed conflicts, which in turn sharpen and further invigorate ideas. But by the end of the sixties conflict turned into mutual destruction. A good reference point for defining the clashing movements of the 1960s is liberalism, which had held latent within itself many, perhaps all, of the antagonistic politics and ideological possibilities. Besides, liberalism in this country has had to do much of the work that in other nations is carried by an articulate, sustained social democratic party. A willingness on the part of liberals more studiously to undertake that task would have made for a more satisfying politics than this country has enjoyed in recent years. Also, much of what today, as a heritage of the sixties, passes for the left wing of liberalism is an encouragement to self-preoccupation at odds with the traditional democratic left. The fortunes of liberalism, then, must be a recurrent subject of this book.

The term "liberalism" as it is employed here refers, as it did during the sixties, to a persuasion founded in the New Deal, leavened by a concern for civil liberties and at least a mild interest in civil rights, trusting to the investigative methods of the academy and the administrative capacities of government, and yet relying to an extent on the good will of popular constituencies gathered during the Great Depression.

Civil liberties rest uneasily with the democracy of which liberals, like conservatives, claim to be guardians. Their defenders are sympathetic to the procedural foundations of democracy, but repelled by such democratic passion as Red-hunting. The connections between government Cold War projects and the scientific and academic communities, staffed in good part by people who considered themselves liberals, compromised academic freedom. But the virtues of self-motivated inquiry claimed by science and the universities made for some champions of civil liberties.

More specifically, liberalism can be observed as ideas in action. The sixties, like any other era but with a special intensity, was a time of a host of ideas struggling for articulation. Establishment liberalism had its ideas, as did the civil rights movement, the counterculture, black power, the Cold War, and several kinds of political radicalism. Ideas directed acts, changed a course of action, and sometimes spun into their own contradictions.

The 1960s were born of a seemingly incompatible parentage: the Kennedy administration and the civil rights movement, one representing the ascendant political and social forces, rational and cosmopolitan, the other embodying a moral renewal that transcended conventions. What the two combined had to offer as complementary opposites were, among the liberals who flocked to the Kennedy presidency, a desire on the part of experts to improve society and, within the rights movement, a determination to transform the terms in which society thought. The Kennedy administration became, in the public mind, a force for transformation. It had an affinity with an age of technological progress that seemed capable of passing from method into magic. That was appropriate to the moment of the rights revolution. So while the space program would dissolve vast physical distance, a walk of a few yards to a drinking fountain would dissolve in an instant the distance that had separated black and white.

The antecedent to the liberalism that came to power with Kennedy in 1961 had done battle, in the time of President Harry Truman and after, with a conservatism that seemed to prize above all else quick emotional satisfactions. Disliking foreign involvements and reluctant to confront the Soviet Union in the earliest days of the Cold War, conservatives dreamed of swift military actions that would rout the communists. During the Korean War they fantasized about bombing China beyond the Yalu River. At home, countless conservatives had sanctioned Red-hunting, which without either heavy expense or great effort brought a pleasurable discharge of anger. Liberals, after some missteps, generally came to prize self-control and emotional constraint. The Cold War, as many of them saw it, should be an exercise in unbounded patience, allowing neither retreat nor rashness, conducted like the finely tempered Berlin Airlift. And in their new President John Kennedy, they had found a symbolic embodiment of crisp coolness and energy under control. The crises of the Cold War during his administration in no way contradicted the liberal relish for the virtues of sobriety and restraint.

The same abhorrence of primitive popular emotions also set liberals against racism. Yet one particular component of the rights movement, the practice of nonviolence, bore a complex relationship to the liberal sensibility.

Nonviolence as civil rights activists lived it, and as the followers of Mohandas Gandhi had lived it in India, was not a simple refraining from violence. Nonviolence was and is a positive discipline in which the practitioners, faced by a mob or hostile police, contain themselves in a veil of calm, neither fleeing nor responding to anger with anger. In common with liberalism, nonviolence seeks a civilized control over passions. Yet nonviolence had its own kind of emotion, emergent in the sixties especially in the southern black evangelical churches and somewhat alien to the ordered world of courts and laws, of science and universities, in which liberals felt most at home.

Every major component of the volatile years that followed had some direct connection or symbolic resonance with these beginnings in establishment liberalism and the civil rights movement. The experiments in style from clothes to mural art, the rock concerts striving for total engagement in the music and the communal experiencing of it, are consonant with the sense of an open future so palpable during the Kennedy and civil rights years. The proliferation in ensuing times of political groups and ideologies as diverse as feminism, gay rights, and deep ecology was a logical expression of energies grown and burst from the movements that had generated them. The escalated American involvement in Vietnam was a berserk application of the pride in technical achievement that had swelled with the first American successes in space.

In the sixties restraints of all sorts shattered. Liberalism helped in that process, and was itself splintered and torn. The bond of humanity to earth had snapped with Sputnik, and John Kennedy's space program further defied it. The bonds of official institutional racism broke because its victims no longer would tolerate them. Conventions of decorum crumbled with the lengthening of men's hair and the shortening of women's skirts. Sit-ins, marches, street theater swept into formal spaces and avenues. Music flooded the air and the times: folk and protest songs, and then hard rock, which in its electronic technology sounded as though it were tapping into the nation's raw physical and social power. The music created and defined a public. Music became a force not only for destruction of conventions but also for cohesion. In whatever way the decade is discussed, the music serves as a soundtrack.

History and politics have not been kind to the 1960s. The Republicans have feasted on the slovenly communes and drug-taking, antiwar actions marked by flag-burnings, sullen student militants, children of the favored classes turning political tantrums into amateur terrorism. They have dined on these delicacies as the Democrats for years gorged themselves on the Great Depression. The civil rights movement in its early years is one major event that still evokes favorable recollections, but even these merge and fade into memories of urban riots and controversial demands for compensatory advantage. Forgotten is the liberation in social customs and behavior that came with the decade and is still with us. Forgotten or recalled with distaste is the widening of the bounds of political discussion, broken out of the staid limits of the fifties, only later to be tucked neatly back into confines that spell security for the comfortable classes. The music alone, or descendants of it, remain as echoes and reminders of a more expansive day.

Yet throughout the decade there was one remarkable absence, as suggestive as the dog in the Sherlock Holmes story that did not bark. Within liberalism and amid the range of ideologies and groups to the left of the liberals, it is almost impossible to discover a major visible movement in the historic American social democratic tradition. It was a heritage that had once flourished among western farmers, Kentucky coal miners, and the militants of Little Steel, and had in the New Deal its most powerful twentieth-century American expression.

In the era of the Great Depression, writers and artists had been drawn to sharecroppers, migrant workers, and union organizers. The attraction risked turning maudlin: *The Grapes of Wrath*, for all its redeeming beauty, is evidence enough of that. But never did middle-class radicals of the earlier period prostrate themselves before representatives of the working classes in the way some white leftists of the 1960s would do before black claimants to revolution. During the 1930s radicals respected the dispossessed, perceiving the unemployed as workers without a job, the uprooted as home-seekers without a home, migrant parents as responsible mothers and fathers who simply had no way at the moment of raising their children in security. It was more typical of the most visible and audible radicals of the late 1960s to define the oppressed as agents and bearers of truths beyond the comprehension of established society, and to do so precisely because they were unable to regard the oppressed as full and productive human beings. Such a view precluded any serious effort to find an equitable ordering of power, property, and work.

It was to be expected that the New Left of the sixties would do battle with the political right. More notable was the rage with which radicals during the course of the decade turned against conventional liberalism.

The numerous causes of that left hostility are reducible to one over-riding fact. Liberals seemed to rule in politics and in the media, yet failed adequately to use their power to advance the purposes that both liberal-ism and the radical left endorsed. They professed, for example, to be ad-vocates of civil rights. Yet the nominally liberal Kennedy administration did not respond quickly to the rights protests in the South. The presum-ably liberal Democratic Convention of 1964 withheld simple unequivo-cal endorsement of the Mississippi Freedom Democratic delegation, rep-resenting the civil-rights insurgency in the state. Though liberals rather than conservatives had been the main prosecutors of the Cold War, many of them repudiated the notion of a monolithic worldwide communist movement. Yet so many of them supported the pointless war in Vietnam. Liberals talked of social justice, but were almost as friendly as conserva-tive Republicans to wealth and privilege. Every opportunity to turn the country toward peace and justice became an opportunity lost, because liberals would not, could not, sufficiently break with the nation's en-trenched ways of thinking and acting. They seemed mountainous in their temperamental immobility. With the expansion of the Vietnam war under Lyndon Johnson the left would come to see them as murderous.

Underlying the particular quarrels between liberals and radicals was a basic difference in temperament and perception. Liberals favored the legal formalities that movement rebels scorned. Liberal thinkers looked confidently to the methods of science and technology. Young radicals were at best ambivalent toward their technological and scientific environ-ment: even as they moved with ease in its more futuristic ambiences, they attacked it as an arm of political and emotional repression. Liberals of philosophical bent were wont to approach even their own convictions with a "Yes, but . . . ," as though the moment of reserve were not only a reasonable check but a fundamentally virtuous act of self-containment. Radicals were more likely to say, "Why not? Why not right now, before one more Vietnamese dies?" Beneath the clashes, then, between liberals and radical insurgents over questions of policy was a fundamental dis-agreement over the character of moral action.

This book begins with the civil rights movement in its phase of nonviolent action during the fifties and early sixties. Both chronology and intellec-tual coherence require this. The civil rights era offers a way of under-standing much of the rest of the decade—both the extraordinary moral and imaginative energy and the many failings of the times. The movement seemed to prove the efficacy of interjecting conscience directly into the public realm without the usual political bargains and compromises. The nonviolent civil rights movement was about as close to moral perfection as American political action has ever come. This statement is not to be taken as hagiography. The rights leaders were as much a collection of squabbling egos as any other group of human beings who find themselves in a position of prominence and heroic endeavor. The moral perfection of the movement was in good measure bestowed on it from the outside by circumstances that encouraged and then sustained the good conduct of the activists. The integrity of the civil rights cause made it a powerful and at the same time deceptive model for later public action.

The perfection of the movement was in part a simple matter of its objective, the overcoming of racism. More precisely, it drew its moral authority from a practice especially equipped for defying racial barriers and inviting even the most virulently racist enemy to recognize their wrongness and obsolescence. A peaceful sit-in was a way of saying to the foe: merely accept my presence at this segregated lunch counter, possibly exchange a courteous word, and you will not be defeated and I victorious; we will both be transformed. And since it was primarily white southern authorities, in their enforcement of segregation, who were in violation of the Constitution, civil disobedience could offer itself as an act in defense of the law. Here, at least, the conscience that in other causes during the era set itself in radical opposition to legal rule appeared to have found a place within establishment American politics.

The spirit in rebellion against rule and law was to reappear throughout the sixties, in protest against rules and formal customs on the campus, in the overturning of sexual and other American mores, and most memorably in sections of the antiwar movement. Even in the face of the most legally declared of wars, which Vietnam was not, the individual who decides that the lives of the victims are worth more than the objectives of the war has to act upon that conviction. But in the time of Vietnam, human beings in rebellion were more clearly at odds with the political process than they had been in the civil rights revolution.

The problem for liberals was that they stood by both the free assertion of conviction and the careful maintenance of laws, institutions, and a well-ordered polity. Between these two advocacies, liberalism was caught and rent to pieces. The sharpest examples were found on the campuses—sharpest partly because these had once been places of the crafting of new social policy. And the university campus for some time had defined itself as being, even in the most conformist of times, a free space for the exchange of ideas. It also identified itself by a set of procedures and courtesies that made that exchange possible. It was as well a place of vast numbers of middle-class students, the sons and daughters of those who had lived the Depression and fought a war for democracy. When students during the sixties demanded a reconstitution of the curriculum, or disrupted a class or a guest lecture, or occupied a building, the liberal academicians faltered in formulating resolute solutions. In their contradictory responses they looked either authoritarian or indecisive. They have never fully recovered from the embarrassments of those days, and the reputation of liberalism in general has suffered.

Issue after issue threw liberals deeper into a quandary. As the American war in Vietnam, which after all had begun as a liberals' war, ripped the nation apart politically, even most disaffected liberals had little traffic with the romanticizing of Hanoi and the Vietcong that bewitched sectors of the antiwar movement. But they could not absent themselves from the movement because of the folly of some of its participants. Nor could they join in the chauvinistic outcries of the right against the puerilities that sometimes accompanied the demonstrations. Black separatists placed liberals in a similar dilemma. In objective and in temper, they were antithetical to liberals. Yet white liberals had accustomed themselves to approaching black Americans with a reticence born of guilt, and they could not bring themselves to a forthright condemnation of the stridency of the separatists.

Still, liberals by the late 1980s, years after their disastrous venture in Vietnam, could argue that they had been vindicated in their perception of the Cold War. In contending that Iron Curtain communism was a mundane, ultimately vulnerable phenomenon, liberalism had been at odds not only with those who thought of communism as the redeemed future but also with rightists who conceived of it as a metaphysical, unchangeable evil. The ultimate liberal warrior was President Truman's secretary of state, Dean Acheson. He had first to construct a diplomatic alliance against the Soviet Union in face of right-wing parsimony and then to continue a policy of confrontation while the same right, confused and emotionally distraught, attacked him as an appeaser. The end of communism in the Soviet Union and Eastern Europe would later prove the prescience of the steely liberal temperament in the conduct of a Cold War that had invited more political anger from the right than from the left. All the same, the damage that the sixties did to liberalism remains.

The revolution of the sixties brought an arrogantly facile notion that the past was irrelevant, the present unique, its new upheavals self-sufficient. Yet the idea that the present is graced, that revelation is immediate, that redemption comes in an instant's openness to it, has long been a major component of Western spirituality in counterpoint to concepts of method and practicality. Numbers of Americans in the 1960s actually believed, for a time, in the possibility of revolutionary change and actually discarded, briefly, the ersatz-tough common wisdom that there will always be wars, that everyone has his price, that reformers are woolly-brained. Like the time of the New Deal, it was a moment when the private soul's ideas joined with the public performance, when stepping outside in the morning was entering a wider drama. Liberals might have drawn on the energy of this moment and offered it the balancing virtues of irony and self-criticism. The momentum in civil rights, the extensions of the welfare state, the transformations that the Second Vatican Council was making in Roman Catholicism, an apparent brightening and sophistication in popular culture all promised a large future for liberalism. Yet liberalism only survived the era divided, confused, and devastated.

This book is selective. It is not a general history of the 1960s. Its choice of topics and its treatment of them aim at extending the interpretation that this introduction has sketched of the temper of liberalism and the character of radicalism.

The examination of the nonviolent phase of the civil rights revolution goes on the assumption that little in the sixties that worked to transcend settled realities would be comprehensible without reference to the rights movement. And the achievement of composure in nonviolence makes for a contrast with the more spontaneous, and of course the drug-induced, forms of transcendence that much of the rebel impulse of the later sixties sought. The discussion of black power serves by contrast to accentuate the virtues of the earlier civil rights movement. The presidency and persona of John Kennedy offer the decade's clearest articulation of technocratic liberalism: mirror image, ally, foe, and victim of the cultural and psychological forces that strove to break through common sense and convention. Looking at the early black movement and the Kennedy administration together should suggest the basic character of the conflicting energies that coursed through the remainder of the era.

Discussion of the counterculture required beginning with some of the Beat authors who preceded the cultural radicals of the sixties. Their sensitivity to the land and to the edges of consciousness itself anticipates certain mental states of the counterculture. The student rebellion is of interest in this book not only for itself but for the ways that it intersected with other phenomena of the time. Some participants quested for the same transformation of experience that the cultural rebels pursued, and occasionally interacted with them; yet the students committed themselves to political organization and political ideas. They were conscious of being trained for elite positions in the technocracy, but wanted control over their skills and a role in overthrowing the corporate and war regime. The thoughtful Port Huron Statement of the early days of Students for a Democratic Society (SDS) captured the best in liberalism and went beyond it. Its call for participatory democracy, in which citizens make decisions in active democratic groupings, accords with what the rights workers were striving to achieve among black Mississippians. The later demands within SDS for ideological conformity meant the abandonment of the personal independence in community that participatory democracy demands, as black power replaced the vision of freedom and equality with the imperative of immersion in blackness.

A commentary on poverty as it was confronted during the decade gives an occasion to reflect on the nation's old habit of shrinking the work ethic to an earnings ethic. That the left of the sixties was unwilling to define a social-democratic alternative to the welfare state was one of the worst failures of the period, as was the inability of liberalism to make a political success of the War on Poverty. The other great failure of the time, the conflict in Vietnam, is examined as another instance of liberal thinking and of the nature of the antiwar movement.

While the chapters herein address main themes, each is also a separate consideration of its particular topic. The book does not deal with every idea of the time, and though the narrative includes events that clarify the ideas or what became of them, it leaves to other historians much of the dense texture of economics, politics, and social life in which ideas happen. So the chapter on the counterculture centers on literature and does not discuss, for example, the sociology of drugs or of communes. The account of Vietnam does not analyze the geopolitics of the Cold War, occupying itself instead with such matters as the fate of the convictions held by Cold War liberals. It is possible, of course, to believe that ideas are the spawn of economic or other forces. But even if this should be the case, isolating some of the ideas that interplay with economics, geopolitics, and personal psychology can aid in understanding.

There had once been, particularly during the interwar years and just after, a composite cultural figure who could be termed the Fighting Liberal. He might be a midwesterner, perhaps a native of one of the old populist or progressive sections, and in photographs on dust jackets he would be in shirtsleeves, exhorting an audience of farmers in overalls. His was the time of a poet like Archibald MacLeish, who sang of the strangeness and newness of being an American on the empty immensity of the continent, the time of the photographers Margaret Bourke-White and Walker Evans, catching in stark images the folk who dwelt on the land in the midst of its Depression-era suffering. The foreign policy of FDR and on through John Kennedy's vocabulary of challenge all carried, arrogantly and yet with a leavening of justice and compassion, the sense that in American democracy lies a goodness that can proudly assert itself abroad, to be mated with its likenesses there.

Liberalism of that grain runs deep in recent American culture. It is not, and perhaps cannot be, the most widely held of persuasions. One of its functions is critical, to be a gadfly of complacencies. And the self-criticism that liberalism encourages makes it as much a burden as a goad against assurance and satisfaction. Advocates of the liberal welfare state, like Franklin Roosevelt or Lyndon Johnson, believe that the good must be constructed and continually reconstructed. They reject the conservative faith in the driftings of the market, and they scorn the Marxist faith in dialectical inevitabilities. However wounded and unsure of itself liberalism may have emerged from the sixties, its New Deal past now freed of some of its more recent fashions may someday regain a confident voice.

 **Sudden Freedom**

Power concedes nothing without a demand;
it never has and it never will.
(*Frederick Douglass, 1858*)

SEGREGATION, sensible people in the South and elsewhere insisted at midcentury, would not yield to demonstrations or to court decrees. On that, President Dwight Eisenhower was of the same mind as Adlai Stevenson, his Democratic party opponent in the elections of 1952 and 1956. You can't legislate morality: so went the inevitable cliché. Americans saw themselves as a people eminently practical in their prosperous economic and political order. Being practical was a matter of ratifying the given, the familiar, the obvious, thinking within the well-established conventions of their country's politics and social relations that appeared to the majority to work so well.

Common sense of this sort sanctions much social evil. In this country it has shielded, among other things, slavery and then segregation. And so what dissolved when black college students sat down at lunch counters reserved for whites, or when the invisible barrier of segregation around a public drinking fountain crumbled, was not only a particular local custom. Vanished also was racial reality itself as people sensible according to their own definition had seen it. And beyond that, civil rights demonstrators were confronting, confusing, and putting to rout the mentality that thinks only by conventions. Much of the rebelliousness of the later 1960s would challenge one or another of the self-satisfied and lethal certainties of political discourse: the abiding conviction, for example, that open resistance to the prosecution of a war is unpatriotic. In this as in many other ways, the rights movement was a prelude to the decade.

It was not only, or even mainly, the physical mixing of races in the South that defied the status quo. The transforming fact, rather, consisted in the way a racial practice was ended. When members of the subject race, instead of waiting for favors from the white caste, simply brushed aside one offensive custom after another, therein began the obliteration of whatever psychological dominance the white community had ever wielded, and whatever sense of mastery it had ever enjoyed.

Nor were most civil rights activists so naive as to see officially decreed segregation as the essence of racial oppression. Segregation was, rather, a component and underpinning in a range of social conditions stretching from inherited poverty to private discrimination in hiring, from the largest institutional arrogance to the slightest personal act of white insolence. Segregation was the most visible instrument of white supremacy, and in denying access to the economic resources that whites monopolized it was among the most effective. The 1954 decision of the Supreme Court in *Brown v. Board of Education of Topeka* explicitly defined segregation as illegal in public schools, and the implications of the Court's reasoning defined it as illegal whenever state or local government imposed it on public accommodations. Later in the 1960s, as segregation in public spaces was becoming obsolete, the rights movement would confront racial injustice in its more stubbornly entrenched economic and social forms.

The sit-ins and other assaults on segregation were not merely a means to an end, as a federal law against racial custom can be a means to its defeat. They were at once means and end: the instant that black and white demonstrators sat together at a lunch counter, the counter was integrated. Such demonstrations were radical in their simple directness, and constituted an assertion of conscience over rule and custom, which frightens people. And they were acts of nonviolence, which challenge common expectations about human behavior.

Yet the concept of nonviolence, drawn in part from the teachings of the Indian leader Mohandas Gandhi, grafted itself onto the civil rights movement from the outside. The Gandhian approach included a sequence of investigation, negotiation, publicity, and ultimately widespread peaceful demonstration and resistance. Gandhi had been able to call out a massive following against a small occupation force and its native cohorts, and he had fashioned a complex philosophy of peace and cooperation within a culture and spirituality distinctively Indian. To adapt his ideas to the American mind required a good deal of distillation. A few groups and individuals with a principled commitment to nonviolence took that idea to the rights movement, and the rank and file accepted, though tentatively and skeptically.

Insofar as white supremacy, like any other form of injustice, is violent in its affront to human dignity, the practice of nonviolent resistance was a fitting response. It addressed the urge to violence that dwelt within both demonstrators and opponents. But the fusion of nonviolence with the issue of racial justice was by no means inevitable, as the black power

movement of the later sixties was to demonstrate. Practitioners of nonviolence, moreover, called for enforcement of the Constitution and
sought federal civil rights legislation; and in the final event, of course, the
law and the Constitution have the backing, armed if necessary, of the
power of the government. For most rights activists nonviolence was more
tactic than spiritual absolute—a tactic, to be sure, morally superior to the
employment of force, an enactment of the best possibilities within human
nature, but dispensable if other means should prove more efficacious.

Fundamental to the civil rights movement in the South, and long-
steeped in the practice of nonviolence, was an institution venerable, dura-
ble, integral to African American culture. The black church—its presence
crystallized in the leadership of ministers such as Martin Luther King, Jr.,
in Montgomery and Fred Shuttlesworth in Birmingham, Alabama, and,
beginning in 1957, King's Southern Christian Leadership Conference
(SCLC)—could pronounce the judgment of the Judeo-Christian tradition
against hatred, against rejection of the stranger. The church could and did
define an ethic of peaceful resistance and prescribe appropriate behavior.
It supplied a formidably large membership ready to be mobilized in a
good cause. It provided meeting places, organizing experience, fundraising, charismatic leaders. Many urban churches were financially solid,
and their ministers were among the few southern blacks who were not
beholden to white society for their income and security. So the southern
black churches—those not too timid to help—were an essential institutional as well as spiritual base of the civil rights movement in the fifties
and the early sixties, in time bringing in as well many northern Christians
and Jews.

Southern black colleges were another important center of the movement from its beginnings, and many of the civil rights leaders had graduated from Fisk, Howard, Tuskegee, Virginia Union, Spelman, or Morehouse. Other black leaders had acquired significant experience and
motivation as labor union members during and after World War II.

Among the organizations more specifically designed to work for equal
rights, the most visible was the National Association for the Advancement of Colored People (NAACP), established early in the century and
enjoying the support of white liberals. The Urban League addressed the
concrete problems of black city dwellers. Also present within the civil
rights movement were groups philosophically to the left. These included
the pacifist Fellowship of Reconciliation, religious but under no denomi-
national control, its World War II offspring and ally the Congress of Racial Equality (CORE), the American Friends Service Committee, and the
War Resisters League. Radicals of this kind have occupied a special place
within the American ideological spectrum: leftist, but with no dogmatic

orientation; aiming less at creating a mass movement than at speaking to the mind and conscience of the individual. In their freedom from rigid and elaborate doctrine, they were similar to liberals.

Another ally of the rights movement was the Highlander Folk School in eastern Tennessee, founded by the southern social activist Myles Horton. Highlander, with an advisory board that had included Eleanor Roosevelt, Norman Thomas, and Reinhold Niebuhr, since the 1930s had been holding workshops in which participants could share and develop ways to realize social renovation. Rosa Parks attended the integrated Highlander for two weeks before her historic act of defiance that launched the Montgomery bus boycott. King spoke there in 1957 and was photographed next to a *Daily Worker* reporter, giving segregationists their evidence, later broadcast across the South on billboards, that the minister was a subversive. One Highlander project during the late fifties, the seeding of citizenship schools throughout the South, instructed the poor in their rights and in registering to vote.

The main antagonist of the civil rights movement was, of course, white racism. Yet a more complex encounter took place between the rights movement, especially in its practice of nonviolent resistance, and mainline American liberalism. Though many liberal politicians had not made the race issue a major concern, they along with more highly principled liberals agreed on the evil of racist institutions. Nonviolence, too, could claim common ground with liberal intellectuals, who have a persistent antagonism toward both personal violence and armed instruments of coercion, along with a trust in the supposedly dispassionate methods of education and science. But nonviolence as spiritual witness is leagues away from the mentality of liberals, ideological and political alike, who are most at home with the worldly vocabulary of law and education and the compromises of government.

The civil rights rebellion had begun years before—centuries before, if measured from the first escape from slavery, or the first slave uprising. Perhaps as good a date as any for the onset of the more recent rights era is 1941, the year when the black union leader A. Philip Randolph planned a march on Washington demanding desegregation in the armed forces and an end to racial discrimination in defense industries. The march was aborted a week before it was to get under way when President Franklin Roosevelt created a Fair Employment Practices Commission, though this was destined to disappoint its advocates. During the 1940s in the Winston-Salem tobacco industry and in Detroit automobile factories, CIO unions nurtured among black workers a militancy that challenged white supremacy even as it also confronted management. In 1947 Harry Truman became the first American President to address the NAACP, and he asked Congress for a federal antilynching law. His government panel report, "To Secure These Rights," brought the phrase "civil rights" into wide usage and created an agenda much in advance of public opinion. Truman also ordered the desegregating of the armed forces, a process that took over a decade. In the presidential campaign of 1948 Truman, though a border-state politician of no very liberal profile, was unsuccessfully opposed on his right by a breakaway southern segregationist faction of the Democratic party, the States Rights party, or Dixiecrats. By 1948 the white supremacist South had reason to worry, more than it knew.

For decades civil rights organizations had been working within American legal institutions, cooperating with liberals engaged in efforts to change the nation's laws. In a series of court cases, lawyers of both races—notably Thurgood Marshall, later to be the first black appointed to the Supreme Court—argued against public school segregation. Then the Reverend Oliver Brown, pastor of the Saint Mark African Methodist Episcopal Church in Topeka, Kansas, filed a suit against the city's board of education, which required his nine-year-old daughter, Linda, to take a long bus ride to an all-black school when a white one was close to her home. The landmark unanimous Supreme Court decision in the *Brown* case declared that "separate educational facilities are inherently unequal" and therefore unconstitutional. The following year the Court added that the desegregation of public schools must be accomplished "with all deliberate speed." It was a triumph especially for the NAACP, which had conducted the litigation.

In its decision the Court had drawn on evidence from research in psychology indicating that segregation in itself, quite apart from the quality of the facilities provided, implanted a sense of shame and inferiority in black children, who could see that the white majority was shunning and excluding them. That, conservatives such as William F. Buckley, Jr., countered, is irrelevant. The Constitution does not traffic in personal psychological states, and requires only formal, outward, institutional equality—which in the question at hand would mean, contrary to southern practice, the spending of a proportionally equal educational sum on each race. But the Court concluded in *Brown* that if the whole, steady, and measurable effect of a legal institution is to do mental harm to a portion of society, constitutional interpretation must take as much account of the fact as if it were dealing with a clearly announced intention to do harm.

For all its sweep, *Brown* was a decorously conducted court case, an argument among members of the country's legal elite over application of its fundamental law. After *Brown* the civil rights demonstrators challenging the South's segregationist practices, which had the support of the local police, could insist that even in their acts of civil disobedience it was they who were the law-abiding citizens, enforcing the Constitution.

But civil disobedience essentially makes a claim of an opposite kind: it presupposes that conscience must obey not statutory or constitutional law but a higher moral law. The legal battle for integration, then, awakened a way of thinking and a method of resistance that in time would defy even law deemed valid under the Constitution. The best-known figure in that dialogue between conscience and the law is Martin Luther King, Jr.

King had decided early in life to follow the career of his father, one of Atlanta's leading Baptist ministers, known for the eloquence of his oratory and his skill in negotiating. Graduated from Morehouse College at the age of nineteen, King earned a baccalaureate in divinity and placed at the top of his class at Crozer Seminary, near Philadelphia. A polite liberal establishment, Crozer was a racially mixed school that employed only white maids. King's favorite theologian, and a favorite at Crozer, was Walter Rauschenbusch, who had argued early in the century for a Christian ethos of social reform. Also prominent in the curriculum at Crozer were the works of the liberal theologian Harry Emerson Fosdick. And King read Reinhold Niebuhr, who recommended the application of Gandhi's practices to the American Negro. Crozer prepared King for a life of respectable ministry in a liberal Protestant tradition. In 1955 King completed a doctoral dissertation in systematic theology at Boston University that would later be found to have involved plagiarism from another scholar. Meanwhile, he had married Coretta Scott, a graduate of Antioch College attending the New England Conservatory of Music.

Returning to the South in the mid-1950s, King became pastor of the upper middle-class Dexter Avenue Baptist Church in Montgomery, Alabama. King's plans for the church included cultural and educational activities of a secular and urban nature; one of his own favorite composers was Donizetti, and he disdained southern church music. He combined, in sum, southern evangelicalism with genteel northern liberalism, believing with his fellow liberals in the redeeming influence of schooling and high culture. His conservative dress and demeanor would please *Time* magazine, as did his support for Eisenhower in 1952.

Montgomery in 1955 was a more tolerant city than others in its time and region. Its mayor had enjoyed some black support in his contest for office, and his regime appointed a number of blacks to the police force. On December 1, Rosa Parks, a seamstress who was also a longtime secretary of the local NAACP, refused to give up her bus seat to a white passenger. Montgomery's bus ordinance, under which blacks could be forced to pay at the front and then board at the back, provided that between the rear portion of each bus reserved for black passengers and the front portion for whites would lie a midsection open to both. There, as occasion required, seating was to be administered in such a way as to keep the races separate. Drawing on local custom and police support, a driver might force as many as a row of black people to stand up in order that a single white person could be seated. Mrs. Parks was in that mid-section when asked to move. Her act fitted with the plans of the NAACP and the local Woman's Political Council, a black civic group, to challenge the bus policy, but she had spontaneously seized the occasion. The police arrested Mrs. Parks, and she soon lost her job in a downtown department store and could find no other full-time work. The black militant Eldridge Cleaver later wrote of that day: "Somewhere in the universe a gear in the machinery had shifted." In 1953 Baton Rouge was the site of a short and partially successful bus boycott, essentially against Louisiana state offi-cials rather than the more yielding city government. As long ago as 1941 there had been a triumphant Harlem bus boycott, organized by Congress-man Adam Clayton Powell to force the hiring of black drivers. But the result of the arrest of Mrs. Parks was a bus boycott that would be instru-mental to the peaceful black rebellion of later years.

Much of the planning and execution of the Montgomery boycott was by the Woman's Political Council led by Jo Ann Gibson Robinson, a local college teacher who, after Mrs. Park's arrest, mimeographed tens of thou-sands of leaflets urging blacks not to ride the buses. The black community also looked to E. D. Nixon, longtime head of the locals of both the NAACP and the Brotherhood of Sleeping Car Porters, who would raise money for the boycott from the United Auto Workers (Dr. King, still the genteel liberal, found Nixon somewhat rough-hewn). Black activism in Montgomery had its genesis in minor political gains already made throughout the South as well as in the hope, spurred by the *Brown* deci-sion, that forms of segregation outside the schools might also crack. Though the specific planning had taken place among the city's black women, leadership still fell, here as elsewhere, to the ministers of black churches.

At a critical meeting King, a newcomer who had attracted no enemies in town, demonstrated his oratorical skill and won the leadership of the boycott. Having taken no important part in creating it and showing the hesitancy that might be expected of a moderate liberal, King became leader almost by default. He doubtless did feel strongly about segrega-tion: he was to recall a trip home from an oratorical contest as a youth when a bus driver demanded that he and his teacher give up their seats to whites: "When we didn't move right away, [I] got up and stood in the aisle the whole 90 miles to Atlanta. . . . I don't think I have ever been so deeply angry in my life." Yet over and again in his career, King was to show an innate caution—tactically choosing not to disobey a federal court injunction, hoping for incremental progress, avoiding the making of enemies wherever possible—therein reflecting the essential temper of American liberalism itself.

In the first days after Mrs. Parks's arrest, the representatives of black Montgomery made a minimal proposal: continue segregated seating, but let a bus fill with the black patrons starting at the back and the whites at the front, until whatever proved to be the encounter point. The protesters also called for more courteous service and the hiring of black bus drivers on predominantly black routes. But the city refused the seating plan and foolishly canceled service in black neighborhoods—a gratuitous contribution to the militancy of black Montgomery. There followed the prolonged boycott of the city's buses that is now legend.

The boycott, coordinated by the Montgomery Improvement Association, included systematic carpooling. Police made a point of ticketing motorists for mild or nonexistent traffic violations. Under dubious legalisms, the city also made mass arrests of participants, including King. These became for the black population a liberating experience, turning into a celebration a procedure that before had meant a fearsome subjection to the white man's power. Harassment by police and city officials, along with more primitive expressions of white anger, made the boycott a perfect occasion for the practice of nonviolent resistance. And that it became.

Many individuals and groups influenced King toward principled nonviolence. In an address on November 10, 1955, at Hampton Institute in Virginia, Harris Wofford, a white graduate of Howard University and later one of John Kennedy's advisers on civil rights, had discussed the applicability of the ideas of Gandhi to the fight for racial justice. E. D. Nixon shared with King a copy of the talk. As the boycott proceeded, Bayard Rustin, black executive secretary of the War Resisters League, came to Montgomery with Glen Smiley, a white Texas minister, who was field secretary of the pacifist Fellowship of Reconciliation. They were to urge upon the demonstrators in Montgomery the philosophy of nonviolent action. Initially there was some scattered violence in support of the boycott. A few black snipers fired on the buses, and a pregnant black woman was shot in each leg for taking the bus. King, his own life threatened and his house bombed by whites, stationed armed guards around his home and applied for a permit to carry a gun. But on the whole the principle of nonviolence held. In January 1956 the Supreme Court upheld a federal court ruling that the city's bus ordinance was unconstitutional.

King accurately described the Montgomery resistance as being a mere withdrawal of cooperation with an evil system. The main action of the Montgomery protesters had not been disobedience. Blacks simply refrained from riding the buses, an act outwardly as conventional as that of any customer who stops buying an unsatisfactory product or service; participating motorists offered prearranged rides, a gesture of impeccable legality. Yet the spirit and method of noncooperation transcended the technicalities of carpooling and evoked the Christianity of the drivers,

their passengers, and the walkers, all of whom had to confront city officials determined to treat them as lawbreakers, or at the least as disreputa-
ble elements. Attending the boycott meetings and not riding the buses
became as much a religious duty as going to church. Insofar as the intention of the segregation ordinance had been to humble the black and exalt
the white community, the very fact of black defiance made it an anach-
ronism, a shell, a fossil, a self-mocking ruin. That was a point of civil
disobedience wherever it was to appear: withdraw cooperation from a
custom, and it at once loses its power over you; join with enough others
in disobedience and it ceases to exist.

Defiance on a large scale by black southerners portended the end of
state-enforced white supremacy. In the mid-1950s the question remained
of whether the executive branch of the federal government would break
with its customary reluctance to confront states when they violated the
Constitution. The affirmative answer came from a leader vastly different
in both temper and station from Montgomery's minister-prophet.

Deeply conservative in his commitment to preservation of the established order, as stolidly noncommittal in public as King was eloquent and
oratorical, President Dwight D. Eisenhower did not publicly support
Brown during the three years following its promulgation, warning instead against "extremism" on both sides. But upon the Supreme Court's
invalidating of segregated schooling in the District of Columbia, Eisenhower pressed quickly for desegregation of the city's schools. He also
greatly increased black representation on the White House staff, appointed the Reverend Theodore Hesburgh of Notre Dame head of the
new federal Civil Rights Commission, and completed the desegregation
of the military. Eisenhower's office along with his conservatism obliged
him to enforce the Constitution, and doubtless his temperament recoiled
from the crudity of the worst racist practices. Events at Little Rock, Arkansas, would put his reticent disposition to the test.

There, at the start of the autumn 1957 term of public schools, Governor Orval Faubus, defying a federal court order, called out the state's
National Guard to prevent a handful of black students from entering
white school grounds. His act was one instance of the massive southern
opposition that *Brown* had sparked even as it also fired integrationist
activism. Faubus insisted that the public peace was in danger; white
mobs, encouraged by his own resistance to the students' admission, gave
credibility to his claim. President Eisenhower ultimately put the Guard
under federal authority, exercising a power granted to him by the Constitution. Thereby for the first time since Reconstruction came a federal
armed intervention in the South, a precedent-breaking warning by the
government that the southern states would not enjoy continued immunity
from obedience to the Constitution. Soldiers who had been keeping black

students from entering Central High School now intervened to assure their admission. To strengthen the federal presence Eisenhower sent in one thousand paratroopers and hundreds of conspicuous FBI observers; he also put ten thousand more military on standby alert. With bayonets fixed, the troops stood outside the school, holding off an angry mob of some eight hundred whites, and for months the soldiers protected black children attending classes. Eisenhower justified his use of the military— which Senator Richard Russell of Georgia likened to an act of Hitler's storm troopers—with an explanation that reflected his distaste for abrupt and sweeping measures. It was meant to aid, in the President's mind, not any particular social policy but the enforcement of the law.

It is difficult today, after the federal initiatives of the 1960s, to realize that for nearly eighty years before Little Rock the United States government, out of caution or indifference, had avoided any confrontation with southern racial injustice. (President Herbert Hoover had once contemplated a scheme for the quick movement of national troops against lynch mobs, but his attorney general rejected the idea on constitutional grounds.) Liberals were cautious: the *New Republic* in 1956 recommended dropping "the emotional race issue" from the political campaign. Eisenhower's intervention not only advanced integration directly but confirmed what the *Brown* ruling had already heralded: that national governmental institutions were now disposed to act in the interests of racial justice. The decision of a conservative President in defense of the Constitution and the courts, a decision resting on established forms and procedures, it belongs to the story of a movement that would later bear prophetic witness against forms, procedures, and establishments.

The city that housed a federal government finding its way into issues of civil rights symbolized the mixture of old patterns and new ways. The District of Columbia, still something of a southern town, was quietly ruled by commissioners appointed by Congress; its citizens did not possess the vote, even on local issues. Though much of the population was black, white Washingtonians thought of their city as white. Black women took buses to comfortable suburbs to cook and clean for white people who thought that their own kind, and their kind alone, counted for something. The District was changing, but with a decorous slowness. A few years earlier, demonstrations by black Washingtonians demanding enforcement of a Reconstruction-era congressional law had achieved some integration of public establishments.

Such was the relatively liberal capital of a nation that in its backwaters was not many social generations removed from slavery. In Mississippi two years before Little Rock a black youth named Emmett Till visiting the South from Chicago had apparently touched a white woman on the shoulder and called her "baby," and thereupon was murdered, his body

thrown into the Tallahatchie River. An all-white jury acquitted the defendants. But by the end of the 1950s, local black activist organizations,
notably churches and NAACP chapters, laced the South. In some cities
brief formal defiance of segregated public transportation met with pro
forma resistance from local governments. Sit-ins dotted the upper portion
of the region. Those at Greensboro, North Carolina, in 1960 began the
phase of continuing nationwide attention, nourishing the movement and
attracting the attention of future rights leaders like John Lewis, Robert
Parris Moses, and Stokely Carmichael. In the next several years surveys
found that the American public considered the race problem the most
important issue facing the nation. Soon some young white people, joining
a growing nonviolent army of blacks, were breaking out of their comfortable middle-class existence and entering a more purposeful life in the
struggle for civil rights. Southern white liberals, having encountered a
movement that forced them to choose between regional loyalties and
their consciences, between their doubts and their hopes about social
change, were among the liberated as desegregation made its halting way
across the region.

King, who moved to Atlanta in 1957, had risen to preeminence in the
civil rights movement. Virginia Durr, a white civil rights activist living in
Montgomery, wrote that he had captured the "devotion of the masses of
Negroes. . . . My wash lady tells me every week about how she hears the
angel's wings when he speaks." Through the remainder of his life he
would occupy a position of symbolic and at times strategic primacy. But
on Monday, February 1, 1960, an event occurred that would accelerate
the civil rights movement into a relentless, unbroken assault on racism.
Stretching far beyond King's Southern Christian Leadership Conference,
the movement's confrontations and setbacks and victories would now be
reported in the press like dispatches from the battlefield.

On that day the relatively progressive city of Greensboro was still segregated, and at the local Woolworth's department store lunch counter
four freshman from the black North Carolina Agricultural and Technical
College requested service and did not get their orders. Ezell Blair, Jr.,
David Richmond, Franklin McCain, and Joseph McNeil were younger
than the youthful American revolutionaries of the 1770s. Their carefully
planned revolutionary act was polite; customers in range of the lunch
counter noted their neat clothes and grooming. To all appearances they
were normal American college students straight out of the 1950s. One of
them, reflecting the times, employed Cold War rhetoric to justify his act,
suggesting that racial justice at home would enhance their nation's struggle against communism in the Third World. Some years later, another as
a veteran of the Vietnam war would heatedly defend his country's engagement in that conflict.

After leaving Woolworth's they formed a circle on the sidewalk and said the Lord's Prayer. Their return the next day with some thirty fellow students brought national press media attention. On the third day, there were sixty-three. An elderly white woman seeking the white ladies' room encountered two black girls and exclaimed, eyes wide with alarm, "Nigras, Nigras everywhere!" On Thursday three white students from North Carolina Women's College joined the sit-ins. After that white youths mobbed the aisles and heckled the demonstrators, and in a mild departure from the original character of the event the A&T football team confronted gangs who waved Confederate flags. "Who do you think you are?" asked an angry white. "We the Union army," a player responded.

On Friday, with more than three hundred students participating, the movement started to spread to other stores, and within a few days it had traveled to other cities. In response to Greensboro, the sit-ins in two months had invaded a total of fifty-four segregated establishments in nine southern states. The activists, most of them young, black, and unknown, but including many whites, were effectively taking leadership of the civil rights movement from slightly older, elite figures. John F. Kennedy, increasingly an inspiration to youth, endorsed the sit-ins during that year's presidential campaign.

The civility of the Greensboro demonstrations did not reassure respectable southerners. North Carolina's governor, Luther Hodges, soon to be appointed secretary of commerce in the Kennedy administration, told the press that the sit-ins threatened law and order. The chancellor of the Women's College, having persuaded the female demonstrators to refrain from further participation, convened a meeting with local black colleges that, after Woolworth's temporarily closed its doors, resulted in an unproductive truce. Moral privileges, a Greensboro business leader explained, could not "be obtained by force or intimidation, but must be secured through the medium of orderly negotiations, reason and mutual respect." It took a resumption of the demonstrations to desegregate the Woolworth's lunch counter.

Though the Greensboro actions came of their own initiative rather than at the direction of the Southern Christian Leadership Conference, they were in no way aimed at challenging the position of King and his peers in that body. But the energies that they released within the movement were consonant with the urgings of Ella Baker, a Shaw University valedictorian of the 1920s. She attacked King's organization for its "glory-seeking," its "arrogant" male ministers, and its middle-class mentality. Urging participation in the movement by the mass of blacks, male and female, after Greensboro she took a major part in forming as a counterpoise to King's influence the Student Nonviolent Coordinating Committee (SNCC—pronounced "snick"), democratic in structure and youthful in staffing. Insisting that the civil rights movement had "made Martin," she argued that the SCLC was merely an expression rather than a shaper of southern black protest. King, nonetheless, was a natural leader, no mere creation of the movement. Ella Baker's distrust of King's leadership foreshadowed a later phase of SNCC's development.

At the moment, however, the quarrels among rights leaders were invisible to the public. The movement sped into 1961 with the Freedom Rides, dispatching bus riders through most of the southern states to test racial discrimination in bus stations used in interstate travel. James Farmer, the first black national director of the Congress of Racial Equality, contributed his organization's years of experience with techniques of direct action. The members of CORE, most of them white, were the first American practitioners of nonviolence in the cause of civil rights. As early as World War II the group held sit-ins in the North, and in 1947 eight blacks and eight whites journeyed throughout the upper South testing acquiescence in a Supreme Court ruling against segregated buses engaged in interstate transportation. Now the Freedom Rides pushed CORE briefly into the forefront of nonviolent confrontation.

The riders, while themselves maintaining strict nonviolence, left behind a long trail of violence they suffered at the hands of southern whites, including the burning of a bus and the beating of its passengers just outside Anniston, Alabama. Politically uneasy with the race question and concerned as any government leader would be with public peace and orderly procedure, President John F. Kennedy would have preferred to see the Freedom Riders stay at home. But when Klansmen greeted riders on a bus arriving in Birmingham—an incident in which John Siegenthaler, an observer from the Justice Department, was beaten unconscious—Washington was forced into action. Attorney General Robert Kennedy, the President's brother, told the Birmingham office of the Greyhound Bus Company to get in touch with "Mr. Greyhound" and said in words quoted widely throughout the South: "I am—the Government is—going to be very much upset if this group does not get to continue their trip." The government sent four hundred federal marshals to the Montgomery bus terminal to protect that contingent of Freedom Riders and obtained an injunction against the Klan and other groups that were interfering with the rides (although in Jackson, Mississippi, Washington allowed the state government to arrest and jail the riders—this was in return for Mississippi's agreement not to leave the demonstrators to the mercy of the mob). In Montgomery federal marshals, whom Governor George Wallace threatened to arrest, gave King protection after white-racist rioting surged outside the Reverend Ralph Abernathy's Baptist church where he was speaking. In further response to the turmoil, the attorney general requested that the Interstate Commerce Commission ban segregation in bus terminals that served interstate passengers. By November 1, 1961, the prohibition was in effect; it achieved immediate compliance in many places and began a process that would eventually end all discrimination in public transport.

From the fall of 1961 through the summer of 1962, rights efforts stalled in Albany, Georgia. Black demonstrators there learned something of the limits of nonviolence. King told a gathering assembled at Shiloh Baptist Church: "Don't stop now. Keep moving. Don't get weary. We will wear them down with our capacity to suffer." Activists filled the jails. But the shrewd Albany police chief Laurie Pritchett confined most of them in neighboring towns, where they were nearly invisible, and schooled his force in the same methods of nonviolence the demonstrators employed. Among his tactics was to get down on his knees and pray with the demonstrators, then arrest them. He thereby deprived the demonstrators of the scenes of white-supremacist violence, enacted before the national media, that his less sophisticated southern compatriots elsewhere so happily supplied.

Meanwhile, another drama had been playing itself out on the nation's university campuses. As early as 1956, Autherine Lucy made a courageous attempt to become the first black student at the University of Alabama. After campus rioting, the university forced her to leave. Then, in 1961, Charlayne Hunter (now the television newswoman Charlayne Hunter-Gault) along with Hamilton Holmes successfully entered the University of Georgia, surviving both mob violence and official maneuvering. In September 1962, Governor Ross Barnett of Mississippi attempted to prevent James Meredith, a twenty-nine-year-old Air Force veteran, from enrolling at the University of Mississippi as its first black student. The Kennedy administration then obtained the governor's apparent agreement to use state troopers to keep order. But Barnett reneged, forcing the Kennedys to send to the campus more than a thousand soldiers, national guardsmen, and federal marshals; in a night of rioting at Ole Miss one reporter and a local white man were killed, thirty-five marshals shot, 340 other people injured, and two hundred arrested. After Meredith's difficult success came the enrollment at the University of Alabama, in 1963, of Vivian Malone and James Hood. In opposition, Governor George Wallace—who in his gubernatorial inaugural address that year had proclaimed "Segregation now, segregation tomorrow, segregation forever"—stood in the doorway of a campus building, a symbolic gesture having nothing practical to do with impeding entrance.

In 1963 the rights movement found in Police Commissioner Bull Conner of Birmingham, Alabama, the ugly opponent that Albany's astute Laurie Pritchett had declined to be. The Reverend Fred Shuttlesworth was speaking for a local movement demanding that downtown department store owners integrate their establishments and hire black clerks. Birmingham, the most segregated large city in the United States, was so tense that Shuttlesworth carried a gun in the trunk of his car. King entered the battle when white business leaders backed out of agreements to work for racial progress. With the local organization in danger and SCLC's credibility at stake, King joined a campaign that faced enormous difficulties. Alabama's Governor Wallace was moving into the leadership of white racism both north and south. The black community of Birmingham hesitated to engage in any radical action, fearing divisions in its own midst and uncertain of the ability of its leaders to control the angrier of the city's blacks, some of whom were near to rioting. Yet by 1963 the civil rights movement was looking toward larger assaults, confidently riding momentum and simultaneously needing to sustain it.

Arrested and held in a Birmingham jail for defying a court order to desist from demonstrating, King wrote to white clergymen who had warned that protests in the city were "untimely, unwise, unnecessary, and illegal." His letter, now regarded as a classic statement of the ethos of civil disobedience, is a passionate claim for conduct that is at once nonviolent and uncompromising. In face of the unyielding brutality of Birmingham's white supremacist regime, King told his colleagues: "[We] had no alternative except to prepare for direct action, whereby we would present our very bodies as a means of laying our case before the conscience of the local and the national community." The Negro's great stumbling block in his stride toward freedom, King observes, "is not the White Citizen's Councils or the Ku Klux Klansmen but the white moderate, who is more devoted to 'order' than to justice; . . . who constantly says: 'I agree with you in the goal you seek, but I cannot agree with your method of direct action'; who paternalistically thinks he can set the timetable for another man's freedom." He warns that if white ministers refuse to support the nonviolent actions of the movement, "millions of Negroes will . . . seek solace and security in black nationalist ideologies—a development that would inevitably lead to a frightening racial nightmare."

What happened in Birmingham during the spring of 1963 vividly impressed and frightened President Kennedy. Bull Conner's fire hoses—carrying a hundred pounds of water pressure per square inch, capable of taking the bark off trees at ninety feet—flattened rows of black protesters. Police used electrically charged cattle prods on demonstrators. Once more, segregationists acted with gratuitous brutality, setting police dogs on demonstrating children, some of whom were bitten. A simple and moving *Saturday Evening Post* cover by Norman Rockwell, best known for sentimental portrayals of the nation as a land of virtuous and comfortable small towns, shows a little black girl dressed in her very best clothes, standing by a wall darkened by the shadow of a snarling dog.

With a tactical stupidity worthy of their ideology, racists managed to offend even the keepers of the country's white middle-class perceptions of itself. Thousands of peaceful demonstrators went to jail, but for the first time hundreds of blacks fought back in an uprising that finally caught the attention of President Kennedy.

Proclaiming that demonstrations could no longer be conducted with order and safety, President Kennedy in a national address on June 11 warned of the "fires of frustration and discord . . . burning in every city, North and South, where legal remedies are not at hand." Meanwhile, after rioting in downtown Birmingham, Kennedy had sent three thousand federal troops to bases close to Birmingham in case the city should erupt. His call for a civil rights bill to end segregation in most "places of public accommodation" at last threw the mantle of the national administration, the Democratic party, and the liberal community over these early goals of the civil rights movement. Disobedience to local rule, even though in the name of the Constitution, had called forth the support of its moral opposite: the procedures and remedies of government. And the aid that these gave to civil rights further encouraged the nonviolent rebellion of the rights activists. Liberalism and a movement that defied the normal terms of liberalism were circling each other warily but ever more tightly.

While Birmingham was to public view a near theater of war, another much less dramatic story was unfolding behind the scenes. Birmingham blacks were discovering an unlikely ally in their midst: white southern businessmen who wanted economic growth and realized that their city would have to prove itself respectable to the national corporations capable of providing it. That meant keeping Birmingham tranquil, and it meant compromising on the hiring of blacks. Thereby the city made itself part of a national establishment of business and government that in the South as elsewhere was beginning to commit itself at least to the more seemly and formal of social and economic rights. Money and perhaps a sense of responsible stewardship had outweighed the maintaining of southern race traditions.

By the end of summer, however, Birmingham was still a tense city. And on Sunday, September 15, a bomb at the black Sixteenth Street Baptist Church killed four young girls. In this worst of moments in the rights movement, riots broke out in the city, and two more blacks were killed. Still, Birmingham whites showed a degree of remorse; and while at the funeral on September 18 for three of the girls no elected officials appeared, among the eight thousand in attendance were eight hundred black and white Birmingham pastors. It is doubtful that any other single event did so much to make white supremacy of the old blatant kind an object of revulsion throughout the country.

Political caution, along with doubts about the pace and tactics of the rights movement, had kept President Kennedy hesitant in his early responses, and the distance between the administration and the activists remained wide. In a telling incident in 1963, Attorney General Robert Kennedy met in New York City with a number of black literary and political figures in an archetypical confrontation between white liberals and black intellectuals. Kennedy probably came to the meeting reasonably full of good will and prepared to talk about what the government was doing for the civil rights movement. What he received was an afternoon of lectures on how little the administration was actually doing and implicitly on the inability of Robert Kennedy in particular to understand the movement. As early as February 1963 Robert was urging the President to permit temporary registrars to sign up voters in the deep South: yet the government was putting more resources into prosecuting the labor racketeer Jimmy Hoffa than into the civil rights division of the Justice Department. The young attorney general made a perfect target for the anger and contempt of the blacks attending that afternoon in New York: sympathetic enough to listen, slow enough in his response to the rights movement to raise the legitimate question, Why had he not been listening earlier?

Yet the attitude displayed toward the attorney general on this occasion was typical only of intellectuals and activists. The black community in general loved President John Kennedy, and in 1968 it would also show its love of Robert as a candidate for the Democratic presidential nomination. Both Kennedy brothers have occupied prominent places in the folklore of the civil rights movement. How did they gain that eminence?

Was it a matter of circumstance alone? Kennedy's presidential campaign year had coincided not with the beginnings of the civil rights movement but with its increase to critical mass. As a moderately liberal President at the head of an administration that attracted liberals more dedicated than he, Kennedy was sympathetic to racial equality, and such events as the attacks on Freedom Riders and on James Meredith drew from him modestly appropriate responses. His administration became therefore the first to commit itself, or rather to be fortuitously committed, to a popular civil rights movement. That it did not initiate but followed the popular lead may have served to increase its symbolic presence within the movement. For instead of bestowing freedom as a gift from the government, Kennedy's presidency took its directions from the rights activists. That granted to the black community what it had never before visibly possessed: a national recognition that it was in control of its own future. The Kennedy administration reaped the benefits of having come at the right time to take up that role. Yet the specific character of the President and his administration also contributed to the nation's memory of the relationship between the Kennedy brothers and American blacks.

Suppose, as is not hard to imagine, that Little Rock had been followed during Eisenhower's incumbency by a sufficient surge of black activism elsewhere, and consequently by a sufficient increase in white mob action, to necessitate some kind of federal intervention. If so, a President's and a soldier's honor might have motivated Eisenhower to uphold federal authority against southern white lawlessness, to use the Justice Department in defense of civil rights demonstrators, and to employ the army against white riots. The probable tones of his accompanying public addresses are fairly easy to surmise. They would have been subdued, vocally flat pleas for civic responsibility—the dignified utterances of a temperamentally conservative elder statesman. They would have implied not the forward march of great redemptive events but the preservation of public order.

The actual words of John Kennedy were not far different. His televised address at the time of the riots at Ole Miss did not speak for the morality of integration or the courage of James Meredith or the self-emancipation of blacks. He called for obedience to the law. Even his speech at the time of the Birmingham disorders spoke of the danger of social disruption. Redress for social wrongs, he said, "is sought in the streets, in demonstrations, parades, and protests which create tensions and threaten violence and threaten lives." Race matters, Kennedy argued, should have their settlement in law and, "above all, in . . . our daily lives." Yet what is said and what is heard can be quite different. People heard Kennedy's speeches, and they have heard them in memory, as alive with movement and purpose and a desire for national renovation. That was how Kennedy's administration perceived and presented itself.

John Kennedy's life had been a progression from a sickly childhood to an act of military courage and then to federal office, all in the face of physical ailments and chronic poor health: a life that seemed straining to surpass itself. He was incapable of being or even looking dull, and he would not tolerate dullness although he gave no evidence of knowing consistently and analytically what to put in place of it. His presidency seemed always close to overturning the given or the commonplace: flirting with nuclear war during the Cuban Missile Crisis of 1962, negotiating a major restraint on nuclear testing in 1963. So the identification of John Kennedy with the civil rights movement had at least an imaginative component beyond the exterior accidents that joined them. He managed to lend to a moment of energy and social change a look of alert and resolute leadership, a role his parents had cultivated in him and that his private struggles with severe illness had strengthened.

Despite the general weakness of his own earlier record on civil rights, President Kennedy represented a strain of traditional custodial liberalism capable of entering into an important symbolic relationship with black aspirations in the early sixties. The language of responsibility, crisis, and social drama came easily to him as to liberals in general. Kennedy's inaugural address had burned with a cold moral fervor that suffered only for a lack of any defined object. For all the cool rationality of liberalism, its devotion to scientific method, its care for the legal forms that are supposed to shield human beings from their own emotions and from one another, the liberal conscience has within it, in close but strained alliance with these things, a perfectionist urge. Both this and the more mundane political and skeptical components of liberalism fostered an endorsement of the civil rights movement.

That movement, at least in its national phase, needed a steady ongoing sequence of confrontations and victories that would enlist the support of men and women of good will, capture the sympathies of the liberal establishment, and impress the opposition with its stride. Media coverage seemed increasingly to sustain the impression of such a momentum as black and white protesters mingled in a segregated bus terminal or demonstrated outside a courthouse. Dramas of immediacy, the act or threat of violence from the opposition, the clear posing of moral issues in physical confrontations all fitted the visual form in which television news is conveyed. But newspaper coverage was probably equally or more important. A century before, John Brown's raid had become known almost as quickly, and stirred as much emotion, as the acts of the civil rights workers. In the South itself, network television coverage of rights events was often deliberately preempted by local commercials, and newspapers carried slanted versions of what had occurred.

Segregation, however, went deep in the North as well, and in the absence of Jim Crow laws and the overtly racist traditions of the South it was less remediable by direct challenge. In 1960, fifty-two thousand people owned homes in Levittown, Long Island, but not one of them was known to be black. In 1963, when demonstrations first began to spread northward, the predictable happened: suddenly many northerners turned against the rights movement. The public protests met with less direct resistance than in the South but also with less accomplishment. Demonstrations against discrimination in the building trades, or Brooklyn CORE's threat to block traffic on New York's expressways during the city's World's Fair in 1964, proved nearly fruitless. The ritual of confrontation that had worked in the South was inadequate. No instant victory and capitulation were possible when the issue was not the ending of some openly segregationist practice but the expansion of opportunity, perhaps at the immediate expense of a white worker whose years of employment had won union seniority. A philosophy of nonviolent protest could not deal effectively with white property owners who, instead of resisting the arrival of black families, simply moved away to the comfortable suburbs. Not only did the northern demonstrations fail both in practical terms and as catharsis; they also threatened the liberal coalition that had now become the primary hope for ending segregation. Northern ethnic Democrats resisted admitting black workers into unions, as well as the migration of blacks to white neighborhoods.

But the movement now had the opportunity to push an antisegregation law through Congress, and with a major triumph so close it could not afford to lose the momentum that had been both its success and its need since Greensboro. Shortly after Birmingham Martin Luther King published a book entitled *Why We Can't Wait*. The urgency of maintaining pressure on Congress brought the March on Washington of August 28, 1963, the symbolic culmination of the freedom marches and a model for many demonstrations in other causes during succeeding years.

The idea was that of A. Philip Randolph, the militant (as well as militantly anticommunist) dean of black labor leaders and originator of the planned 1941 March on Washington for Jobs and Equal Participation in National Defense. The 1963 march was planned by Bayard Rustin, long an important activist for nonviolence and socialism. But this new enterprise, initially intended to press for federal action on jobs, was quickly transformed by white leaders, notably the clergy, into a demonstration principally in support of the civil rights bill pending in Congress. Determined to keep the event peaceful, Rustin drafted dozens of black New York City policemen to assist in maintaining order at the march. White liberals succeeded in discouraging the use of radical vocabulary, in keeping the march away from Capitol Hill, and in heading off any plans of civil disobedience. Attorney General Robert Kennedy closed the city's bars. President Kennedy, initially reluctant, effectively endorsed the event at a press conference on July 17. Several liberal congressmen and senators joined the march, as did a few labor leaders, including Walter Reuther of the United Auto Workers. But the AFL-CIO national council declined to endorse it, and AFL President George Meany did not attend: his absence was more than a hint of the strains to come between blacks and organized labor, which chiefly represented ethnic whites.

The gentle army of more than two hundred thousand, the majority black but with as many as a third white, assembled in the shadow of Daniel Chester French's Lincoln Memorial to hear speakers and performers who caught the mood of the day and the moral direction of the times. In the largest demonstration to this date in American history, Randolph saw a hope over twenty years old brought to reality. The NAACP president Roy Wilkins eulogized W.E.B. Du Bois, a founder of the organization who as much as any other individual had created the forces in apparent triumph that August day. Du Bois had died in Ghana two nights before at the age of ninety-five, an expatriate from the nation that only now was showing some willingness to confront the questions he had posed.

On the steps of the Lincoln Memorial and facing the Washington Monument, King delivered the speech that has entered history under the title "I Have a Dream," eloquently capturing the movement's vision:

> I have a dream that one day on the red hills of Georgia the sons of former slaves and the sons of former slaveowners will be able to sit together at the table of brotherhood . . . and when *this* happens . . . we will be able to speed up that day when *all* God's children, black men and white men, Jews and Gentiles, Protestants and Catholics, will be able to join hands and sing in the words of the old Negro spiritual, "Free at last! Free at last! Thank God, Almighty, we are free at last!"

Few have been privileged to hold an entire nation in their moral debt. Those who heard King's entire address learned, if they did not already know, why he had become the preeminent leader of the movement.

Afterward John Lewis, chairman of the increasingly radical SNCC, in remarks that he had tempered when the local Roman Catholic archbishop, Patrick O'Boyle, threatened otherwise not to participate, argued that only a revolutionary change in American institutions would allow blacks to achieve equality. (Originally Lewis had written, "We will march through the South, through the heart of Dixie, the way Sherman did. We shall pursue our own 'scorched earth' policy and burn Jim Crow to the ground." Lewis had offered to amend this last sentence by adding the word "nonviolently," a sincere sentiment in his case.) The black nationalist leader Malcolm X was on hand to insist that blacks had been had, and he awarded Oscars for best performances by white speakers. Malcolm said of King: his speech was a "nightmare, only he's too dumb to know it." Many SNCC people, including Robert Parris Moses and Stokely Carmichael, had refused to attend the march, out of resentment against the modesty of the demands and the imposition by march organizers of various restrictions, such as specifying what could appear on picket signs. But one SNCC participant observed that the march had been a "tremendous inspiration" to poor blacks from the deep South brought there by the organization. President Kennedy called the event something of which "the nation could properly be proud." The March on Washington of 1963 was one of the great moments of self-definition on the part of a country that has been in continuing quest of its own moral identity.

The nonviolent, direct-action phase of the civil rights revolution did not end at the Lincoln Memorial that August day. But now considerable attention shifted to legislative and political activity: lobbying for a civil rights bill, registering voters, and acting to counter the emerging white backlash already reflected in municipal elections in Philadelphia and Chicago.

Rights leaders found themselves in a strategic crisis. What liberals and the President had contributed to the struggle, as far as activists like those in SNCC could judge, amounted mostly to expressions of good will and pleas for restraint and moderation. The movement leadership recognized that the aid of establishment politicians would be necessary: a federal public accommodations bill was in the works. But in time activist leaders, and not only those who were tempted by black counterracism, would come to decide that the proper course was to do honestly what out of need they had been doing in fact all along. That was to organize black people separately so that they would define their own goals, develop their own sources of power, and act without trying to appease cautious liberal politicians.

Quite another kind of assertiveness meanwhile was going to add confusion to white perceptions of black militancy. Ghetto riots in Harlem and Newark during 1964, and particularly in the Watts section of Los Angeles in 1965, sounded the end of the fragile moment of nonviolence over which King had presided. Watts, some have argued, was in reaction to California voters who had recently voted down a statewide fair-housing proposition. Forty-six square miles of Watts turned turbulent: thirty-four people died, and a thousand were injured. King of course deplored the riots, predicting that the "more there are riots, the more repression will take place, and the more we face the danger of a right-wing take-over, and eventually a fascist society." Yet the basic tenor of events was changing. In 1964 CORE members entered a segregated restaurant in Atlanta and urinated on the floor, which prompted the city's mayor to ask whether urination was nonviolent. The civil rights movement would soon fragment in a time of riots, social friction in the North, and growing black nationalism.

Before that, however, came a harvest of legislation.

When Lyndon Johnson assumed the presidency, he strengthened the bill that, as initially sent to Congress by his predecessor in June 1963, had called only for partial desegregation of public accommodations. Construing civil rights legislation as a remembrance of the recently assassinated Kennedy helped its passage, as did the support of a southern President whom liberals had not recognized as one of their own. By 1964, moreover, some exemplary state and local laws had been passed. In the Senate, religious institutions would take on a special role, bringing their influence to bear on churchgoing midwestern members whose support was needed for shutting off debate. Senator Everett Dirksen of Illinois, Republican minority leader and head of his party's uncommitted moderates, was besieged by church leaders, as well as by liberal Republicans and a President who, a White House assistant has remarked, "never let him alone for thirty minutes." Dirksen, after a show of hesitation that was likely for the benefit of conservative constituents, announced his support, observing that "no army can withstand the strength of an idea whose time has come."

A Senate vote in June 1964 to end the southern filibuster, taken after ample time had been allowed for a full expression of views, tallied seventy-one to twenty-nine. It was the first time the Senate had ever invoked cloture on civil rights—a signal of the decline of the once-powerful southern bloc in the upper chamber. The bill then passed by a slightly greater margin. Those in opposition included few nonsouthern Democrats and only five Republicans from outside the South, most notably Barry Goldwater, who was to be his party's presidential candidate that year. Two Republican politicians outside the Senate who would later become Presidents of the United States also opposed it: Ronald Reagan and George Bush.

Notwithstanding criticisms that the bill did not attack the subtler forms of discrimination or the underlying problem of black poverty, and that it contained loopholes and limitations, the Civil Rights Act of 1964 was a milestone. The law announced that equal access was now enforceable as official national policy. It banished into history much of the country's unofficial but ingrained practice of discrimination. In a comparatively short time numbers of corporations and universities would cease to be co-conspirators in the racism that had afflicted the country from its beginnings.

The act empowered the Attorney General to file suits to compel school desegregation. But unlike the Supreme Court's *Brown* decision, the law was more than a measure to halt, in the name of the Constitution, the racist practices of governments. It attacked private as well as government manifestations of racism. It outlawed discrimination against people seeking services in hotels, motels, restaurants, theaters, and all other public accommodations engaged in interstate commerce, although a provision exempting "private clubs" without defining them made it possible for some groups to evade the law. An important weapon for later use was a provision withdrawing federal funds from discriminatory programs. The law banned prejudicial hiring practices in all businesses employing more than twenty-five people and created an Equal Employment Opportunity Commission to investigate and review complaints, though granting it little power to ensure compliance.

While pushing national legislative objectives in the mid-1960s, the civil rights movement had also been broadening the character of its local activism. Sit-ins and similar techniques of nonviolent confrontation made sense only in dealing with the kinds of racism that could be ended immediately. Deeper changes required voting power on the part of black southerners, which in turn required bringing blacks to the polls in spite of prejudiced registrars and campaigns of intimidation, and their own conditioned discouragement and apathy. Wherever in the deep South blacks were largely absent from the polls—in Orangeburg or Jackson— demonstrations had failed. Even the Birmingham agreement registered only partial success for the local demands of the civil rights forces. Without voting strength, direct confrontation had no future.

Encouraged by support from liberal charitable foundations and urged on after the Freedom Rides by Robert and John Kennedy (who promised participants draft deferment), SNCC and CORE increasingly turned to the strategy of getting blacks in the deep South to register to vote. The winning of the vote promised not merely the incremental victories over white supremacy that the movement was already achieving, but ultimately a transformation in the region's whole power base. The task civil rights workers faced in Mississippi was especially daunting. That state's population had the highest percentage of blacks of any state in the union. They had been subject to a lifetime of intimidation and of enforced subordination. Rights workers had to encourage them to overcome their fears and their sense of inadequacy and attempt to register. They had to train prospective registrants in the process: by the end of the several years of work in Mississippi, freedom schools teaching black Mississippians their rights along with the historical and legal knowledge they would need to qualify for registration had become a well-recognized part of the process. Rights activists coped as well with the harassment and danger that they and their clients risked from local police and Ku Klux Klansmen. They had to do this despite the knowledge that after all it took in persuasion and courage and preparation to get applicants even to enter the local government office, a registrar could reject them for contrived reasons.

From one point of view, the effort at voter registration constituted an adaptation to establishment politics and institutions. Yet if voter registration was in a formal sense more moderate than confrontational techniques and did not imply the reconstitution of human behavior that nonviolence demanded, it was simultaneously a radical action. It meant working with the poorest blacks, and the twentieth-century American polity is even more uncomfortable, if that is possible, with issues of poverty than with questions of race. Voter registration also threatened the southern white establishment with the loss of political control and required challenging the white South at its most dangerous rural outposts, where sheriffs and vigilantes ruled, or thought they could rule, with impunity. Integration of restaurants and bus stations merely symbolized the end of white supremacy; the black vote, the possession of concrete power, would ratify that ending. Although the voter registration campaigners addressed the workaday details of law and political institutions as the rights demonstrators did not, they glowed with the same resolute and visionary fire and composed the same participatory community that had given rise to the civil rights demonstrations.

One of the preeminent leaders of the voter registration movement was Robert Parris Moses, a 1956 graduate of Hamilton College in upstate New York. Some years later, Moses would recall being "deeply bitter about some of the realities of the campus and of the white attitude," which he summed up as amounting to: "Well, we have to do our part—the society has the over-all problem, and our part as an educational institution is to try and open a door for two or three Negroes, and let's see what happens." Moses' anger had turned southward. Arriving in Mississippi during the late spring of 1960 and again in 1961, he was the first SNCC member to be jailed. He went to jail repeatedly, and was beaten there repeatedly. On one occasion automatic rifle fire tore into his car, seriously wounding another SNCC occupant. Moses continued his work. Another time, on returning from a field assignment, he found the local SNCC headquarters ransacked; he simply made up a bed and went to sleep.

Moses lacked, or possibly stifled in himself, that urge to capture an audience which makes for the power relations he despised. He deemed it manipulative to speak from a pulpit, preferring to talk from the back of a room; if at a rostrum, he asked questions in a conversational tone. Speaking slowly, pausing frequently, monotonous in cadence, he turned reticence into strength. His style anticipated, yet was quite different from, the studied inarticulateness of many student rebels of the late sixties.

Moses in the early 1960s used the SNCC budget to bring food to Leflore County, calling it food for those who wanted to be free and observing that the minimum requirement for freedom was registering to vote. In Mississippi he was seeking to enact a modest version of what would shortly manifest itself as participatory democracy. At once new and with ancient precedents, it was a concept of a community expressing its democratic will not primarily through plebiscites or elected representatives but through the cooperative action of its diverse and autonomous members. Radicals of the late sixties would conceive of it both as a means of conducting protest movements and as the proper form of a reconstituted American society. It could disperse the power and authority that had congealed into the giant corporations, the military, the whole of a centralized imperialist regime. The empowerment of black Mississippians would come to be equivalent to revealing to them their own latent power, making them conscious of the strength they had always possessed. Moses' constituency comprised those most oppressed and most isolated from the general white culture. Society had robbed black Mississippians of their power, which is to say their consciousness of possessing it. To study for registration, and then attempt it, was for Mississippi's black poor an achievement in itself, whatever its results.

In those times of fear, hope, and vision, SNCC and its efforts to awaken the black South meant for the more spiritual of the rights workers a reality beyond the democratization of politics: they felt the presence of what Martin Luther King called the "beloved community." The white Mississippi Methodist pastor Edwin King, a leader in the movement who was often arrested and often the target of segregationist violence, recalls the closeness among the SNCC members, who had to entrust their very lives to one another. They wished to enlarge their community as far as it could reach, so that it might embrace black southerners redeemed from shame and whites redeemed from the sin of racism. To this extent, the civil rights movement stands within a Christian tradition reaching back two thousand years. It recalls the Kingdom theology of the turn of the twentieth century, envisioning a Kingdom already present to whoever wishes to step into it, a realm also to come in the fullness of time.

While rights activists were pursuing the aim of voter registration, some were attempting to reach the supposedly moderate middle-class church-going Mississippians. Groups of blacks would go to white churches, on the supposition that Christians might see their way to admitting their fellow Christians to worship. Church after church turned away the seekers, thereby defining the character of white Mississippi Christianity.

In Mississippi's capital of Jackson, meanwhile, the state NAACP's director, Medgar Evers, had been leading a campaign of boycotts, demonstrations, and civil disobedience in which several hundred people went to jail. The national NAACP had by now become known for favoring establishment channels, and within the organization Evers was a maverick. Among black people the Jackson movement awakened the kind of spirit and participation that activists were seeking to evoke throughout the state. Mississippi imposed an injunction against planning boycotts and other actions, and the federal courts failed to block it. The injunction, added to massive police repression, put up a formidable obstacle to the Jackson protests. Civil rights workers had reason to think also that toward the Jackson movement as toward other forms of confrontational activism liberal Washington was unsympathetic, wishing for a more sedate pace of social change. Evers, one of the strongest and most stubborn of rights leaders, defied the injunction. Then, on June 12, 1963, he was shot to death; it took over thirty years to convict his killer.

In the same year rights organizations in Mississippi under the umbrella Council of Federated Organizations (COFO), which Medgar Evers had been instrumental in forming, executed a new, daring, and impressive maneuver demonstrating the readiness of black Mississippians to vote.

With Aaron Henry—a black pharmacist and state president of the NAACP as well as COFO—as their candidate for governor and Edwin King for lieutenant governor, they prepared for a mock election, to be held at the same time as the official vote. Explaining the vote to the black population and encouraging participation added to regular staff work, stretching the resources of SNCC and the rest of COFO too thin. So with the aid of Allard Lowenstein, remembered today as a promoter of liberal causes, the project recruited students from northern universities such as Michigan and Yale. The Freedom Vote garnered from eighty to ninety thousand votes, the base for a separate political organization, the Mississippi Freedom Democratic party. That enterprise was a factor in the decision to wage a major drive the following summer.

Among the organizers for 1964's Freedom Summer, the thorniest question was whether to repeat, on a much larger scale, the use of northern students. There was reluctance to bringing in people who might change the character of the Mississippi movement. But the designers of the project calculated—accurately, as it turned out—that the risks and perils undertaken by the white young would hold the attention of the nation's majority and its power structure as the tribulations of black SNCC workers had not. That meant that the black staff would be proceeding on the rankling knowledge that it was precisely the privileged whiteness of the white volunteers that would make them useful to the enterprise. The planners also recognized the immediate benefits of increasing the number of rights workers. Moses was influential in winning over the organizers to the idea of inviting white participation. In the end, the project brought to Mississippi some nine hundred northern white volunteers, with a heavy representation from such elite schools as Berkeley, Yale, and Swarthmore.

After an initial training in Ohio the white volunteers, many of whom had expressed a desire to honor the memory of John F. Kennedy, went on to encounter a world far outside their upbringing: the grinding poverty of tarpaper and wood shacks where a people poorly fed, clothed, and educated clung to existence. Here they also encountered increasing violence. Three white and six black rights workers were murdered during the summer of 1964: and in the most widely publicized killing, when a rural Mississippi sheriff picked up three activists and turned them over to the Klan, the white northerners Michael Schwerner and Andrew Goodman died together with James Chaney, a black southerner, whose body was the most severely mutilated. (That a white southern jury in 1967 convicted the killers of the federal crime of depriving the victims of their civil rights—the federal government had no jurisdiction to try them for murder—has been interpreted as a watershed act of southern justice. An advance only in the sense that white southern juries had previously shown no disposition to convict in cases of whites murdering blacks, it was nonetheless a conviction heard throughout the South.)

The triple murder brought to visibility in the rights struggle a figure whose relationship to the movement is still disputed. Director J. Edgar Hoover of the Federal Bureau of Investigation, who had gained a reputation among liberals for being a right-wing bigot, under orders from the President publicly committed his forces to assist in solving the crime. Hoover and his Bureau had been lily-white in composition and mentality. The FBI, like comparable agencies in the federal government, including its parent, the Justice Department, employed almost no black agents in the early 1960s. In fairness it should be said that until that time most white Americans of Hoover's generation in the District of Columbia were lily-white in outlook and scarcely gave it a thought. Hoover was capable of giving it a thought. He had, for example, opposed the vicious treatment of Japanese-Americans during World War II. But his thinking on most subjects was narrowly focused and literal, fixed and loyal to conventions. His preoccupation with propriety also dictated some scrupulousness about the proper limits of a national investigative force and the legal constraints within which agents should operate in a federal system. In the era of McCarthyism, liberals held up the FBI as the appropriate institution for investigating subversion, as the discreet and competent alternative to congressional Red hunts. On occasion, Hoover expressed an essentially modest role for his Bureau. "I am inclined toward being a states' righter in matters involving law enforcement. . . . I consider the local police officer to be our first line of defense," he said, articulating a view that, of course, was quite congenial to southern white local police. During much of the civil rights movement he was constrained by the federalism of the Constitution and by public opinion. His temperament expressed itself in administrative rigidity and a protective obsession about the reputation of the Bureau. A typist, goes a tale about him, once left too little space on a memo. Hoover scrawled a note "watch the borders," and his staff telegraphed offices near Mexico and Canada to be on the alert.

Consistent with the temper of this champion of law and starched respectability was his long, inveterate hostility to the Ku Klux Klan. As early as 1922, President Warren Harding sanctioned an investigation of the Louisiana Klan on condition that the state conduct the prosecutions. FBI agents uncovered evidence linking the Klan to a number of murders in Louisiana, but state grand juries refused to indict. Hoover successfully embarrassed the Imperial Kleagle, Edward Y. Clark, by prosecuting him on white slavery charges. The Klan, supposedly devoted to upholding the purity of American womanhood, was humiliated. The Klan largely fizzled out a couple of years later after financial and sexual scandals; yet for some fifteen years beginning in the 1950s, the FBI wiretapped the phone of Bobby Shelton, the deep South's best-known Klansman.

SNCC workers in Mississippi found the FBI, along with much of the federal government, maddeningly reluctant to protect the effort at voter registration. Attorney General Robert Kennedy defended Hoover: "I don't agree with this sort of general criticism that's been made that the FBI doesn't do anything in civil rights." Burke Marshall of the Kennedy administration's Justice Department instigated voting rights suits throughout the South, but he shared Hoover's apparent concern about constitutional constraints. The difference is that Marshall was tormented by the problem, while Hoover seemed comfortable enough. Still, from 1964 on, the FBI waged nothing short of war against the Klan. Hoover sent 153 agents to Mississippi to investigate the deaths of the civil rights activists Schwerner, Goodman, and Chaney, and 258 took part in the subsequent investigation of the Klan. The Bureau requested and got the assistance of four hundred sailors to comb the swamps looking for the bodies of the victims; Hoover's call for two hundred marines was denied after Mississippi's Senator James Eastland objected. After the murders Hoover flew to Jackson to open an FBI office, and the presence of this zealous anticommunist and superpatriot must have had symbolic meaning in the conservative South. His investigations were being hampered, he complained, by "water moccasins, rattlesnakes, and rednecked sheriffs, and they are all in the same category as far as I am concerned." He gave Governor Paul B. Johnson, whom he carefully described as "a man I have long admired from a distance," and Highway Patrol Commissioner T. B. Birdsong the names of state troopers who had joined the Klan. By the time Hoover was through the FBI had some two thousand informants in the Klan, which he called "a group of sadistic, vicious white trash. . . . You can almost smell them." His agents had interviewed 480 of them, he said, "just to let them know we know who they are." The FBI subsequently arrested dozens of Klansmen involved in the murders of Mississippi blacks.

Hoover in Mississippi broke the terrorism that southern authorities as well as what he termed "private scum" had waged against blacks. And thereby he gave a preview of how he would go about attacking what he later perceived as black terrorism. Hoover would violate legal procedures that, at other times in his public life, he had publicly made a point of observing. The FBI, for example, raided Black Panther headquarters in Chicago in 1969 and confiscated records; the agency had a warrant only for the arrest of a murder suspect thought possibly to be on the premises.

In Martin Luther King, Hoover confronted a force immeasurably different and more perplexing. When President Kennedy, the time of McCarthyism not many years in the past, asked King to stop associating with a couple of rather important ex-communists—most notably Stanley Levison, King's ghostwriter and perhaps his closest adviser—the civil rights leader had agreed but soon broke his word. The Kennedys, worried about political damage to the administration, thereupon closely monitored King. With the permission of the attorney general, Hoover tapped King's phone and learned about his active extramarital sex life. The director was particularly repelled by a sexual joke that King made in a reference to John Kennedy's funeral. "King's a 'tomcat' with obsessive degenerate sexual urges," the puritanical Hoover announced. When *Time* named King its man of the year for 1963, the director protested: "They had to dig deep in the garbage to come up with this one." Imagination reels at the thought of Hoover's reaction to King's winning the Nobel Peace Prize the following year: all we have is his scrawl that King qualified for the "'top alley cat' prize" instead. King's opposition to the Vietnam war doubtless further infuriated the unreflectively patriotic director.

Whatever in Hoover's detestation of King derived from contempt for sexual behavior unbecoming a minister and married man should differentiate him from a strict old-fashioned racist. A bigot from the past would not have expected sexual self-restraint of a black man—might have considered sexual honor to be a code appropriate only to the master race. But Hoover's ideological objection to King may have centered on the practice of nonviolent disobedience to legal authority.

Hoover once expressly denounced King for "the idea that you can violate a law if it is wrong." Here was the point at which everything the director stood for appeared to clash with everything the clergyman stood for. That King and his nonviolent protesters disobeyed the law publicly and then willingly accepted the penalties for their principled actions bespoke their concern for civil order. But such finer points could easily escape the notice of an unquestioning guardian of the law. A common criminal might be more understandable, less threatening to the majesty of the law, than a person whose civility in the act of disobedience overthrows the law's moral authority. To Hoover such acquiescence in the legal penalties must have signified not submission to law so much as condescension to it. What King represented in the 1960s—indifference to communist ties, to conventional morality, and to the rule of law—summed the phenomena that Hoover detested in the decade.

If Hoover could not understand civil disobedience, much of the liberal leadership of the Democratic party, it seems, could not even understand Freedom Summer. At the party's August 1964 national convention in Atlantic City, the limits of establishment liberalism fully revealed themselves.

The delegation selected in Mississippi's separate Freedom Democratic caucuses challenged the regular delegates on the grounds that they had been chosen in voting that excluded blacks and most had declined to sign a loyalty oath to support the party's nominee. A Freedom delegation spokesperson, forty-one-year-old SNCC staff member Fannie Lou Hamer, had good reason to know about Mississippi justice. A few years earlier, local health authorities had sterilized her, without her knowledge, after surgery. Mrs. Hamer testified eloquently to the convention's credentials committee of her savage beating at the hands of the Winona police in June 1963. She described being whipped until her skin turned blue and she had no feeling left in her arms: "All of this on account we want to register, to become first-class citizens," she said, weeping, "and if the Freedom Democratic party is not seated now, I question America." After her attempt to register, her farm employer had fired both her and her husband. The Freedom Democrats were lobbing a live moral issue straight at the heart of the nation's political process.

The more liberal of the nation's two parties proved unable to handle it. Party leaders were more concerned about the need for unity against the challenge posed by Republican presidential candidate Barry Goldwater. In the primaries of Maryland, Indiana, and Wisconsin, conservative Democrats had voted in large numbers for Governor George Wallace of Alabama. So concerned was President Johnson that he arranged to interrupt the television coverage of Mrs. Hamer's testimony by holding a trivial press conference. But the evening news carried much of her moving speech.

A compromise was offered to seat two members of the Freedom Democratic delegation. The remainder would be allowed on the convention floor as "honored guests," and the party further pledged to institute full racial representation and a ban on segregated delegations at the next convention. Of the state's regular Democrats only the five who signed a pledge to support the convention's nominee would be seated, but, as planned, under the unit rule they could cast the full vote of the delegation. That only two Freedom Democratic delegates were to be seated, and that the Democratic establishment was to select these two, constituted a double insult. Nonetheless, important liberal figures—Hubert Humphrey, Walter Mondale, Wayne Morse, Walter Reuther, and the party's own counsel, Joseph Rauh—along with many black leaders urged the delegation to accept the proposal as a moral victory.

The Freedom Democratic party refused to accept the offer, choosing, as its members saw it, to maintain its integrity rather than to compromise and accept a demeaning tokenism. The Freedom Democrats, moreover, had ample reason to doubt that the Democratic party, fearful of backlash and virtually incapable of binding itself from one election to the next, would keep its promise to ban segregated delegations in 1968 (in fact, it did). Fannie Lou Hamer patiently explained to Humphrey, whom the President had not yet anointed as his running mate, "If you lose this job of Vice President because you do what is right. . . , everything will be all

right. God will take care of you." More concerned than disappointed at
Humphrey's inability to distinguish right from wrong, Mrs. Hamer told
him, "I'm going to pray to Jesus for you."

Wiretapping and a deceptive meeting that made a show of working
toward a compromise after the issue had actually been decided were
among the backroom tactics against the black delegates that bore the
imprint of President Johnson. He also blackmailed one woman member
of the Credentials Committee with the threat that her husband might not
receive the judgeship for which he was being considered. Johnson, something of a southern bully who believed that he was on the side of the
rights workers anyway, wanted an undiluted electoral mandate for his
reform program. As for the regular Mississippi delegates, even the voice
vote on the convention floor for the liberal compromise was too much for
them, and all but three Johnson loyalists promptly went home. These
three could have outvoted the two Freedom Democrats.

Robert Moses and his coworkers quite legitimately felt betrayed by
the liberals. The Freedom Democratic party's fate at Atlantic City was a
turning point in a shift from nonviolence and toward black separatism.
The Convention represented the negotiability of moral issues along
with the connection between the southern racist and the northern liberal
Democratic party, even Democratic liberals like Humphrey. The escalation of the war in Vietnam in the ensuing months cemented the inclination of members of SNCC never again to trust liberals or the national
government. SNCC could perceive a kinship between the poor of Mississippi and Vietnamese peasants for whom the rhetoric of liberalism came
accompanied with napalm, pacification of hamlets, and right-wing generals like Curtis Le May, who wished to use atomic weapons in North
Vietnam.

For their part, the *New York Times* and many prominent liberals insisted that an inability among civil rights activists to accept the inevitable
ambiguities, compromises, and frustrations of politics would have dangerous consequences in the long run—and that was true as well. "An
awful lot of them . . . were in love with death," Robert Kennedy once said
of some seekers after purity on civil rights. RFK had a politician's, albeit
a moral politician's, preference for progress achieved by compromise. His
own eruptions of angry moralism—ranging the political spectrum from
his early Red-hunting days with Senator Joseph McCarthy to his final
liberal scorn for Americans indifferent to suffering in Vietnam—signify
that a morality of absolutes and a morality of strategic compromise can
coexist within a single person. At the moment, though, the primary concern among liberals was their anxious search for national consensus. As
they saw it, they had an election to worry about and the possibility, however remote, of a Republican victory that would bring to power right-

wing ideologues who would have re-created reality in ways even less appetizing to the rights activists than were the events at Atlantic City.

Notable liberals dissociated themselves from SNCC. As early as 1963 Theodore White, the author of a series of popular liberal books on American presidential elections, had called its members "lunatics" and alleged that "unidentified" elements had infiltrated it. SNCC also incurred the hostility of old-line socialists like Irving Howe, who described it as "bureaucratically deformed, manipulative and undemocratic." The southern liberal journalist Ralph McGill suggested in his nationally syndicated column that Cuban communists had taken over SNCC and were financing it. To such accusations Moses responded: "We have decided that we aren't going to let the politics of the '30s, '40s, and '50s guide our movement in the '60s. It is irrelevant."

Gradually, the Freedom Democratic party and SNCC moved apart. Mrs. Hamer left SNCC in reaction to a meeting in Waveland, Mississippi, in late 1964 at which separatist ideas found expression: "I think blacks and whites have still got to work together," she said. "I'm not one of those who go around hating all the time. If I were like that, I'd be a miserable person. I keep remembering that righteousness exalts a nation." In 1968 Fannie Lou Hamer and other Freedom Democrats were part of an integrated delegation (its leadership still picked and controlled by the White House), which may be seen as a vindication either of the refusal of the Freedom Democrats to compromise or of the good faith of Democratic party officials. The party's rules four years thence in 1972 went very far to bring black and other minority delegates to that year's national convention.

The winter after Freedom Summer, the major confrontation in the South shifted to Selma, Alabama, an old slave-trading city just downstream on the Alabama River from Montgomery. Early in 1965 Selma's police force, using ropes, whips, and clubs, repelled freedom marchers attempting to register blacks to vote. The white South lived up to its stereotype as block-jawed deputy sheriffs in sunglasses obligingly beat blacks in full view of media cameras. Selma's main attraction, Sheriff Jim Clark, habitually lost his self-control on catching sight of black demonstrators; a state trooper in a nearby town chased down a young black church deacon, Jimmy Lee Jackson, who had been protecting a relative against white bigots, and shot him to death. The Reverend James Reeb, a white civil rights activist, died of a beating by whites.

The killing of Reeb moved King to start a protest march from Selma to Montgomery, the state capital, to be held the following Sunday. Had King not done so his power over the movement might have been severely weakened. At the far end of Selma's Edmund Pettus Bridge state troopers halted the marchers, setting on them with tear gas and clubs. Fleeing back into the city, the demonstrators met Jim Clark's forces acting under his command to use tear gas and "get those god-damned niggers." SNCC's chairman, John Lewis, and others were severely beaten. Bloody Sunday appeared on the nation's evening television news and included film of troopers clubbing and gassing black women. King's tactics had worked again, but his absence at the march angered SNCC members. A second march shortly after Bloody Sunday ended with King and his SCLC leadership halting upon reaching the other side of the bridge when confronted by ranks of police blocking the way. After singing "We Shall Overcome," the marchers turned back at the direction of King, who was under a federal court order not to march. "If we can't sit at the table of democracy," raged one SNCC leader in parody of King, "we'll knock the fucking legs off."

King's campaign received some unlikely support from a figure who in a letter of December 1961 had said to "Mississippi youth": "[We]'re with the efforts to register our people in Mississippi. . . . But we do not go along with anybody telling us to help nonviolently." A Baptist minister's son who had cast off the family name inherited from the time of slavery, Malcolm X had been a leader within the Nation of Islam, or Black Muslims, a religious group that proclaimed the white race to be genetically evil and that numbered by the early sixties a membership of about a quarter of a million. Malcolm, having become a powerful figure, had recently broken with Elijah Muhammad, the head of the Black Muslims. Now, in January 1965, Malcolm went to Selma and spoke with Coretta King about the softening of his views toward the white race: "I want Dr. King to know that I didn't come to Selma to make his job difficult. I really did come thinking that I could make it easier. If white people realize what the alternative is, perhaps they'll be more willing to hear Dr. King." Within a month Black Muslim assassins had gunned down Malcolm X in New York City.

King finally triumphed when President Johnson, following a court order by Judge Frank Johnson, secured the highway to Montgomery with helicopters, federalizing three thousand members of the Alabama National Guard. The ensuing successful five-day march, beginning on Sunday, March 21, brought thousands of northern clergy and liberal celebrities to join in solidarity with the black participants. King compared the event to Gandhi's great twenty-six-day march to the sea in 1930, a massive act of civil disobedience against the British in India covered by the world press. On reaching the capital King delivered another memorable speech in the cadences of southern black revivalism:

How long will it take? . . . it will not be long, because truth pressed to earth will rise again. How long? Not long, because no lie can live forever. How long?

Not long, because you still reap what you sow. How long? Not long, because the arm of the moral universe is long but it bends toward justice. How long? Not long, 'cause mine eyes have seen the glory of the coming of the Lord.

On the night of King's speech Viola Liuzzo, a white volunteer and mother of five from Detroit, was driving with a black passenger along the route followed by the marchers to Montgomery, when Klansmen overtook her car and shot her through the head. It was to take authorities over thirteen years to catch and punish her killer. Lyndon Johnson sent condolences to her family as well as that of James Reeb. Blacks noted the absence of any message from the President to the family of Jimmy Jackson, the other casualty of Selma.

Shortly afterward President Johnson—speaking in King's own rhetoric and using the signature phrase from perhaps the best-known protest song, "We Shall Overcome"—presented before both houses of Congress a new tactic for voter registration in seven southern states, and the result was the Voting Rights Act of 1965. Under this law, where patterns of exclusion existed voter registration would proceed thenceforth not by tedious lawsuits but immediately by federal examiners. Its passage, added to the ratification in 1964 of the Twenty-Fourth Amendment outlawing the poll tax as a qualification for voting in federal elections, completed a legal base of protection for the right to vote. Before long many localities in the deep South were electing their first black officials since Reconstruction. By 1966 black voter registration in the region had increased 40 percent from that of the early sixties, and it would subsequently go well beyond that. Johnson, for all the uneasiness of his relationship with the civil rights forces, had made an enormous contribution. He pushed victims of discrimination through the door, encouraging them on their way to freedom. To be more cynical: this consummate politician may also have calculated that the Democrats by the midsixties had lost the South unless a new voting coalition might emerge between voting blacks and white moderates. With the substantial ending of institutions of political inequality and the shift of activities from the South to the North, attention now went increasingly to the problems of social and economic inequality of which segregation had been the surface instrument and expression.

American history can be seen as an ongoing quarrel between common sense and the visions of reformers—recurrent visions, eruptions from within a culture normally disposed to fix on what it considers the immediate and practical task. For inherent within the workaday American enterprise has been a will to recast the shape of things. It is a will that can express itself in its daily labors of reworking a career or a piece of steel; or it can seize upon visions. That is what the civil rights movement did. It did so in the same unpredictable, sometimes random fashion that characterizes all social movements.

The initial goals of civil disobedience were clear: a meal at a lunch counter, a seat on a bus, a swim at a pool, the use of a book in a library, a ballot in a voting booth. The ordinary had dignity conferred upon it. And the activists could do more than compel integration; by the simple act of entering or sitting down, they could make it a fact. By its immediacy and clarity, integration of this sort implied the Christian drama of conversion; speaking from his religious training, Martin Luther King called upon whites to throw off in an instant their racist past. Meanwhile, the practice of nonviolence, requiring training and a confrontation of the fear and the primitive anger welling within the practitioner, articulated a morality of self-reformation and a recognition of the difficulty of it. These perceptions together kept with the evangelical traditions of both the black and the white South, and the belief ingrained in American religion generally that the Kingdom of Heaven is a spiritual presence on earth, even as it works toward its earthly realization.

A society training its poor for jobs, arranging for a better distribution of wealth, or integrating and improving its schools is engaging in the mundane work of making things better. But in the gesture of stepping across an invisible line, Americans asserted their faith in the possibility of rebirth.

 **Killers of the Dream**

THE RIGHTS MOVEMENT sought, in effect, to bring black Americans under the Declaration of Independence. It stood for one of the truest beliefs of the American experiment: that it should be an aim of a good society to eliminate, as far as possible, the arbitrary and vicious barriers that background and surroundings erect against the full achievement of personal identity. That principle will never, can never, become fully realized, but it is an imperative toward which American politics should strive. Nonviolence was fitting for a movement demanding liberation from arbitrary constraints, for that conduct fosters self-discovery and self-making. But another aspirant to the liberation of black Americans had been long present, and in the middle and late 1960s this alternative vision gained prominence once again. This was the concept of race as the nearly exclusive foundation of the identity of African Americans. As beguiling as nationalism, that corrupter of recent Western and world history, as seductive to American blacks as white racism has been to whites, that impassioned embrace of blackness came close to negating the civil rights movement.

So terrible were the racial conditions out of which black power grew, so justifiable the angers, so *wrong* does any out-of-place remark about black fury seem that it has proven difficult to write forthrightly about the black militancy of the late sixties. Whites, understandably enough, are hesitant to do so; and perhaps many black scholars carry such anger themselves, or are so conscious of their own middle-class status, that they feel a similar reticence. White commentators who do criticize black power risk being put down as resentful liberals, nursing a sense of grievance over their rejection by blacks with whom they had thought to be allied. But somewhere it needs to be said that the separatism following the decline of the nonviolent phase of the civil rights movement was a disaster. It muddled the goals of civil rights. It seriously diminished the support, or at least acquiescence, of the white community that black progress required.

Above all it trampled on a persuasion of nonviolence, civil disobedience, and integration that had been the heroism, the glory, and the promise of the earlier movement. Enticing its followers to look first not to their individual resources but to their skin to tell them who they are, it remains ensconced in enclaves within the black community, where its adherents may celebrate their collective blackness and, if they so please, invent histories that will help them do so. The narcissistic absorption in the group content of self-identity, the nearly sensual preoccupation with the wrongs inflicted by the other, later found another expression in some segments of radical feminism.

Yet black power had origins, or immediate forebears, more rational than that. It was not blacks in general so much as the black poor, for example, whom SNCC had wanted to take command of their collective fortunes. SNCC's strategy envisioned the fashioning of alternative black political, social, and economic structures. Of the Mississippi Freedom Democrats who went to the Democratic National Convention in 1964, the rural poor constituted some 80 percent; most of them opposed the compromise offered by cautious Democratic liberals. In this Robert Parris Moses achieved something that much of the left of the sixties, for all its energy and diversity, did not work hard enough to acquire: a viable, homegrown American plan for popular mobilization and for a social and economic remaking of the country. In Mississippi, SNCC had worked for empowerment, and it was the local black poor who were to become the authors of their own liberation; no mystique of Africanness was required. The ultimate purpose was to empower individuals as free participants in community, to give them an awareness of the power already latent within them. Such awareness and its consequent expression in action would constitute not only the means to freedom but its essence. The winning of the vote itself promised to give to blacks their own power base.

The aim to awaken this kind of power and freedom governed Moses' hesitation to exert direct leadership. After 1965 he dropped out of the Mississippi movement, saying that his position there had become "too strong, too central, so that people who did not need to began to lean on me, to use me as a crutch." Leadership, he wrote, "is there in the people." He suggested that SNCC abolish all its committees and that the field workers walk out the door and, in the words of the freedom song, "go where the spirit say go, and do what the spirit say do." Perhaps Moses was himself unsure of where the movement should go next: in an epigram he summed up the perplexing limits of democracy: "If you want to make a slave, you take a free man and give him the vote."

Between the mainline civil rights movement and black power there were resonances. Awakening the suppressed black populace, summoning it to enterprises of courage and self-restraint, enlisting the African American church, the rights movement had been from the first an occasion for pride. It had pursued substantive equality—economic, political, social, cultural—an equality beyond the formal bringing together of black and white into the same physical spaces. The desirability of integration of that technical sort lay in large part in tangible benefits that could plausibly be expected to accompany it. Integration of the schools promised an improvement in the education—and ultimately the economic status—of black children, if only because it would prevent a white majority from siphoning off the bulk of public resources for the children of the privileged race. Integration in itself could be a compelling statement of human community, as it was when black and white demonstrators sat side by side at a counter or marched together through a racist mob.

But in the mid-sixties other issues became more pressing. As civil rights activists turned their attention increasingly to economic and social problems that would not yield to formal integration, their tactics and concerns of necessity began to take on a black separatist cast: community organizing, improvement of neighborhood schools and of slum housing. The most immediately gratifying way to attack poverty was to nourish the economy, the schooling, the neighborhood pride, the political awareness of black communities. One idea that was to become associated with black power called for community control—of schools, federal funding, and other government and private agencies in black neighborhoods. Some advocates may have seen the separation of ghetto schools from the control of the citywide white leadership as merely a temporary expedient, not entailing hostility toward the larger society. Rather, they perceived it chiefly as a means of building up black institutions so that they could effectively interact with white ones. Private loans and government help, for example, might nurture black business until it could take its place beside white enterprises. Community control of black schools could demonstrate to African Americans that they were eminently capable of taking charge of their own education, and of cultivating their own intellectual resources. Such control was desirable also for encouraging broader participation, a prerequisite in any democratic polity. And a concern for practical community control led quite reasonably to the question, Why did whites run the banks in black ghettos, and own the slum buildings? The relationship of whites to inner-city blacks combined the worst of flight and the worst of visibility: flight to the clean air, spacious homes, good schools, and safety of the suburbs, to which whites took their tax money and their skills; visibility in the form of financial institutions that possessed the cities like distant conquering empires.

Beyond the political considerations were the discovery and the articulation of African American culture that black power furthered. Here black power's benefit greatly outstripped its capacity for mischief. Black power attended, if it did not necessarily instigate, a cultivation among black Americans of styles and forms of creative expression that were better aligned with their own spirit, history, and outlook. Hair straightening and skin bleaching went out of fashion. Soul food became recognized for the cuisine it was. Soul music was a more self-conscious expression of ethnic distinctiveness than the older, and perhaps more African, black American rhythms and tones. Theater companies arose to explore black life and experience. The presentation of culture was in itself as liberating as is the awareness and cultivation of any ethnic or regional identity as an integral part of personal identity. There is reason in Barbara Ann Teer's declaration in 1968, "The way we talk (the rhythms of our speech which naturally fit our impulses), the way we walk, sing, dance, pray, laugh, eat, make love, and finally, most important, the way we look, make up our cultural heritage. There is nothing like it or equal to it, it stands alone in comparison to other cultures. It is uniquely, beautifully and personally ours and no one can emulate it."

As to the more aggressive assertiveness that accompanied black power: some of this found its rationale in a selective reading of a subtle and insightful book, *The Wretched of the Earth*, by the psychiatrist Frantz Fanon, born in Martinique and a resident of Algeria at the time of his death in 1961. Though he wrote not of the United States but of the Third World, Fanon had wide renown, and black power leaders, among them Stokely Carmichael and Eldridge Cleaver, were drawn to his work. Fanon's thesis is that only through active resistance to their oppressors can oppressed people achieve inner as well as outer freedom, and an authentic collective identity. Translated to the American situation, such resistance, as Fanon viewed it, could take spiritual and cultural forms. The embracing of the color black, of the festivities of the black community, of the pain and endurance that entexture black history, of the grace and courage of the civil rights movement itself—all this had the potential for nurturing a vigorous cultural life.

And the embrace of black role models made sense within a population that has traditionally begun its education with little white Jack and Jill running up the hill and then sustains its pride with tales of lily-white nation builders, some of whom were slavemasters. The historian Eugene D. Genovese observes that instead of bringing over with them a culture like the white ethnic groups, blacks shaped out of resistance to slavery and white supremacy a powerful new culture. If Genovese is right about that, then black ethnicity belongs also the larger American ethos, which has expressed itself in a continual act of making and remaking.

The elaboration of black culture promised to the individual black American the kind of self-identity, assertively pursued, that other Americans and other peoples had always taken as a birthright. It affirmed the common recognition that a person is not simply an instance of universal humanity, a naked mind settled in a body. Mind and character are grounded in a particular time and place and set of circumstances: a turn of speech, a twist of humor, a way of respecting parents or rebelling against them, the knowledge of a shared familial and ethnic past. Black consciousness, to that extent, could have been a means of ensuring that as its participants were in the process of freeing themselves from an older set of abstract imposed definitions—the Good Negro, the Ungrateful Negro, or whatever—they need not simply have a new set imposed on them: the Oppressed, the Victim, the Liberated. The black individual would not continue invisible, like the protagonist of Ralph Ellison's 1952 novel *Invisible Man*, who in his journey from his Georgia childhood to full self-awareness must overcome the conflicting definitions that both white radicals and black racists fix upon him, definitions that have hidden him from them and from himself.

Among these, however, is one definition that in varying forms is a special temptation to Ellison's searcher: that of Blackness itself. He ends his journey of self-discovery not in some kind of easy reconciliation to black or any other culture but in an ironic awareness of the many things he has experienced and endured. And it is this clear-headed detachment, which Ellison sets in a hidden room bathed in electric light, that along with the particulars of his racial and individual past constitutes the protagonist's achieved identity. He can return to his black Georgia upbringing because he has found a lucid perspective upon it and for that reason can choose to accept its presence within him.

Ellison's artistically mastered idea of self-identity, then, can clarify the interplay between personhood and culture. But parts of the black power movement spoke at their shrillest as though race and culture were, and should be, the commanding and unyielding absolute within identity. During the days of black militancy, Ellison went out of fashion, since he did not reduce blackness to the simplicities that would win favor among purists.

The assertion that an ethnic, national, or racial group must possess a self-consciousness and a sensibility is, in fact, tautological; such a group exists as a collectivity only insofar as it has such things. It does make sense to learn more about yourself, either individually or collectively; there is something in the notion of becoming what you already are—as, for example, in systematically studying the grammar of your native language. To that extent a black studies program, like that in women's studies or in some particular ethnicity, is a valid exercise in introspection. But people who self-consciously determine to cultivate a collective sensibility are trying to form themselves into a group, which says that they are not one already. And people who belong to an already definable group and share its collective mentality may with profit consider what in that sensibility should be discarded. A Serb, for instance, or Zionist or Arab nationalist of ethnic-purification bent, or an adolescent whose peers bond by getting into the drug trade, would benefit by freeing himself from what he may take to be the group consciousness. Otherwise it would have to be assumed that a white Mississippian, say around 1960, was obliged out of group loyalty to get more thoroughly into the Experience of Being White.

Having decided, at some time during the middle to late sixties, that it had been wrong to assume that race was one of the less important things about people, radicals came to assume that race and sex are the most important. And so, instead of thinking of words like *black*, *white*, *female*, *male*, *homosexual*, *heterosexual* as adjectives designating qualities that go into the complex whole of a person, a portion of the left came to think of them nominally: someone is a black, a woman. In defense of that notion of identity, black separation had in effect to accept social reality as it then was, insist that it would always be so, and hug the passive pride of being indelibly different. Martin Luther King, Jr., had offered a vision of how the future might be, and the courage and perseverance to bring it about.

Still, the assertion of culture and ethnicity that took place in the sixties had its healthy connections to the American past. It was a reminder of the cultural pluralism that has always been a distinctive though not a unique fact of the nation's life. In so being, it had at least a capacity to teach tolerance and a healthy curiosity not only toward differing groups at home but toward the outside world, toward which Americans have held contradictory attitudes of generosity and provincial dislike.

Long before the public eruption of black separatist impulses after Freedom Summer in 1964, charismatic leaders had appeared, preaching the incompatibility of the two races or, more mildly, the necessity of constructing a self-determining black community free of white impurities. Earlier in the century Marcus Garvey articulated a form of black nationalism that envisioned a return to Africa. The best-known of these nationalists, then and today, is Malcolm X.

Malcolm pulled himself out of petty crime and street hustling into a life of social purpose; he possessed a quick eloquence; and toward the end of his life, and even on occasion earlier, he demonstrated an ability to transcend fixed racial attitudes. These qualities, along with his ability to awaken a sense of pride among some underprivileged African Americans who might otherwise have surrendered to drugs and casual crime, have revealed him as a man of strength and depth. The call to genuine pride was inherently attractive. As for the racism of his Black Muslim years, there is no reason to expect black Americans to be any more immune than the rest of humankind to the appeal to collective superiority, especially if it is perceived as a reaction to generations of pain and suffering. More surprising is the patronage bestowed on his separatist notions by some white liberals.

Memories and myths about Malcolm X, born Malcolm Little, have remained a powerful presence in black militancy. Light of skin, he later held that a white man had raped his maternal grandmother, but there is no evidence for that or for the claim that his father, a follower of Marcus Garvey, was murdered. The elder Little had spent much of his time organizing for Garvey. If, as Malcolm's mother told him, the Klan had forced the family to move from their home in Omaha, the local Klansmen did not know that Little worked for Garvey's movement and that Garvey was one of the Klan's favorite Negroes. Relatives and scholars have disputed both stories, and Malcolm himself recanted on the assertion of his father's murder. He also insisted that arson had claimed both his childhood homes, in Omaha and Lansing, Michigan.

In 1946 Malcolm was sent to prison for armed robbery. Converted to the Nation of Islam while recovering from drug addiction in jail, he read dictionaries and other books to compensate for his having left school after the eighth grade. A confirmed black nationalist, Malcolm held to the goal of separatism even after he broke with the Black Muslims and softened in his perception of whites. "Coffee," he would say, "is the only thing I like integrated." In accord with a widespread practice among the Muslims, he rejected the slave name that he claimed plantation owners had bestowed upon his forefathers. In fact, many surnames had been deliberately and freely chosen by freedmen. The later idea of turning Mississippi into a romantic Spanish civil war for a generation of white college kids repelled Malcolm; he detested what his ideology told him was the vapid sentimentality of freedom songs.

The decades-old Black Muslim faith, led by Elijah Muhammad, looked vaguely in the direction of Islam but departed from it in preaching not a message to all humankind but a gospel of racial antagonism. The white race, the Muslims were taught, was the creation of Yakub, a black devil who with 59,999 of his followers had migrated to an island in the Aegean. The Black Muslims followed an austere code of living. Forbidden were sexual promiscuity, sleeping late, ball games, movies, dancing, smoking, drinking, and drugs. Muslims were allowed only one meal a day, were required to bathe often, and made their prayers five times daily facing Mecca. They rejected Marxism as one more political ideology invented by white men for white men and favored instead black capitalism based on the bourgeois virtues of hard work and thrift. The Muslim persuasion and moral code unquestionably contained at least some of the ingredients of successful community self-development. To this day the Black Muslims have remained active in combating the drug blight in black neighborhoods.

Paroled from prison in 1952, Malcolm lived for a time in Chicago with Elijah Muhammad—another black leader who earlier had developed leadership qualities while in prison, in his case for refusing to participate in World War II—and eventually became the Muslim leader in Harlem. Malcolm proved to be at least as powerful a public speaker as Martin Luther King, though he often strove more for effect than for substance. On a Los Angeles talk show he rejoiced in the death in a plane crash of white Atlanta cultural leaders: "I got a wire from God today. . . . He dropped an airplane out of the sky with over 120 white people on it because the Muslims believe in an eye for an eye and a tooth for a tooth. We call on our God, and he gets rid of 120 of them at one whop." When his radio host objected, Malcolm rejoined: "Sir, just as America thanked God when He dropped the bomb on Hiroshima that wiped out 100,000 Japanese, I think that we are well within our rights to thank God when He steps in. . . . Because we have no bombs and have no guns and have no weapons, when someone attacks us, we rely on God . . . and I think the white man has a whole lot of nerve, after all of the injustices that he has been committing against Negroes in this country, to be offended or surprised when someone says that God is after him." At times Malcolm, who made himself up as he went along, could injure himself by his own words, which King rarely did. When President Kennedy was killed, Malcolm observed, "Chickens coming home to roost never did make me sad; they've always made me glad." His racial invective was sometimes the inverse of the spewings from flatbed loudspeakers of Klan rallies: "The dog," he said of whites, "is their closest relative. They got the same kind of hair, the same kind of skin, and the same kind of smell, oh, yeahhh!"

Not a few of Malcolm's fulminations were directed against Jews. "Everybody talks about the six million Jews," he complained, "but I was reading a book the other day that showed that one hundred million of us were kidnapped and brought to this country—*one hundred million*. Now everybody's wet-eyed over a handful of Jews who brought it on themselves. What about our one hundred million?" Malcolm said that when he thought of a child bitten by rats he thought of a slumlord on a Miami beach. For black Harlem in the 1950s, Jews were most visible as marginal storekeepers, slum owners, and welfare workers. Though Malcolm in his later days was to reject anti-Semitism along with black racism, after his death some other Black Muslims and nationalists advanced both notions.

It was fitting that the Muslims and another group that harbored anti-Semitic race supremacists should find each other. On January 28, 1961,

Malcolm sought the aid of the Ku Klux Klan in behalf of Muslim separatism. The Klan implicitly agreed not to hinder Muslim activity in the
South.

Intrinsic to Malcolm's message was a swaggering vocabulary of violence. Nonviolence, he once announced, is "unmanning"—a statement
dense in its ignorance of the discipline of nonviolence and later dismissed
by the black scholar Henry Louis Gates as "macho bullshit." Against the
ideas of Martin Luther King Malcolm orated:

> There is no such thing as a nonviolent revolution. The only kind of revolution
> that is nonviolent is the Negro revolution. The only revolution in which the
> goal is loving your enemy is the Negro revolution. It's the only revolution in
> which the goal is a desegregated lunch counter, a desegregated theatre, a deseg-
> regated park, and a desegregated public toilet; you can sit down next to white
> folks—on the toilet. That's no revolution. Revolution is bloody, revolution is
> hostile, revolution knows no compromise, revolution overturns and destroys
> everything that gets in its way. And you, sitting around here like a knot on the
> wall, saying, "I'm going to love these folks no matter how much they hate me."
> No, you need a revolution.

Anticipating the romance of guns that has made black ghettoes into
shooting galleries between urban gangs or street criminals and their prey,
Malcolm in 1964 recommended that blacks form rifle clubs for self-
defense in areas where the government was not protecting them. He could
exhibit a more disciplined strength: once in a protest against police brutality he had led a band of Muslims to stand silently in front of a Harlem
precinct station.

Along with Malcolm's posturings about violence went a denunciation
of liberalism, the only major persuasion that pointed a way out of violence. King he labeled a "fool," handpicked by white liberals intent on
keeping blacks subjugated. He denounced as racist the spending of three
million dollars by the federal government to protect James Meredith at
the University of Mississippi. In 1963, the year of the March on Washington, Malcolm during an interview with *Playboy* urged separate white and
black societies.

Standing in contrast to the separatist militancy of the Muslims was the
persistence of black Americans who managed, even in bad times, to break
the color line. Among them was Jackie Robinson, who in 1947 had become the first African American baseball player in modern times to enter
the major leagues. The *New York Herald Tribune* for April 26, 1964,
quoted Robinson as saying that Malcolm "has big words," but no actions
in civil rights. "He is terribly militant on soap boxes, on street corners of
Negro ghettoes. Yet he has not faced Southern police dogs in Birmingham
as Martin Luther King has done."

Malcolm ultimately broke with Elijah Muhammad over the Muslim leader's attempt to keep him from making political statements. After two journeys to the Islamic heartland in the Middle East revealed to him that the faith did not require hatred of whites, he shed much of the racism that had infused his earlier pronouncements. In the mid-1960s a more complicated Malcolm emerged.

Of the deaths in 1964 of Andrew Goodman and Michael Schwerner in Mississippi, Malcolm said, "I've come to the conclusion that anyone who will fight not *for* us but *with* us is my brother." (In contrast, the poet-activist LeRoi Jones—he would change his name to Amiri Imamu Baraka—called Schwerner and Goodman "artifacts" whose deaths caused him no regrets. But in his 1984 *Autobiography* Baraka remarks: "Schwerner and Goodman were out there on the front lines doing more than I was.") At a meeting at Wayne State University in 1964 where Malcolm spoke, the Jewish moderator recognized for a question a black member of the audience who thereupon launched into an anti-Semitic rant. "I suspect," Malcolm interrupted, "that our moderator today is Jewish and I won't put him in the position of silencing you. So I will. Shut up and sit down."

"In the past, I have made sweeping indictments of all white people," he observed late in his life. "I will never be guilty of that again." He was now terming "sincere" the moderate black leaders James Farmer of CORE and particularly the Urban League's Whitney Young, whom he had previously denounced as Whitey Young. In a telephone statement for the French press early in 1965 after that government had denied him entrance into the country, he showed how far he had moved away from his old beliefs:

> I don't advocate violence and I'm not a racist, and I'm against racism and against segregation. I'm against anything that is immoral and unjust. I don't judge a person according to the color of his skin, I judge a person according to what he believes, according to his deeds and his intentions. I do not advocate violence—in fact, the violence I constantly refer to is the violence that the Negro in America is the victim of.

Malcolm in his last days was thinking of bringing the black condition in the United States before the United Nations, where African and Asian countries might vote to condemn this country's racial policies. Then, in February 1965, he was gunned down in full view of some four hundred followers, a victim of the violence he had helped to foment. There were foreshadowings of his violent death: his accusation that the leader of the puritanical Muslims had sired eight illegitimate children with six teen-aged girls; a declaration by the official Muslim newspaper that Malcolm deserved to die; Malcolm's report of observing Muslims shadowing him for months and his claim that they had firebombed his home; and his own admission that he had trained many Muslims how to kill. In an interview with *Ebony* on March 10, 1964, Malcolm said that the Black Muslim leaders have "got to kill me. They can't afford to let me live." The night after the murder, Elijah Muhammad's mosque in Harlem was torched, presumably by followers of Malcolm. (Earlier Muslim leaders Drew Ali and W. D. Fard had been mysteriously killed in power struggles within the Muslim movement.) Three Muslims were accused of killing Malcolm; all were indicted, tried, convicted of murder in the first degree, and sentenced to life in prison. In spite of all this, claims are made, depending more on what was possible than what was probable, that a CIA or FBI plot was responsible for Malcolm's death. Only slightly more plausible is the suggestion that Malcolm was the victim of narcotics interests in Harlem. James Cone, the author of a 1991 book on Malcolm, concludes that "there is much evidence to support [Muslim] complicity and very little to contradict it."

After his death Malcolm became a saint of sorts—a streetcorner Jean Genêt speaking anger in lean and simple metaphors. His posthumous influence both implanted pride and encouraged irresponsibility. His spiritual heirs (Malcolm bequeathed no material estate, whereas Elijah Muhammad would leave $74 million) include Kwame Touré (Stokely Carmichael) and H. "Rap" Brown (Jamil Abdullah Al-Amin) of SNCC, Huey Newton, Bobby Seale, and Eldridge Cleaver in his Black Panther phase, as well as Imamu Amiri Baraka (LeRoi Jones) and George Jackson, a black hero with literary skills who was killed in a shootout while trying to escape from prison. As Touré wrote, Malcolm knew "where he was going, before the rest of us did." To one teenaged boy growing up on the Mississippi Delta, Malcolm was to become pure words, pure thought: "I have no personal feelings about his conduct, [but] . . . he saved my mental life." In the 1990s it is usually not the tempered Malcolm of his final years who appears on the posters and book covers that have proliferated through the black community but the image of Malcolm during his Muslim days, the glaring and finger-spearing separatist.

It is as a personal model that Malcolm remains most deserving of study. In the posthumously published *Autobiography*, written with Alex Haley, the young Malcolm is a seeker, curious and at times generous in his relations with a white world he had no reason to trust. His time in the Nation of Islam involved the faithful mastery and elegant presentation of an arcane creed. His liberation from the most bigoted implications of the Black Muslim ideology and his effort to combine separatism with a wider view of the human race bespeak a large capacity for self-criticism and self-remaking. That he spent much of his career inviting others to define themselves by the unitary experience of blackness contradicted the example of his own complex and independent life.

Soon after Malcolm's death, separatism ceased to be confined within the sectarian boundaries of the Muslims and came to infect the civil rights movement itself.

There were understandable reasons. To battle-weary veterans of the voter registration years, the treatment of the Mississippi Freedom Democratic Party at Atlantic City in August 1964 appeared to be cause for veering away at least from white establishment liberals. Real or suspected instances of paternalism on the part of whites toward their black allies and co-workers in the rights movement naturally awakened resentment. "Negro students, you know," Robert Moses once observed, "actually feel this is their own movement . . . , that this is one thing that belongs to them in the whole country; and I think this causes the emotional reaction toward the white people coming in and participating." And perhaps it was impossible to sustain indefinitely the extraordinary composure and temperate conduct implicit in the civil rights movement. Pride founded effortlessly in the fact of racial identity, resentment rendered into a political principle, and an indrawing against the difficulties of full integration into a demanding world must have seemed at times the easier course. It was, in any event, a course that grew steadily in appeal among rights activists.

In 1966 the rupture between liberalism and black militancy, the rupture in fact within the black civil rights movement itself, became fully public. It emerged in June during a march across Mississippi calling on Washington to send marshals to enforce the right to vote as guaranteed in the Civil Rights Act of 1965. The march came after James Meredith, the black student who had integrated Ole Miss, was shot and wounded during a protest walk across the state.

Stokely Carmichael, the SNCC activist who was now the most vocal spokesman for separatism, was a major organizer of the event. Martin Luther King was there, determined to uphold the old spirit of integration. Unlike Roy Wilkins and Whitney Young, who refused to join with the black militants, King remained after Carmichael promised to allow whites to join in and to maintain nonviolence. But King was not in friendly company. Militants were increasingly calling him "de Lawd" and mocking the church cadences of his speeches. Attending the march were some armed black guards, the Deacons for Defense. Carmichael, recently renowned for brave voter registration work in Lowndes County, Alabama, appropriated from his adviser Willie Ricks the cry "black power" and during the march shot one of King's SCLC white associates between the eyes with a water pistol. One white marcher from the University of Michigan remembers the anger of Ricks, who "lashed out at whites. As he talked . . . there was a feeling of a rising storm." The black power chant "seemed like a hit on well-intentioned whites like me, that the message from Willie Ricks was 'Go home, white boy.'" The student did return to Ann Arbor and led the antiwar protest there, one of the first of many allies to depart from the rights movement in view of the swelling black separatist tide. The marchers turned down Wilkins's request that the demonstration be used in support of the civil rights bill of 1966, which was to desegregate housing.

Apologists insisted that the phrase "black power" was nothing more than a rallying cry to build political strength around the issue of the vote. But journalists seized on Carmichael's newsworthy but ill-defined phrase, and in Mississippi King warned him that the new tone "would confuse our allies, isolate the Negro community and give many prejudiced whites, who might otherwise be ashamed of their anti-Negro feeling, a ready excuse for self-justification." Carmichael, however, a veteran of some forty days in a Mississippi penitentiary, deliberately baited nonviolent blacks into leaving the march by making up new words for freedom songs: "I'm gonna bomb when the spirit say bomb . . . cut when the spirit say cut . . . shoot when the spirit say shoot." He was soon traveling across the country calling integration "irrelevant," a "subterfuge for the maintenance of white supremacy"; the President was a "bigot." Later he moved from predicting urban ghetto violence to advocating it.

A native of the Caribbean island of Trinidad, 96 percent of whose population was black, Carmichael soon was urging African Americans to sever all ties with whites. The media, on hand to record the face of southern white hatred, now aided in the creation of a public figure as harmful to the cause of integration as the acts of southern white louts had ultimately been beneficial to it.

After the Mississippi march, with its verbal violence among participants and tear gassing by police, a SNCC group operating as the Atlanta Project gained prominence through its hostility to the presence of whites within the civil rights movement (black separatist ideas in the organization had appeared as early as 1964). Several of the Atlanta militants belonged to the Nation of Islam, and SNCC now included other members unschooled in the practice of nonviolence that had seasoned the earlier activists of the civil rights movement. The influence of the North Carolinian Robert F. Williams, the author of *Negroes with Guns* (1962), also contributed to the wayward course of SNCC; eventually Williams had to leave the country for Cuba and then China following disputed charges of kidnapping.

SNCC, so argued the militants, must expel its white members. "The TRUTH," one Atlanta position paper declared in 1966, "is that the civil rights movement is not and never was our movement. . . . [T]he civil rights struggle since slavery (except for the *revolts* during slavery and the *riots* now) has been one of advancing our positions as slaves, but not abolishing slavery." The authors declared: "All white people are racists; that is, no white person (when you really get down to the nitty-gritty) can stand to deal with black people as humans, as black people ruling over them or ruling independently of them." Whites henceforth should not come into direct touch with the black poor, since they were "not equipped to dispel the myths of western superiority. White people only serve to perpetuate these myths." Organizing must be done by "Black people who are able to see the beauty of themselves, are able to see . . . that this country was built upon the blood and backs of our Black ancestors." Whites were a "contaminating" influence. Carmichael did not endorse the paper, and initially criticized it as reflecting a wish to be "blacker than thou." But he soon capitalized on it, running successfully against John Lewis to become head of SNCC. Carmichael was then twenty-four. The Atlanta Project's ideas came to dominate SNCC, which in 1967 officially though narrowly voted to expel whites, the ban to go into effect the following year. Thereby the organization, having achieved the philosophical purity and the exclusiveness that ideologues so relish, destroyed the possibility of its winning a power base and a future. The separatist mood, by making color the issue of preeminent importance, postponed the day when it would matter less.

The logic of black power dictated severance from establishment politics. Carmichael, whose behavior ranged in tone from soft-spoken and moderate to eruptive, pronounced it "as ludicrous for black people to join [the Democratic party] as it would have been for Jews to join the Nazi party in the 1930s. Our ideology must be pan-Africanism, nothing else. . . . We have to have a land base. I think that the best place for that is Africa and in Africa the best place is Ghana." President Kwame Nkrumah of Ghana, an authentic revolutionary, had another view of black pride: "When I speak of Africa for the Africans this should be interpreted in the light of my emphatic declaration that I do not believe in racialism. . . . The concept . . . does not mean that other races are excluded." Increasingly Carmichael fostered a scorn among poor blacks not only for leaders like King but also for members of their own race who aspired to self-improvement through education. "Integration today," he wrote, "means that the man who 'makes it' [leaves] his black brothers behind in the ghetto as fast as his new sports car will take him. It has no relevance to the Harlem wino or to the cotton picker making three dollars a day."

Along with the idea of black power often came a rhetoric of violence that Martin Luther King had long argued against. Carmichael, though telling King he opposed "aggressive violence," had argued during the

Mississippi march that every courthouse in the state should be burned to the ground "so that we can get rid of the dirt." In Cleveland he said: "When you talk about black power, you talk about bringing this country to its knees. When you talk of black power, you talk of building a movement that will smash everything Western civilization has created." H. Rap Brown, who succeeded Carmichael in 1967 as head of SNCC, came up with the epigram "Violence is as American as cherry pie." He told reporters in Atlanta that he had come to blow up the city. (Willie Ricks said SNCC militants there would "make Vietnam look like a holiday.") "Get your guns" and "burn this town down" were among Brown's contributions to clarifying the issues. Like Carmichael, who ultimately became prime minister of the Black Panther party, Brown had high-spirited moments: after meeting with President Johnson in 1965, he told reporters, "I stole some stuff out of the White House. . . . I was trying to figure how to get a painting off the wall and put it under my coat. I figured it belonged to me anyway."

The vocabulary of violence among black power militants, then as later, has essentially the sound of drama and the intoxications of language. It is not to be taken seriously as literal statement. But insofar as it gave cheap thrills to white radicals, confused liberals, and alienated masses of Americans whose support was necessary for social progress, it polluted discussion.

Among the prominent black power groups of the middle and late sixties, SNCC was in the running for the most doctrinaire. With the purity of vision characteristic of ideologues, the group in its later days refused to support President Johnson's civil rights legislation. Some of SNCC's Freedom Summer schools disdained the Great Society's Head Start program on the ground that it lured the young away from their black heritage. Nationalists declared that since Fannie Lou Hamer would not acknowledge the need to expel whites from SNCC, she was "no longer relevant" to the cause of black liberation. Some SNCC members abandoned any serious effort to make their organization effective. They coasted along on racial ideals, romanticized the black poor, talked of guerrilla warfare, and welcomed the ghetto riots of the mid- and late sixties as "rebellions." Stretches of time were spent in discussing hidden meanings of racial expressions and terminology; buzzwords like "oppression" and lists of "demands" cluttered discourse. Brutal infighting became common. At one point SNCC expelled Carmichael for failing to conform to what at the time happened to be its ideological position. In its last days SNCC, its leaders sometimes high on pills (Eldridge Cleaver complained that the group was "composed virtually of black hippies"), acted as though it were intent on making more enemies for blacks than any number of southern Klansmen could do. Most of the organization's affiliates at

black colleges disappeared. As SNCC declined in Mississippi and elsewhere in membership and influence, the NAACP added dozens of new
branches and doubled its membership. SNCC disbanded in 1969.

While SNCC was starting on its downward spiral, Martin Luther
King, who had won the Nobel Peace Prize in 1964, began devoting more
of his energies to protesting the war in Southeast Asia. He also concentrated more and more on class as opposed to racial tensions and, in his
call for redistribution of wealth, took a distinctly radical turn. King had
once remarked that the three worst problems were racism, economic exploitation, and war. His opposition to the war redeemed him among
many younger radical students, black and white, even as most politicians
and older civil rights leaders like Bayard Rustin and Roy Wilkins dis-
approved of his lending his prestige to the antiwar movement. One of
President Johnson's advisers, the irrepressible Professor John Roche of
Brandeis University, called King's New York City Riverside Church address of 1967 clear evidence that he "has thrown in with the Commies."
In early 1968 King initiated plans for a poor people's demonstration in
Washington, D.C. Representatives of the poor—black, Mexican-American, old-stock white, American Indian—would later set up a camp on the
Capital Mall that became known as Resurrection City. It was an attempt
to connect the civil rights movement to fundamental social and economic
issues and to mobilize the poor and disadvantaged across racial lines.
Had it continued beyond 1968, it might have constituted an initiative at
once more radical and less sullen than black power: more radical in addressing basic questions concerning the distribution of wealth and power,
less sullen in aiming at transcending resentment and racial exclusivity.

On April 3, 1968, in a speech supporting a strike by garbage collectors
in Memphis, King said:

> We've got some difficult days ahead. But . . . I've been to the mountain-
> top. . . . Longevity has its place. But I'm not concerned about that now. I just
> want to do God's will. And he's allowed me to go up to the mountain, and I've
> looked over, and I've seen the promised land. I may not get there with you. But
> I want you to know tonight that we as a people will get to the promised
> land. . . . Mine eyes have seen the glory of the coming of the Lord.

The next day, at the age of thirty-nine, King was murdered by a white
assassin.

In reaction to King's death, ghetto riots broke out across the nation.
Black power already had been popular among a few of the Memphis
garbagemen who had smashed windows and looted stores along with a
gang of young blacks known as the Invaders. In the District of Columbia,
Carmichael advised blacks to "get guns" and predicted that "guerrilla
warfare will rapidly develop in the cities." Rap Brown added his rhetori-

cal flourish, declaring to an audience in Washington, DC, to "do more shooting than looting when you riot. . . . If you are going to loot, loot yourself a gunstore." From 1965 through 1968, 169 people were to be killed in riots, seven thousand wounded, and more than forty thousand arrested. Few if any civil rights organizations had roots in the ghettoes, and their leaders could not stem this self-destructive rage.

The riots suited well a view of cities that this now largely urban nation has inherited from its rural past. The conviction that cities at their core are brutal, disordered, rotted with drugs and crime may have more to do with flight to the suburbs than does any simple racist objection to open housing: blacks with the means to do so have joined the flight. The urban disorders of the sixties altered the terms of cultural and social confrontation. In place of the traditional hostility between heartland and city, it was now the lawned communities against the inner city.

To investigate the riots President Johnson in 1967 appointed the National Advisory Commission on Civil Disorders, which, in a major statement of liberalism, labeled as racist the state and local institutional patterns that gave power to whites and denied it to blacks. Holding that the nation, after moving for a time toward integration, was once more becoming two societies, separate and unequal, the Commission recommended specific policies to improve life in the ghettoes and to provide for their eventual dispersion. As is well known, conditions of life there have since deteriorated rather than improved; in this the report has gone the way of similar documents after major riots—in 1919, in 1935, in 1943, and in 1965. All, in the words of the black psychologist Kenneth Clark, amounted to "the same analysis, the same recommendations, and the same inaction."

Martin Luther King had lived his dedication to ending racial injustice in this country, but his religious faith committed him to a particular ending of it. He wanted a conquest of the sin of bigotry and a reconciliation between racist and victim. Achieving this resolution to injustice would have brought an enhanced sense of dignity to black people. But it would have been significant also in its enhancement of the real as opposed to the self-perceived dignity of whites. King's understanding of the racial question rested on an ethic that defines the struggle for personal authenticity as just that: personal, interior, incapable of being subsumed under some social category such as race or class. King's Southern Christian Leadership Conference, along with the NAACP, continued after the 1960s to be at the forefront of the effort for civil rights long after SNCC and CORE had faded. Still, the anger that the death of King stirred against whites fed the black separatism that he had tried to combat.

Supporters of that persuasion set about to achieve the properly simple and unitary mindset among black Americans. Determined to make black children identify with the culture of ancient Africa, a few separatist mentors by the end of the sixties were attempting to shield them from the world outside, much as ideologues in school systems throughout the globe keep their charges from encountering divergent ideas and cultures that might awaken in them curiosity, irony, or skepticism. But try as hard as they could to filter out the culture that lay beyond their contrived nation of American blacks, the larger American nation is an ever-present fact— projected into homes every night by television—and achievement within it an ever-present need as measured by the wishes of young blacks themselves. In the end black separatism simply made less accessible the norms and qualities of a society that the good sense of black youth defined as desirable, or at least inescapable.

Roy Wilkins, a cultural conservative and an older veteran of the black combat against racism, persistently spoke out against the black militant attempt to reject the dominant society. What black power preached, Wilkins observed in his presidential address to the annual NAACP convention held in Los Angeles in 1966, was no more than the inverse of the South African formula: it was "a reverse Mississippi . . . a reverse Hitler . . . a reverse Ku Klux Klan." He wanted, Wilkins has explained, "to include Negro Americans in the nation's life, not to exclude them. America was our land as much as it was any American's. The task of winning our share was not the easy one of disengagement and flight but the hard one of work, of short as well as long jumps, of disappointment— and of sweet success." Wilkins's autobiography strikes out at the "ersatz, dashiki-built instant culture" of black power. "Did we," he asks, "destroy *Plessy vs. Ferguson* [the 1896 Supreme Court decision that permitted separate but equal facilities] after so many decades of pain and struggle only to Jim Crow ourselves with superficial ideas of black nationalism? Where had separatism led Marcus Garvey in the twenties? . . . I wasn't arguing against separatism in the abstract. I had seen it in action off and on for nearly forty years—and it didn't work."

A figure central to the theory and practice of black power was the poet and dramatist LeRoi Jones, born in Newark, New Jersey, who took on the African name Imamu (spiritual leader) Amiri (prince) Baraka (blessed one). He defined race not so much by genetics as by feeling, identity, and culture, and his definition of culture included politics. Black Americans, he declared, were a "cultural nation striving to seize the power to become a political nation." Black art "is change, it must force change, it must be change." If it was racist—in the play *Jello* Rochester gets to kill Jack Benny, who wears white face—that was a taste of the whites' own medicine.

In New York Baraka was arrested for encouraging looters during a power blackout, cruising Lenox Avenue in a sound truck. In a riot in

Harlem he stenciled a black-power fist on building walls and would greet people on the street with the consciousness-raising question "What time is it?" hoping for the response "It's Nation time!" Baraka's poem "Black People" counseled ghetto residents to say "magic words" ("Up against the wall mother fucker"), take "magic action" (smash windows together), and do a "magic dance" in the street ("take the shit you want"). At his trial for carrying firearms and resisting arrest during the 1967 rioting in Newark that left twenty-six dead and over a thousand injured, the judge read the poem, calling it "a diabolical prescription to commit murder and to steal and plunder." Baraka asserted that he was "sentenced for the poem." His conviction was later reversed.

Fundamentally, however, Baraka was committed to sparing his own children the destructiveness of the ghetto, and to working for the improvement of his birthplace, Newark, and its black community. "It is not hatred that nationalism is about but development of self," he observed. His efforts for voter registration and his use of performances for fundraising contributed to the electicn of Kenneth Gibson in 1970 as Newark's first black mayor. In 1974 Baraka and his Congress of African Peoples looked to Marxism, which pointed away from racial exclusiveness and toward an inclusive politics. Posters for his plays now announced that "poor whites are welcome." "Cultural nationalism," he wrote in the 1980s, "uses a historical, unchanging never-never-land Africa to root its hypotheses."

A black power venture oriented to culture was Ron Karenga's US movement, based in Los Angeles. Baraka became one of its chief supporters. US urged the teaching of Swahili, and it sponsored arts events based in the black community. The movement aimed at substituting black cultural and language studies for "slave" habits like "smoking reefers, and dropping pills, and drinking wine." In time Karenga, like Baraka, turned in some degree away from exclusiveness.

One of the organizations involved most strongly in black power advocacy and activities was CORE, which a few years earlier had carried out the integrationist Freedom Rides. Thereupon, however, it shifted increasingly toward separatist militancy. To this, members gave expression particularly at the 1966 convention, not long after the march across Mississippi and the black power pronouncements within the Atlanta wing of SNCC. Floyd McKissick, who that year replaced James Farmer as director of CORE, moved the group's headquarters from downtown Manhattan to uptown Harlem on 135th Street across from the Truth Coffee Shop. At the convention McKissick proclaimed nonviolence "a dying philosophy" that had "outlived its usefulness." The group's new separatist leadership rejected any alliance with the Democratic party and envisioned a millenarian future. Lillian Smith, the southern white liberal author who had been on CORE's national advisory committee for two decades, resigned in reaction to McKissick's policy and, echoing the title of her anti-racist novel of 1949, condemned the new "Killers of the Dream." CORE, she said, "had been infiltrated by . . . nihilists, black nationalists, and plain old-fashioned haters, who have finally taken over."

Members of CORE came to adopt the styles that were then becoming popular among militants of both races. There were whites from CORE who, in the complaint of a black woman, visited her apartment and put their feet on her coffee table, perhaps displaying their liberation from manners, one of the early casualties of ideologies of all sorts. With the advance of black power ideas in the organization, some white chapter leaders resented having to step down from leadership positions on racial grounds in an organization dedicated to wiping out racial discrimination. Other whites doubtless concluded that they had no right to question anything coming from the black community. One young white woman member of CORE remembered that during her visit to the Watts area in Los Angeles she had found poverty, and beyond that—"Truth. There does not seem to be the need for glamour or falseness that is so obvious in the white world. This truth and honesty are everywhere, in the food, the music, in the talk, and in the faces of the people. . . . My feeling is that the role of whites [in the civil rights movement] should be one of almost silence."

In 1967, the year that SNCC officially excluded whites from membership, CORE did the same. At CORE's convention in Columbus, Ohio, members debated the coming black nation-state. Some demanded that seaboard states from Florida to Maryland be emptied of whites and turned over to black separatists. Roy Innis, who succeeded McKissick as president of CORE, called for "organizing two separate and distinct races of people" by "sealing the borders" around black ghettoes and building a "membrane" around the community.

As it aligned more assertively with black power, CORE went into a sharp decline. After the Voting Rights Act of 1965, CORE chapters had less to do with registration and politics than with attacking the existing power structure. But members encountered enormous difficulties in trying to organize the poor. Berkeley's campus CORE secretary, for instance, reported that her group could obtain "no significant involvement of Oakland's black community" in its job demonstrations there. Members of Denver's middle-class CORE chapter established a freedom house in a vacant store in the city's poorest neighborhood but were reluctant to go into the area at night. The few neighborhood blacks attracted to such efforts remained silent at meetings, inhibited for want of education and confidence, or they drifted away. Association between CORE members and such groups of armed militants as the Deacons for Defense alienated both blacks and whites repelled by violence.

Perhaps the most sensational product of the new militancy was the Black Panther Party for Self Defense. Borrowing its name and its panther emblem from Stokely Carmichael's militant SNCC Black Panther party in Lowndes County, Alabama, the new group was founded in October 1966 in Oakland, California, by Huey Newton and Bobby Seale. It took as a leading text Chairman Mao's dictum that political power grows from the barrel of a gun. Newton was fascinated by *Negroes with Guns*, the tract by the black expatriate Robert Williams. "When the masses hear that a Gestapo policeman has been executed while sipping coffee at a counter, and the revolutionary executioners fled without being traced," blustered Newton in an expression of the violent fantasies that aroused the Panthers and a species of white leftists, "the masses will see the validity of this type of approach to resistance." After serving a prison sentence for a knifing incident, Newton had turned from a life of crime and violence to attend Oakland City College, and he would attract to the Panthers some other blacks who had quick minds and a talent for critical analysis. But Newton chiefly recruited "brothers off the block," and he disdained young blacks who held regular jobs, though he and other Panthers like Seale and Bobby Hutton accepted paychecks from the Great Society's antipoverty program. Unlike Stokely Carmichael, the Panthers generally welcomed white radicals as allies and held a vision of world revolution among all peoples.

From its inception the Black Panther party adopted a mystique of armed aggressiveness, and its gun fetishism was an invitation to pop psychology. Its particular object of hostility was the police, which made some sense: urban blacks had ample experience of police prejudice and brutality. To monitor the white police force in the Oakland ghettoes, its leather-jacketed members carried cartridge belts and guns, including M1 rifles, twelve-gauge shotguns, .45-caliber pistols, and carbines: California did not then bar the open flourishing of such arsenals. Part of the money for the growing arsenals came from sales of *Thoughts of Chairman Mao* on the Berkeley campus.

Eldridge Cleaver, for a time the Black Panther minister of information and then its field marshal, wrote for *Ramparts* magazine of his exhilaration on first meeting the Panthers:

> I spun round in my seat and saw the most beautiful sight I had ever seen: four black men wearing black berets, powder blue shirts, black leather jackets, black trousers, shiny black shoes—and each with a gun! In front was Huey P. Newton with a riot pump shotgun in his right hand, barrel pointed down to the

floor. Beside him was Bobby Seale, the handle of a .45-caliber automatic showing from its holster on his right hip, just below the hem of his jacket. A few
steps behind Seale was Bobby Hutton, the barrel of his shotgun at his feet. Next
to him was Sherwin Forte, an M1 carbine with a banana clip cradled in his
arms.

He had served nine years for rape in Soledad Prison, where he educated
himself and wrote the memoir *Soul on Ice*, which first brought him to
public attention. He told *Playboy* magazine that "for the young black
male, the Black Panther party supplies very badly needed standards of
masculinity." Such was one role model of black power. It is a comment
on the self-destructive impulses within white radicalism that in 1968
Cleaver became a presidential candidate of the Peace and Freedom party,
winning 195,135 votes. Cleaver spread his hostilities widely: besides
turning on SNCC and eventually on the Panthers themselves, he denounced the black author James Baldwin as a faggot and referred to King
as Martin Luther Queen.

In May 1967 thirty Black Panthers achieved considerable visibility
when in military garb, some of them toting guns, they sought entrance to
the visitors' gallery of the California state assembly in Sacramento, but
instead walked inadvertently onto the assembly floor. They had intended
to protest a bill making illegal the carrying of unconcealed weapons. Photographs of the incident would appear around the world.

That October, Huey Newton was charged with the murder of a patrol-
man in a shootout with police in which he was wounded. Eldridge
Cleaver beat and pistol-whipped dissenters within the Panther ranks to
force agreement to institute a forthcoming nationwide Free Huey movement, which was publicized by *Ramparts* magazine. Electrifying meetings
before thousands promoted the campaign, and Cleaver announced that a
merger with SNCC had resulted in the appointment of H. Rap Brown as
Panther minister of justice and Stokely Carmichael as prime minister.
Brown fired up one crowd of six thousand with, "How many white folks
did you kill today?" Even the mild-mannered James Foreman of SNCC
joined in, calling for thirty police stations to be blown up and five hundred policemen dead in return for the killing of one Panther. A Bay Area
organization named "Honkies for Huey" gushed of its hero: "His love for
people is so strong that it is impossible not to feel it." Celebrities rushed
to the defense of the Panthers. Luminaries like Donald Sutherland, Otto
Preminger, Leonard Bernstein, Jane Fonda, Harry Belafonte, and Dick
Gregory raised large sums. The radical attorney Fay Stender—who was
later to commit suicide after having been shot and paralyzed by a black
militant—got Newton's charge reduced to manslaughter on the technical-
ity that he might have been wounded prior to shooting Officer Frey, so

that his judgment in firing back was clouded. Of the crime of manslaughter he was never convicted.

Following his release from prison to the cheers of a crowd of some ten thousand in 1969, Newton became a cocaine and, some years later, a crack addict. Soon he began to support his drug habit by appropriating funds the Panthers had raised to provide free breakfasts for children of poor people. In 1973 Newton murdered a prostitute and fled to Cuba, but returned after he paid off a witness to withhold evidence against him. As the 1994 book *Shadow of the Panther*, written by the black journalist Hugh Pearson, makes abundantly clear, Newton was guilty of both murders, and almost certainly many more.

Two decades afterward it is sometimes hard to tell what in the Panther program was guerrilla theater and caricature and what was murderous. In the late sixties, local police forces and J. Edgar Hoover had palpable difficulty making the distinction. All new members had to sell on the streets a newspaper called the *Black Panther*, which reached a circulation of 140,000 by the end of 1969. It was loaded with pictures of policemen characterized as pigs and Panthers shooting police. Like the Nation of Islam's publications, it frequently demanded retribution. The *Panther* called for freeing all blacks from prison. At their free breakfasts, the Panthers indoctrinated poor black children; one stanza of a song taught to some of them went, "I want a porkchop. Off the pig!" But Cleaver's shootout with police in Oakland, during which he was wounded, was not mere theater. Other Panthers became involved in lethal clashes with police, some provoked, some not. David Horowitz and Peter Collier, editors of the leftist *Ramparts* during the sixties, would later claim—after turning politically rightward—that the Panthers had killed some of their brethren in remote areas of the Santa Cruz Mountains and executed their bookkeeper, Betty Van Patter, whom the two had recommended to Newton. In Oakland and other cities the breakfast program for children, often used in justification of the Panthers, was increasingly based on extortion. Convenience stores that did not contribute food were in some instances firebombed. The Panthers almost from the beginning also ran a protection racket in Oakland, whereby crime was allowed to flourish. One breakfast program in New Haven, Connecticut, does seem to have operated without criminality.

Much was made of the police killing of the young Panther Bobby Hutton. Cleaver, according to numerous sources (including the Panther leader David Hilliard and Cleaver himself), in April 1968 had organized four carloads of Panthers to do "some shooting." They planned to ambush a policeman while transporting a cache of weapons to one of numerous safe houses in the San Francisco area. They achieved their purpose, but several officers backed Cleaver and Hutton into a house. When the two men came out with hands raised, Hutton stumbled, dropped his hands, and was killed by a policeman. Since Cleaver claimed at the time that a police car had pulled up and started shooting for no reason, Hutton became an overnight martyr among young blacks and equally credulous radical whites. Seventy-five law students at Berkeley signed up as Panther supporters. At a New York City rally to raise legal defense funds for the Panthers, Amiri Baraka told the interracial gathering of some two thousand that "the white people who killed Bobby Hutton are the same white people sitting here." He received applause.

In 1969 the Panthers' program of black nationalism had the endorsement of Students for a Democratic Society, which helped precipitate the split within SDS later that year. Carmichael, working with Eldridge Cleaver, successfully urged the establishment of Black Panther groups throughout the country. The Panthers' news organ engaged in calculated diversions and disruptions. The group seemed to join with the conservative NAACP in condemning "fools running around who declare that they are 'just trying to be black' by wearing Dashikis and Bubas and . . . telling black people that they should relate to African customs and African heritage that we left 300 years ago, that this will make them free." The Panthers' program included a proposal to set up a black state in the South where polygamy would be practiced. The president would be Robert F. Williams of the Deacons for Defense, then wanted by the law. With chapters in most large American cities and elsewhere, it became for a time the nation's leading symbol of black resistance to the American power structure. Sometime in 1969 the SNCC contingent among the Panthers pulled out, convinced that the group's behavior was becoming pathologically vigilante. By 1972 only about two hundred Panthers remained.

Among the enemies that the black power movement perceived, American Jews had a special place. Heirs to a history of persecution and traditionally in the vanguard of liberal thought and action, politically active Jews were major participants in the civil rights movement. But after the Six-Day War of 1967 between the Israelis and their Arab neighbors, black militants attacked Israel as a racist Western nation imposing an imperial dominion over the Palestinians. Policy clashes in New York City with the teachers and administrators, many of them Jewish, who presided over predominantly black urban schools furthered the mutual alienation. In 1967 the Ford Foundation made a grant to advance community control of the Ocean Hill–Brownsville public school system in Brooklyn. When blacks took over control of the school board, instituted an Afrocentrist curriculum, and tried to transfer some Jewish teachers out of the district, the teachers struck. Demands for quotas in universities for blacks also antagonized Jews, for in the past quota systems had been employed against them. All this added to a waning in sympathy toward black political causes within what had perhaps been the single white ethnic group most helpful to them. More generally it posed a dilemma for liberals who in the past had believed the educational system to be one of their special responsibilities.

Black power was much infected with macho swagger, and militants portrayed women as bitches, bimbos, or subordinate to their revolutionary men. Therein it alienated much of its own potential constituency. Men of the black power generation were capable of rejecting white mores and yet accepting a *Penthouse* concept of relations between the sexes. Stokely Carmichael's alleged remark that the only position for women in SNCC was prone sharpened the growing fury of the women's movement. Huey Newton and David Hilliard were among the Panther leaders who beat party women regularly; it was a normal part of Panther life. Eldridge Cleaver, in *Soul on Ice*, spoke of white women with an arrogance, passing for existential anger, that some white radicals failed to condemn in the midst of things they wanted to cheer.

Would black power accommodate itself to white radicalism? At the 1967 antiwar demonstration in front of the Pentagon, some black militants gave an example of their attitude toward the camaraderie of resistance. They refused to join white protesters and withdrew to hold meetings by themselves while confrontations were taking place.

The growing numbers of enemies their movement was making left black power orators untroubled. Neither by talent nor by desire were they equipped for winning friends. Militants could not stop at repelling Jews, women, and as much of the antiwar movement as possible. They also turned on one another, splitting into factions that clashed over whether the goal was to be black capitalism or African communalism or some kind of Marxist utopia.

Black guerrilla theater had its moment on at least one major university campus. For a brief time early in 1969, Cornell University was the location of a singularly bizarre disturbance, an acting out of wishes, fears, and gestures that rendered the sixties as public theater.

Blacks on that campus had been troubled for some weeks by a variety of incidents. A young black woman from New York City had enraged roommates by playing soul music at peak volume and otherwise being in their view obstreperous. The school authorities referred her for psychiatric assistance and finally asked her to leave. But she and other black students found that unacceptable. The school gave in by setting up some black women's cooperative residences. In another instance, black students who objected to a visiting professor, a Jesuit priest from the Philippines whom they held to be racist, drafted a statement for him to read before his class. But they rejected his insistence on being allowed to look it over beforehand, and he dismissed the class; thereupon his black students held hostage the professor's department chairman and secretaries. In the interest of coming "to grips with the agonies of our society," as the liberal President James Perkins phrased it, the university refrained from taking action against the students.

Getting away with these tactics emboldened the militants to do more. The center of controversy was a program in black studies that the university was planning to put into effect for the next academic year, following Yale's successful introduction of a similar program in 1968. Black militants came to think that the committee charged with setting up the program was engaging in stalling tactics, and they demanded full control over its establishment and the admission of black students. Black militants invaded the president's office with water pistols, took hundreds of books from library shelves, and dumped them as "irrelevant." At one point some militants invaded a meeting of the black studies advisory committee and declared the body dismissed; then they issued an ultimatum that included the setting up of an autonomous degree-granting college within Cornell. When President Perkins resisted, black students physically pulled him from the podium during a conference on apartheid that included only three blacks out of twenty-five participants.

On Friday, April 18, a flaming cross thrown on the porch of a black female–student cooperative gave black students a legitimate reason for outrage. Many fraternities and sororities at Cornell, at least until the very recent past, had been notoriously anti-black and anti-Semitic, and some campus officials dismissed the incident as a "thoughtless prank." Male blacks, however, thereupon seized the Student Union and ejected visitors using rooms there during Parents' Weekend. White Delta Upsilon fraternity members tried unsuccessfully to recapture the building. Their skirmish was not an entirely unreasonable action on a campus in which force now seemed to have become the chief means of inquiring into academic questions.

Then two shotguns and thirteen rifles were passed in to the people occupying the student union. At that point the will of the administration crumbled. Acceding to the militants' terms, Perkins agreed to put the new program of black studies under separate and essentially black militant direction. After a representative of the college administration announced agreement to virtually all the black demands, news photographers snapped away as the black students marched out in Panther fashion with guns raised, therein bringing to the American public one more revolutionary fantasy in a campus that had become wonderland. The faculty at first rejected the agreement or, more correctly, capitulation that college officials had made; the administration started to call in the police; militants announced that Cornell had three hours to live; the faculty council recommended reversal of its initial rejection and in a voice vote gave in, asking for a "restructuring" of the university. The conflict was over. Cornell had nothing left to surrender.

Several prominent faculty members left Cornell in protest, among them Allan Bloom, who would write the bestselling book *The Closing of the American Mind*. Clinton Rossiter, a prominent political science professor, committed suicide in his despair over the events. In justice to the professors at Cornell who submitted to the militants, some residual awareness of a college's traditional role of serving *in loco parentis* may have guided them at their second meeting—had guided Perkins from the beginning—and they doubtless recognized that the situation was building to a point where, sooner or later, some student would get killed.

At San Francisco State as well that year, black activism led to guerrilla theater. During troubles there militants wearing stocking masks invaded campus offices, smashed equipment, and cut telephone wires. Black students of Wisconsin State at Oshkosh presented a list of demands and ransacked the presidential suite. But Oshkosh was not Cornell. Protesters were jailed, and the Board of Regents expelled 90 of 114 black students from campus.

Acting both on FBI director J. Edgar Hoover's obsessions and on two years of President Johnson's urgent requests for intelligence on urban rioters that might reveal and discredit their leaders, the FBI in August 1967 launched an essentially criminal policy of repression, particularly against black urban splinter groups such as the Panthers. Other organizations—Asian, Latino, and white—were under surveillance as well, but the Panthers had at more than one point encouraged the murder of police officers. The Bureau was operating under the COINTELPRO program, which had originated in the 1950s for the purpose of identifying communists. FBI strategy included attempts to tie down black leaders in expensive and time-consuming legal problems as well as the use of provocateurs to incite violence among black radicals. State and local officials loosely cooperated with the FBI but often pursued independent strategies. Between 1967 and 1969 nine police officers were killed and fifty-six wounded in confrontations with Panthers; ten Panthers were killed and a sizable number wounded. The blame was by no means entirely on the Panthers; racist police would commit murder if the circumstances were right.

In 1969 Fred Hampton, a leader among the Chicago Panthers, went to prison for the crime of stealing $76 worth of ice cream bars. While he was in jail, the police raided several Chicago Panther offices. That November a shootout took the lives of two policemen and a former Panther. When city police, operating on information supplied by an FBI informant, the next month raided the now freed Hampton's apartment, they shot and killed him and another Panther. Leading tour groups through the apartment, Panthers showed people the bullet holes made at 4:45 A.M. and Hampton's bloody mattress. Survivors sued the city government and in 1982 won out of court a settlement of $1.85 million. But after some one thousand arrests and nineteen killings, the Panthers were in disarray.

After the FBI's efforts, combined with the militant groups' own internal disorder, led to their disintegration, the inflammatory rhetoric of black power burned on, scorching the ideals of brotherhood and love that Martin Luther King had preached until his death. Funds from white liberals and northern foundations to civil rights groups, which the public now easily confused with the emergent New Left, were dropping. Rap Brown went into hiding in Canada but returned in 1971, only to be wounded in a shootout with New York police following a robbery in Manhattan. He spent most of the 1970s in prison, adopted the Black Muslim faith, and encountered further difficulties with the law during the mid-1990s in Atlanta. Huey Newton, titled Supreme Servant of the People, by the 1980s had an extensive record of murder charges without convictions. Newton, who went on to earn a doctorate in the History of Consciousness Program from the University of California at Santa Cruz, was shot to death by black drug dealers in 1989 in Oakland. The black mayor of the city declined to come to his funeral, citing Newton's constant involvement in criminal violence.

As an epilogue to the violence of the 1960s came the riot in 1971 at New York State's Attica prison, during which thirty-nine people died. Preliminary reports in the press claimed that black rioters had killed hostages, but autopsies found that all deaths in the recapture of the prison had been from bullets of the state troopers and prison guards.

While on the one hand the black power movement was an outcome of passions and ambitions released during the civil rights days, its appearance also indicates that by the mid-sixties the rights activists had done about all they could do. Formal legal equality was in the courts and on the books, yet poverty and discrimination remained. Black power, then, was a thrashing about for some progress beyond that achieved by rights marches and new laws. But black power had little of lasting value to offer toward overcoming poverty, and nothing substantial over time as an alternative to integrated prosperity and opportunity.

"Put too much power in any one son bitch's hands, it's too much," complained a disillusioned member of the North Carolina branch of the Deacons for Defense, an organization formed for protecting blacks against white violence in the South. "How can you work with a son of a bitch that every time you look up he is throwin' up his fist talkin' about black power?" The potentially most convincing claim, that integration did not address fundamental economic inequities and only the establishment of a separate, autonomous nation within a nation could serve, was undermined by the failure of black power to address economic concerns in any major way. Black power, then, could subsist only on one belief, essentially a formula for psychological and objective defeat: the conviction, King observed, "that the Negro can't win." Dismissing as self-destructive the violence fantasies of black revolutionary rhetoric, Theodore Cross's *The Black Power Imperative* contends that integration—the active physical entrance into the spaces occupied by whites—is the indispensable means of access to the economic and other forms of power that whites in the United States now monopolize, and thus the true way to genuine black power. Black nationalism, argues Harold Cruse, wants "sovereignty, but a subsidized sovereignty. It seeks to develop the rudiments of a new black nation, but merely succeeds in producing a new form of a black ghetto." Irving Howe in *Dissent* summarized black separatist control of the ghettos: "Black people would then acquire possession of their own slum tenements, control their own crowded and segregated schools, do battle with their very own rats. They would still receive the crumbs—no, the garbage—from the table of this affluent society, but they would take title to that garbage."

While the black poor have not yet turned despair into an ideology, they have responded in one way to the logic of hopelessness: their voting turnout is notably low. SNCC workers risked their lives to win the vote in Mississippi. Many Democrats, at their own considerable political expense, have championed African Americans. Democrats need the black vote, and blacks need the Democrats. A variant of the failure to vote at all has been the creation—at the insistence of black leaders and with the support of both Republicans and Democrats—of voting districts so carved as to be overwhelmingly black. These districts—evidently outlawed by the Supreme Court in July 1995—have facilitated the election of a number of African Americans to the House of Representatives. But most calculations indicate that clustering black votes densely in fewer districts has contributed to the election of more conservatives from predominantly white districts to Congress. The black power movement cannot be blamed for the neglect of the vote among the black poor, but it can be blamed for a failure to urge the black constituency to vote, and not only for African Americans but for white candidates who would represent their interests. Malcolm X was on the same path to self-destruction at the time when he declared of the American Peace Corps workers showing villagers how to string electric lights, put in windows, build schools, and read their native languages that they were spies and agents of colonialism. And to the extent that some American liberals patronized separatist black militancy or in its presence became guilt-locked in silence, liberalism became complicit in its own political decline.

Amid all this, the mentality born of black power survives, and comes close to being the dominant politics of the black community. The bluster of the separatists is still romanticized. Black politicians who tolerate black anti-Semites have enjoyed the toleration of white liberals. Affirmative action, justifiable as a tactical way of correcting present wrongs, has gained approval as compensation for the wrongs done to past generations, as though one person can inherit in his blood a treasury of merits for the injustices others have suffered. Thus the black power ethos strives to encrust black Americans into a single mass, and whites into another, mutually isolated, lacking the kinds of rebellious individuality capable of thinking outside the norms of the group. And the liberal tradition of civil rights and civil liberties, affirming the integrity of the individual, fades alongside the social democratic tradition, once articulated in the best of the New Deal, affirming the community of workers across class and racial lines.

The black power treatment of women was only part of an illness that still afflicts the ghettoes, a mark of the failure of the movement to build an enduring separate community. By the 1990s the number of young African American men either in jail, on probation, or on parole exceeded the total number enrolled in the nation's colleges by more than 170,000. Black power had claimed to strengthen individual character and foster an alternative black nationhood. In fact, its vocabulary and style went more easily with the violence that has grown with the drug trade.

The black power years led many Americans to recognize as a more desirable alternative the integrationist activism that in the time of early rights demonstrations they had thought radical. Quite contrary to its intentions, black power contributed at least indirectly to making the civil rights movement of Martin Luther King and SCLC, of the marches and the sit-ins, part of American history, to be enshrined with the Lincolns and Franklin Roosevelts who in their own times had so angered defenders of older ways. Civility, so much a part of the integrationist outlook that black power had opposed, speaks in the reaction of Rosa Parks to rioting in 1967 in Detroit, where she was then living: she was horrified that looters had attacked a grocery store in her neighborhood run by "good, good whites." In 1994 she herself became the victim of a young black thug who struck her repeatedly and robbed her. Characteristically she forgave him but wondered what "has happened to our young people." It was activists of the temper of Rosa Parks who established the moral terms of race relations that the country at large has now come to honor.

However great the damage black power did to it, the achievements of the civil rights movement in many respects remained intact. John Lewis, a respected leader in SNCC and later a United States congressman from Georgia, comments in a recent oral history:

The civil rights movement that I was a part of has, in a short time, changed this region. There are still problems, no question about it, but when you go around this area, you see people working together in a way that is simply amazing. It's a different climate.

You go back to some of these communities where we had marches, and you see some of the same people. I was in Selma not long ago, and the mayor who was mayor then gave me the key to the city. You go to lunch or dinner with some of the people who were in power then, and the guy will say, "John, I was wrong. I was on the wrong side. I tried to keep you all from marching. I had you arrested. We thought you were an agitator. We were wrong. We made a mistake." In recent years, I've met with Governor Wallace and with other officials. I met with the son of the major who gave the orders for the troopers to advance at Selma, and this young man said to me, "We're sorry about what happened, and about what my father did."

I'm telling you, they are entirely different people now, and I think one thing the movement did for all of us in the South, black and white alike, was to have a cleansing effect on our psyche.

I think it brought up a great deal of the dirt and a great deal of the guilt from under the rug to the top, so that we could deal with it, so that we could see it in the light. And I think that in a real sense, we are a different people.

We are better people. It freed even those of us who didn't participate—black people, white people alike—to be a little more human.

If Lewis sounds perhaps too optimistic in the face of today's dismal conditions of urban decay, his words must be read against the shadow of the horrors he had known in his early years. There could be no better testimony than Lewis's to a fact known to Americans of both races old enough to remember the years before the rights revolution. "Those who sardonically claim 'not much has changed for American blacks,'" observes Mary King in *Freedom Song*, "must not know how bad it was. . . . The word *integrated* has lost significance in the American lexicon. To say that 'the car was integrated' . . . was once a frightening statement."

Visible integration among characters in television dramas, integrated entertainment, integrated news teams, a host of major cities governed by black mayors, Birmingham among them, a black governor in the old Confederacy: such phenomena today appear ordinary and normal. The reason they have become normal is that they are victories of a movement that forty years ago challenged a country in which all of them were unthinkable. Also taken as normal, and also unthinkable in the past, is the swelling presence of blacks in the American middle class.

Racism of the old vintage persists. To that, among other examples, the conduct of elements of the Los Angeles police department testified as recently as the 1990s. To this day almost any black, whether lower- or middle-class, can relate stories of mistreatment by white police. In other ways, however, the character of racism itself has changed. The smugness that today bears the name of racism is so evolved from its recent ancestor as to need, perhaps, some name of its own. Racism, or whatever it should be called, is no longer a matter of assigning to black people a defined subordinate place in society, an intricate ritual of white privilege assumed and black deference expected. Even right-wingers now take for granted the assertive, nondeferential presence of black Americans in the social, economic, and political realms and bestow their quite genuine congratulations on those who have joined the affluent classes. Most conservatives are now preoccupied by evidence of violence, crime, unmarried mothers, and other forces of social disintegration among the rest. Today, they find in such evidence proof of the superiority of the comfortable middle classes or the failure of liberal antipoverty programs. The color of the excluded classes makes their identification the easier and more convenient, but it is a secondary fact.

Tangible results of the civil rights movement live on in the courts. The judiciary is not supposed to be responsive to political movements: much of its value lies precisely in its ability to protect minorities against majority sentiment. This is what it has done, or largely done, in the case of the black minority, therein acting as an independent force within the rights revolution. The Supreme Court under Chief Justice Earl Warren, together with the lower federal courts, cut the heart out of the South's caste system. By 1972, 40 percent of southern blacks attended a public school in which whites were in a majority. One among many forces responsible for blocking greater progress in northern schools was black nationalism. Some of the most important decisions of the Warren Court concerning criminal procedure and the rights of the accused offered a degree of protection to blacks, who had been so often victim of wrongful arrest and maltreatment by the police. In *Gideon v. Wainwright* (1963), the Court, in siding with a white convict, guaranteed in all felony cases the right to legal counsel regardless of the ability to pay. Three years later, in *Miranda v. Arizona*, the justices affirmed that before answering questions prisoners must be told their rights. The Court's most critical decisions affecting urban political life came in legislative apportionment cases beginning with *Baker v. Carr* (1962). This ruling ended some of the extreme instances of a rural area's enjoying power disproportionate to its population, and thereby incidentally helped elevate to an equality relative to numbers the voting power of the black urban masses.

The antipoverty measures of Democratic administrations, backed by vigorous affirmative action programs, gave capable blacks the opportunity to attend the nation's best colleges and postgraduate institutions. Many determined black students without family help could manage to go to a state university or junior college with the assistance of government grants and loans. To accommodate the distinctive needs of black students as well as to enrich the curriculum, many universities have also established black studies departments or programs.

Had traditional classes and textbooks done what they ought to have been doing all along—discuss black culture and the status of women or Hispanics as a matter of course, just as they treated English Americans or the settlement of the West—the campuses might long ago have had programs in black and women's studies, examining their themes with breadth and curiosity. Excellent scholarship does come out of such programs, and other respectable field studies also came out of political ferment. "There was no black revolution in the United States," correctly observes the black intellectual Harold Cruse, "without cultural revolution" and an education in what that culture is. But the rethinking from the 1960s onward of university curricula has at least on a few campuses come close to inviting any group claiming a record of oppression to engage in a solipsistic examination of itself.

Roy Wilkins of the NAACP spoke of "racial breast-beating" among those black students who say they need to get together in their own dormitories to build a common strength:

> Who can declare them completely wrong? Certainly they are right about the usefulness of study of Afro-American history and culture. They are right, also, in calling for increased enrollment of Negro students and in requesting more black faculty members. But in demanding a black Jim Crow studies building within a campus and exclusively black dormitories, they are opening the door to a dungeon. They do not see that no black history becomes significant and meaningful unless it is taught in the context of world and national history.

Segregation on campus was detestable in its traditional white forms—the fraternities and sororities that excluded not only minorities but white students who did not conform to the petty standards of the group. Self-imposed, sometimes racistoid apartness suggests a need to continue the condition of oppression and conflict: a need among some students and faculty who find indignation and rage to be the most manageable states of mind. Resegregation in schools is, like traditional segregation, pernicious on any number of counts. It deprives black students of the contacts that make for successful careers in the larger society, the society that black militants are the first to define as possessing all the desirable wealth and power. It closes down minds and imaginations. Compartmentalization into fields and subfields had already fractured the intellectual life of the university, even before it became a fashion among some students and faculty to withdraw from the continuing discourse that ought to be proceeding throughout every campus.

Though the civil rights movement won formal and in many ways informal equality and brought sizable numbers of blacks into the middle class, it failed to cut the Gordian knots, the most enduring social problems that came out of the country's racial past. Since the great days of the rights demonstrations, black Americans have been prey, more than the rest of the country, to forces corrosive of social order. Especially visible is a black underclass, trapped in a world of drugs, crime, illiteracy, and shattered families. The instabilities of black families, a growing number of them headed by women and mired in welfare dependency, were at the core of black social malaise. So argued the sociologist and politician Daniel Patrick Moynihan in a controversial position paper published in the mid-sixties. Today far more blacks die annually, victims of other blacks, than were killed in all the lynchings in American history. Others are living victims not of the Ku Klux Klan but of street drugs supplied by their black brothers. Drugs, disintegrating families, street violence—these are the ills that threaten black communities, and no vocabulary of black rage will begin effectively to address them.

Meanwhile, there is the black parent in a ghetto or middle-class neighborhood who gets up at six in the morning, eats a fast breakfast and dresses her children for school before she goes off to her computer training, the construction worker who at the same hour drinks enough coffee to prepare him for the work that will someday buy his family a larger home. They are heirs of the civil rights movement, heirs as well of the American tradition of work and family and a carefully nurtured future. They can use social programs out of the liberal past; but these are about to be victim to white middle-class selfishness, aided by the conduct of the separatists, the criminals, and the compensation mongers. Not all is lost: a few entrenched black-nationalist professors will continue to do well, as will politicians in carefully gerrymandered black districts, along with the crack dealers.

In the early 1960s Norman Podhoretz, then a liberal and editor of *Commentary*, published an essay, "My Negro Problem—and Ours," that rivals in complexity James Baldwin's *The Fire Next Time*. It addresses hostility between black and white. The article's strength lies in Podhoretz's evocation of his childhood when his antagonism to young blacks began, and in his acknowledgment that the adult must leave the child behind.

As a Jewish youth in New York City belonging to people not much less poor than the nearby black families in the Depression-ridden 1930s, Podhoretz could not understand the claim that American blacks were a persecuted race. That is because his own experience—the concrete, intimate experience that makes up a child's reality—taught him that it was black kids who were apparently more confident, superior in strength and ruthlessness, the aggressors in youthful violence against whatever local white child invited their enmity.

Norman Podhoretz the child was touching on a truth that he did not know, ideologues cannot grasp, and his essay does not explicitly define. This truth is that the oppressor, at any specific instant, is not whoever is politically definable as the Oppressor but whoever at that moment has power and is using it against whoever at that same moment is alone and afraid. Norman Podhoretz the adult came to know that beyond the limits of personal experience lie realities that the mind must recognize even when the emotions cannot respond. Reality in this case, of course, is that in the greater world white Americans have been collectively the arrogant street gang and black Americans the powerless victims, in economics and politics and society and often enough on city streets and backcountry roads. The adult Podhoretz, now remembering the security and encouragement he had found in his own household, chose to endorse not the emotions of the child that were still with him but the intelligence and conscience that could respond to facts the emotions did not feel.

Podhoretz the adult, and at that time the liberal, had come to grasp something about human nature that was the triumph of the nonviolent civil rights movement and in another way the strength of American liberalism. The rights movement bore witness against the primitive emotions of racism and, in its own self-restraint, the primitive angers that must have surged time and again within the protesters. Liberalism has worked to build up a buttress of laws and customs against institutional racism and a buttress of education against the aggressiveness of the individual. In uneasy partnership the two had a time of achievement during the sixties, before a backwash of black fury and white self-centeredness and the entrepreneurship of the drug trade smashed against the edifice of reason and justice that they had begun to construct.

**Resolve and Restraint:
The Cold War under Kennedy**

AN ACHING-COLD SUNLIGHT etched the public figures who performed the inaugural rites. It blinded the poet Robert Frost as he tried to read the poem he had composed for the ceremony. Thereupon he discarded it in favor of another poem he spoke from memory. But the words remembered today from January 20, 1961, are those that the speechwriter Theodore Sorensen had composed and the forty-two-year-old John Kennedy delivered to set the tone of his presidency. The country, Kennedy proclaimed in his clean harsh New England twang, was ready to "pay any price, bear any burden, meet any hardship." That the prices and the hardships, along with their objectives, were unspecified does not diminish the appropriateness of the address. It was as right for its era as the crowd-flattering pronouncements of the Reagan presidency, no hint of price or burden in them, were to the 1980s. And if the tone of the inaugural presaged an increase in defiance of the Soviet Union, it ushered in an administration that was to modify the terms of the engagement with the communist superpower.

Kennedy spoke of action, heroic if necessary. Action was to come, but in a form that the government had few resources for understanding. Baton Rouge, Montgomery, Greensboro: these and uncounted civil rights actions in the years before Kennedy's tenure had prepared for the character of the decade more than had the President's own career. The encounter between Kennedy liberalism and the religious witness of the nonviolent civil rights protesters constituted much of the dialogue within liberalism during the 1960s.

—————————

John Kennedy was born to money, to high ambition, and to ill health. Money gave the Kennedys access to the education, the manners, the sports, the power of the patrician class to which they aspired. The envious insecurity of the Irish Catholic Joseph Kennedy toward upper-class Protestants drove him to school his children at once to emulate their ways and to a competitiveness that the well-born are ordinarily supposed to despise. Perhaps illness as much as anything else made Jack somewhat more bookish and private than might have been predicted of a Kennedy, brought him to admire resolve and courage as inward counters to weakness and adversity, and drew him as a boy to reading biographies of great historical figures. This disposition would give Kennedy a manner that went well with Democratic party liberalism on the eve of the 1960s, as it called for a quickening of national energies. Kennedy family appetite and competitiveness would express themselves in this presidency that seemed forever eager to do something grander: evoke a national purpose, confront the Soviet Union, get to the moon.

Both family and ethnic ambitions had ridden on the education of Jack Kennedy and his brothers. Shacks on an island in Boston harbor for a time housed Bridget Murphy and her future husband, Patrick Kennedy, fugitives from the Irish potato famine of the 1840s. Patrick, working with a cooper's adze and croze, survived only into his early thirties. But that was long enough to found with Bridget an American family that would acquire great wealth and political influence. The marriage of Bridget and Patrick's grandson, Joseph Kennedy, to Rose Fitzgerald, daughter of Boston's Irish mayor Honey Fitz, further solidified the cachet of the Kennedy name. Socially prominent, endowed with all the social graces, and at the same time very strictly Catholic, Rose Kennedy brought elegance to the alliance. But the distance both families had put from the gritty struggles of Irish immigrant experience was not enough to satisfy the aspirations of the driven, aggressive Joseph Kennedy. He wanted more money, which he piled up in banking and moviemaking, and by manipulating the stock market. And he wanted either acceptance by the Anglo-American social hierarchy or some form of vindication that could transcend acceptance. Meanwhile he had determined, with Rose Kennedy's eager assent, to prepare his sons for achievement and his daughters for refinement.

For the young female Kennedys, education was to be in Catholic schools, while Joe, Jr., John, Robert, and Edward each had in large part a Protestant schooling. But the most notable component of the four boys' upbringing was the discipline their parents provided.

The summer compound at Hyannis Port was ideal for rounds of calisthenics and daily practice in the patrician sport of sailing—the father, bullhorn in hand, following his sons in a separate boat and shouting out their errors. A lax showing could bring banishment to supper in the kitchen. The training was in winning and not in the graceful manners of the aristocracy, but it was also in intellectual excellence and civic responsibility. Confiding that she too wanted to rear her sons to greatness, Rose Kennedy schooled her children in proper speech and the correct use of "I" and "me." She would pin to their pillowcases reminder notes like "memorize the Presidents" and would post news items on a bulletin board for discussion at dinner; the children might then be put to arguing issues raised in *The Federalist Papers*. On rainy days a game of Monopoly was common. The children also had their parents' love.

Joseph Kennedy sent his sons to Harvard. They were to execute their father's revenge on the Boston uppercrust, who had snubbed him and kept his daughters out of the season's list of debutantes at Cape Cod.

The businessman father was an early supporter of Franklin D. Roosevelt for President and campaigned for him "for my own security and for the security of my kids." The country, he had decided, needed reform; he worried about "how ugly and menacing hungry men" were becoming during the early years of the Great Depression. Under the New Deal he became a public servant, regulating as head of the Securities and Exchange Commission the activities of his fellow corporate barons and then, as ambassador to the Court of St. James, invading with his assertively Irish-American presence the highest citadel of the Anglican establishment. Victory, honorable service, self-aggrandizement: father and sons perceived these as a single indivisible compound.

Added to the externally imposed elements of Jack Kennedy's raising was recurrent sickness. As an adult he would often appear somewhat distant even from the politics in which he was so successful a striver, and it is reasonable to suppose that his days in bed, in confronting his own helplessness, translated the Kennedy values into a more ironic, inward-looking concept of strength and achievement than the family had consciously instilled in him.

What specific political outlook was the future President receiving in all this? The family belonged by tradition to the Bay State's Irish Democracy. The claim of the father that Democratic policies were necessary for the preservation of an enlightened capitalist system was hardly a radical position—if anything, it was slightly to the right of Democratic liberalism in general. The education in competitive aggressiveness tempered by public spirit, or in public service competitively pursued, might belong anywhere within either major party. A rhetoric of strife and the overcoming of challenges was to characterize Jack Kennedy at whatever point on the spectrum he happened at the moment to be. His father, as ambassador to Britain on the eve of world war, urged conciliation with the fascist powers and an isolationist course for the United States. His rough-and-tumble eldest son, Joseph, Jr., perhaps because of his devout Catholicism, was sympathetic to the Spanish fascists. But Jack's Harvard senior thesis, soon published with editorial help as *Why England Slept*, is an unfavorable commentary on Britain's inaction as Germany was preparing for war. Joe, Sr., bought thirty thousand copies of the book, storing them in his attic, so that it would reach the bestseller list. Such was his ambition for his sons.

At Harvard Jack's grade average rose to B+ in his upperclass years. He was "very argumentative in a nice way," one friend would recall. "He questioned everything. He had a great intellectual curiosity and the best sense of humor of any of the Kennedys."

The navy had at first rejected Jack because of a bad back, but with the elder Kennedy's influence he became an intelligence officer in 1942. Then, when an indiscreet affair with a Danish beauty earlier admired by Hitler and Hermann Göring threatened Jack's fortunes, the father again intervened, this time to have him transferred to seamanship school. Jack lacked the qualifications to be a Sea Scout, but he was given command of a PT boat in the South Pacific. That assignment had something of the family's characteristic panache. More generally, it went with the style of gentry and patrician youth at war in a conflict in which, as the old cavalry vanished, swift motorized horses of the land, sea, and air appeared in its place. Though largely ineffective as a weapon, the PT craft seized the public imagination. Gallant young men of wealth and family with experience in sailing were considered desirable for such assignments. What followed is the best-known incident of Jack's early life. Under circumstances that suggest his own negligence, a Japanese ship sliced his boat in two. Kennedy rescued a badly burned crewman, swimming and towing him to safety over several miles of sea. Jack deservedly won a hero's reputation. It would soon jumpstart him in politics.

It is reported that after hearing of Jack's heroism in the South Pacific, his brother Joe, Jr., a navy flier in Britain, had brooded in rage, "clenching and unclenching his fists" as toasts were raised. In an experimental assault, he piloted a drone loaded with TNT that was bound from southern England to attack a supposed enemy V-1 rocket site in France. The plane's engines seemed sluggish as he slowly maneuvered down the muddy runway, and the wheels left the ground dangerously late. The plan was for him to set the drone on its way and then parachute to safety. Minutes later, in the largest airborne explosion over Britain during the war, the plane blew up before he could abandon it. Before taking off, young Joe had scrawled a note: "If I don't come back, tell my dad . . . that I love him very much."

The father, having lost the son whom he had intended as the first aspirant for major political success, now turned to Jack, the second oldest. He encouraged the novelist John Hersey to write the story of PT-109; *Reader's Digest* carried a condensation of Hersey's *New Yorker* article, and in the congressional elections of 1946 in Massachusetts a reprint materialized on the seat of every subway and bus in Boston. In that state's

Democratic primary for the congressional district that Jack was contest-
ing appeared a candidate named John Russo; Jack's resourceful father
put up a second contender of the same name to divide the Italian vote.
The father, his fortune further boosted by enormous sums he had earned
in mid-Manhattan and Chicago real estate speculation after the war, then
sent contributions to deserving ethnic associations and religious causes.
Jack, who as a journalist for the Hearst chain had been reporting on the
United Nations and the Potsdam Conference, learned the business, un-
congenial to his withdrawn temperament, of shaking working-class
hands and kissing babies. At the age of twenty-nine, he walked away with
the election.

The population of his district was partly of Irish origin, partly of Italian. For both the Kennedys and the Fitzgeralds, even as they acquired
wealth, the city's Irish Catholics remained the base constituency. Well
before the Civil War much of that community had been notable for its
conservative resistance to reform: opposition to abolitionism, for example, and antagonism to public schools with their inculcation of an essentially Protestant religious training. That the seaboard Irish were Democrats and, in the Great Depression, many of them impoverished had given
them sufficient reason to be New Dealers. But patriotism and a loyalty to
a church that defined communism as not merely an earthly but a spiritual
evil prepared the Boston Irish community for a nationalistic hostility to
the Soviet Union more visceral than liberal Democratic anticommunism.
Along with that evolution came a susceptibility to the antileft sentiments
that soon were to take the form of McCarthyism.

Kennedy began his congressional term in 1947. His Massachusetts colleague Thomas O'Neill, Jr., said he had never seen a congressman get so
much press attention while doing so little work. However that may be,
the work of the first-term representative gave little indication of a clear
political profile.

The young congressman supported the confrontation with communism abroad that the national Democratic party was developing against
the opposition more of the isolationist right than of the tiny domestic left.
Joseph Kennedy, in fact, for a time sounded much like an isolationist
himself, less from the xenophobic motives that made right-wingers antagonistic to foreign aid and American involvement abroad than from
doubts about the good that our meddling in foreign politics would bring.
John Kennedy favored the Truman Doctrine, sketching the containment
of communism, and the Marshall Plan, the European recovery program.
But he also indulged in rightist rhetoric, saying that at the Yalta Conference Franklin Roosevelt had sold out to the Soviet Union. Once, in opposition to foreign aid, on the House floor he dismissed potential recipients
as "Hottentots."

1. Freshmen at Southern Illinois University, 1960. Photograph by Francis Miller, courtesy of *Life Magazine,* © Time, Inc.

2. Suburban housing, 1960. Photograph by Charles Gatewood, courtesy of Magnum Photos.

3. Allen Ginsberg outside of the Democratic Convention, 1968. Photograph by
Dennis Brack, courtesy of Black Star.

4. Bobby Dylan. Photograph by Fred W. McDarrah.

5. Mrs. Rosa Parks sits at the front of a city bus, December 1956, Montgomery, Alabama. Photograph courtesy of UPI/Bettmann.

6. Martin Luther King, pensive, chin in hand. Photograph courtesy of AP/Wide World Photos.

7. This Greyhound bus, carrying the first Freedom Riders into Alabama, was set afire by a mob outside Anniston in May 1961. Photograph courtesy of AP/Wide World Photos.

8. Firefighters spray civil rights demonstrators in Birmingham, 1963. Photograph by Charles Moore, courtesy of Black Star.

9. Kennedy-Nixon televised debate. Election year, 1960. Photograph courtesy of Archive Photos.

10. A Peace Corps volunteer teaching English to Philippine Islanders. Photograph courtesy of UPI/Bettmann.

11. John F. Kennedy. Photograph courtesy of the John F. Kennedy Library.

12. Castro and Khrushchev hugging and grinning. Photograph courtesy of AP/ Wide World Photos.

13. Art reproductions, 3 for $1.00. Photograph by Ken Heyman, courtesy of Woodfin Camp and Associates.

14. LBJ at Job Corps Center in San Marcos, Texas. Photograph courtesy of UPI/Bettmann.

On domestic issues, Kennedy's early record was mixed. He complained about liberal "do-gooders" and voted against aid to the Navaho and Hopi Indians, hospital construction, rural electrification cooperatives, and a bill prohibiting discrimination in employment. Yet he favored an extension of social security benefits, a minimum wage law, and a modest national health program. In his spare time, he was devoting some attention to domestic affairs of another sort.

Sexual adventure is not uncommon among politicians and men of wealth, and the popular psychological explanations probably account for them adequately: a craving to receive from lovers further instances of the admiration that society has already bestowed; a hunger to exercise in private relationships the power that money, politics, and governance provide in public matters. In Kennedy an additional reason might have been the ill health that was a leitmotif of much of his active life. In the late 1940s he learned that he had Addison's disease, which, if not for the discovery of cortisone, would probably have killed him. In the mid-1950s he suffered from acute back pain and nearly died during an operation. Dangerous illness may often make for a retreat into passivity; that was not in the Kennedy upbringing. Another reaction, more in the Kennedy style, can be to pursue all the more ardently and restlessly ambitions or appetites. A woman Kennedy dated would recall that he seemed driven to grabbing everything, including her. Another remembered his listening to news broadcasts incessantly, even while they made love.

About Kennedy's repetitive sexual exploits, a couple of things can be noted. The tolerance or admiration of his behavior among liberals in the early sixties, at a moment when enlightened sexual liberation was identifying itself with the James Bond manner, marks the distance between that time and the full midday of the women's movement. Kennedy's continued sexual prowlings were to fatten the notes that FBI director J. Edgar Hoover kept on him as on other public figures and no doubt contributed to the security of Hoover's tenure at the Bureau while Kennedy was President.

In 1952 Congressman Kennedy ran for the Senate. "We're going to sell Jack like soap flakes," observed the elder Kennedy, and using the full armamentorium of modern advertising he proceeded to do so. Among his acts of salesmanship was to make a desperately needed big loan to the McCarthyite editor of a Boston newspaper. Money went again to charities—lots of money, and to a wide variety. "With the money I spent," Joe was to remark, "I could have elected my chauffeur." Much of what went on was quite respectable, simply a matter of the meticulous organization that money and a family of long-fermented ambition could achieve. Jack's energetic brother Robert Kennedy, next in age to him, did much of the organizing. He gathered, for example, fifty times the number of citizens' signatures necessary to nominate Jack; before the election, each signatory was sent a letter of thanks. Hersey's account of Jack and PT-109 was mailed to every home in the state. The handsome candidate was widely appealing to women. Kennedy, moreover, did solid work on the issues, once outdebating on international questions his liberal Republican opponent, Henry Cabot Lodge, Jr., an expert in foreign policy then seeking reelection. Kennedy, barely victorious in the year of Eisenhower's first sweep to the presidency, replied to criticisms of his campaign: "I worked for what I got. I worked for it." As for the spending of personal fortunes on campaigns, it would have been asking a good deal of the Kennedys to demand that they rise above the conventional belief that money deserves its privileges.

Senator Joseph R. McCarthy's brand of Red-baiting in the early 1950s offered to his admirers not so much a specific program for internal security as a perception of the communist enemy as ubiquitously and insidiously present, a vocabulary of angry awakened patriotism. As late as 1954, John Kennedy attacked a classmate for denouncing in the same breath both Alger Hiss and McCarthy, whom Kennedy called "a great American patriot." And Jack's younger brother Robert was for a time a counsel on the investigative subcommittee that McCarthy chaired.

Once elected a Senator, however, Jack began putting distance between himself and McCarthy—at a time, to be sure, when the Red-hunter from Wisconsin was becoming increasingly discredited. On the television news program "Meet the Press," Kennedy commented that the government had rid itself of most subversives, a remark not calculated to reinforce the gloomy gratification that right-wing ideologues—or ideologues of any sort—take in seeing the forces of the enemy prosper. Privately, he expressed disapproval of McCarthy. But in the 1955 Senate vote to censure the Wisconsin senator, he did not confront the issue. In the hospital for a major back operation, he could have paired with another Senator on the opposite side—whatever the opposite side would have been for him. Jack, however, had an eye to his Massachusetts Catholic constituency, and beyond that to an unpredictably large number of McCarthy supporters across the nation who might some day be included in his constituency. His father's friendship with McCarthy, and perhaps some notion that in McCarthy's state of besieged desperation it was no time for friends to turn against him, warred in Kennedy with disapproval of his colleague.

Kennedy's first term in the Senate also brought forth *Profiles in Courage*, largely ghostwritten by Theodore Sorensen, though the senator had produced a couple of draft chapters. The book is a set of essay sketches of Senators who in exercising political integrity risked their reputations or their political future. It takes, of course, no courage to sign a book about courage. Readers and voters think that they admire bravery: they merely fail to recognize it in politicians who defy their wishes. Kennedy is not especially to be faulted for putting his name to a ghostwritten book. The practice, among public figures who lack either the gift or the time for writing, has been widespread in the present media-sent political generation. The ideas in such a book are assumed, at any rate, to comport with those of its signatory. Kennedy seems to have reflected a good deal on courage: his war record, along with a lifetime of ill health and the boldness with which he had earlier exposed his illness-wracked frame to injury in sports, gave him some right to fix his name to a book about bravery. The book received a Pulitzer Prize, one explanation being that the awarding committee, in overruling the advisers' choices, had concluded that the book would inspire youth; the other, that lobbying by Joseph Kennedy bagged the trophy.

A war hero chose to sign a study not of courage in battle, its most dramatic and quickly admired form, but of inner fortitude. Kennedy at moments demonstrated something of the thoughtful reserve—courage of a sort, or at least a condition of it—that went with what would later be known as the Kennedy style. He did so when, invited by Eleanor Roosevelt to join in a postmortem condemnation of McCarthy, he responded with an honest self-perception not usually found among politicians that he was in no moral position to enlist retroactively among the anti-McCarthyites. His sponsorship in 1960 of repeal of the requirement that graduate students take a loyalty oath before receiving federal loans would have to do for an apology. President Kennedy's responses to the Berlin Wall in 1961 and the missiles in 1962 in Cuba were to require of the national temper demands as serious as the subjects of *Profiles in Courage* had faced. They denied to the public, on the one hand, the quick relief that visible retreat would have brought and, on the other, the spasm release of hostility, at least of the safely verbal kind that superpatriots crave. Perhaps, then, *Profiles in Courage* is not without symbolic fitness for a putative author who, at least in manner, was introspectively self-contained in the presence of crisis.

In 1955 and 1956 Martin Luther King in Montgomery had demonstrated a different idea of inner strength from that offered by standard military and political models. But the question of civil rights did not figure very prominently in Congress during this period. Two of Kennedy's votes were in support of civil rights and two against (he voted in favor of jury trials for accused violators of the Civil Rights Act of 1957, at a time when it was widely known that southern juries would not convict in such cases). Vice President Richard Nixon, at this time a strong supporter of civil rights, denounced the Senate's adoption of the jury-trial amendment, calling it "a vote against the right to vote."

Still, Kennedy's senatorial years did mark a somewhat liberal bend in his thinking. Choosing Theodore Sorensen, a midwesterner who had become a prominent lawyer, in 1953 as his political adviser says something about the range of his associations. Sorensen could play very hard politics, harder than the intellectual liberal sensibility is expected to sanction, and he apparently shared Kennedy's preference for practicality over sentiment. But Sorensen, a conscientious objector during World War II, had made an early commitment to civil rights, which included founding a chapter of the Congress of Racial Equality. By the late fifties, simplistic anticommunist verbiage in foreign policy had given way for the most part in Kennedy to observations, liberal in tone, on the complexity of the world, the possible clashes within the communist orbit, the necessity for respecting nationalist struggle, and the virtues of foreign aid.

In the 1956 Democratic Convention, Kennedy made a bid for the vice-presidential nomination, helped by Democratic fears that Eisenhower had won dangerously strong Catholic support. Kennedy lost out to his Tennessee colleague Estes Kefauver, whom he tersely described as "the kind of person who kept looking over your shoulder for someone more important as he talked with you." But Kennedy's presence at the convention and his narration of a film history of the Democratic party, and his later energetic campaigning for the ticket led by Illinois governor Adlai Stevenson, raised his stature within the Democracy. He gained further visibility as a member of the highly publicized McClellan committee, charged with investigating corruption within organized labor, and he wrote some labor legislation that passed the Senate but died in the House.

In "view of the international prestige at stake," the journalist asked Eisenhower, "why were we not straining to catch up with the Soviet Union in space?" This was three years after the launching of the first satellite by Moscow. Sputnik had given the USSR a spectacular triumph, and administered the United States, so proud of its technology, both a humiliation and a shock. At the President's request, the reporter started the question again. "I said, in view of the international prestige at stake . . ." Eisenhower, parrying, questioned whether American prestige was on the line.

Eisenhower was a conservative. That word is as elusive as the word "liberal," and has managed to mean a range of things from a stable community to competitive market economics, from the composed manners of ladies and gentlemen to the crassest entrepreneurial craving for wealth. If the word has anything to do with what it sounds like, if it implies a determination to conserve a workable present and a careful questioning of any restless eagerness for change, it fits Eisenhower to the core of his modest and reserved soul. His exchange with his interrogator may have been merely a defensive posture in the face of Soviet success in space. In retrospect it appears a wisely measured calculation of how transient was the temporary Soviet spurt in space technology. That is not, however, how the technological advances of the Soviet Union looked then to liberals. And one of the liberal complaints against McCarthyism had been the belief that in raising a false scare over domestic communism, Red-hunting distracted attention from the need to counter the solid threat of Soviet weaponry.

Most self-described liberals in the late 1950s above all demanded activity, renovation, the application of scientific and technological expertise to the problem of the moment. Civil libertarian by tradition and in most cases by virtue of their opposition to McCarthyism, liberals nonetheless were certainly not interested, for example, in the radical cultural dissent that the Beat writers presented; they preferred more sober and institutional kinds of questioning. Liberals wished for an eventual end of racial injustice, but the issue was not at the center of their thinking. They would have agreed that government must work for the lessening of poverty, but for a number of reasons, including a complacent belief that the liberal New Deal had provided effective protections against want, poverty was not a particularly visible phenomenon politically. The strident variety of anticommunism that the right favored was not to the taste of most liberals: they welcomed the signs of conflict between Moscow and communist China that made the world more confusing than right-wingers could handle.

In the end, however, liberals were cold warriors. What concerned liberals of the 1950s were questions of national character and will, and especially the question that has haunted Americans from the time of the Puritans onward: have we gone weak and slack, lost our purpose? Commentators were now questioning whether American education was undemanding of the intelligence and effort of students, enfeebling our science and technology, and for that matter our arts and letters.

The dominant thrust of the liberal ethos of the time was the promotion of growth. A revived national will would commit itself to economic and cultural development as an activity in itself and as the precondition for a more activist national policy; in return the demands of development would toughen the national character. Growth should be worldwide: Walt W. Rostow, an adviser to Kennedy, published in 1960 *Stages of Economic Growth: A Non-Communist Manifesto*, urging the West to promote in underdeveloped countries an economic ripening to eliminate communism from political competition. The idea of economic growth was a central part of the Kennedy liberal agenda.

It was the Cold War that drew the fiercest emotions and occasioned the most pressing arguments for growth, in this instance as a basis for military and related spending. Here the thinking of liberals made up yet another compound that would turn out to be a contradiction. The worldwide confrontation with communist powers that had been the project of the liberals of the Truman years seemed to them to require an urgency of attention that the Eisenhower administration was not giving it. The *New York Times* late in 1957 announced that a "feeling of emergency grips the people of the free world"; and this canonical institution of liberalism called, in the tones of a later neoconservatism, for recognition that we were in a "race for survival." Especially disturbing, liberals decided, was the missile gap, a presumed Soviet superiority in missile weaponry. But liberals scorned the kind of fear of communism that drove right-wingers to Red hunts, and during the Korean war they had stood against the demand from the right for a quick strike against China with nuclear bombs. The Cold War, to the liberal mind, meant an enterprise measured, continuing, free of emotional convulsions. It also meant watching the world for signs of division among communists—the most notable instance of which, the split between China and the USSR, confused and therefore angered American rightists by its incompatibility with their view of a simple, unified communist evil. In time, the liberals' determination to see the world in its complexity would contradict the commitment to the Cold War. But not yet.

So the liberal concept of foreign policy defined for itself, in effect, not one obstructive force at home but two. There was the far right with its sullen view of the world, its refusal to confront the possibility of rupture among communist nations and the consequent moral ambiguities. But the far right, though its rhetoric had to be reckoned with politically, was not in power: it had lost the Republican party to the moderate Eisenhower in 1952, and by 1955 McCarthyism was in the past. So the major obstacle to a good foreign policy, as liberals judged their times, was the course pursued by the conservative Eisenhower administration, which they attacked for its inactivity.

An activist foreign policy needed as its grounding an energetic economy. And that, according to the liberal persuasion of those days, required rigorous schooling. A good educational system could instill in the young technical skills and humane judgment that would also fortify the national resolve in international relations. In questions of prosperity and education, liberals defined tangible problems, though not very specific villains or solutions. The nation's economy late in the 1950s was sluggish compared even with that of the Soviet Union, and there was the kind of public dissatisfaction that accompanies not the hardships of depression but the irritations of economic stasis. And our public schools, having been shown up when the USSR took an early lead in space, did not look good in comparison with the demanding educational systems attended by at least the elite in various other nations. American students, it appeared, did too little homework and too much socializing. As the 1960 presidential campaign approached, the schools and the economy were central liberal preoccupations.

Though liberals were taking no major account of Kennedy, alliance with him was logical. Kennedy had the kind of education that they could identify with. A language of energy, motion, the conquest of large problems, belonged to him by upbringing and temperament, and his presence radiated energy informed by intellect and self-possession. Given the right issue or the right speech, he could exude resolute force. In his vote for removing the provision in the National Defense Education Act requiring a loyalty oath for applicants, he argued that the oath would bar from federal funding the kind of intelligence needed in our competition with the USSR. That claim tightly combined good inherent liberalism with the idea of enlisting trained minds in the national service. And Kennedy was a member of the World War II generation that seemed, by age and by that epic of virtuous conquest, the fit inheritor of the mantle of leadership.

In foreign policy, which would furnish the most articulately defined questions of the presidential election of 1960, Kennedy had for some time been sounding quite squarely a liberal. In a Senate speech denouncing a cut in funding for United Nations humanitarian programs and a failure to work for reciprocal trade agreements, he warned that "we have damaged the respect of our allies, unity among free nations, and our reputation [for being] a friend of underprivileged nations and . . . an enemy of colonialism." Having endorsed in 1949 the right-wing condemnation of the Truman presidency for losing China to the communists, in 1957 Kennedy attributed the loss not to failed diplomacy but to fundamental revolutionary conditions. He urged trade with Poland, recommending that the United States recognize the differences within the communist bloc. That same year he attacked France's colonial policy in Algeria. All this is the thinking not of a dissident from the Cold War but of a liberal. Kennedy was in liberal terms a nationalist who, through a generous foreign policy sensitive to the world's diversity, wanted to win the "respect of our allies," "unity among free nations," and in time an end to communist totalitarianism. Kennedy's anticommunism, in short, did not share the political right's concept of an absolute, changeless communist evil. The Cold War, he later presciently told the journalist Richard Rovere, "would not be won or lost"; it would simply peter out.

With their gains in the House and Senate in 1958, the Democrats could sense that as the presidential tenure of the popular Eisenhower neared its end, political momentum was in their favor. Liberal Democrats had their own hopes. Surely the most faithfully liberal candidate was Senator Hubert Humphrey of Minnesota. But Humphrey's liberalism belonged spiritually to the days of the New Deal, when questions of economic suffering dominated, and he addressed such issues directly and with passion. That was not the political mode of a time in which enough Americans were well off to leave the poor submerged, "invisible" in the description of Michael Harrington's *The Other America*, a book that would soon have an important part in making poverty visible once again. More appropriate to the issues that interested liberals in the late fifties would be some candidate wearing the polish of university education, a manner of understatement and crisp competence.

Kennedy's victory over Humphrey in the 1960 Democratic primaries hinged on the important early West Virginia vote, where Franklin D. Roosevelt, Jr., brutally contrasted the candidates' war records. Humphrey's later autobiography claims that a hernia disqualified him for service, but a medical procedure to correct it came conveniently after the war. Kennedy also handled his Roman Catholicism skillfully enough to neutralize it politically: he engagingly invited and comfortingly answered questions about the compatibility of his faith with the religious neutrality of American political institutions. Sorensen advised the candidate, "Make it clear that you are a victim of . . . bigotry by always so stating in passive tense, 'I have been called' . . . 'it has been suggested that' . . . 'people are being asked to vote against me because.'" Winston Churchill had given the presidential candidate similar advice. It became something of a sign of bigotry to oppose Kennedy, and of enlightenment to favor him.

In the 1960 contest with the Republican candidate, Vice President Richard Nixon, Kennedy's cool good looks played well on television against Nixon's tense demeanor. The contrast made Kennedy look the winner in their debates, whereas, in the opinion of radio listeners as opposed to television viewers, Nixon made the better presentation. In the debates Kennedy set forth the inaccurate liberal claim that a missile gap existed in Moscow's favor. Neither in the debates nor in other campaign talks did Kennedy establish a clear ideological or programmatic distinction between himself and Nixon, but the thrust of his message was that the country must be astir with new energies, particularly in the economy, and must develop a more sophisticated and versatile system of defense. As hard as it is for commentators to tell in retrospect exactly what Kennedy's campaign was about, every sharp and confident New England syllable made it sound as though he knew: it was "to get this country moving again."

Kennedy in 1960 won a substantial victory in the electoral college but a thin popular margin, probably aided by some vote manipulation in Chicago and Texas. Many Catholic voters favored his election, particularly in the large states where their votes were concentrated. But despite his successful attempt to conduct a campaign different from the parochial contest waged by Al Smith over a generation earlier, the candidate, according to social scientists, lost more votes on account of his religion than he gained. His was the final triumph, nonetheless, for an Irish-American Catholic, the vindication of a heritage and an escape from its burdens. That election night also had powerful meaning for fellow Catholics of varying ethnic strains and for other minority groups—Jews, blacks, Hispanics, Asians. Kennedy's achievement represented the fulfillment of a national promise that Americans even of definably immigrant background might aspire to wealth, homes, education for their children, national leadership, or an ideal of justice.

Among the sectors of the public most satisfied with the new President were liberal academicians. The inaugural address had impressed them. A time would come of falling respect for the address, which has as its best-remembered line a contrived play of opposites: "Ask not what your country can do for you—ask what you can do for your country." But it is a rare speech on a ceremonial occasion that is taken seriously enough to receive continued reviews of any kind. The address is noteworthy for the somberness with which the new President chose to lecture his compatriots. He appeared actually to be thinking about his subject, in this respect breaking with political convention. During Kennedy's occupancy of the White House, and for a short time thereafter, much was made of the culture that the administration was supposed to represent, manifesting itself especially in Jacqueline Kennedy, whose attractiveness and social finish lent so much to the Kennedys' public image. That the First Lady spoke French impressed intellectuals in a nation where people do not customarily learn foreign languages well enough to use them. All this bespoke a hope that intellect allied to Democratic liberalism had entered the White House. That hope attended a sense of confidence that in the West ideological conflict was no longer relevant, that science, technology, and civilization had advanced to the point that problems were now solvable by the application of intelligence and impersonal knowledge. Kennedy seemed the right leader to preside over the severe but ultimately benign technical forces of the age.

The administration's new appointments must have displayed to liberals a fitting polish. Robert McNamara, the cost-conscious president of Ford Motors with a mind as clean as a statistical table, became Secretary of Defense. "He really runs, rather than walks," a cabinet colleague remembered of this man who would subdue the Pentagon brass. McNamara had been a student and teacher at the Harvard Business School, a member of the NAACP, and at Ford something of an outsider who lived in the university town of Ann Arbor rather than in conservative Grosse

Point. Later to be an object of scorn for his part in the war in Vietnam, McNamara perfected the technocratic impulses of liberalism. For State, Kennedy first wanted Democratic Senator J. William Fulbright, but for political reasons this Arkansan voted against civil rights measures, and his appointment would not have sat well with emerging African nations. Instead, the President appointed the imperturbable Dean Rusk—a Rhodes Scholar who had been a peace advocate before World War II, an open opponent of McCarthyism, and a supporter of Adlai Stevenson even in 1960. Rusk belonged to an almost forgotten company of old-line liberals. When such gestures meant something, he once had broken a color barrier by going with Ralph Bunche of the United Nations to a Pentagon officers' mess. Rusk would try to restore the China experts who had been purged from the State Department during the Red hunts. A prime adviser who became chair of the Joint Chiefs of Staff was Maxwell Taylor. A scholar who could speak several languages and write serious books, Taylor was a liberal's general. Others on the staff—McGeorge Bundy, Walt Rostow, Chester Bowles, and Arthur Schlesinger, Jr.—constituted virtually a university faculty headed by a President whom Norman Mailer once described as resembling a detached young professor.

JFK's first major test occurred during April 1961 in the attempted invasion of Cuba, ending in disaster at the Bay of Pigs. The effort had its origins in the Eisenhower years, when the Central Intelligence Agency had done every bit of the planning for the invasion. Yet the scheme was much in the spirit of the liberalism that attached itself to Kennedy's presidency. Fidel Castro represented the type of leftist regime—repressive, speaking and thinking in slogans, instilling a militant ideological conformity—that liberals despised as a travesty of the idea of social and economic democracy. The CIA, taking the place after World War II of the wartime Office of Strategic Services, in its early years had attracted liberal intellectuals, and its combination of panache and expert knowledge reflected the style of the Kennedy presidency.

Yet the Bay of Pigs invasion looked like the work of amateurs. The planners had picked a landing site inadequate for defense or advance into the interior. The invading force, using old freighters supplied by the United Fruit Company, was badly equipped and poorly supported. Promised air cover proved inadequate and untimely (the airplanes were operating on Eastern instead of Caribbean time); the boats' hulls ripped apart on coral reefs.

One explanation—aside from a belief within the military that the President would if necessary call in full military support—for so careless an operation was apparently the prevailing belief shared by the invaders, the CIA, and the Kennedy administration that under communist regimes the people longed for freedom and at the first real opportunity would rise up spontaneously. Comments subsequent to the Bay of Pigs, made within the government and not for public propaganda objectives, indicate the sincerity of this conviction. During the discussions in the policy committee directing the American response during the Cuban missile crisis, the danger was noted of taking action that would excite the Cuban people to revolt and force the United States to intervene. In the early days of this country's deepening involvement in Vietnam, Lyndon Johnson, in a document for White House circulation, spoke of taking measures that would keep up the morale of the North Vietnamese people. His observation based itself in the assumption that the North Vietnamese must be miserable in their captivity to the communists, and that their hope and their morale would of course be invested in our continuing resistance to communism.

In supporting the Bay of Pigs invasion, the members of the Kennedy administration were being faithful to the liberal Cold War heritage. In the administration's final decision not to send in air support for the beleaguered rebels, Kennedy was overcoming a major element in his upbringing: win, win, never think of losing. In doing so he was living up to that idea of him as self-composed that some of his admirers had until then, perhaps wishfully, perceived in his deportment. His refusal in the final instance to use force conformed to the liberal idea of force exactly measured, stripped of any motives of self-gratifying belligerence. And this would be the rule throughout his presidency. Behind the language of confrontation, he and his lieutenants brought to foreign policy a large degree of caution and temperance.

After the failure of the invasion, however, Washington's hostility to Castro intensified. The CIA, under instructions from the Kennedy brothers, made a plan to disrupt the regime, and according to the later Senate investigations, chaired by Senator Frank Church of Idaho, eight attempts were made to assassinate Castro, a more frustrating target seemingly than Rasputin. While President Kennedy probably did not know the details of the bungled plots to kill Castro, he shared in the ill will and showed no serious interest in treating the Cuban rulership as simply one more of the world's bad regimes, to be accepted and dealt with as Washington dealt with Paraguay or South Africa. Cuba was too proximate for that. In its $10 billion aid program for Latin America, the Alliance for Progress, the administration committed itself in 1962 to land and tax reform. But the Kennedy presidency essentially continued the Cold War policy of assuming that even vaguely Marxist governments and movements are in a separate category of evil. Under the Agency for International Development, funds went for training local police in counterinsurgency measures as well as for technical aid assistance to sanitation and transportation. Except in his dealings with some African states, notably Kwame Nkrumah's

Ghana, and his lack of sympathy for the white supremacist government of South Africa, Kennedy's foreign policy maintained along with its more directly humane objectives the government's conventional hostility to the left. That implied also willingness to befriend even the most brutal rightist regimes as a bulwark against revolution.

In the wake of Vietnam it has become common on the left to argue that this nation's singleminded hatred of revolutionary governments and movements is a lunatic obsession. In Central America during the 1980s, at any rate, that lunacy was to play out its delusions so visibly as to suggest the psychotic's plea to be stopped. The Kennedy administration's unremitting hostility to Castro is part of the earlier history of this national preoccupation with the sins of the far left. And reconstructing the mentality of the Kennedy years requires recognition that the instructive carnage and failure in Vietnam lay in the future, and that Kennedy's policy faced no large and audible domestic criticism as did the Reagan policy toward Nicaragua.

The Cold War had begun out of an understandable fear of the Soviet Union, after a world war against a state that the Stalinist monstrosity closely resembled. From the early and limited programs for protecting the Western European democracies, the confrontation with Moscow spread by its own moral and strategic logic to the rest of the world, growing hazier in its definition of the enemy, now waging war on the brutal North Korean regime, now overthrowing a progressive democracy in Guatemala. Castro's Cuba was, within the most moderate and intelligent Cold War thinking, a correctly chosen target. It killed its opponents or subjected them to brutal imprisonment; its connections to the Soviet Union were close; and it was so located as to seem a geopolitical danger to the Western Hemisphere. (It was also taking measures to raise literacy and health standards; but that, on the part of a communist regime, meant nothing to cold warriors.) At its simplest, the American waging of the Cold War, as at the Bay of Pigs, represented not power-hungry nationalism but an idea: eventually, in Vietnam, to be driven to disaster by its own relentless rationality.

A crisis in Berlin brought the Cold War back to the continent of its origin. The Berlin airlift of 1948—when President Truman kept intact the Western presence there despite Stalin's attempts to choke the city by cutting off all land routes—had been the first head-to-head confrontation between the allies and the Soviet Union. It had been the West's clearest triumph. In 1961, Soviet Premier Nikita Khrushchev revived the threat to the city. He announced that unless the Western powers entered an agreement favorable to East Germany, Moscow was going to sign a separate peace treaty with its satellite power, whose status from the first days of Soviet occupation had been considered to be in suspension until the reunifying of all of Germany under free elections. What Khrushchev was proposing, in effect, was to make East Germany a (nominally) sovereign republic surrounding and endangering the freedom of West Berlin, the part of the city not under Soviet occupation. Khrushchev suggested that West Berlin become a free city under United Nations guarantees. But the allies did not relish making the city hostage to the good intentions of East Germany or that prospective nation's Soviet overlord. At a summit meeting in Vienna during June 1961, Kennedy and the Premier had argued inconclusively over the issue. There Khrushchev received a view of Kennedy as something of a weakling, and it is speculated that for a time the Soviet leader acted on that impression.

In the case of Cuba the moral question had seemed relatively simple: if the Cuban government was sufficiently repressive to dissidents and others, sufficiently a danger, and easy enough to overthrow, then an attempt to do so would be justifiable; if not, not. In the matter of Berlin, the issue was more complex, with conflicting and almost equally plausible claims.

The USSR had serious and legitimate concerns. Germany had won against Russia, Czarist and Bolshevik, the Eastern phase of World War I, extracting a favorable peace before suffering its own defeat on the Western front. That Germany in the Second World War had proved a monumental and unspeakable threat to the Soviet Union needs no argument. Now, under postwar conditions, a greater Germany would become an instrument of Western power against the Soviet bloc. A separate Eastern German nation would preclude that danger. A more immediate problem for the Soviet Union was the accelerating exodus to the West, through the border between East and West Berlin, of Germans whose education and skills were essential to the economy of eastern Germany and implicitly to the social stability of Moscow's other European satellite nations. As part of his scheme for Germany, Khrushchev insisted that the communists have authority to prevent exit through the border within Berlin. Khrushchev could have had domestic considerations in mind as well. He had achieved a slight relaxation of the police-state system in his country, and something of a shift to consumer needs. To his right were enemies who wanted more military spending than he favored. A tough posture toward the West could strengthen him politically at home.

The West had its own intractable concerns. In the light of what politicians chose over the years to perceive as being within the free (because anticommunist) world, the concept became so debased that it seems almost naive to say that West Berlin was free and East Germany unfree. That happens, however, to be true. The Western allies believed they had a commitment to defend the freedom of the West Berliners, who having lived under freedom would suffer its loss more grievously than East

Germans suffered its absence. Khrushchev's plan was to establish East Germany permanently as a separate republic. It would therefore have none of the obligations that bound the Soviet Union, as one of the postwar occupiers of Germany, to act in concert with her wartime Western allies in any future governance and disposition of Berlin. Whatever assurances the Western powers might get on paper for the safety of West Berlin, they feared the practical result of the Soviet demands.

Another consideration balanced against this. The Western allies had their own stake in the stability of the Eastern bloc. They knew that Moscow could not then afford the economic collapse of Eastern Germany, and it was unpredictable what Khrushchev would do if, as observers at the time believed, a continued flow of refugees brought that collapse nearer. To allow the communists to prevent passage into a freer society was ugly. But even uglier might be the reaction in Moscow to the possibility of economic and social disaster in Eastern Europe.

Resolution, then, had to balance against compromise, the needs of Berliners against the needs of peace. The adversary force was too powerful, and its wants too urgent, to make possible any satisfyingly easy use of Western force. At the same time the rights of Berliners were too important to be accorded a merely rhetorical heroism as their defense. The problem was of the kind that could not accommodate the palpitating emotions of the right.

Much of the Kennedy administration's response was an increase in belligerency, and not merely of words but of actions. The President called for an extensive civil defense program and on July 25, proposing an increase in military spending and in the armed forces, announced a doubling of draft calls and a mobilization of some fifty-one thousand army reserve troops. But in the summer of 1961 there occurred a curious incident. On July 30, Fulbright, who was chair of the Senate Foreign Relations Committee, observed on television that the communists might have the right to close off the border to the West. Fulbright subsequently retracted the statement. Yet responding at his August 10 press conference to a question concerning Fulbright's remark, Kennedy was silent on the issue of whether East Germans had a right to free exit. Was Washington giving Moscow a hint—take, if you must, the course that will save the East German economy? Khrushchev was losing East Germany and could not permit that, Kennedy is said to have mused, and the Premier would need to halt the flow of refugees, perhaps by a wall.

Later that month, the communists began restricting egress through the Berlin border and started construction of the infamous wall. That the act was ostensibly an East German rather than a Soviet initiative constituted in itself something of a challenge to the West. Although the German Democratic Republic had not yet signed a treaty with the USSR, it was acting like a sovereign power, precisely the status that Moscow wanted to force the West to acknowledge. But such technicalities did not preoccupy Western public opinion. The clearest result was that East Germans seeking freedom or opportunity in the West were now sealed up, unless they should find a means of escape. And then there was the added fear that construction of the wall might be the prelude to some attempt to swallow up West Berlin within East Germany.

Kennedy's reaction had the appearance of resoluteness. Denouncing the Berlin Wall as an outrage, he called up more military reservists and sent fifteen hundred troops to West Berlin along the Autobahn through communist Germany (former Secretary of State Dean Acheson advised sending a division, but he hailed from a more primitive stage of the Cold War). Vice President Lyndon Johnson visited West Berlin to affirm an American pledge to defend it. As his representative to Berlin, Kennedy appointed General Lucius Clay, who had conducted the airlift of 1948 that ended in a triumph of Western skill and resolve. A further crisis arose over the question of who in East Berlin was to regulate the movements of whatever Western military had business there. Under the four-power agreement among the victorious occupiers of Germany, the Soviet Union as custodian of East Berlin was to exercise that authority. But when the USSR began transferring to the East Germans control over the movements of Western personnel in the city's eastern zone, the United States saw a further attempt to nullify the postwar arrangements and to establish the German Democratic Republic as a nation that would in time claim rights over West Berlin as well. In October at the border between the two Berlins, there was at General Clay's initiative a moment's face-off of tanks snout to snout that ended only when the Russians pulled theirs back.

If the Kennedy administration had previously been sending hints to the Soviet Union that shutting off East Berlin would be understandable and acceptable, then why the militancy of the American response once the communists had acted? The President may have reflected that although he could not prevent Khrushchev from fencing in the East Germans, he could still rally the allies to the defense of West Berlin. Perhaps, then, while the administration later in August was sincerely repelled, if at the same time relieved, at the communist strangulation of the exodus from the East, its intent was to channel the West's indignation into solidarity with the West Berliners, whose freedom, unlike that of the easterners, could be saved.

As Kennedy was piecing out his confrontation with Khrushchev, the two men began a lengthy correspondence. Early in September the Premier told the *New York Times* of his willingness to meet with the President as he had inconclusively in Vienna the previous June, suggesting the solution of a dispute in Laos in return for a solution of the Berlin question. On September 25 Kennedy made a conciliatory address before the United Nations. To General Clay, who wanted authority to take quick unilateral action in Berlin as occasion demanded, Kennedy recommended instead cautious determination and coolness. The general was brought home the following May to the distress of the American right.

The Berlin crisis did not end with a signed document. Rather, after months of hostility, both sides tacitly agreed to a certain accommodation. At the expense of those Eastern Germans who wanted freedom, the communists did what they believed was needed to rescue the East German economy, which in the interests of geopolitical stability was not displeasing to the allies either. Khrushchev, on the other hand, had not imposed his deadline for allied recognition of a separate communist republic as a condition for retaining Western access to West Berlin.

The administration's response to the Berlin crisis was, in sum, a carefully managed fusion of confrontation and restraint, the general strategy of liberalism in its argument with the right. The confrontational element was not in itself the sending of military reinforcements to West Berlin— the minimal action required to make clear the will to sustain the enclave—but rather the original decision to preserve it. The Cold War policies crafted by liberals had committed the United States to Berlin as a symbol of its solidarity with West Germany and beyond with Western Europe. Here the nation probably went far beyond the actual frontiers of its self-interest. In the fantasy world of the right, on the other hand, the sacred mission of the United States was to drive communism back, preferably to the borders of the Soviet Union, and more preferably to oblivion. For this enterprise, the right had no plan: in power, it would be hesitant to make even small demands on the nerve or resources of its American constituencies. The Kennedy administration did not encourage the Western alliance to undertake the destruction of the Berlin Wall. Washington indicated its willingness to accept the wall, its determination to protect West Berlin, and its desire to do both as economically as possible. Its policy was spare and well calculated to those ends, an instance of the prudent statesmanship that qualified the somber militancy of the inaugural address.

In contrast to the way he had embarked on the Bay of Pigs invasion, then, Kennedy's behavior during the Berlin crisis reflected the very essence of the liberal cold warrior: measured, exact, cool, and patient. His hard line adviser on Latin America, Adolf Berle, did not like the performance: "The evidence coming in now," he wrote in his diary, "suggests that a little nerve would have stopped the [wall]."

While restrained, carefully calibrated military confrontations were defining in part the Kennedy presidency, his administration was shaping other programs that added to the definition. The Peace Corps and the Green Berets, a new version of the special military unit of the 1950s, had a number of things in common. Both were intended as instruments of the war against communism. Each was, at least according to its original intellectual architects, to convert that war as far as possible into a project for social reform and technocratic economic progress. The Special Forces warriors and the Peace Corps volunteers must be elites of purpose, intelligence, and technical sophistication.

The Green Berets, whose official title was the Special Forces, were in the same tradition of a mobile, autonomous elite to which the PT-boat officers of World War II had belonged. Kennedy, along with Secretary of Defense Robert McNamara, included them in the administration's design for the renovation of the country's arms. The Secretary had an appetite for efficiency and a reliance on modern methods of gathering information. Our need, the administration reasoned, was for a more versatile and flexible defense than the existing city-killing nuclear weapons, for if an emergency should arise, they would limit us to choosing between doing nothing and incinerating the globe. Kennedy and McNamara developed a system that targeted Soviet missile sites rather than cities. Troops of the Special Forces as the administration imagined them looked something like a human equivalent of this projected missile force. They were supposed to be independent, skilled in individual combat, sensitive and knowledgeable in working with civilians. Any Special Forces personnel parachuted into Hungary, it was suggested, ought to be familiar with the major Hungarian poets.

The idea for a Peace Corps had in fact been around for some years before Kennedy's presidency. The notion, which Kennedy took up in the 1960 campaign, stood in counterpoint to an unflattering image that many Americans had come to have of their compatriots abroad—an image to which a novel published in 1958 by William J. Lederer and Eugene Burdick had notably contributed.

The figure from whom their book *The Ugly American* takes its name is physically ugly, a sign of plain moral character, and he is committed in a blunt earnest way to service and good work. He is an engineer whose ideas of appropriate technology, shaped to the needs and resources of traditional impoverished communities, have no appeal for the American, French, and Asian officials he encounters. Living simply in an Asian village, he demonstrates how bicycles can be used for water pumps. His wife, observing the bent backs endemic among the elderly women of the village, shows them that by using long-handled brooms they can liberate themselves from an affliction brought on by constant stooping. Standing in sharp contrast to the protagonist and his wife are the pleasure-seeking, the time-serving, and the merely incompetent Americans who live luxuriously in Third-World cities as pampered representatives of their country and its policies. The point of the novel, of course, is that the United States needs fewer of their kind in the rest of the world, and more Ugly Americans bringing unvarnished honest skills and knowledge to people who need them. In conformity to their times, the authors were concerned above all about the fortunes of the war against communism, which they believed American blundering was losing in the Third World.

The title, though not the argument, of the novel was quickly misconstrued. "Ugly American" soon came in common parlance to designate Americans who were the opposite of the novel's virtuously homely figure: Americans who flaunted their money, made loud demands for American standards of comfort, disdained knowledge of the language and culture of the country they were invading, and in general insulted their host population and embarrassed their homeland. The point of the Peace Corps was to field American teachers, agronomists, road surveyors, and the like who would be rewarded only by pride and commitment to the work: "Ugly Americans" in the original meaning of the book title.

No program advanced during Kennedy's presidency so perfectly fitted his call as did the Peace Corps to "ask what you can do for your country." During the presidential election campaign on October 14, 1960, he questioned extemporaneously a huge crowd of University of Michigan students about how many of them would be willing to spend years in Asia, Africa, or Latin America. His call to sacrifice stirred the audience. In San Francisco on November 2 he further developed the theme, observing in an address that people "without compassion" had been sent to represent the United States in countries suffering from poverty, disease, and illiteracy.

Once in office, Kennedy put his brother-in-law, R. Sargent Shriver, in charge of the Peace Corps. Installed before Vietnam and the dynamic of the civil rights movement radicalized much of the nation's politically articulate youth, the Corps attracted volunteers who could accept the government as a vehicle for social change. Peace Corps volunteers became the pride of their home communities. The program was, to be sure, meant to be an arm of the battle against communist infiltration of the Third World, and participants had to take a loyalty oath. But the designers of the Peace Corps sincerely intended the lessening of illiteracy and poverty as goods in themselves and perceived economic and social justice as integral to democratic pluralism. The condensed training was rigorous; Americans were actually required to learn to speak foreign languages; volunteers prepared to serve in the outlands, far distant from any access to exported

American luxuries. The liberals of Kennedy's time shared in the continuing American preoccupation with the nation's character and ethos.

The Peace Corps was designed to target specific pockets of need in impoverished regions. In this it spoke more directly to the problem of deprivation and injustice than does the most militant of ideologies, Marxist or other, in which there is an intrusive element of love for the internal architecture of the ideology itself. The enlistment of idealists was superior to revolutionary philosophies that can define no way of relating individuals to one another save by some sort of exterior historical or social logic.

The Peace Corps has not limited itself to any age group, but it was intended to appeal especially to the young. Kennedy's identification with youth, which was an element in the ambience of his presidency, began in a simple and direct fact: he was young. And like the celebrants of youth during the later sixties, his admirers made much of it. But events had not yet moved to the near self-worship of youth. The Peace Corps' hundred thousand volunteers with a median age of twenty-four are the most lasting of Kennedy's legacies to a responsible idea of youth. By respecting the cultures of their host nations, those members of the Corps who were not seduced by the American golden ghettos abroad built a good will whose face is as unsusceptible to measurement as is President Kennedy's effect upon them.

The administration was moving toward articulating a persuasive alternative, and counter, to communist ideology. Previously the democratic West had offered little as an answer to communism: either mere anticommunism, which is no more than definition by opposition and therefore devoid of substance; or militant capitalism, which has little that is convincing to say to the world's poor and excluded. Kennedy, for example, seems to have intended so to distribute Alliance for Progress funds as to lessen somewhat the structural inequalities of power and wealth in recipient countries.

The essential problem lay in the anticommunist element in the mix. Anticommunism belonged there quite logically; it would have belonged on purely philosophical grounds even if it had not been an expression of this country's perceived self-interest. But the war with Third-World movements allied to Moscow or Beijing dictated that American policy would do business with repressive regimes of entrenched privilege claiming to be a bulwark against communist revolution, as has been the case in Washington's dealings with Latin America. And as long as extremes of structural inequality remained—and structural inequality was exactly what such regimes were determined to protect—even the best-intentioned programs of economic relief could offer no more than relief. Anticommunism, which might have found its appropriate partner and likeness in social democracy abroad, could not in its American form remain true to the partnership.

The Kennedy administration had yet to face its most dangerous moment. That moment could not have been predicted. Its origins lay in considerations that in 1962 led Nikita Khrushchev secretly to begin installing missiles in Cuba, some of them supplied with nuclear warheads.

Perhaps the most plausible explanation for Khrushchev's actions has to do with the fate of Cuba. Both Cuba and the Soviet Union were convinced that the United States still planned a full-scale attack on the island. Operation MONGOOSE, the CIA's program of sabotage against the Castro regime, was well known to both Cuba and the Soviet Union, and similar operations under Eisenhower had predated the Bay of Pigs. Placing nuclear missiles in Cuba would in effect bring the island within Soviet military territory, and constitute a way of saying to the United States that an attack on Cuba would be an attack on the Soviet Union. Further political advantages would be an increase in Soviet prestige throughout the world, and in the domestic standing of Khrushchev himself, who as an architect of de-Stalinization was in a precarious relation to the hard-line Soviet right.

In the early autumn of 1962 air photographs confirmed the existence of Cuban missile sites, and without revealing the findings to the public, the administration quietly prepared a response. Kennedy had learned from the disaster at the Bay of Pigs. He wanted counsel more balanced and thoroughly debated than a single group of advisers could give him. For the purpose he drew together from the National Security Council and elsewhere an executive committee, or ExComm, as it became called in crisp alignment with the cold, swift decisions that the moment demanded. ExComm was an assemblage of the government's highest civilian and military officials, and they ranged in persuasion from the dovish Ambassador to the United Nations, Adlai Stevenson, to the Joint Chiefs of Staff, who, like former President Eisenhower, wished to take out the missile sites with an air strike. General Curtis Le May advocated a wider attack on Cuban military targets. Senator Fulbright argued for an air strike as less aggressive than an attack in international waters on a Soviet ship defying a naval interdiction. As tapes of the ExComm meetings reveal, President Kennedy himself at first inclined toward a strong military response. McNamara and Robert Kennedy opposed the idea of an air raid, RFK comparing it to Pearl Harbor. After several days a consensus was reached within ExComm on establishing a quarantine—the word "blockade" seemed too provocative—of ships that might be bringing in equipment for the completion of the missile system. The navy was not to be trusted with supervision of the quarantine; that job belonged to Mc-Namara, the Pentagon's civilian chief.

Not until Monday, October 12, did the public learn that the world was in a grave crisis. On television that evening the President revealed the presence of the missiles and the decision to impose a quarantine. Some have retrospectively criticized him for bringing the matter to public attention, which very likely made it more embarrassing for the Soviet Union to withdraw. To that the response has usually been that diplomatic efforts were then under way and the purpose of the speech was to mobilize international opinion on the side of the United States. For about two days the world waited to see what its future was going to be. Then on Wednesday, after the navy allowed a tanker to pass through, a Soviet ship containing equipment that could be used for the missiles turned back. But it had been a close thing. Some 180 warheads, many with nuclear warheads installed in the missiles, were already being assembled in Cuba, and local Soviet commanders had discretion over whether to use them. Kennedy knew nothing of this. And some forty-five thousand Soviet troops were on the island, far more than Washington had estimated.

Privately, Moscow and Washington had meanwhile been negotiating their mutual preservation. Khrushchev, frightened by Castro's desire to launch a preemptive attack against the United States, sent a telegram proposing a removal of the missiles in return for a promise not to invade Cuba. Then he sent another asking for the removal of Jupiter missiles in Turkey, which the Department of Defense had not yet dismantled as Kennedy had long since ordered. These antiquated European missiles were vulnerable to a strike, and in the event of nuclear war the Soviet Union surely would have eliminated them before they could be launched in retaliation. Thus they were of no significant use as a deterrent to such a war, and were usable only in a war begun by the United States. That made them provocative, as did their closeness to the Soviet Union. The United States, indignant at the emplacement of Soviet missiles in Cuba, had itself not hesitated to locate missiles near Soviet borders. Robert Kennedy suggested a tactful response: ignore the second telegram, publicly accept the substance of the first with a private agreement not to invade Cuba, and privately let Moscow know that dismantling the Cuban missiles would bring dismantlement of ours in Turkey. On Sunday morning, Americans awakened to learn that the Soviet Union had decided to withdraw the Cuban missiles.

A judgment of Kennedy's behavior that October has to begin with the prevailing American consensus, in which he shared, that nuclear arms are legitimate as deterrents. That consensus implied acceptance of the continuing risks of nuclear war that come with their possession. Was Kennedy acting as responsibly as a commander of nuclear arms could act under the circumstances? He gambled the danger of a nuclear war—in fact, Soviet troops in Cuba had tactical nuclear weapons ready there against an American attack—against the hope that in gaining removal of the Cuban missiles he would restore and strengthen a stability that Khrushchev's bold act had threatened by its very boldness. Having determined to force the removal of the missiles, Kennedy carried out that decision with as much care and restraint as it would allow. Norman Mailer once observed that Khrushchev, by recklessly installing the missiles, had rescued the United States from the moral disadvantage the Bay of Pigs had imposed upon it.

In the wake of the crisis, in fact, the two nations became more civil toward each other than they had been at any time since the beginning of the Cold War. Kennedy's June 1963 speech at American University warned against having "a desperate and distorted view of the other side." Teletype communication, which Khrushchev had proposed over a year earlier, was established between Moscow and Washington—the hot line it became popularly known as for use in times of danger. (In the initial testing of the line, the first reply from the Soviet Union was a perplexed inquiry as to the meaning of the phrase that has a quick brown fox jump over a lazy dog.) The American public began to acquire something close to a liking for Khrushchev's earthy exuberance—at times he seemed the classic peasant of folklore—and for the happy resolution of the moment of high tension that he, his country, and the American people had gone through together. The warming of relations was both cause and effect of the successful negotiation of a treaty banning the atmospheric testing of nuclear weapons.

Earlier, in the days of anger over Berlin, Khrushchev had resumed nuclear testing, and the United States had followed quickly in September 1961; the next spring the light from an American Starfish test brought false daylight to Hawaii and flashed the skies as far as Australia. But in the spirit of friendship, or of the discovery of the precariousness of peace, or of the simple giddy relief that followed the Cuban missile crisis, Soviet and American leaders negotiated in late 1963 a treaty banning testing above ground.

Americans on the right, of course, denounced the treaty as appeasement. A later and opposite accusation has been that the treaty, rather than embodying a sense of equity on the part of the administration, merely halted the process of testing at a state of weaponry favorable to the United States. But partly in reaction to Herman Kahn's controversial *On Thermonuclear War* (1960), even the notion of nuclear superiority was becoming obsolete by the early 1960s. It was generally understood that in a nuclear exchange, no matter which side might have the slight advantage of instigating it, the results would be intolerable devastation to both sides. The simplest explanation for the treaty, therefore, is the soundest. The missile crisis had rightly scared both camps. In view of existing nuclear arsenals and knowledge, atmospheric testing offered few if any practical advantages, while it was a psychological irritant and a great expense. Radiation spread through the air, moreover, was a proven health hazard. Right-wing critics at the time, who saw the treaty as an act of self-interest on the part of the Soviet Union, and later American critics on the left who labeled it an act of self-interest on the part of the United States, were both quite obviously correct: otherwise there would have been no treaty.

The agreement had still to win two-thirds of the Senate. Here Kennedy found two allies only apparently unlikely: Republican Senator Everett Dirksen of Illinois and Republican Congressman Charles Halleck of Indiana. Halleck, as a member of the House of Representatives, would not take part directly in the debate or the voting, but as a leading Republican politician was an important influence on opinion within his party. The same two legislators also supported civil rights legislation. On both issues they demonstrated not only moral sensitivity but the difference between simplistic rightist negativity and a conservatism alert to the distinction between changes that threaten the health of institutions and those that enhance it.

The treaty's victory in the Senate in September 1963, by a vote of eighty to nineteen, represented in foreign policy what the victory of civil rights legislation was to signify on the race issue. It meant that a consensus was forming to the left of where American ultranationalists had for a time believed and hoped that it had fixed itself—in the case of the treaty, that unremitting hostility to the Soviet Union as a transcendent evil was giving way to a posture of armed watchfulness. Part of the story of the decades to follow lies in the right's attempt to reestablish the anticommunist certainties of an earlier day.

Hostility had been more sustained in Truman's presidency than it was during the sporadic clashes of Kennedy's tenure; the relationship between Mikhail Gorbachev and Ronald Reagan would be warmer, perhaps, than any that Kennedy toward the end of his days achieved with Khrushchev. But in Kennedy's time the stretch of conflict and conciliation between the two powers surpassed the range during any other presidency. What more particularly qualified the conflicts of the time, on both sides, was a character of measure and meticulousness in the actions that accompanied and in some degree resolved them. It is as though the liberal idea, expounded against the jangled nerves of the right, of how to wage a protracted though cold war had found an opportunity to take the stage in the intricate moves of Berlin and the Cuban missile crisis, in the Peace Corps, the Green Berets, the test-ban treaty. And for that liberal idea to achieve the proper staging, it needed the unlikely cooperation of Nikita Khrushchev, who seemed to understand the motions of the dance.

The result of it all might have been an era of freedom— nervous freedom—from major international war. But meanwhile in a corner of Southeast Asia, John Kennedy was almost ignoring his own basic policy.

 **The Rucksack Revolution**

Americans should know the universe itself as a
road, as many roads, as roads
for traveling souls.
(Walt Whitman)

IN 1961 Ernest Hemingway died in Ketchum, Idaho, of a self-inflicted gunshot wound. More than any other American figure, Hemingway had defined the sensibility that critics have called modern. He invented, in the words of the literary critic Leslie Fiedler, "a major prose style viable in the whole western world." He catches the speech of men and women who had experienced the upheaval in European and American culture during the era of World War I. Hemingway's men, laconic, ironic in temper, are driven to feats of heroism by a purely personal sense of honor. For all the physical sweep of their adventures, his heroes fulfill themselves not by widening the range of their vision but by contracting it to the accomplishment of some private act of daring. They risk everything to complete a particular moment—in the bullring or a war, on the hunt or the seas. They fight for no cause but their own integrity; they endanger their lives for nothing beyond those lives, and only to give them definition. Hemingway describes manhood in flat, minimalist terms in and for an age when causes and ideals had proved invalid.

It was not unlike the style of John Kennedy that folklore would come to image, though the Kennedy presidency projected the kinds of hopeful enterprises that are foreign to the Hemingway manner. By the time of Hemingway's death, a new generation of writers had established itself and was exploring more expansively the meaning of identity and fulfillment. While the civil rights movement in its early days was probing beyond the limits of settled social reality, the Beat Generation was composing works that would contribute in their own ways to the widening of sensibilities in the years to come.

The first impressions a reader will take from the best-known writings of the Beats are rootlessness, rebellion, great gobs of primal undigested experience, and in the generation's chronicler novelist Jack Kerouac a

vigor and sense of the open land suggestive of Jack London. Other readings yield subtler moods. The lost sound of jazz drifting above the city
from the back rooms of the poem's seekers catches one tone of Allen
Ginsberg's *Howl* (1955). Kerouac's novel *The Dharma Bums* (1958) portrays a search for moments as finely etched as a Japanese watercolor,
immaculate like the pure mountain water in which the two central characters brew cups of tea. No single theme predominates in Beat writing,
nor was all the Beat rebellion on the political left. While Ginsberg was an
antiwar activist, Kerouac admired William Buckley and supported the
war in Vietnam. William Burroughs could be something of a reactionary.
The rebellion, rather, was against what the authors took to be the timo-
rousness of the nation's culture, the narrow limits it placed upon experiencing. They sought, and stored reflectively in their writings, experience
gained in encounters with the physical world—archetypically, a car craving its way through the bountiful continent that had once sustained
among the pioneers and then the hoboes a restless American folk culture.
And in the belief that experience, mundane or mystical or in whatever
conjunction, lies for the taking beyond the bounds imposed by social conventions, the Beats anticipated a decade that was to be about the ruptur-
ing of boundaries.

In 1957 a substitute book reviewer at the *New York Times*, Gilbert
Millstein, wrote a favorable review of Kerouac's powerful novel *On the
Road*. "It is possible," he said,

> that [the book] will be condescended to by, or make uneasy, the neo-academi-
> cians and the "official" avant-garde critics and that it will be dealt with superfi-
> cially elsewhere as merely . . . picaresque. . . . But the fact is that "On the
> Road" is the most beautifully executed, the clearest and the most important
> utterance yet made by the generation Kerouac himself named years ago as
> "beat," and whose principal avatar he is. Just as, more than any other novel of
> the Twenties, "The Sun Also Rises" came to be regarded as the testament of the
> "Lost Generation" so it seems certain that "On the Road" will come to be
> known as that of the "Beat Generation." There is, otherwise, little similarity
> between the two: technically and philosophically Hemingway and Kerouac are,
> at the very least, a depression and a world war apart.

Kerouac had a sense of place and family that he evoked in *The Town
and the City*, a fictional work preceding *On the Road*. He came from an
ethnic French Canadian section of downtown Lowell, Massachusetts. As
a boy he had played adventure games, wearing a cape, always running,
like Doctor Sax in his 1959 novel *The Subterraneans*. He longed for a job
on the railroad. He loved the trains near his house, especially the locomotives with their steaming breath; later his favorite writing place was to be
within earshot of locomotives chugging and railroad cars being shunted

in the yards, and he would work for a time as a railway brakeman. Football offered him a way to college, a good college, Columbia, in New York, a city he was already in love with from the movies.

Kerouac quit college after two years in 1942 but spent much of the time until 1950 on Columbia's Morningside Heights, which must have offered to his expanding imagination a feeling of neighborhood, of urban and literary community, dense against the openness of the continent that called to him, and yet alive with a comparable energy. He joined the navy briefly but was kicked out after he laid his rifle down and marched off in his own direction during close-order drill.

Early in the summer of 1947 Kerouac consulted a map and traced the red line of U.S. Route 6 westward from the Bear Mountain Bridge near West Point, not knowing that this old highway had fallen into disuse. He hitched a ride to that starting point and stood in the rain for hours before returning to buy a bus ticket to Chicago. Then he hitched to Denver and San Francisco.

On the Road is about a community dotted across the continent, shifting like the patches on a kaleidoscope. In its way it is a foreshadowing of the rebel communes that in a few years were so to bemuse establishment liberals. It consists of Kerouac's first-person narrator Sal Paradise and his reckless driver companion Dean Moriarty, and their friends drawn from life such as Carlo Marx, who is Allen Ginsberg, as Moriarty is the legendary Beat vagabond Neal Cassady. By the time he was twenty-one, so the story goes, Cassady had stolen five hundred cars. In the novel it is the road trips that connect the characters, continent-devouring trips by Sal and Dean with stopovers wherever a friend is living and welcoming. What they share is talk, notably the exultant, delirious monologues of Dean; and beyond that, the American land, for the community in *On the Road* is unthinkable apart from the American spaces that make the novel a rush of wind against car panes. Plot does not unfold in *On the Road*; character does not develop. Nor would there be any point in either. The novel presents a way of life more traditional than the work's reputation would suggest: a cross between bohemian and hobo. It offers as a phenomenon of immeasurable energy the nation's continental stretch and the seekers who move and scatter across it, which again puts the story in a venerable tradition, a distinctively American sensibility to the land.

On the Road has an underpinning of ideas. They are crystallized in the word "beat," which Kerouac equated with "beatific." Here the Roman Catholic Kerouac, who would experiment in Buddhism but never divest himself of his heritage, turned to Catholicism for nomenclature if not theological understanding. The experience that his generation was reaching, so he decided, could be understood only as approaching a mystical apprehension of reality. There are chemical means of ecstatic experience in *On the Road*, marijuana and alcohol. But ecstasy, the state of being outside yourself, is achieved and conveyed more convincingly in the primal states of the novel: the land, the distances, the talk that is more chant than talk.

On the Road has been spoken of as a road map for the sixties. "You who are on the road," Crosby, Stills, and Nash were to sing to the youth of that time, "must have a code, / That you can live by, / And so become yourself." Kerouac, loyal to his nurturing New England French Catholic family and heritage, conscious of the generations of train-hopping migrants who had preceded him in his questing, might not have agreed with them in the next line, that the past is just a goodbye. Nor would his later politics accord with those of the rebels of the 1960s, for whom physical rootlessness was an expression of disaffiliation from their society and government. But the endless movement, the refusal to become encumbered by property and social station, the journeying that is at once spatial and internal, the sense that the finding is in the looking: all this makes the book a glimpse into the decade to follow. Fourteen-year-old Jim Morrison and Bob Zimmerman, later Dylan, at fifteen copied passages from *On the Road* into their notebooks.

The Dharma Bums, published in 1958, reflects Kerouac's discovery of Buddhism. Here as in *On the Road*, much of the strength of the tale rests in Kerouac's direct and naive representation of land and mountains, of homings and of beginnings out on the road. Like Sal of the earlier novel, Kerouac's narrator-self Ray Smith is a wanderer, here accompanied in much of the story by Japhy Ryder. Modeled on the Beat philosopher Gary Snyder, poet and translator Japhy has a northwestern logging background, has discovered Eastern culture and languages, and practices his own idiosyncratic form of Zen Buddhism. Ray has adopted what he understands of a Buddhism more mystical than Japhy's, viewing the phenomenal world as purely illusionary. At the same time, Ray takes an innocent pleasure in the things of this earth: a hot breakfast, camping equipment simple and compact, an act of charity. If there is a latent logical contradiction between this robust earthiness and Ray's world-denying spirituality, it is merely logical and not experiential.

The world, meanwhile, is there to be explored, all its splendors to be savored even as consciousness contemplates its own recognition of nonexistence and observes the beauty of the phantoms that dwell in that nonplace. Japhy, sharing not Ray's transcendental denial of existence but his search for perfection of experience, foresees "a great rucksack revolution, thousands or even millions of young Americans . . . going up to mountains to pray, . . . all of 'em Zen Lunatics who go about writing poems that happen to appear in their heads for no reason and also by being kind and also by strange unexpected acts" bringing images of freedom to all human and other creatures. It was eleven years to Woodstock.

Yet Kerouac, who became for a generation an iconic figure of rebellion and spiritual questing, was at bottom quite simple and conventional in outlook. He could not withstand the glare of publicity, and after *On the Road* never truly got his compass back on north. Heavy drinking came later, when he moved with his mother to a house in Northport, Long Island, and hung out with high school kids. Asked "How do you like fame?" he answered, "It's like old newspapers blowing down Bleecker Street." As Kerouac neared his alcoholic end, Ginsberg spent hours on the phone with him, trying to get through. He died in 1969.

Kerouac's novels swallow the land as they rush through it. His friend Gary Snyder offers a more philosophically finished means for perception of its detail. "Water in motion," says a note that Snyder made while he was a forest ranger in the Northwest during the summer of 1953, "is precise and sharp, clearly formed, holding specific postures for infinitely small frozen moments." Such glimpses fleck the writings of Snyder's early years: "A dead sharp-shinned hawk, blown by the wind against the look-out. Fierce compact little bird with a square head . . . on the west slopes creek beds are brushy north-faces of ridges, steep and covered with snow slides and old burns on dry hills." Existence forms, from instant to instant, into minute shapes as clean and transient as water ripples. From his forest watchtower the writer captures it in snatches of imagist verse.

Snyder's world appears cold, distant, fleeting. It is in fact completely available to the observer who wishes not to possess it but rather to know it with attentiveness and detachment. That is the purpose of Zen as Snyder, studying that discipline in Japan in 1957, was defining it: "As Zen goes to *anything* direct—rocks or bushes or people—the Zen Master's presence is to help one keep attention undivided, to always look one step farther along, to simplify the mind: like a blade which sharpens to nothing." The reconciliation of the spiritual and the material is clearer in Snyder's work than in Kerouac's *The Dharma Bums*, or rather, there is no need of reconciliation for there is no duality: mind empties so as to be filled with the reality of things.

When the rucksack revolution of the 1960s came, Snyder made important contributions to it. Zen had explained the relation of self to world: Snyder could conclude that what was astir amounted to an effort to restore the primal rightness of the relation. Throughout the course of human existence, he held, there has been a Great Subculture stretching from ancient Shamanism and cave-painting to European witchcraft, Bengali Tantrism, English Quakerism, and manifestations in China and Japan on down to San Francisco hippies. It has preached trust in our natural being, along with a recognition, acting out, and exorcising of the demonic forces in the unconscious. This tradition has been subversive of civilization, which involves a ruling class and its law—and law takes hold of the social psyche most effectively if people doubt their nature, more particularly their sexual nature. To doubt human nature is also to doubt outer, wilderness nature, and therefore aim at control over the natural environment rather than to seek to live in harmony with it.

In Snyder's writings of the sixties, nature, sex, the unconscious—basic materials for much of the counterculture—take the place of the exacting personal encounters with the outer and inner world that he had once sought in Zen discipline. Ecology and the tribal community, the need for humankind to relearn intimate connection with a particular place and soil, are the essential themes of his essays in *The Old Ways*, collected in 1972. Of the knowledge that a people acquires of its locality, Snyder writes, "*a spirit of what it was to be there* evolved, that spoke of a direct sense of relation to the 'land'—which really means, the totality of the local bio-region system, from cirrus clouds to leaf-mold." A knowledge of place contributes to knowledge of self, for the self is composite. "Part of you is out there waiting to come into you, and another part of you is behind you, and the 'just this' of the ever-present moment holds all the transitory little selves in its mirror." Such is the wisdom of peoples who have learned to keep within their ecological limits. In dark contrast stand the imperial peoples, who have discovered that by invading another ecological system they can drain energy from it. From wisdom comes a perception of the soundness of the whole universe. Snyder tells of the concept in India of the universe-as-energy as a voice, a song stirring within the still and silent Brahma: mantra chanting is a chanting of the fundamental syllables of that voice, a return to the first energy of the universe.

Snyder represented a cultural movement that distrusted modern technology, practiced simple crafts, and thought to return to fundamental impulses of the body and compositions of nature. Its partisans exalted the folk traditions of peoples such as the Vietnamese and American Indians whose primary communities seemed to be under siege by Western imperialism with its technological and scientific apparatus.

People of the United States have never quite come to terms with their continental land as an Irishman knows his plot or a Guatemalan Indian her village. The friendship of Kerouac and Snyder brought together ways quite divergent and yet complementary in their apprehension of the land. In *The Dharma Bums* Kerouac melded the motor and the continent, as Carl Sandburg had anchored his boundlessly energetic Chicago in the boundless prairie. Kerouac embraced the land hurriedly as he sped from place to place. He could perceive detail and nuance: "The trail had a kind of immortal look to it, in the early afternoon now, the way the side of the grassy hill seemed to be clouded with ancient gold dust and the bugs flipped over rocks and the wind sighed in shimmering dances over the hot rocks." But ultimately that trail, that hill, that dust will be lost in the immensity of a continent that offers an infinity of rocks and hills and color tones, glimpsed in passing. Snyder, nomad though he has been, has demanded fixity, and close knowledge of a particular place whether won by the Zen discipline of the individual perceiver or carefully received and tended from generation to generation. Kerouac's characters fore-shadow the restlessness of the cultural rebels of the sixties, a restlessness that they, like him, expressed and gratified with the very considerable and unabashed aid of modern technology. Snyder foreshadowed and then ar-ticulated their conviction that nature and her relation with the human community had been maimed.

Prominent among the writers who had learned to live with the maim-ing and make poetry of it has been Allen Ginsberg. His mother, Naomi, had gone mad; and he was a homosexual at a time when homosexuality most often evoked repugnance and social ostracism, but Ginsberg was open about his sexuality as he was about all matters. He would have to live his days outside the many conventions that give shelter to the timid. If his work reveals much curiosity about nonviolence, perhaps it is all traceable to experiences that induced a constant self-examination and concern for how to live within yourself, knowingly, acceptingly, and well.

The public history of the Beats has a prologue in Ginsburg's days at Columbia College after his enrollment in 1943. In the dust of his dirty window he wrote of the university's president, "Butler has no balls," and, for the benefit of his anti-Semitic cleaning lady, "Fuck the Jews." When Kerouac's football coach found Jack sharing Ginsberg's room, Allen was suspended. In 1949 Ginsberg was back at Columbia, again working on a B.A., and again he managed to get into trouble. Friends stored stolen goods in his apartment, some booty wound up in his car, and he was arrested. The police confiscated his copy of the *Bhagavad Gita*, telling him that only religious books were allowed in jail. It is remarkable, not-withstanding the generally staid academic atmosphere at the time, that Columbia's faculty stood by him. The redoubtable art historian Meyer Schapiro commented that the arrest reminded him of the time he himself had gone to jail in Europe. Even Lionel Trilling, the embodiment of high culture, though horrified, was helpful, and advised Ginsberg to see Her-bert Wechsler of the law school, who told him to plead insanity. Faculty members testified at a hearing, and he ended not in prison but in effectual incarceration in the mental ward of Columbia Presbyterian Hospital.

It was doubtless preferable to jail. But mental institutions, in addition to doing their work of curing or tending the sick and suffering, have had in the United States as in the former Soviet Union a second purpose, to a far milder degree here than that of Soviet psychiatric imprisonment but at least distantly comparable: to adjust people to society on its terms. Ginsberg's stay in the mental ward was not intended to help him realize his desire for life to be a "sweet humane surprise." Ginsberg tried to conform, returned after several months to Paterson, dated women, and found a job. He was miserable until he moved to California in 1954 and began seeing a $1 an hour psychiatrist at the university in Berkeley. In San Francisco Ginsberg saw another psychiatrist, Philip Hicks, who asked him what he would like to do. "Doctor," as Ginsberg recalls his answer, "I don't think you're going to find this very healthy and clear,"

> but I really would like to stop working forever—never work again, never do anything like the kind of work I'm doing now—and do nothing but write poetry and have leisure to spend the day outdoors and go to museums and see friends. And I'd like to keep living with someone—maybe even a man—and explore relationships that way. And cultivate my perceptions, cultivate the visionary thing in me. Just a literary and quiet city-hermit existence. Then *he* said "Well, why don't you?" I asked him what the American Psychoanalytic Association would say about *that*, and he said . . . if that is what you really feel would please you, what in the world is stopping you from doing it?

Ginsberg was free, and he lent some of that freedom to the 1960s.

Ginsberg's "A Supermarket in California" addresses Walt Whitman. The similarities between the two poets—"shopping for images," Ginsberg entered the supermarket "dreaming of your enumerations"—are clear enough: the listings of objects, the energy, a poet's sweep across a city or a continent, the clutter of metal and brick and people that, according to the poetry's metaphysic, resolve into a transcendental One. Ginsberg is also, to be sure, angrier than Whitman and far more private, so that great stretches of his work give a reader nothing except the mood and presence of the poet half revealed among the jumble of sensations. Yet he is as significantly in the tradition of that nineteenth-century singer of enumerations as Kerouac is in the tradition of the hoboes. The primal American land and the cities, primal in their energies, had entered both poets.

"Look in my eyes and speak to yourself, that makes me everybody's lover," announces Ginsberg in "Fragment 1956." It is among Ginsberg's Whitmanesque statements of a transcendent unity among the particulars of existence. Yet Ginsberg's poetry is grainier with people and things than Whitman's, and will not so easily dissolve into some principle of oneness. If Ginsberg can join himself to his world, it is by the activity of love or of thought, person mated to person and consciousness to object.

Ginsberg's scenes of modern urban life and technology are harsh. But there is in him and in his poetry that which absorbs and transforms them.

It is in part, of course, his transcendentalist embrace of the world around him, along with a necessary identification with surroundings that have belonged to his life: in one poem Ginsberg goes up to the top of the RCA building to "gaze at my work, Manhattan." And the metallic tangle, the rusty discarded slabs and bars of iron, are aesthetically and morally appropriate to the poetry of hard, abrupt imagery that presents a world beautiful not in formal architecture but in raw and lonely objects transformed by love and imagination. The tough, dusty old sunflower on the riverbank of industrial discard in "Sunflower Sutra" is in one way a triumph of life over its industrial setting of broken metal. But it also resembles the rusted and forgotten iron around it; and if ultimately it is not metallic refuse but life, so too is the refuse.

Among the Beat writers, the writing and the way of life were complementary, becoming together an argument by example for traveling light and exploring the moment's experience—visual, auditory, kinetic, sexual. Ginsberg has always been among the most publicly visible of the Beats, and the public figure as well as his verse contributed not only to the Beat phenomenon but to the politics and counterculture of the sixties. The poems are a vehicle for the public Ginsberg. The poetry as a whole is revelatory, reciting some episode in his life, expressing anger at his country's brutalities abroad. Ginsberg's life yields a politics, a protest against both his nation's imperialism and the totalitarianism of the left. And the whole of his experience as the poems recall it, along with the impulses and discordances of the poetry itself, constitutes in effect a politics of dissociation from collective power and in quest of true community, at moments as small and loyal as community with a lover lying drug-sick in a city room.

It followed that his writing lent itself to a direct expression of political and cultural protest. That is what Ginsberg made of *Howl* as early as 1956, when he did a reading of the poem to a Berkeley audience. The listeners responded with jeers and hisses to the repeated name of the demonic superforce "Moloch!"—the deity who receives the sacrifice of children and the poem's emblematic representation of the forces interior and exterior that in our time stifle life. "Moloch! . . . Boys sobbing in armies! . . . Moloch whose mind is pure machinery! Moloch whose blood is running money! . . . Moloch who entered my soul early! Moloch in whom I am a consciousness without a body! Moloch who frightened me out of my natural ecstasy!" The thundering denunciations appealed to a listener who would one day be president of Students for a Democratic Society—"Moloch . . . the vast stone of war! . . . Moloch whose soul is electricity"—and has remembered thinking that Moloch should be unplugged. Opening with lines now generally familiar, "I saw the best minds of my generation destroyed by madness, / starving hysterical naked," the poem catches in microcosm much of what is distinctive in Ginsberg's work and thought. It has the compact imagery, the essentially private references to the anger, the identification of imaginative sensuality with life and of political with emotional repression, the transcendentalist equation of mental with physical states, so that Moloch is at once a desiccated human consciousness and a war machine.

The Beat event was an intersection of technique and style of living, and a good deal of the best-known Beat writing was reportage of a sort, a carefully wrought account of incidents the authors had lived or observed. The Beats had an excitement about literature that now seems archaic and naive, a conviction that literature could clarify even the briefest of moments. Soon to be depicted by the media as a slothful, self-indulgent literary rabble, they were in truth submitting literature and themselves to experiment and examination, determined to mine every vein of vitality that an incident can yield as Snyder, for instance, could find it in seeing a hawk's body whipped by the wind. They were living in times when gentility ruled literary circles. The sensations of the flesh, so it was and ever has been common to assume, are nihilistic. But Ginsberg, the relentless Jewish intellectual, approached even drugs in a spirit of seriousness, and he was disappointed in the 1960s when marijuana became a drug for partying, not for study and exploration of the inner self.

While many on the left were being selectively indignant about repression abroad, Ginsberg's loyalty to freedom was uncompromising. Ideologues like social uniformity: it appeals to their architectonic sensibility. It is consequently a practice among totalitarian regimes to reinforce conventional sexual intolerance. In Castro's Cuba, a dissenter-hounding state that enjoyed the favor of some dissenters in this country, Ginsberg in 1965 singlehandedly attacked the persecution of homosexuality. He was also irreverent, which is corrosive of totalitarianism: he announced a desire to sleep with Fidel Castro's brother Raoul. Though he did succeed in getting a few men freed through some fracture in the system, he was deported from Cuba and went to Czechoslovakia, taking with him like a good Jewish boy a very bourgeois electric toothbrush such as people in Prague had never seen. Again, Ginsberg spoke more openly than was acceptable. His phrase "afraid of the red police" could not be published, nor would the authorities go with his helpful revision "pink police." In Czechoslovakia, however, Ginsberg found far more freedom than in Cuba, reading *Howl* and even his poem about the red police: "They let me loose, I talked freely, the walls of the State didn't fall." Ginsberg moved on to the Soviet Union to meet some cousins who had returned there in the early 1920s. To his surprise he found himself something of a hero among Russian intellectuals who had read his work in *Evergreen Review* during the 1950s. He also met the poet Yevtushenko, who like other Russians simply could not fathom Ginsberg's interest in drugs or homosexuality, calling them "juvenile preoccupations." Stopping in Poland on his return home, Ginsberg had difficulty explaining to the Russian writer Voznesensky the meaning of "wow." Polish students elected Ginsberg May King, and some hundred thousand revelers gathered in the Park of Culture and Rest at midnight to greet him. Afterward a man rushed at Allen shouting "Bouzerant! Bouzerant!"—homosexual—and knocked him down. The police came, Allen chanted the Hindu mantra "om!" as was his wont, and his visit was terminated as of that day for "grossly violating the norms of decent world behavior."

At a party with John and Cynthia Lennon in London that same year, a drunken Ginsberg took his clothes off, put his shorts over his head, and hung a hotel-room "Please do not disturb" sign over his penis; the Lennons got up to go, John explaining to him, "You don't do that in front of the birds!" Yet his presence at a poetry reading at the Royal Albert Hall was a major stimulus for the great international poetry festivals that were to become fashionable in Europe throughout the decade.

By the midsixties Ginsberg was a celebrity, his likeness seen everywhere on posters, his ideas and persona a matter for international discussion. The French saw him as a study in fashionable coolness. The whole world regarded him as stoned most of the time, though in reality Ginsberg took fewer drugs as political protest increased in the sixties. He was dedicated to nonviolent protest against the Vietnam War, lending to the movement his massive integrity, chanting "om!" to still the passion of a crowd or the forces of discord and war, giving away his considerable income to war resisters, underground papers, and legal defense campaigns for dissidents pursued by the police and the FBI, which were by then actively infiltrating the antiwar movement. He had become, it has been said, the students' "ultimate faculty adviser." Ginsberg wore well. In 1996 he was a teacher at Brooklyn College, in look and authority rabbinical. It is among his accomplishments that he was a leading figure in removing from homosexuality much of its stigma as a metaphor for evil.

Neal Cassady—the original of Dean Moriarty in *On the Road* and of the beatific Cody of later works, and like Ginsberg a feature of the Beat Generation—looked like Kerouac even down to his crewcut. Both literature and life have associated him with the role of driver, whether of the cars that take Sal and Dean rushing to the next place to rush from, or of the day-glo bus that in 1965 Cassady would drive across the country, even through forest fires, with a celebrated band of protohippies, its destination proclaimed as "Further," a microphone slung over his head for broadcasting his own concept of travelogue as he explained that the gas pedal had turned to spaghetti.

Orphaned at thirteen, the handsome Denverite had gone to a reformatory when he was fifteen. He hungered for books as he hungered for the road. He read Proust and Kant, yearned to express himself in writing, and has left fragments of autobiography and stream-of-consciousness letters written on stolen typewriters. His style, apparently, was simply to touch ground whenever he needed for whatever he needed. A car he drove might be stolen, or it might be the kind that people leave at agencies to be driven to other cities. Unable to afford a flophouse, he and Jack once slept in the balcony of an all-night movie theater for thirty-five cents and watched a singing cowboy epic and a spy thriller with Sidney Greenstreet and Peter Lorre. Psychologists who need labels might call Cassady a sociopath for acting out so much or so heedlessly on the instant's impulse, the impulse generally being to go somewhere. If Dean Moriarty of *On the Road* is a true likeness, Cassady could be monumentally irresponsible in his treatment of friends and lovers, but he was neither ugly or violent.

In 1958 Cassady, possibly set up by undercover police, went to San Quentin for possession of marijuana. Ginsberg, as always compassionate, sent a letter of appeal to the California Adult Authority, promising a job and pointing out that his friend had fathered three children. A decade later Neal Cassady was dead in Mexico of a careless drug overdose. His life had been his art, except that in its spontaneity his life was artless.

Kerouac offered the continent as a space for freedom; Snyder commanded a careful sensitivity to its detail, as though each acre within its disordered whole were as minutely perfect and logical as a Japanese garden; Ginsberg protested a politics and culture that war against that freedom. A novel published at the close of the heyday of the Beat Generation brought into clear and compact opposition the open continent and the political culture that was stifling it. The author was less a Beat than an early representative of the counterculture.

Randy McMurphy of Ken Kesey's *One Flew over the Cuckoo's Nest* (1962), the outlaw who has maneuvered himself into a mental hospital to avoid a criminal sentence, is a primal figure arising out of the clean American earth itself before moralists and businessmen had subdued it into suburbs. His strength is in his innocence, most notably his assumption that no one chooses to surrender freedom. It is that lusty innocence and primitive strength that he introduces to the mental hospital and attempts through his own rebellion to impart to the cowed inmates. One of them, Chief Broom, has a more refined intellect and imagination as well as immense physical strength. These are what enable him to understand the hospital and the outside forces that have shaped it. And these are what give him his greater power, allowing him even in his sickness to step outside the institution into the picture of fresh open nature hanging on the wall, and revealing to him that he must free McMurphy by death, himself by flight, and his fellow inmates by destruction of the nerve center of the hospital.

Then there is the enemy that Kesey labels "the Combine," the collective force of unfreedom as Chief Broom's mad exact imagination discovers it. The Combine has succeeded in appropriating the nature and livelihood of his tribe as it crushes the other sufferers who have voluntarily committed themselves to the hospital. As Broom sees with his vivid mental sight, it runs a vast factory machinery under the institution for the total control of the patients.

One Flew over the Cuckoo's Nest should not be read as a fashionable celebration of insanity. Chief Broom's madness is in a mind so finely powerful that the madness turns to insight and vision and ultimately to health, but he begins as a broken invalid, unable to recognize even his physical might. The other inmates are fear-ridden husks of human beings, their sickness carrying possibly a hint of some deviance from the plastic conforming complacency that defines the Combine's good Americans, but sickness nonetheless, terror without confidence to confront it, self-contempt based on lack of self-awareness.

Aristocratic and aloof, favoring conservative vested suits, William Burroughs lived as much as Kesey, Kerouac, Snyder, and Ginsberg the cultural dissidence that was also the matter of art.

A patrician upbringing placed Burroughs outside middle American society and within his self-contained mind and manners. Drawn to the elan of combat, during the Second World War he tried unsuccessfully to get into the navy and dreamed of elite service, finally reacting as likely as not to the threat of military regimentation by cutting off the tip of his left little finger. As is the option of children of privilege, he turned from advantage to the life of the streets, washing windows, working as an exterminator, engaging in petty theft, and imagining the life of a second-story burglar. He was a practicing bisexual. Much of his life he has been on drugs, hard drugs, and one night he awoke with something squeezing his hand: it was his other hand. In an accident, he shot and killed his wife during a game of William Tell. "All liberals are weaklings," announced this cultural radical who stands at the anarchist point where far right and far left curve to intersect, "and all weaklings are vindictive, mean, and petty." He longed for a return to "our glorious frontier heritage of minding your own business." Mexico City at midcentury appealed to him for its frontier lawlessness.

Yet Burroughs did not secede from society. He just had his own ideas about what society needed. He dreamed up schemes that include a home dry cleaning machine and concrete houses that would last forever. He became interested in Timothy Leary's experiments with psychedelics, at one point suggesting to Leary that through widespread use of such drugs "whole areas of neurosis could be mapped and eradicated in mass therapy." Yet he grew horrified at the waste and conspicuous consumption of the Leary household, the undiscipline of the children, and Leary's indiscriminate distribution of magic mushrooms. Such were the judgments of a gentleman of background who combined individualism with a sense of proper limits.

Naked Lunch, Burrough's best-known work, was several years in reaching the public in final form. As early as 1959 the *Chicago Review* at the University of Chicago published excerpts from it, which the university promptly moved to suppress. After Boston authorities ruled *Naked Lunch* obscene, Norman Mailer and others in 1965 before a state court testified in its behalf. The court ruled that under the Constitution only work utterly lacking in redeeming social importance could be banned and so found in favor of *Naked Lunch*. The book, which had already been published in Europe in 1963, appeared in full in the United States in 1966. Like the Supreme Court's previous decree in the case of Henry Miller's *Tropic of Cancer*, the verdict was a landmark in the liberation of literary expression. Now in the art of the novel as in politics, the decade was set free.

The novel has no plot; it is essentially a series of rapid-fire sketches through which move characters like Clem Snide the Private Asshole and the Paregoric Kid. The antihero is a drug addict: junk is a refuge from the pain of living. Addiction is a metaphor for society. Power and junk are symmetrical and quantitative. Bureaucracy is one of the chosen instruments of control. For power addicts, corruption is another. Politics is a red cloth, images and illustrations that the public is trained to chase. *Naked Lunch* is the work of an aristocrat and anarchist, an individual who will neither exercise nor submit to power.

The Beat subculture sprouted in many different places here and there through the length and breadth of the continent. *On the Road* refers apparently to events of the late 1940s, and a long unbroken prehistory can be conjectured, stretching back through countless artist bohemias or fellowships of drifters. The novel enhanced the cohesiveness and communal self-awareness of the Beats and gave them a new visibility. But while its setting is the open land, Beat public coffeehouses, jazz audiences, and poetry readings fixed them as an event of the big cities, especially New York and San Francisco. And some Beats undoubtedly wished that their distinctive sensibility might leaven in some general way the mindset and manners of the world beyond them.

Yet there was nothing to suggest that such a wish might be fulfilled. For it was the very apartness of the Beat subculture that gave it at once the ironic detachment and the pacific rebellion that were central to its character. These qualities were inseparable from whatever its adherents might offer the rest of the country as exemplars of independence, introspection, awareness of the mystery and fleeting nature of experience, and exact craftsmanship. Although the Beats attracted wide public notice, they centered their lives in small jazz and poetry gatherings, or in friendship and love sheltered in rent-cheap apartments. What the greater society had to offer to the Beats, in turn, was to keep things going in the daily tasks that had little interest to them. The dialectic of the encounter required that the two remain distinct from each other.

Beat writing has now settled into a solid place within American literature, studied and included in anthologies. Time and legend have incorporated into American tradition the coffeehouse poetry readings and jazz, the hobo wanderings, the anarchist politics and ways. But to win a place in our traditions, to gain authenticity as an insurgent movement within a national experience that is a tapestry of jeremiads and insurgencies, the Beat Generation had to begin as outsiders. Critics obliged. Norman Podhoretz denounced the phenomenon as "a revolt of all the forces hostile to civilization itself, a movement of brute stupidity and know-nothingism"; "what juvenile delinquency is to life, the San Francisco writers are to literature." A reviewer in *The Nation* said of Kerouac that he presents "a blend of nihilism and mush, . . . a proof of illness rather than a creation of art." It was typical of liberals to dismiss as illness any deviation from what they considered good sense or behavior, including homosexuality. Such critics wrote of the Beats—much as others would later treat the student radicals—psychoanalytically (although a few, like the poet Louis Simpson, were to repent: he called himself "obtuse" and embraced the writings of Ginsberg, which as late as 1967 he had refused to include in a modern poetry anthology). In the other camp were readers who liked the Beats precisely for the energy, the violation of academic literary form, the social revolt caught in the cadences of the writing.

By the late sixties the Beats had become replaced, as far as the public could see, by a movement deceptively similar and claiming Allen Ginsberg as a spokesman. The counterculture, as it is now known, could also exist in small gatherings. Far more insistently and programmatically than the Beats, it proclaimed a liberation of the imagination and the senses. It too conducted an existence apart from that of the majority of Americans. Its practitioners proposed, and attempted to achieve in their own lives, a new society in place of the civilization of the majority. Yet subtleties of expression and aim distinguish the Beat Generation from its successor.

While Gary Snyder looked to the redemption of American nature from its European invaders, his colleagues belonged to the world of cities and machines. The characters in *On the Road* hunger for the continent; but it is not as untouched nature but as space, distance, hugeness, that the continent calls them, and it is gears and combustion and metal that claim the spaces for them. Beat writing catches the clean edges of what it describes, and this is as true of Snyder as of the more urban Beats—Snyder, whose sensibility had honed itself in his study of Japanese culture, as precisely and rigorously wrought, as *un*natural as any culture on earth. Appropriate to the Beats and to the cities of glass and steel they inhabited was jazz, a music distinguished for detached analytical technique. Clarity, craftsmanship and self-definition in craft, the establishment for the writer of a particular identity or mode of perception—these characterize Beat artistry.

Except in the workmanship of their preindustrial arts, the practitioners of the counterculture, to the contrary, did not concern themselves for the most part with verbal articulateness and the separate properties of things. Jazz draws a small group of careful listeners; rock creates an impassioned community. And though perhaps more hippie communes have existed in cities than on the countryside, the love generation of the sixties proclaimed a return to nature: pastoral nature along with open sexuality and unrepressed emotion.

Beyond its antecedents among the Beats, the emergence of the counterculture has no single satisfactory explanation. No one planned it, no organization mastered and directed it, and few would remain in it for years to keep it going. It had no canonical texts of its own: it neither acknowledged nor had the patience for canons. Hippies believed that some new fact was on the way. The counterculture, like the political left, lived in expectation of its coming.

Even to call the counterculture a culture is to make the best of nomenclature. Unlike the phenomenon generally defined as culture, it had no real history beyond romantic imitation. For all its exaltation of nature and spontaneity, it was a construct, by its members and observers. The counterculture, therefore, had a deliberateness, as if thinking out blueprints for itself, that is the mark of the modern technological mind—itself a part of culture, though not a culture in itself. Yet despite that attribute of the counterculture, and despite its own considerable use of the technology of its day, exemplified in its embrace of electronic music, it appeared the enemy of its technical and scientific surroundings. Foreseeing a future of nationalization and administrative planning, a society run by programmers, executives, and systems analysts, a portion of liberalism dismissed the counterculture as retrograde.

The counterculture did, however, have thoughtful commentators whose perceptions of a form within it amounted to the only form and collective reality it would ever have, much as Kerouac's announcement of the presence of a Beat Generation had imposed a Gestalt on the scattered lives and experiences of his friends.

The most visible observer of the counterculture is Theodore Roszak, who was responsible for popularizing the term "counterculture" and identified within it an intellectual structure that owes more to his own analytical powers than to the intrinsic qualities of his subject. *The Making of a Counterculture* (1969) introduces the reader to the happening that is both discovery and conceptualization on Roszak's part. *Where the Wasteland Ends* (1972) tells where he thinks Western civilization has gone wrong and, by implication, how the cultural rebels are setting it right.

The counterculture as Roszak portrays it confronts a Western ethos that, he argues, has severed the cerebral and observational faculties from the physical and sensual. The world, the body, whatever is visceral and untidy, is viewed as Out There, distant from the observer, to be analyzed and used. In Here is the rational consciousness, methodical, ascetic, disdainful, subduing the rich vital world to its modern scientific and industrial aspirations. The task of the counterculture is to find means of healing the fissure, learning through communal ways of living how to relocate consciousness at the nerve ends. The enterprise is not one of frenetic pleasure-seeking but a phenonemon at once of physical feeling and of meditation, the body sending its reports more freely to the mind, the mind hearing and sensing in a careful reflective way the material existence with which it has reconnected. This suggests the connection between that rebellion and the political radicalism that by the late 1960s was resisting especially the Vietnam war, a war fought by the most impersonally land-scorching, life-crushing forces of modern times.

By that time culture and politics were flowing together. In turning away from the concept of private property as enshrined in the country's institutions, communal living made an insistently ideological statement. Music, psychedelics, love-ins, festivals were expected to expand minds that capitalism had attempted to press within its frozen geometries. When Ginsberg chanted his mantra at a demonstration to still the forces of war or the hostility of the police or the fury of the demonstrators themselves, he was engaging in spiritual insurgency against the mind of politics and government as practiced in every country of the world. It was the insurgency of the rock musicians the Fugs, who in 1968 during the repression of the Prague Spring thought of going to Czechoslovakia to masturbate in front of the invading Soviet army. More broadly the counterculture acted on the most insurrectionary of convictions. It assumed that the transformation of politics, culture, economics, and society begins not with some revolutionary machinery of change but with any number of personal decisions to live the transformed society at once: to learn the expressive skill of a handicraft or the supple knowledge of computer technology perhaps, or to cultivate and preserve nature on a plot of earth.

Yet the absence of acknowledged traditions or models suggests that the counterculture was in fact located in a tradition it might not have recognized. This is the strain of antinomianism within Christianity that places inspired passion at the center of morality and sets it against all natural and human laws and institutions. From the beginning, Christianity has set a perplexing problem for adherents who feel some obligation to live in the world. If truth can break in on earth in human guise, preaching a sharing that gets a death sentence from authority; if the spirit of a new age can burst forth at Pentecost, in declarations of freedom that override conventional understanding, then what use is there for hierarchies, governments, and theologies? In time, of course, Christian churches made a comfortable peace with the world, and became champions of law, wealth, and rank. But the notion has persisted in Western culture that something in civilization itself is fundamentally awry, that the proper business is to listen in stillness, to speak in tongues, to practice—Chief Broom practices it—the madness that is the final clarity. So thought St. Francis and the early Quakers, and in their own way so have thought the most ardent of the present-day witnesses to nonviolence. Impulsive, reckless of property, the counterculture might have claimed, with some show of plausibility, to be a continuation of the original spirit of Christianity.

But the counterculture was not early Christianity. Few of its adherents had the power to commit themselves fully, for, unlike the spontaneity of pentecostal and antinomian Christianity, the impulsiveness of the counterculture had no foundation in a belief that what is sought lies beyond momentary gratification of desire. Francis of Assisi had enlisted for the duration; most communes of the sixties lasted only briefly (though numbers have stubbornly held on in enclaves in New Mexico, Vermont, Texas, Oregon, and elsewhere, living by farming and craftsmanship). The counterculture acted not upon a conviction that something eternal is always breaking in upon the present moment, but upon a belief that the present moment is all there is. All that was best in this antinomianism unarmed by a more rigorous creed—its contempt for property, its celebration of a simple, uncluttered life, its recognition of the need for immediate good acts—revealed itself for a moment late in the sixties among the Diggers who operated in the hippie Haight-Ashbury district of San Francisco.

Taking their name from a seventeenth-century English sect that preached love and denounced property, the Diggers practiced a form of street theater. They stole food, turned it to stew, and distributed it. In a free store they gave out stolen goods. With equal generosity, they passed out free marijuana. The logic of freedom, of immediacy, and of right action dictated their conduct: to live without clinging to property is to be free, to give food to others in defiance of the law is to behave in accord with a liberated will, to feed the hungry is to act rightly. The Diggers went in for stunts and theatrics. In the best-known of them, in August 1967 Abbie Hoffman with some companions dropped dollar bills on the floor of the New York Stock Exchange, which sent some brokers scuttling for them; they then burned money as reporters tried to figure out what was happening. But spontaneity also permitted the Diggers to assume that they had privileges over the unliberated. There is a story of a Digger invasion of a June 1967 Students for a Democratic Society (SDS) conference in Michigan, insulting the earnest conferees for their earnestness.

On New Year's Day, 1968, Hoffman, Jerry Rubin, and others founded YIP, the Youth International party. When the journalists and the Yippies, as they were called, discovered each other, one of the dangers inherent in Digger spontaneity began to exhibit itself. The style of outrage and pranksterism, undisciplined by ideas, stiffened into an imitation of itself, and its adherents began performing the part of free spirits according to public expectations.

Still, there was sophistication of a kind in the decision, among some of the cultural radicals, to constitute a counterpolitics as well, counter to the solemnities not only of Washington but of the left. The recognition that, if not inevitably lethal, political solemnities can be at the least a lethal bore makes Abbie Hoffman's *Woodstock Nation* a defter commentary on the SDS in its later days than any number of the earnest things adults uttered at the time decrying the radicalization of American youth.

Hoffman had come from politics as much as from cultural revolt. Not long before he became a media personality he had been engaged in civil rights work, which included a stint in Mississippi. The Yippies were among the activists calling on the antiwar forces to come to the Democratic Convention of 1968 in Chicago, and after the riot that Mayor Richard Daley and the police blamed on the demonstrators and the demonstrators blamed on the police, Hoffman became one of the Chicago Seven: defendants in a lengthy trial for conspiracy to incite riot. Hoffman was at Woodstock in the summer of 1969, and soon afterward wrote *Woodstock Nation*, in longhand, so the paperback claims, "while lying upside down, stoned, on the floor of an unused office of the publisher," Random House, and in five days.

The title proclaims the major assumption of the book. Woodstock in Hoffman's perception represented a nation of cultural radicals, struggling like the internal black nation for freedom from Pig Nation, the United States. Woodstock Nation is an anarchy realizing itself in the act of anarchic rebellion. He wants to be tried in Chicago, Hoffman writes, not for supporting the National Liberation Front but for having long hair. "Not because I support the Black Liberation Movement, but because I smoke dope. Not because I am against a capitalist system, but because I think property eats shit. . . . Finally, I want to be tried for having a good time and not for being serious." The citizens of Woodstock Nation act with simple honest directness, and do not take orders. Hoffman's attorney at the Chicago trial refused to characterize his client's work as employment. "He has worked for the causes he believes in. He is not employed by them." Hoffman added: "Work is something you do for money, isn't it, or for some other reason? I never worked, ever. If that is what work is, it is a dirty four-letter word."

Hoffman was impatient with the conventional New Left. In Eisenstein's brilliant though politically conformist Soviet silent film *Battleship Potemkin*, the sailors revolt after they discover maggots in their food. The SDS of later days, Hoffman concludes, "would have shouted 'maggots are reformist' and called the sailors irrelevant or petit bourgeois, or lumpenproletariat, or outside the Third World, or white, hence unreachable." *Woodstock Nation* recalls an SDS convention Hoffman attended in Chicago, thick with politicspeak about "male chauvinism," "petit bourgeois revisionist," and "members of the proletarian vanguard waging the relentless battle against imperialism." Perhaps the choice moment came when members of one group holding up their red books shouted Mao's name: "So not to let them slip by their left vanguard, up pops Progressive Labor party in the balcony and shouts in unison, 'Beware of those who wave the red flag to oppose the red flag.'"

Woodstock Nation, in its contempt for the vanguardism of SDS, seems near to a complete dismissal of the ideological enthusiasm of Hoffman's time. But then he goes on to praise, as an alternative to vanguardism, the spirit of Mao.

One matter on which Hoffman did not go even slightly astray was his recognition of what was coming to be known as hip capitalism. The most direct money exploiters of the counterculture were of two kinds: the drug merchants (chiefly of marijuana: smart anarchists shunned the hard stuff) and the rock profiteers, which included the wealthier bands as well as the promoters. On the fringes were the straight-world advertisers and financiers who cultivated the youth-culture market. Yet *Woodstock Nation* recognizes that capitalism is not only a world of sellers but on the other side, among denizens of that world affluent enough to participate, a realm of consumers, with a consumer mentality.

In countercultural literature there is a hint of awareness of this. Several months after Woodstock came Altamont, the California concert featuring the Rolling Stones that ended in terrorization and murder by motorcycle gangsters hired to police the event. In a mood of self-examination, survivors of the concert brooded over their acquiescence in the hiring of the outlaws, their hypnotized inert willingness, after the day's violence had begun, to remain passive receptors of the music. We had dreamed, reflects the journalist Sol Stern, of marching on the Alameda County sheriffs and freeing prisoners they were holding from the People's Park conflict at Berkeley. But in our retreat from Altamont we left the broken body of one of our own. "And the only ones who cared for that battered body, made sure it got from the coroner's office to a funeral parlor, informed the parents, and now the only ones trying to bring the killers to justice, are the Alameda County sheriffs."

It was not a question of cowardice. A small, cohesive body of warriors can hold at bay a disordered throng many times its size, whatever the character of the individuals on either side. The point is that the audience was not the commonwealth of autonomous individuals whom philosophical anarchists of the last century had projected. It was an audience of consumers. And that, rather than any ripoff of middle-class youth with enough money to be ripped off, was the mockery that hip capitalism made of the counterculture: it had the cooperation of hip consumers.

Hermann Hesse, whose work was popular among the cultural radicals for teaching an intellectual and sensuous self-cultivation, would not have made that mistake. There is coldness in his disdain for politics and for mass movements. But his *Magister Ludi* projects a future in which, without social compulsion, a vast interconnected community of scholars pursues knowledge and aesthetic appreciation.

These ascetics of the intellect have intense consciousness because they have rigorously schooled and controlled it. Few denizens of the counterculture would have begun to attempt that. But one variant among the children of the sixties made for a notable exception. A few responded especially to the critique of American civilization for having debased honest workmanship, and they sought some form of work requiring skill, producing a specific and tangible object, and uncorrupted by submission to the country's capitalist and military institutions. Their taste was for the fine arts or for artisanship, for music, or for organic farming. Or they could look for guidance to Paul Goodman, a cranky older commentator on his times and unaccepting of its political hysterias, who argued that much of modern science and technology too could be redeemed at the hands of workers who respect its inherent austerity. Today, in pockets of the American economy, there remain farmers and woodworkers, programmers and musicians, who give some continuing meaning to the idea of Woodstock Nation.

 **Do Not Spindle:
The Student Rebellion**

ALLEN Ginsberg caught the atmosphere of the midcentury American liberal arts campus when he related the words a dean used to chastise him for writing an offensive scrawl on the dirty window of his room: "Do you realize, young man, the *enormity* of what you have done?" Today what he had done would vanish from memory, along with the words themselves, after the next window cleaning. But in the years after World War II universities and colleges were bastions of gentility, and peer review of faculty was often little more than checking for proper behavior. A professor who called a student by a first name was being conspicuously friendly; a student who addressed a professor by a first name was being impertinent. Scholarship and pedagogy, the academic profession still believes, require a space separate from the vulgar clamors of the outside world, a quiet place inhabited by faculty devoted to knowledge and great ideas, sedate in manners, perhaps faintly supercilious.

The idea of the university as a haven for research and reflection derived in part from nineteenth-century Germany. German scholars advanced the notion of pure research uncontaminated by outside considerations. Americans borrowed this model and superimposed it on the ideal of a genteel academic life in which distance between student and professor must be maintained. This refuge might be disturbed by occasional student uprisings, but these were primarily displays of adolescent high jinks. Then, in the earlier years of the Cold War, the professoriate came under attack from a force unmannerly and mindlessly vicious: the mobocracy that some congressional communist hunters wished to lead against leftists in government, the universities, and everywhere else. In face of this assault, the decorum and the carefully reasoned disputation of the campus looked all the more worthy of preserving as a civilized defiance of popular hysteria. That was so even though as the Cold War mentality gelled, there had been spying for the government on campuses and firings of radicals.

In 1963 Richard Hofstadter, something of a presence on the American campus, published *Anti-Intellectualism in American Life*, arguing for the virtues, at once serious and playful, of a life of thought: a theoretical coda to the defense of academic manners. Scholarly investigation and research, the book claims, can do practical good for humanity, but that is not its primary impulse. Submission to standards makes its own demand; the play of ideas brings its own joy. The book is a catalog of American attitudes and movements that Hofstadter saw as antagonistic to the life of pure inquiry, and therefore to intellectual freedom itself. The movements range from communism on the left to fundamentalism on the right. The enemies of intellectual freedom include technocratic educators as well as businessmen. One threat that Hofstadter overlooked comes from the academic detachment he championed. That detachment risks both trivializing the academic enterprise, robbing ideas of any direct connection to practical political and social problems, and at the same time denying political action the critical judgment and analysis that academic inquiry might give it. This man of unassailable intellectual integrity nonetheless offered in *Anti-Intellectualism* a powerful case for the apartness of the academy.

This was the orderly liberal arts realm that students awakened by the causes of the day violated in the mid-1960s; many younger faculty members joined their disruptions. Colleagues who refrained from political action had a point. Academia is supposed to live by civilized discourse, in class, in faculty groups, in journals and books. If it is to accomplish its reasoned goals, the conversation must be suspended in judgment, courteous and tolerant of opposing views. Still, an aloof academic style that appeared to deny the connection between discussion of a moral issue and acting on it could perplex a student who, for example, innocently thought that a pointless war ought to be stopped right now, before anyone else got killed. The situation that arose in the sixties, then, could not help but foster mutual misunderstanding and rage among politically active students, genteel professors, and bewildered administrators.

Distrust on the part of student radicals had something specific to feed on. The claim by universities and their faculty to a broad critical detachment was open to question. Some Soviet studies programs were in effect Cold War institutes. In 1965 Professor Gabriel Kolko, a historian at the University of Pennsylvania, discovered that research in chemical and biological warfare was going on at the university. This he learned from his student Robin Maisel, who while working at the campus bookstore had discovered the enterprise by noticing the kinds of books that were being ordered. Maisel was fired for noticing. In 1967 the trustees of Penn put a stop to this project. But the willingness of academicians to engage in such projects suggests that some scientists will subordinate dispassionate intellectual curiosity to the requirements of the war machine or, of course, to money. Or to the contrary they are so possessed of the imperatives of objective inquiry as to overlook its consequences, however predictably horrible.

The revolution that overtook the campuses was partly demographic in origin—one result of the baby boom following World War II. Before the war only about 14 percent of college-age students had attended college (in 1900 it had been about 7 percent). By 1961 the percentage increased to 38 percent, and by 1970 to over 50 percent. In the mid-1950s three million students had pursued higher education; well before 1970 the post–World War II baby boom was swamping the stately yards and quadrangles of academe. Most college students in the early 1950s had attended private schools of higher learning; in 1970, of some eight million students well over two-thirds studied at public institutions. The faculty became steadily younger overall. In 1966, for every faculty member who retired five young instructors were hired. Customs like parietal hours and compulsory chapel became insupportable not so much because of any principled philosophical assault upon them as for the sheer weight of the student body's numbers and diversity.

Once the campus had been the domain of proper lettered intellectuals; now increasingly it was the venue of bohemian poets, sculptors, novelists, and painters. Courses in film as well as studio and performing arts entered the curriculum. In some classrooms young teachers might use offensive language for effect, and some students would do the same. The social sciences proliferated as the study of ideal systems steadily gave way to the examination of class structure, the assembly line, streetcorner culture, deviant personalities, and survey data of every type. By the late sixties 9 percent of college students were black as against some 3 percent in 1960; larger numbers of women attended, and in increasing force took up disciplines traditionally reserved almost exclusively for men. Yet even as the student body became more democratic, it remained relatively affluent, which increased opportunities for political activism. Still, only 28 percent of college students even in the chaotic year 1969 engaged in any demonstrations.

By then the university had become a target for whoever wanted to complain about the direction of the country. Rightists called faculty members ideological mesmerizers of youthful minds. Leftists accused both liberal and conservative faculty of being professionalized servants of the military-industrial complex, and whatever modicum of critical detachment the liberal universities retained the left despised for its coldness in the face of the world's agony. While few schools long retained the strict curricula that had prevailed in the name of liberal arts, most students, spurred by the idealism of the civil rights and antiwar movements, remained serious about life and study. It was their demand for meaning in their education that impelled students to denounce their schooling as irrelevant. An admissions officer spoke of reading essays that in their idealism "soared"; there is a good chance that an essay today will be about becoming successful.

Two of the largest student rebellions—at Berkeley in 1964–65 and Columbia in 1968—mark the distance between substantial numbers of radicalized students and their liberal elders.

Between 1963 and 1964 the number of entering freshman at the University of California at Berkeley increased by 37 percent. In the previous decade students majoring in the more socially conscious humanities and social sciences had jumped from 36 to 50 percent. Clark Kerr, president of the multicampus University of California system, had planned for the arrival of masses of new students. But he failed to see the attendant problems. He presided over an institution, committed to acting *in loco parentis*, that in this new time of student ferment and enormous growth could no longer do so. Academic conservatives complained that administrators and faculty members were no longer supervising their young charges' thought and behavior; students were soon complaining of the vestiges of that supervision.

Kerr, a liberal Quaker and a Democrat, had helped squelch a faculty loyalty oath imposed by the California legislature back in the McCarthy era. Yet he often compromised. In 1961, he refused to allow Malcolm X to appear on campus; his grounds were that Malcolm was a sectarian religious leader. But he did not block the less controversial Billy Graham, the prominent evangelical preacher. On another occasion he kept Herbert Aptheker, editor of the American Communist party's theoretical journal, from speaking. In 1963 Kerr lifted a ban against communist speakers, but to get the university Regents' approval he instituted a yardstick he himself disliked: spokesmen for traditional views would have to follow controversial speakers. In all, he was a prototype of the liberal who would be caught in the conflicting demands of his time. That is likely a fair description of much of the administration at Berkeley. The maneuvers, at times ham-handed and at others conciliatory, of Berkeley officialdom in 1964 and 1965 attest to the dilemmas of liberals confronted by a radicalism that they had neither the wish to stifle nor the will to embrace.

By the late fifties a new student left, some of it led by children of liberal and radical professionals, had begun to emerge on campuses. At Berkeley a student party named SLATE, dedicated to ending nuclear testing, capital punishment, Cold War rivalries, and other off-campus ills, began in 1957 to run candidates for student affairs elections. SLATE then incorporated civil rights into its agenda. Soon after, at the University of Wisconsin, students in history and the social sciences with a similar social and political profile launched an ambitious journal, *Studies on the Left*, committed to the "radicalism of disclosure." A visit to Berkeley in 1960 by Tom Hayden, editor of the *Michigan Daily*, the student newspaper at Ann Arbor, led on the University of Michigan campus to the formation of VOICE in imitation of SLATE. And there were stirrings of dissenting politics on other campuses as the Red-baiting era wound down in the late 1950s.

As early as 1960 Berkeley students delivered a blow for dissent when several hundred protested the hearings of the House Un-American Activities Committee (HUAC) in San Francisco. No group during that Cold War era more vividly represented than HUAC the general disregard for civil liberties. Police arrested many of the protesters or simply washed them down the steps of the city hall with fire hoses. The next day thousands of demonstrators returned to chant, "Sieg Heil!" and to bear witness that in California the days of unchallenged Red-hunting were over. *Operation Abolition*, a film put out by HUAC to show that these demonstrations had been the work of subversives, was so addlebrained that it strengthened the case of liberals against HUAC. *Operation Abolition* ultimately became a cult movie among campus sophisticates and dissenters.

In September 1964 Mario Savio, the son of a Roman Catholic machinist proud of his son's commitment to social justice, returned to campus after teaching at a freedom school in McComb during that greatest of Mississippi summers. Savio discovered that the campus authorities had declared off limits for advocates of civil rights and other causes a stretch of Telegraph Avenue, the Bancroft strip, just outside the main gate to the Berkeley campus. For years the strip had been accepted as a place where students could hand out pamphlets, solicit names for petitions, and sign people up. But recently it had become identified with demonstrations against Berkeley and Oakland businesses that practiced discrimination. One of the demonstrators' chief targets was the *Oakland Tribune*, the East Bay newspaper published by William Knowland, the conservative United States Senator. The students' activities antagonized conservative university Regents and they pressured Berkeley to close the campus as a recruiting ground for activists and restrict student agitation in adjacent areas.

The ban set off a firestorm. Students who had taken on HUAC, Mississippi racists, Senator Knowland, and the East Bay business community were not about to be denied their rights by the likes of Clark Kerr. Groups representing SLATE members, anti-HUAC demonstrators, civil rights militants, and ordinary students, some of them conservative, protested the university's actions.

On September 29 the demonstrators defiantly set up tables on the Bancroft strip and refused to leave when told to do so. The next day university officials took the names of five protesters and ordered them to appear for disciplinary hearings that afternoon. Instead of five students, five hundred, led by Mario Savio, marched to Sproul Hall, the administration building, and demanded that they be punished too. Three leaders of the march were added to the list of offenders, and all eight were suspended.

The event that converted protest into rebellion occurred on October 1. As students arrived for classes that morning they were greeted by handbills declaring that if they allowed the administration to "pick us off one by one . . . , we have lost the fight for free speech at the University of California." Soon after, CORE, SNCC, the Du Bois Club, Students for a Democratic Society (SDS), and six or seven other groups set up solicitation tables in front of Sproul Hall, the administration building. At 11:00 A.M. the assistant dean of students went up to the CORE table and asked Jack Weinberg to identify himself. Weinberg refused, and the dean ordered campus police to arrest him. A veteran of the civil rights movement, Weinberg went limp in standard civil disobedience mode when the guards carried him to a waiting car. Bystanders and observers quickly came to his rescue. In minutes hundreds of protesters, singing the civil rights anthem, "We Shall Overcome," and chanting, "Let him go! Let him go!" surrounded the car, preventing it from leaving to cart Weinberg off to security headquarters.

For the next thirty-two hours Weinberg and his police escort remained captive in the car while speaker after speaker climbed atop the vehicle to address the growing crowd. Savio, here and later the most civil of militants, removed his shoes so as not to damage the police car. He compared the protesters to Henry David Thoreau, who had briefly defied the authorities to protest the Mexican War that would enlarge United States slave territory. He was followed by other speakers, who were pelted with eggs and lighted cigarettes by about one hundred fraternity brothers and athletes.

The standoff ended with an agreement between Kerr and the warring parties that submitted to a committee of faculty, students, and administrators all issues of campus political behavior and turned over to an academic senate committee the question of suspending the eight students. Weinberg would be released without charges.

But the rebellion had only begun. A new organization, the Free Speech Movement (FSM), was formed with a large executive committee representing its constituent campus organizations. Despite the FSM's growing fear that the administration was not dealing with the students in good faith, the next few weeks were relatively quiet on campus. Yet incidents were accumulating that would provoke the students and help trip off another confrontation. Berkeley's chancellor Edward Strong refused a request that he reinstate the eight suspended students while the senate committee deliberated their fate. Kerr, who dismissed the FSM as "a ritual of hackneyed complaints," failed to realize that faculty, graduate students, teaching assistants, and undergraduates alike would perceive the issue as amounting not to how many restrictions had been removed but how many remained. Here the liberalism of the Berkeley administration, disposed to compromise, crashed head-on into the moral objectives of the student movement, as the liberalism of Kennedy and Johnson collided with the visionary purity of the civil rights activists.

The FSM proposed that the freedom defined in the First Amendment be considered the only guide to political activity on campus. Savio denounced a compromise reached by the senate committee for imposing prior restraint on student actions. On November 9, in defiance of the administration, Savio and his allies once again set up literature and solicitation tables. As a preliminary to disciplinary action, campus police took the names of seventy-five students supervising the tables. Now the student movement had antagonized not only the administration but also many of the more conservative student groups. On the other hand, it was gaining support among graduate students, many of whom were poorly paid, overworked teaching assistants. The graduate student organization declared that it would preside over tables. The administration, the TAs said, would not dare suspend them since their role was vital to the university's functioning. They were right. When almost two hundred graduate students set up tables nothing happened. Many undergraduates, deciding that the administration was choosing to pick only on the weak, shifted back to the FSM. What the incident really proved was that in a university essentially liberal in structure, students who were also teachers could undermine administrative authority.

On November 13 the dilatory liberals on the faculty senate committee finally made a report. Six of the eight suspended students should be reinstated; Savio and Art Goldberg should be kept on suspension for six weeks. By what one administrator described as a "mealy-mouthed liberal nondecision," Savio and Goldberg's sentences, however, should be made retroactive to the incident, more than six weeks in the past. With that problem out of the way, focus returned to the question of campus advocacy and solicitation for off-campus causes. The FSM leaders decided to confront the university's Board of Regents, who were scheduled to meet on the campus on November 20. To assure a good turnout, movement leaders prevailed on Joan Baez, the popular folk singer and a sympathizer with the FSM, to give a free concert during the meeting.

Baez brought out the crowd. Three thousand students gathered near Sproul during the Regents' meeting to listen to speeches. They then snake-danced their way to the west gate of the campus and sat on the grass to hear the singing and await the results of the meeting. The results disappointed most of Berkeley's students. No campus facilities could be used to further causes deemed "unlawful," and the Regents overruled the faculty and increased the punishments on Savio and Goldberg. The student militants could have wondered, like the SNCC workers in Mississippi in their dealings with liberal Democratic party forces in Washington: just what did the establishment want?

In the few remaining weeks of the semester, the FSM won increasing support on the Berkeley campus. Among administration blunders that brought the militants success was Chancellor Strong's against Savio and his associates for unlawfully hindering campus police from performing their duties. The graduate students decided to go on strike. On Wednesday, December 2, from four to five thousand people, spectators as well as FSM partisans, gathered around Sproul Plaza.

In his indictment of the alienating, impersonal machine that he believed the university had become, Savio found his own authentic eloquence. Martin Luther King in the "Letter from a Birmingham Jail" had spoken of "direct action, whereby we would present our very bodies as a means of laying our case before the conscience of the . . . community." Now Savio announced:

> There's a time when the operations of the machine becomes so odious, makes you so sick at heart, that you can't take part; you can't even passively take part. And you've got to put your bodies upon the gears and upon the wheels, upon the levers, upon all the apparatus, and you've got to indicate to the people who own it that unless you're free, the machines will be prevented from working at all.

This is poetry that combines the exaltation of the civil rights movement with the splendor of the existential vision. It moved the listeners. And it placed the Free Speech Movement at about the point in the spectrum that much of the student left then spoke from: with no suggestion of violence, thinking of concrete change, its discourse as yet unthickened by dogmatic pseudorevolutionary verbiage.

Soon after the demonstration in the plaza, student supporters began to fan up and out across four floors of Sproul Hall singing "We Shall Overcome" and Bob Dylan's "The Times They Are-a Changin'." Savio, Weinberg, and others urged people on the plaza to join the sit-in. From one thousand to fifteen hundred went inside the building.

For a time it looked as though the administration would not act. Late that afternoon, university officials declared the building closed and sent employees home. As hours passed and nothing further happened, students inside Sproul relaxed. The FSM leaders designated separate areas and floors for special activities. There was a room for movies, another for a Spanish class, an area for quiet study, and a spot for square dancing.

But off campus the forces of the establishment began to stir. To some observers the Berkeley rebellion seemed a heinous violation of the rules of university decorum, an outrageous defiance of rules and procedures by a privileged group of young people, beneficiaries of a generous taxpaying public. Around midnight the deputy district attorney of Alameda County told Governor Pat Brown in Los Angeles over the phone that "temporizing would only make the eventual blow-off more dangerous." Brown gave permission for the police to move in. Shortly after 2:00 A.M., six hundred California highway patrolmen and Alameda County sheriff's deputies cordoned off Sproul Hall. In the middle of the night Chancellor Strong appeared with a bullhorn admonishing students to leave the building. The Free Speech leaders now began spreading the word that students should go limp to slow down the removal process. That way, the bust would still be going on at the time classes resumed in the morning, and uncommitted students, on the way to lectures and labs, would observe the cops manhandling their fellow students.

The police charged with resisting arrest any student who went limp. At first removals were gentle. Then, as the police tired, they became less careful. They twisted some arms and banged some students' heads on the stairs as they were dragged out. Such treatment by police of students was still an unfamiliar experience. In all it took twelve hours to clear the building, but by midafternoon 773 of the occupiers had been arrested and booked for trespassing. Most were shipped off to the county prison farm at Santa Rosa, where a Black Muslim prisoner, Huey Newton, looked on in amazement; all the students were released on bail the following day to return to Berkeley. It had been the largest mass arrest in the history of California.

The bust electrified the campus. By noon, when the police were still busy loading demonstrators into vans, as many as ten thousand people jammed the plaza, craning to see what was happening. It was a "sea of outraged faces," a witness noted. The crowd spilled over onto the roof of the Student Union across from the plaza and onto the adjacent playing fields. As they watched, many found FSM handbills thrust at them proclaiming a universitywide strike to protest the tactics of the authorities.

That afternoon eight hundred faculty met at the invitation of Professor Seymour Lipset of the sociology department to consider the sit-in, the strike, and the police action. Much of the Berkeley faculty, especially in the humanities and the social sciences, was liberal, prepared to react against heavy-handed authority backed by the police. And faculty members were quite genuinely appalled at the violation of the haven for scholars to do their research, teaching, and learning. Students belong on campus; police do not.

The faculty recommended that all action pending against the students be dropped, that a faculty committee hear appeals from administration disciplinary decisions connected with political action, and that these appeals be final. It also approved a statement that no student be cited by the university for participating in off-campus political action. When a member of the bacteriology department condemned "the presence of the State Highway Patrol on the Berkeley campus," and demanded "the prompt release of the arrested students," the assembled professors cheered. After the meeting, many of the faculty headed for Alameda County Court House to post bail for the arrested students. For all the hesitancy of liberalism in the presence of agitation to its left, liberal faculty now acted in solidarity with their young academic offspring, and not least in parental solicitude for them.

Over the next few days the Free Speech leaders proved that they were capable not only of arousing strong feelings but of channeling them effectively. A Strike Central coordinated all strike activities and churned out thousands of flyers and handbills, many of them run off on the mimeograph machines of academic departments with friendly chairmen.

Support of the strike was not total. In the engineering, technical, and business fields, the turnout was weak. But in most disciplines teaching assistants and many faculty canceled classes to express support or to free themselves and their students to work for a solution of the crisis. Perhaps three-quarters of Berkeley's twelve hundred professors contributed to the strike by choosing not to hold classes.

Hoping to end confrontation, Kerr proposed a "new era of freedom under law." All Monday classes, he announced, would be canceled so that students, faculty, and administrators could meet at the Greek Theater to hear the proposals. Free Speech supporters came to the meeting in force along with many students sympathetic to the administration's tone of moderation. In all, by noon, sixteen thousand people filled the amphitheater.

Kerr read to the crowd a statement that dozens of department chairman had approved. It endorsed "orderly and lawful procedures" and condemned the sit-in as "unwarranted" and as likely to obstruct "fair consideration of the grievances brought forward by the students." The department chairmen then recommended against imposing further penalties on the arrested students and urged the resumption of classes forthwith.

During Kerr's reading, sections of the stands most sympathetic to the Free Speech Movement sometimes booed and jeered. Its leaders had demanded more: that the university intercede with the courts in favor of the arrested students. This display of feeling was a mere foretaste of what came at the end. Professor Robert Scalapino, chairman of the political science department, adjourned the meeting. Savio, who had been sitting in the press section just in front of the rostrum, walked onto the stage and attempted to speak. He never made it. Two campus guards immediately stopped him, pulled him from the rostrum, and dragged him backstage to an empty dressing room. Before a mass gathering in an open-air Greek theater, the free speech leader was being physically denied free speech. Even the most dogged parliamentarian might have allowed that granting brief access to the microphone would not have threatened good order at the event that was about over. There was nothing Kerr could do to remedy the situation. Pandemonium broke out. "Let him speak! Let him speak!" the crowd demanded. Savio was allowed to return to the stage, where he merely announced that his organization had scheduled a rally to follow immediately at Sproul Plaza. The students, he shouted, should leave "this disastrous scene and get down to discussing the issues."

The academic senate meeting the next day, December 8, was the zenith of the FSM arc. It was the largest turnout within memory for a body much given to routine discussion of courses, rules, and minor university policy. Outside, several thousand students gathered to listen to the deliberations carried from the room by loudspeakers.

The discussion revolved around the proposal of the senate's academic freedom committee endorsing the Free Speech Movement's basic positions on the disciplinary proceedings and the time, place, and content of speech and advocacy. In effect, it left the university authorities with only minimum traffic-cop powers to prevent physical disruption of the campus. A group of faculty moderates and conservatives led by Lewis Feuer of philosophy and Nathan Glazer of sociology opposed the committee's proposal. Feuer offered an amendment that committed the university to nonintervention in matters of speech and advocacy only when they were "directed to no immediate act of force and violence." He observed to his colleagues that the failure of the German universities in the early 1930s to insist that students be disciplined for off-campus attacks on Jews, liberals, and socialists had enabled Nazi students to destroy German freedom and prepared the way for the rise of Hitler. The liberals counterattacked. Owen Chamberlain, a physics Nobel Prize winner, deplored the paternalism implicit in the Feuer amendment. Others endorsed the right to mount boycotts, stage sit-ins, and establish picket lines to protest injustices in the outside community without university interference. Several noted that the students were watching them, a view that struck Feuer's party as a threat of mob violence if the faculty did not accept the original proposals.

The Feuer amendment was defeated 737 to 284; the vote on the original proposals carried 824 to 115. As the faculty filed out of the building the masses of student spectators greeted them with cheers and loud applause.

Within hours the Free Speech Movement called off the strike and issued a statement headed "Happiness Is an Academic Senate Meeting." Apparently Jack Weinberg's pithy slogan warning against trusting anyone over thirty had been proven wrong. The next day the movement won another victory. At the annual student government elections, SLATE, a part of the Free Speech coalition, swept into student government offices. Every SLATE candidate won. With double the usual voting turnout, the student government's existing conservative leadership was totally repudiated.

The eagerly awaited Regents' meeting on the 18th did not turn out well for the Free Speech supporters. The Regents refused to accept the academic senate's assumption of ultimate disciplinary authority over the students. The group did not pass on the substantive proposals of the senate's December 3 resolutions and promised only to appoint a committee from among its members to consult with students, faculty, and others to make recommendations at some later date. Pending completion of this process the existing rules would remain in force. But then fortunes shifted. On January 2 the Regents fired Chancellor Strong and as acting chancellor in his place appointed Martin Meyerson, dean of the College of Environmental Design. Meyerson had been a supporter of the Free Speech Movement, while Strong had been responsible for the Sproul bust. The Regents were clearly offering the student activists peace. Meyerson's first act was to accede almost totally to the Movement's fundamental demands. Henceforth students would be allowed to set up tables on the Bancroft strip and at other designated places on campus. Student organizations using these tables could receive donations, distribute literature, recruit members, and sell such items as buttons, pins, and bumper stickers.

The major issues now in the past, FSM was on its way to demise. Then, on March 3, a nonstudent drawn like others to the ferment at Berkeley sat down unobtrusively on the Student Union steps opposite Sproul. Possibly he uttered nothing; his sign, with two words, said it all: "FUCK (verb)." A Berkeley city policeman reported it to the campus police, who promptly came and arrested the sign carrier. Again the campus flared.

A small demonstration at which speakers peppered their remarks with the word in question had led to eight arrests by campus police. But now the militants were divided. Radicalism had not yet reached the stage of verbal overkill that would characterize its violence-obsessed wing within the next few years; it was still deeply founded in the liberal academic traditions that respected precise and seemly speech. Savio, denouncing the new controversy for endangering rights hard-won, withdrew from FSM. The Filthy Speech Movement, as the latest agitation was termed, soon died.

"I am a human being," went in essence one of the more remembered student laments of the sixties: "I am not the sum of my data on a computer card. Treat me as well as you ask that our university cards be treated." Reduced to a message on signs that Berkeley students were carrying, the plea read: "I am a student. Do not fold, bend, mutilate, or spindle." If this is to be understood as a call for an education allowing for closer exchange between students and teachers, more respectful of students as potential contributors to the learning process, it is not only well phrased but eminently reasonable. But some student rebels came to want more: to equate their condition with that of a people for whom resistance is the only alternative to suffering. Modern life, in fact, had little to impose on American students that countless people during the Great Depression, or in any earlier time, would not have been envious to share. Savio, for all the sense of balance that distinguished him from many of his successors, announced that the police were "*fam*-ily men, you know. They have a job to do. . . . Like Adolph Eichmann. He had a job to do. He fit into the machinery." The equation of American cops with a bureaucratic Nazi architect of the Holocaust was a portent of the rhetorical confusions to come. Savio, moreover, had drawn parallels with the black freedom movement in the South. There was one critical respect in which the comparison was unsatisfactory: the nature of the enemy. At Berkeley, the antagonist was no more than the managerial liberalism of the university administration. Martin Luther King faced palpable evil; the students at Berkeley confronted paternalism.

Still, students were right to recognize that what happened, and happened to them, on their sheltered grounds belonged to the larger monstrous world. Their universities contributed to the institutions of wealth and war, which they were being trained as much to serve as to question. To acknowledge, without self-abasement, the extent to which they were privileged; to define, without self-dramatization, the ways in which they were exploited; to find the points of intersection between the cool critical methods of the academy and the impassioned issues of the time or any time: these requisites of a well composed student politics would have been difficult for the strongest of campus leaders to meet. Savio himself was hard-put to keep the balance.

When Berkeley's FSM students invited a speaker to help clarify their goals, they chose Paul Goodman, a philosophical anarchist who advocated a life of self-discovery in community. Much of Columbia's student rebel leadership, drawn from Students for a Democratic Society and reflecting that organization's growing Marxist-Leninist sectarianism, was composed of glowering ideologues who sought little wider insight. Their spokesman was Mark Rudd, an arrogant young man who in 1968, soon after taking a three-week trip to Cuba, wrested leadership of the campus chapter from moderates. Savio's rhetoric had drawn on Herodotus; Rudd favored obscenity. He would later confess that the "Vietnam War had driven us crazy." For his purposes, Rudd was fortunate to encounter at Columbia an administration that harked back to the 1950s and even more than Berkeley's was steeped in the academic culture of the past.

Columbia's liberal arts students had been largely politically moderate and quiescent; their curriculum was the most traditional in the Ivy League. During the sixties radical activists on campus never amounted to more than 10 percent of the undergraduate population. They had little reason, moreover, to quarrel with the faculty, over 70 percent of whom opposed the Vietnam War. By 1967 many faculty members, defying the Selective Service practice of drafting academically weak students, voted to discontinue both the ranking of students and the release of student grades to draft boards: Columbia was the first major school in the country to adopt such a policy. But Columbia's liberal leaders, President Grayson Kirk and Vice President David Truman, had learned little from their counterparts at Berkeley. In dealing with student protesters they were alternately indecisive and punitive. Eric Bentley, the university's eminent drama teacher, said of Kirk, "He hasn't spoken to anyone under 30 since he was under 30." When Truman told him the police were coming to the campus to end the demonstrations, Bentley announced, "I resign"—which he did.

An issue contributing to the uprising against the administration was Columbia's connection with the Institute for Defense Analysis (IDA), a consortium of leading universities, including Stanford and Princeton, that contracted to do research for the Pentagon on weapons systems. IDA connected Columbia to the Cold War as well as Vietnam and made it seem an integral part of the detested military-industrial complex. When SDS and a number of liberals protested Columbia's participation in IDA, the university severed its corporate connections with the institute, though Kirk as a trustee retained his personal membership.

The other major point of contention was a proposed new gymnasium to be built in Morningside Park, the border between Harlem and the Columbia neighborhood. The university was prepared to allow Harlem residents to use the gym at specified times, but in the interests of safety it mandated a special entrance for the local people at the bottom of the park. It was all perfectly well intentioned and even reasonable, but the public look of it was terrible. With good intentions, a rich, privileged, and largely white institution was intruding into a poor and sensitive community. It seemed to tell blacks that they were being patronized; it struck many activists, black and white, as emblematic of race relations generally.

The Columbia chapter of SDS in early 1968 was not strong as were branches on other major campuses, and it sought to augment its local following. In this apocalyptic year, moreover, Rudd and his lieutenants were also hoping to make their contribution to the final overthrow of liberal capitalist society in line with the prevailing new mood of SDS's national leadership. Rudd later declared, "We are out for social and political revolution, nothing else."

On April 23 SDS mounted a rally to protest Columbia's continuing association with the Institute for Defense Analysis. Meanwhile, the Student Afro-American Society denounced the university's gym construction plans. When a dean failed to respond to Rudd's demands that the university yield forthwith on both issues, the activists proposed taking a hostage. They rushed into Hamilton Hall and prevented Dean Henry Coleman of Columbia College and two other administrators from leaving the building.

The invasion of Hamilton Hall soon turned into an occupation. SDS and its allies established a steering committee that presented the administration with six demands including amnesty for whatever the students had done or would do, total withdrawal from the defense consortium, and suspension of gym construction. The black students asked the white radicals to leave Hamilton Hall and kept it for themselves in the spirit of the new black separatism. The whites thereupon occupied Low Library, administration headquarters, smashing a glass door to enter. The black occupants of Hamilton, who proceeded to put up posters of Carmichael, "Che" Guevara, Lenin, and Malcolm X, maintained a strong system of leadership that contrasted to Rudd's attempt to hold to participatory democracy.

The students in the occupied buildings quickly reached the media to get their story out and invited potential allies to join them in their protest. Morningside Heights became a magnet for New York's literary left. Susan Sontag, Norman Mailer, Dwight Macdonald, and Robert Lowell all came to the campus. New Left notables, including Tom Hayden, also visited to observe and advise. Hamilton Hall drew black power leaders H. Rap Brown and Stokely Carmichael. Lesser-known folk were also drawn to the action. Mathematics Hall was overrun by an East Village counterculture crew that rejoiced in the name of Motherfuckers.

In the buildings life was intense. The students debated how to make universities more democratic and how the world would look after the revolution. One visitor during those heady days was the philosopher Herbert Marcuse, whose ideas, merging Marx and Freud, appealed to young revolutionaries around the world. Marcuse disappointed his Columbia admirers by telling them that even in their imperfect existing forms universities were worthy institutions. In Fayerweather Hall two students were married by a Protestant minister who pronounced them "children of the new age."

The university trustees rejected the demand to drop the gym and refused student proposals to make disciplinary hearings a courtroom procedure. A student Majority Coalition attacked the rebels' tactics as "tasteless, inconsiderate, and illegal." The faculty divided. The largest group advised the students to leave the buildings, but promised to support most of their demands except amnesty in advance. Liberal faculty members tried desperately to mediate the dispute. Rudd's troops occupied the President's offices, smashed his cigars, and raided his files.

Despite attempts over the weekend to negotiate a settlement, an impasse had developed, and the administration concluded that it must call in the police to evict the occupiers. Fearing a dangerous racial incident possibly involving the nearby Harlem community when the police entered Hamilton Hall, New York City Mayor John Lindsay and moderate black leaders negotiated for a peaceful withdrawal by the Afro-American students when the police arrived. As tension built, the radicals prepared for a confrontation that would reveal to the world the "naked face of power."

The bust, when it came on Tuesday morning, was not pretty. Some one thousand members of the New York Tactical Police Force, few of whom could expect their children to enjoy an elite college education, pummeled students with their nightsticks and dragged them roughly down the stairs. Outside the buildings they went a bit berserk and beat bystanders, including some faculty. Over a hundred people were injured and sent to hospitals; some policemen were injured by rocks hurled from the crowd. Seven hundred students were carted off to the Tombs jail for booking. An exception was Hamilton Hall, which the black occupiers left peacefully. The police were busy enough: in New York City that spring you could Dial a Demonstration.

The brutal police eviction did the job the rebels wanted. It radicalized the campus. One previously conservative freshman from Connecticut declared: "My attitude changed as soon as the cops charged. Whatever enmity I had against the demonstrators, I now have against the administration." The activists declared a strike, which the administrators sought to preempt by suspending classes for a week to consider healing measures. The upshot was that Columbia's 1968 spring semester virtually ceased. A few students went to a few classes; others went home, starting their summer vacations early. Most student grades in the law school and elsewhere were entered as pass or fail.

Columbia was the high or low point of the student rebellions of the 1960s. Across the country, college demonstrators on differing occasions brought out not only the police but the national guard, which was called on some two hundred times to maintain order on campuses. However drastic the reaction, these occasions were not comparable to the clashes between Appalachian coal miners and guardsmen during the bitter days of labor war. At some point, in the case of the students, parental restraint was sure to be invoked. That alone ensured that students would remain ignorant of the grimmer realities of power.

The liberal academicians who recoiled from the manners and tactics of radical students and their insistence on absolute ideological purity could have made a good case. During the 1930s moral absolutism on some campuses had taken the form of Stalinism. The language and at times the action of radicals during the Vietnam years demonstrated the capacity of moral impulse to run berserk. Are whites guilty of racism? No, that isn't strong enough: say rather that white Americans are guilty of imposing misery and oppression on the entire world. Better still, whites are a blight on the human race. (That last was a contribution of Susan Sontag.) If the empowering provided by a university training in skepticism had no more than the practical purpose of moderating such fevered fantasies, it would be justified. But in fact it offers more. At its best it serves the development of intellectual autonomy as a virtue in itself. And the winning of freedom from the institutions of racism, predatory versions of capitalism, the warfare state, and all other alienating forces (among which many radicals included the university itself) was a central project of the rebel movements of the time.

The problem was to separate intellectual independence from genteel detachment, and such a separation was difficult. The Vietnam war was going on, and real people were getting killed while much of the academic establishment was being detached and reasonable. Given the situation the country was confronting, the morality of questioning and restraint that defined the practice of academia risked ceasing to be a morality at all, shriveling into mere propriety. It was also true that the moral passion of the campus radicals continually threatened to spill over into a lethal travesty of its essentially humane beginnings.

Even had each side kept to its better self, the events of the sixties would have presented the university with the question, How can academia most fruitfully examine, with due distance and analytical rigor, the greater world in its immediate grief and need?

While radical students and their liberal mentor-antagonists were struggling early in the decade over the antithetical claims of reflection and immediate moral action, a radical movement based both on and outside the campus had been attempting to define the very nature of the good society. At the center of American radicalism during the sixties was the New Left; and at the core of the New Left was SDS, Students for a Democratic Society.

In the remote history of SDS was the League for Industrial Democracy, or LID, a radical organization dating from 1905. Among its founders were the roustabout writer Jack London, the novelist and social reformer Upton Sinclair, and Clarence Darrow, a lawyer remembered for his defense of unpopular individuals and causes. These were three insurgents in the American grain, eccentric, individualistic, experimental in ideas and in life, unfettered by any polysyllabic ideology. In 1925 the organization acquired its long-term title. It became during the Soviet era militantly anticommunist, in the way of independent European and American radicals who recognized the USSR as a mockery and betrayal of the ideals of the left. LID had a student wing, SLID, which just before the Kennedy era it reconstituted as Students for a Democratic Society. SDS, then an obscure group, was one of several cosponsors of a decorous antiwar action in February 1962, a convergence of several thousand students on the nation's capital, where they conducted demonstrations and lobbied government officials. Prominent among the groups present was Tocsin, an organization founded at Harvard College and committed to reasoned opposition to American military policy. In a moment that symbolizes the contrast between these early days and the later rage between the government and its left opponents, President Kennedy had coffee brought to demonstrators outside the White House, and they accepted it.

That June, however, a clash between LID and its offspring foreshadowed the gulf that was destined to open between the young left, even at its most temperate, and its old radical parentage. The confrontation took place over the Port Huron Statement drafted in Michigan at the FDR camp of the United Automobile Workers in 1962.

Some fifty-nine delegates attended the meeting. Most were members of Students for a Democratic Society, but the delegation included representatives of SNCC, the National Student Association, the Young Peoples Socialist League, the Student Christian Movement, and the Young Democrats. The chief proponents of what would become the final draft were Al Haber and Tom Hayden. Hayden, who was to have continuing visibility in the radical politics of the decade, had read Kerouac and then hitchhiked in 1960 to San Francisco and Los Angeles, the city that was then hosting the Democratic National Convention; and for a time John Kennedy impressed him. By 1962, then, he had experienced both the Beat phenomenon and Democratic liberalism.

A condemnation of the Soviet Union severs the Port Huron document from the tiny portion of the Old Left that had clung to that delusion. Yet the great majority of the older radicals found the architects of the Port

Huron Statement insufficiently anticommunist in suggesting that blame for the Cold War should be distributed in roughly equal portions between the communist and the Western world. The Port Huron Statement had observed, for example, that the Soviet Union was "more disposed to disarming" than the United States, which had developed "an economic commitment" to continuing the arms race while the economic situation of the USSR gave it a greater incentive to reduce arms. A LID member asked, "Does the Berlin Wall show the desire or possibility for disarmament?"

Especially vocal among the critics of SDS was Michael Harrington, author of an influential book, *The Other America*, which with no clutter of dialectical class analysis documents the persistence of poverty in the United States. Harrington, about a decade older than the college students who were supposed to be the constituency of SDS, was not the most likely opponent of the leaders of the fledgling organization. He did not bear the burden of sectarian disputes that weighed down his still older comrades, and his practical, reflective consideration of concrete social problems indicated that he might make an effective nondogmatic mediator of in-house conflicts. But so menacing was the shadow of communism he saw hovering over the democratic left that he not only joined but was a major spokesman for the older generation unable to tolerate even what looked like a hint of tolerance toward the enemy of the free world.

As to the Port Huron Statement itself: even the manner of its adoption was in keeping with the nascent ebullience of the era. The convention had split into smaller groups, in effect seminars, people jumping freely from one discussion to another. Port Huron was a talkfest: participants made friends and discussed issues as they sat on the grass on a June afternoon and stayed up to witness the dawn breaking over Lake Huron. Out of it all came a signed document that at once reflected and embodied the early intellectual orientation of SDS and revealed the outlook of the left at a fleeting moment of American history.

The Statement can be read almost as easily as a production of American academic liberalism in a self-critical mood. Its stress is on cultural issues. Its concern is for the lack of integrity in American society: "The goal of man and society should be human independence . . . finding a meaning of life that is personally authentic. Human relationships should involve fraternity and honesty." The declaration complains of the world's poverty and the nuclear threat, seen not only as evils in themselves but as giving the lie to American society's claim to virtue. Its attack on the rule-making bureaucracy in colleges and universities became a major underpinning and inspiration for the Berkeley Free Speech Movement. Also central to the Statement is the concept of participatory democracy, in essence though not in name a traditional aim of anarchism and democratic socialism and newly articulated by a philosopher at the University of Michigan, Arnold Kaufman.

A concept of democracy not in formal voting procedures but in the daily ongoing action of life, conducted by people in control of their own minds and skills, may be considered the very core of the young democratic left. It is roughly equivalent to the original socialist idea of a commonwealth of workers. The cooperatives of the southern and western farm rebels in the late nineteenth and early twentieth centuries were participatory democracy in another form, and they were characteristically American in being not collectivist but entrepreneurial. Even earlier, Puritan congregations and the town meetings of New England had practiced their democracy of engaged participants. The Beats lived their own disorderly cooperative community: *On the Road* describes such a community, speckled across the continent, seeking perfection of experience. The civil rights movement found realization in the voluntary cooperative action of black students and church members. The SDS advocates of a democracy through a broad ongoing engagement among its members recognized what the civil rights demonstrators had already shown: that democracy is not only a means to an end but an enactment of the future it strains toward—"prefigurative politics," as Wini Breines expressed it.

In the spirit of the essentially cultural and moral preoccupations of the early SDS was the work of a Columbia sociologist popular within the Port Huron generation. At a time when the ideal of consensus dominated academic analysis of American society, C. Wright Mills stood out as a defender of old-fashioned progressive values of the sort he had imbibed at the University of Wisconsin in his graduate student days. In an American rebel tradition, Mills looked for the good in experiential things: he lamented the decline of the old entrepreneurial class, independent professionals, the family farm, pride in work. In this respect Mills is closer to articulating a socialist ideal of bringing autonomy and intelligence to the act of work, fusing the freedom of craft with the advanced skills of the machine, than to endorsing the centralized consumer socialism of the twentieth-century Western world. In 1960 he had written a "Letter to the New Left," a manifesto published in the British *New Left Review*, in which he declared that the future of radicalism no longer rested with the proletariat. The working class had been bought off. It was young intellectuals around the world who would make the revolution. Mills's brief article identified a new agent of revolutionary change.

The college campus of which the young SDS members were both committed members and, in time, dedicated opponents was well exemplified by Tom Hayden's University of Michigan. Operating heedlessly within the terms and money that the prevailing American institutions provided, professors there developed missile guidance systems that could kill any number of people who had never intended them any harm. Michigan had more contracts with the National Aeronautics and Space Administration than any other university in the country. In his annual report for 1958–59, Michigan's president observed that "various areas of University teaching have recognized the cold-war struggle and have reflected their concern. . . . It is imperative that our progress at this University be rapid, continuous, and strong. Otherwise, the [Soviet Union] might overtake, surpass, master the Americans." This was the thinking of university people when the passions of Americans to their right had gone not into spending on military and economic resistance to international communism but into the clobbering of the most marginal leftist nonconformity at home. Here lay the choice, so a member of the Port Huron generation might have decided, that the country was foisting on the young: join in brain-clogged Red-baiting, or join in the polite and reasonable academic liberal promotion of global technological death.

After the drafting of the Port Huron Statement, relations between LID and SDS remained uneasy. The board of the parent organization complained that the partisans of the Statement had "adopted a popular front position," "bitterly scored [American] foreign policy," and placed blame for the Cold War largely on the United States while "making the merest passing criticism of Soviet action," and allowed a communist seating and convention rights at the convention. (The "communist" in question was a seventeen-year-old boy who had just graduated from a suburban high school.) The LID board decided to censor all SDS materials leaving the central office and to fire Hayden and Haber. Although LID subsequently retracted some of its more hostile actions, at the beginning of 1966 it cut all its connections with an SDS grown increasingly militant.

The intensity of the conflict between LID and SDS in its earliest days was in fact disproportionate to the actual degree of moral and ideological differences. It was a disagreement less between philosophical positions than between generations, each fixated on the events that had formed it, each shunting somewhat to the side that to the other was absolutely central. The position of the LID people on the evils of the Soviet Union was quite compatible with major criticism of the nation's Cold War policies; the libertarian and democratic commitments of the Port Huron generation set it poles apart from the totalitarianism of the Soviet Union and its Western apologists.

The adherents of the Port Huron Statement considered it to be fully responsive to the older radicals in its condemnation of communism. But LID refused to be satisfied, though Harrington himself would later regret his failure to recognize that SDS had taken his concerns into account.

That the anticommunist old left continued to Red-bait some of the most promising young recruits after they had sought an accommodation was among the first of the innumerable wounds that radicalism was to persist in inflicting on itself during the years to follow.

Still, the older radicals had their case. Their battle to fend off totalitarians within the left had been brutal. A LID member once pulled off his shirt to reveal the scars of a communist assault on him during a Madison Square Garden rally over a quarter century earlier. Democratic leftists could remember the manipulations of communist infiltrators. They had accustomed themselves to perceiving communism along with fascism and capitalism as the century's embodiments of maldistributed power. And beyond that were the stain and slander that the Soviet Union and other communist regimes had brought to the idea of socialism, at times with the silent or temporizing acquiescence of noncommunist radicals. All this suggests the solidity of the concerns that pushed the LID people over the edge in their reaction to Port Huron. The fondness that the early SDS had for Fidel Castro's regime in Cuba suggests that it could have learned from its more seasoned elders.

At the very end of 1963 SDS had only a few dozen college chapters and at most fifteen thousand members. That year the organization selected twenty-year-old Todd Gitlin as its president. Then came the Berkeley FSM, the intensification of the civil rights struggle, and the escalation of the war in Vietnam. And along with the war came the pressure of the draft on college students precariously protected with deferments. That was, of course, a threat to their self-interest. But students who, for one reason or another, were not threatened by conscription also opposed the war. The draft meant the further presence on campus of a war machine already massively supported by university research.

The turn of events might have made SDS a presence clearly and self-consciously confined to colleges. Meanwhile, it was being torn internally over the question of how important campuses were in themselves. Some members were willing to affirm and live their academic status. Others, though still on or fresh from the campus, disdained as trivial the issues of university life and insisted that to become genuine radicals, students had to cease centering themselves in being students and work among the poor. Their vehicle of action was ERAP, the Economic Research and Action Project, an arm of SDS that flourished, though only briefly, in the mid-sixties. ERAP, begun in 1964 with a grant from the United Auto Workers, sent its members into poor neighborhoods, with the mission of organizing their residents around issues of immediate local concern. The aim was to effect a democratic redistribution of power to help the poor regain some measure of control over their daily lives: to enable welfare recipients, for example, to have a say in the way welfare programs were run. ERAP, in sum, like the Mississippi voter registration project, sought to stimulate participatory democracy on the community level.

On the college campus, there was a prospect of translating into reality the ideal of participatory democracy, at least to some degree and if only temporarily. Students, after all, were supposed to be trained both in independent critical thought and in the difficult art of listening to people with whom they disagreed. But ERAP organizers, in attempting to take the principle into impoverished neighborhoods, faced a far more daunting task: to bring to people schooled chiefly in the lessons taught by a daily struggle for existence an understanding of an idea originated in academe. The organizers were committing themselves to live in a constant state of anomaly. Themselves well born and well educated, they sought to become at one with the dispossessed, and to do so without a whiff of condescension or anxiety-ridden good fellowship. They wished to act not as directors but as catalysts for organized action conducted by neighborhood residents themselves. Yet in practice they might have to decide whether to run a project hierarchically or let it disintegrate. For full success, a neighborhood project would probably require some smooth dealing with government bureaucrats and old-vintage politicos, the kinds of people from whom SDS especially recoiled. ERAP workers also had to preserve a core of belief and commitment amid realities that shattered romance: the poor were apathetic, ERAP people were beaten or robbed, some women were raped. By the end of 1965 it had largely faltered, though it retained a legacy in a few Great Society efforts. But what also turned SDS away from community organizing, and gave it the character that would determine its fortunes in its few years remaining, was the issue of Vietnam.

In the autumn of 1964, even before the massive American bombing of North Vietnam, the campus-bound wing of SDS had been conducting antiwar activities. At the University of Michigan the group helped bring about the seminal teach-in of March 1965. An April rally of some twenty thousand demonstrators in Washington, D.C., largely the work of SDS, greatly boosted its membership, and by the end of the month thirty campuses had held teach-ins. That same year, SDS chose as its president Carl Oglesby, a determined opponent of the war. Estimates of SDS's membership vary widely. One of them has the organization peak in 1966, counting perhaps sixty thousand casually affiliated members and a great number of supporters in spirit. One problem is in deciding how to identify members in an organization with an enlistment scattered through local chapters. But it is clear that in the mid-sixties the organization leaped in size, much of the new recruitment coming from the vast hinterland between the coasts. "Prairie Power" it was termed, less reflective, less likely to come from well-educated families, more prepared for spontaneous action than was the old guard of an earlier generation.

In 1965 SDS also attempted to push the organization to the limits of democracy, debating at its December convention in Champaign, Illinois, for example, the abolition of national officers. The Chicago headquarters decided on egalitarian principles to share among staffers the task of putting out the mail. The last to send something would be expected to mimeograph and prepare another sending. That seems an inoffensive enough responsibility. But Paul Booth, a leader in SDS at the time, reports that since nobody liked such tasks, the processing of mail lagged. Booth, who later would switch to working with the labor movement, was already arguing in 1965 that SDS was too large to operate by consensus and should accept ordered forms of setting policy. The hostility to structure, like the widespread presence of marijuana among members at the Champaign convention, had its close parallel in SNCC at the same time, where unattached floaters and practitioners of what was called "freedom high" made constant trouble for those members more interested in effective organization. The extension of democracy, with whatever absurdities attended it, at least as an experiment was consonant with the original vision of SDS. But forces soon to flood the organization made meaningless a democracy that could have functioned only amid reasoned civilities.

The new membership, the intensification of political anger on the left, and the predominance of the issue of Vietnam transformed SDS. Committed to democracy though disaffected from the Cold War, it had pronounced its antagonism to the USSR, and its early constitution contained a clause opposing membership for anyone favoring totalitarian principles. In 1966, however, SDS threw out this stipulation, and before long members of the Du Bois Clubs, favorable to Moscow, and the Progressive Labor party, looking to Chairman Mao, were infiltrating the organization's chapters as well as its national office. Simultaneously, as the nation polarized ideologically, increasing numbers of insurgent students felt the appeal of totalitarian radicalism, at least in the Third World. At the beginning experimental, broad in principle, curious about a range of wide economic and cultural questions, the organization now hardened into factions defining themselves by the ideological rigor of their positions. From thoughtful, intellectually exploratory beginnings, SDS came to adopt the postures of shrill hostility, even toward apparent comrades in struggle, that by the late sixties had become typical among young American claimants to revolution.

The war was incalculably important in the hardening of the mood of SDS and the left in general. Yet for all the strength of the war's maddening, corrosive presence, SDS failed to make it the commanding issue that, in the retrospective judgment of participants, would have given the organization focus and solidity in its later years. If it had seized leadership of at least the student wing of the antiwar movement, SDS could have had a unifying focus, its members arguing only over tactical questions. And the peace issue, which by the late sixties was attracting an increasingly large segment of the American people, might have brought SDS to attempt winning the broad blue-collar and middle-class public. Instead, it became fixated by the close of the decade on defining what had to be done to transform society totally. Through the efforts of its factions to identify revolutionary races or classes or nationalities in the larger world, it ended by arrogantly alienating itself from the real public.

Members of SDS meanwhile had maintained that connection with higher education which they might have been expected to desert for its apparent irrelevance to the increasingly volatile world outside. The social space between the campus and the nation at large was actually something of an attraction, establishing the community of student radicals as an outpost in hostile country. Then too, higher education presented its own set of issues that, however vastly different from that of the war, were capable of eliciting the attention and involvement of radicals. Since the Free Speech Movement at Berkeley, radical students had learned to perceive the university as an oppressive institution, imposing meaningless curricula, supporting military research, and processing students for jobs as technicians in the service of capitalism and the state. Precisely for such evils, it was worth the attention of SDS members and sympathizers, who in resistance were confirming themselves at once as radicals and as students. A further advantage to rebelling against university authority was that it was the only authority in the land that students could effectively rebel against, certainly the only institution that might up to a point tolerate their rebellion.

SDS managed for a brief moment later in the decade to create a potentially enduring perception of the working class that would include students in its ranks. The problem was that most workers in Western society were comfortable enough with their status or at least with their opportunities and the general shape of things. By the 1960s, the working classes as customarily defined were clearly estranged from any idea of revolutionary change. This, added to the wish of student leftists to be recognized as real people engaged in authentic employment, required some rethinking of the nature of the working class and of what grievances might in time bring revolution. A conference at Princeton University in February 1967 sponsored by the local chapter of SDS explored a theory of Robert Gottlieb and others expressed in a long paper, "Toward a Theory of Social Change in America." It suggests an important place for the student generation within the work force.

The study finds three subclasses in the new working class: wielders of technical and professional skills; industrial workers requiring more education than blue-collar producers; and workers in the social services, among them teachers, physicians, and artists. The problem facing the new working classes and the possible occasion for their insurrection would be their lack of control over the purposes their labors served. Students, trainees for the new working class, so the theory implies, must learn the necessity of taking control of the forces that otherwise would control them, and to that end they must have control over the university, from which they can bring to the larger world their vision of self-directed workers. The concept fits with the vision of participatory democracy, and in all that it suggests of the centrality of work to integrity comports with the convictions of generations of socialists and anarchists. But by the late sixties, SDS had lost the quality of reflectiveness that might have given its pronouncements a wider hearing.

The student uprising at Columbia in 1968 gave SDS an occasion to flex what power it had. But it had no means of allying, or will to ally, with any major element of the American people. It boycotted the campaign of Eugene McCarthy, one of the few political events of the time that had the potential of combining with a traditional appeal to voters a mentality that by American standards was moderately to the left. Seeking as middle-class radicals are wont to do a closeness with the officially oppressed, some members of SDS became drawn to the idea of violence and enamored of the Black Panthers. Fred Hampton called it right: "Custeric violence." The national office of SDS, notably represented by Bernardine Dohrn, looked to the Panthers. For both, revolutionary violence was an entrancement, revolutionary posturing an aesthetic. They wished to connect with Third-World revolutionary movements against American imperialism: blacks in this country were seen as an internal colonized people. The national office partisans also argued, conformably to the Princeton conference of 1967, that in the advanced industrial world the old forms of oppression of the working class had given way to such ills as meaningless work and consumption. Against this faction of SDS stood Progressive Labor. PL since the midsixties had calculatingly moved into SDS opposing long hair, beards, drugs, and casual sex, and espousing a Marxist embrace of the working class as traditionally defined, along with a version of Maoism. Its concentration on economic and social exploitation entailed a rejection of nationalism. PL perceived the radicalism of the national office of SDS as undisciplined.

In an internecine brawl at the June 1969 Chicago convention of SDS, the Revolutionary Youth Movement (RYM) under Bernardine Dohrn succeeded in expelling Progressive Labor, though it could just as well be argued that PL remained as the true SDS. But by this time, SDS no longer had a future worth fighting over. Indicative of that is its 1968 convention, when a garbage can nominated for a national office was only narrowly defeated. It did not matter, for SDS was ceasing to matter. Severely riven by the conflict between its two major factions, and by a radical feminist hostility to the male left in general, drawn to the fury and romance of violence, the organization was no longer amenable either to leadership or to leaderless self-direction. The garbage can could not have done worse.

As SDS disintegrated, the violence that took verbal and sectarian form within it spilled outward in an organization calling itself Weatherman. The name, referring to a talk-song by Bob Dylan, implied that the members knew which way the wind blew and what to do about it. In their ranks were some of the best-known names among the radicals in the later years of ferment: Bill Ayers, Kathy Boudin, Cathy Wilkerson, Mark Rudd, and Bernardine Dohrn. The militants perceived themselves as allies of the Third World; in contrast to Progressive Labor, they went in for drugs and sex, perhaps as expressions of the spew of nihilistic energy that they wished to release into society and politics; they intended to inspire by violence. Some of their leaders were children of privilege whose behavior suggested the expectation that whatever they demanded they were entitled to get, with tantrums if necessary and certainly without punishment. They conceived the idea of politicizing working-class white youth. To this end they organized raids into high schools in several cities. One feature was physically to push teachers around, which was supposed to be a revolutionary statement and inspiration to the blue-collar young. The Weathermen's main effort to reach hearts and minds was the four Days of Rage in October 1969, "bringing the war home" by trashing Chicago. About five hundred participated. That the People were more offended than aroused to revolutionary action did not enlighten the Weathermen. At a meeting in Flint, Michigan, in December 1969, Bernadine Dohrn praised the murders committed by the California drug cult led by Charles Manson. Thus ended an organization that had once combined radicalism with civility and a loyalty to the unfinished promise of the American past.

The Weather rampagers had by then severed themselves not simply from American society as a whole but from the larger and more civilized antiwar movement. Fury for its own sake, mayhem for its own sake, the exercise of power for its supreme sake had became their revolution, their identity, their meaning, and most of all their fantasy. Just after the Days of Rage, peace activists held a great demonstration, the October 15 Moratorium. While coordinators planned for action to follow in Washington during November, a group of Weatherman activists suggested to them, darkly, that they consider a contribution toward the payment of legal expenses in the wake of the Chicago caper as a way of averting violence in Washington. The Moratorium leaders impudently failed to perform the role of cowed peaceniks. Thereupon, and perhaps to show the terrible things that could happen when anyone defied their will, on November 13 Weathermen split from the main demonstration in Washington and did some window-smashing and cop-fighting. All this doubtless did its small bit to antagonize some portions of the population toward even measured antiwar activity. Two days later the Weathermen had a chance to measure their relative size within the resistance to the country's politics. Something like three-quarters of a million demonstrators in the nation's capital heard mainstream politicians such as George McGovern, listened to folksingers who had inspired the movements of the sixties, and for a moment in their coming together took back the decade. The *New York Times* was probably accurate in portraying the typical antiwar marcher of the era as "a middle-class adult." It was, of course, the media to a large extent that fixed on more catching images, making much of Vietcong flags, or bearded and sandaled figures.

Continuing to take itself seriously, Weatherman would in its brief later history adopt the laboriously unsexist name Weather Underground. In New York City in March 1970 an accidental explosion in a townhouse converted into a bomb factory killed three revolutionaries. The victims' fate may have been worse than what they had contemplated for others: American left terrorists of the time imagined bombings planned to be disruptive but not lethal. A few small affinity groups went completely underground, conceiving hit-and-run attacks that would disrupt the remnants of Pig Amerika.

In violence of language and, in a few cases, of acts, a portion of the student movement had ruptured every possible connection with the American people at large. Some young radicals learned to put in more theoretical form their distance from the public. They got much of their instruction from the German émigré scholar Herbert Marcuse, who for the time was the country's most visible left academician.

Marcuse shared with other European intellectuals an interest in Karl Marx as a visionary not merely of economic and social revolution narrowly conceived but of a transformed human mind and sensibility. Marcuse's revisionist fusion of Marx and Freud transfers from economics to consciousness the revolutionary dialectic of history. As an event of the mind, the dialectic consists of an ability at any moment to imagine a remaking of a given condition. By reasonable extension, this means that a carpenter can be said to act dialectically, seeing a pile of boards as a table and proceeding to translate that vision into reality. Every valid revolutionary thought is therefore dialectical. But more: revolution, an expression of the consciousness that is constantly rethinking and remaking the world, should also make for a further liberation of that consciousness, which is the very being of freedom and creativity.

This rendering of the dialectic seems in itself respectful of the best in ordinary experience, and in no way antagonistic to common life as Americans or any other people lead it. Work, as a revisionist understanding of the dialectic can perceive it, is a determination to recraft the world and the worker. That makes sense, and offers a particular comprehension of experience in itself at its strongest as a continual overcoming of indolence, a heightening of sensibility, a discovery and rediscovery of the world. But Marcuse contended that capitalism had succeeded in destroying among the people in general the very ability to think and act dialectically. It had done so, the argument suggests, by buying off the working class with a superficial prosperity that masked the meaningless life under its dominion and rendered the population incapable of serious thought. It was therefore necessary for intellectually advanced revolutionary movements to take over the job of thinking. Here, some student radicals apparently decided, lay their destiny. And ideas that clash with those of the revolutionist, Marcuse proposed, might have to be suppressed.

Participatory democracy, as SDS defined and the Mississippi activists practiced it, was the most intriguing intellectual formulation of the New Left; its later betrayal by newly converted enthusiasts for repressive regimes in China, Vietnam, and Cuba is a commentary on the waywardness of events and people but not on the idea. Yet within the concept and its practice lurk clashing possibilities.

Participatory democracy is founded on the conviction that freedom is a continuing exercise in decisionmaking. Freedom is not the possession of the vote or the protection of the First Amendment but an acting from moment to moment in accordance with intelligence and conscience. Participation requires not only concern for others but an ability to cooperate in group undertakings, a decision to forego individual impulsiveness. Act only out of your own spontaneous notion of right and wrong, and participation becomes impossible; act at each moment in accord with the will of the majority, and you cease to be free. At their very worst, of course, personal willfulness and group conformity may coalesce in that most participatory and most democratic of institutions, the lynch mob. But the 1960s were rich in enactments of personal freedom, and in the spontaneous formation of groups, projects, and communities. When freedom and community came together, they constituted just what is meant by prefigurative politics: they became not simply means to the future but the future itself as its adherents would imagine it.

In Oakland, California, in 1967 an instance occurred of what it might mean to make freedom synonymous with action and cooperation. It was a draft resistance action that took place on October 16, and again on the 19th.

The Oakland protests represented a form of civil disobedience that differed from the sit-ins of the earlier civil rights movement. In Greensboro and elsewhere, the demonstrators had merely placed themselves where they had a moral right to be: side by side with white customers. No confrontation was intended in itself; it was up to white patrons and owners to decide whether to welcome the newcomers or to treat them as intruders. But demonstrations on the Oakland model, while still nonviolent, were of a more active character. They involved blocking roads or entrances to buildings, peacefully inasmuch as the demonstrators used no force beyond the presence of their own bodies or other obstacles to passage. The purpose might be to draw attention to an evil—the war in Vietnam, as the example in point—or to announce by deeds that business as usual would not be permitted to continue so long as the evil persisted. Like participants in the less deliberately confrontational sit-ins, demonstrators of this mode might allow themselves to be struck without striking back, and like their predecessors and contemporaries in resistance they might wish ultimately to convert temporary antagonists into permanent friends. But this newer type of demonstration was directed, willy-nilly, against even uninvolved or possibly sympathetic bystanders.

The purpose of the Oakland resisters was to seal off temporarily the city's draft induction center. On October 16, police clubbed demonstrators. Three days later, thousands of activists clogged one intersection, then another, for several hours, shifting as opportunity or police attacks dictated. Some protesters dragged parked cars into the streets, letting air out of the tires.

The Oakland event raised difficult or even unanswerable questions, the most obvious being, Do protesters' consciences take precedence over a bystander's rights? Since the activists were cooperative and participatory only among themselves, moreover, their action could not offer a full prototype for a society in which participatory democracy prevails. This action nonetheless embodied a more convincing enactment of freedom and participation than either the antics of the Yippies or the thuggery of the Weathermen. A degree of courage was displayed. That it was not the courage of the anti-Nazi underground of World War II, or of dissidents in the Soviet Union and its satellites, is beside the point. While the Oakland activists did not confront the police of torture regimes, they faced the clubs of police forces only somewhat restrained by law, and clubs are frightening enough. The Oakland resistance, on balance, stands in the lineage of Port Huron and the civil rights movement.

So does one of the mildest and least obviously political events of the time, the creation in Berkeley of the People's Park.

In 1967, the University of California bought some old houses just off the south campus, in a neighborhood that the administration found unsavory and cluttered with hippies. Thereupon Berkeley condemned the buildings and tore them down. In 1969 a number of community activists decided that the unused land should be planted and turned into a park. They were operating on a long-standing principle that can be found even in the writings of John Locke, the classical formulator of a modern capitalist idea of property: anything in nature that its owners are allowing to go to waste should be applied to the social good. As though affirming the identity of freedom, spontaneity, and action, the organizers began cultivating the field. Soon hippies and some of their more conventionally respectable neighbors were working together in shaping a public park.

The routinized stupidity of large organizations is a phenomenon well known to social theorists. Whether because the People's Park was thought to attract hippies and loose living or because it was an invasion of property, the university decided to destroy it. On May 15 bulldozers flattened the gardens while police took control of the area. Chancellor Roger Heyns's actions recalled those of the administrators in the free speech movement: he described himself as a business manager working for a landlord confronted with an unauthorized tenant. Partisans went to the defense of the park; some of them threw rocks; the police used shotguns, firing not only at the defenders but inadvertently at passersby. After someone was killed, Governor Ronald Reagan sent in the National Guard. Property, capitalist property, was saved. But for a moment, in building and then in defending the park, its champions enacted democracy.

The larger problem in the effort to bring about participatory democracy is inseparable from the concept itself. Autonomy by its nature cannot be programmed. Autonomy must realize itself again and again over time. Without resisting a downward drag toward conformity and submission, it cannot even be an active and definable principle. The supporters of freedom can work to eliminate massive obstacles to it in the form of capitalist or collectivist political and social structures. They can be alert to sham imitations of autonomy. They can, above all, labor to ensure— against self-indulgence masquerading as spontaneous freedom or mob psychology masquerading as democracy—a proper understanding of participatory democracy, as the work of individuals trained in self-questioning, civilized disagreement, and cooperation. In this participatory democrats could be both the embodiments and the antagonists of liberal academia. But freedom cannot guarantee its own perpetuity.

Participatory democracy, at any rate, was among the most intriguing ideas to emerge out of the radical impulses of the time. The worst, in its continuing presence on the campus and its continuing embarrassment for the left, is scarcely an idea at all; it is the state of mind that today is known as political correctness, or PC. It is a phenomenon that for all the commentary that has been devoted to it needs still more if its relationship to the 1960s is to be clearly understood.

To make political correctness synonymous with left persuasions will not do: within those many quarreling parties will be found some of the most insistent enemies of PC. It is not a particular political canon but a way of claiming beliefs. A suggestion that would bring the phrase close to its recent signification would be this: PC is the political equivalent of the mentality that in the artistic and cultural sphere has been called philistinism.

A defender of tradition, or the American Way, or Marxist realism who rejects abstract expressionist painting as a threat to order is an artistic philistine. So is a culture snob who dismisses simple representational art as too easily accessible to the public. In none of these cases is there any genuine critical evaluation of the object in question for its excellence or its flaws on its own terms. The philistine chooses instead to adopt the appropriate fixed or prefabricated posture: defense of tradition and convention, affirmation of proletarian artistic standards, rejection of popular taste in favor of a sophisticated modernism. That definition of philistinism translated well into a definition of political correctness but of a kind that fits at any point in the political spectrum.

On the left, PC has an exact illustration in the New Politics conference in Chicago in 1967. Taking direction from the black militants was among white participants a matter of correctness, a posture of submission to the rightly defined embodiment of revolution. So the white radicals endorsed a program they had never seen that black militants had forced on them. Militants made the most of it: at a box marked "Contributions for Our Black Brothers in Prison," they made a point of laughing loudly whenever a white put in money. A like preference for correctness as opposed to untidy reality showed itself among American conservatives unwilling early in the 1960s to recognize the split between the Soviet Union and communist China. The rupture, while entirely open and demonstrable, was a scandal to conservative doctrine, which postulated a single world communism: it became therefore incorrect to believe demonstrable fact. The same proclivity was evident decades later in the bewilderment among some conservatives at the reformism of Gorbachev. There was no room in the most determinedly conservative ideology for imagining the existence of a reformist communist, or of a Soviet Union over which the hegemony of the communist party could become limited and confused. Torn between correctness and reality, conservatives fixed on the idea of the unchangeable metaphysical evil of communism had to await some new configuration of events that might appear to align itself with their customary system of beliefs.

Still, the question remains: if political correctness, properly understood, inheres not in any particular ideology but in a state of mind, why, then, does it appear to be the special vice of the left movements of the 1960s and their present-day academic heirs?

The explanation may lie in part in the influence of Marxism among the rebels of the later sixties. Marxists in general have been among the world's most obsessive concept-splitters since the medieval scholastics. There have been times in parts of the world where differing with a fellow Marxist over what was at the moment the disposition of class forces in the dialectic of history could get you killed. Only a handful of American Marxists in the time of the disintegration of SDS were that lethal, even in imagination. But doubtless polemicists infected their young listeners with something of the determination to be doctrinally precise that has characterized Marxists of many strains.

It was perhaps more, however, an opposite characteristic among American radicals in the sixties that implanted in some of them a taste for correctness. Precisely for lack of a rigorous intellectual structure that might unite the American left or at least give it a common ground on which to argue, radicals sought truth in experience, emotion, immediate events. Or they sought it in the suddenly emergent concerns for self-identity that made for black power, for radical feminism, for the sense of the radical community as an entity on its own. All this invited a preoccupation with the delineating of right relationships: of, say, white radicals with the black race, which some whites thought they must defer to as the revolutionary vanguard; or of radicalized men with women toward whom ideology commanded that they feel guilt. The possibilities for defining not truth but correctness were endless.

By the late 1980s and into the 1990s the conviction that a contagion of ideological purity was gripping universities across the nation had become common, if not quite PC, among some conservative commentators. But whatever the real extent of PC on the campus, and whatever its sources, its existence will be a continual reminder of the clench-jawed earnestness and the beliefs, commingled of passion and cold abstraction, that came to characterize the left of the sixties as it moved toward its disintegration.

 **The Poverty Wars**

IN 1798 the Reverend Thomas Malthus, in his *Essay on Population*, condemned the English Poor Laws as "futile and dangerous." By encouraging early marriages, he wrote, they fostered overpopulation and alleviated the misery needed to goad the lower orders to lead more provident lives. Human beings, as Malthus and other laissez-faire thinkers presented them, are solely economic creatures impelled by the hope of material gain and repelled by both the pain of poverty and the pain of work. The trick, then, was to make the threat of poverty so vivid and the possibility of gain so elusive and yet so tantalizingly visible as to overcome the normal human aversion to work. The best instrument for the job of forcing the poor to work, the classical economists believed, is the free market. They did not consider that men and women might work also out of an obligation to society, a will to artistic excellence, the quest for self-authentication: motives that might go contrary to the demands of the market and the spur of greed.

Moralists joined the laissez-faire economists in praise of work driven by necessity. Some people clearly could not work: the sick, the lame, the halt, the aged, the honest workers who in a time of economic crisis could be excused from what the moral world would otherwise demand of them. Society must support these afflicted people, for their poverty was not their own fault. But the others—the lazy, the vicious, the improvident—could not claim support by right. They were the authors of their own condition. Society could not let them starve, perhaps, but it must make help difficult lest a generous response encourage others to join their ranks. The moralists, in effect, created two categories of the poor. One was "deserving," entitled to society's decent care without much stigma; the other was "undeserving," to be kept alive, but reluctantly and only after being stigmatized. The mixing of moral with strictly economic justification of the market has continued to be particularly appealing to the well-to-do. Some of them like the idea that since poverty is the fault of the poor, the propertied classes have only limited obligations to assist them.

Market economics has been not only economically but politically dominant throughout most of American history. But it has softened in the twentieth century, in part because the enormous productivity of modern technology made it seem that poverty might ultimately drown in a flood of material goods. By the time of President Herbert Hoover in the late 1920s, for example, bounding prosperity had inspired a measure of optimism that poverty would someday be abolished. The "poorhouse is vanishing from among us," proclaimed Hoover in his 1928 speech accepting the Republican presidential nomination, not long before the Great Depression. "We shall soon . . . be in sight of the day when poverty will be banished" from the country. While in office, this wealthy and very generous philanthropist announced, in words that contradict the laissez-faire belief in the spur of want, that "intellectual, moral, and spiritual progress are not the products of poverty." As a Quaker and a representative of the more progressive wing of the Republican party, Hoover did not begrudge collective support to various classes of the economically afflicted. He sponsored government loans to farm cooperatives and during the early days of the Depression made some stabs at the direct relief of poverty. But with his defeat and the handing over of the wrecked economy to the Democrats, it fell to the party of Franklin D. Roosevelt to enact the first practical nationwide social welfare programs.

The slowness with which this country has moved to expand its welfare system contrasts to the swiftness of response in Western Europe to disruptions brought by the industrial revolution and to the social possibilities of its enormous productivity. At the prompting of landed conservatives whose ideology championed a more interdependent society than that of the free market, Great Britain in the nineteenth century passed legislation protecting factory workers. Imperial Germany built a social insurance state in the 1880s, and in the second decade of the twentieth century Britain began instituting substantial welfare measures. Western European political parties, conservative as well as socialist, have come to take for granted the obligation of the people and government to provide basic living and medical services for everyone. But tradition in this country has fostered the idea that poverty is the fault of the poor. The New Deal and Fair Deal only modified this mentality, which purred along into the postwar world.

Even after World War II, then, it remained a widespread conviction in the United States that poverty is the just punishment for people who have not tried hard enough. What welfare existed, specifically the New Deal Aid to Families with Dependent Children (AFDC), was widely regarded simply as making a decent provision for the unfortunate poor, notably widows with children or women whose husbands had deserted them. The authors of the original Social Security Act anticipated that the typical

AFDC beneficiary would be the wife of a West Virginia coal miner killed in an accident. This was not how things worked out. Beginning in the mid- to late 1960s increasing numbers of women on the rolls were unmarried mothers. Most had been white, but in the public mind the typical welfare mother has been black.

Even in the years when the Cold War, McCarthyism, and questions of the mediocrity of American culture dominated public discussion, liberals never completely abandoned the issue of poverty. One of numerous muckraking books that presaged the sixties, John Kenneth Galbraith's *The Affluent Society* (1958), along with its larger message of private wealth and public squalor announced that poverty still existed in the United States. Galbraith's point about poverty was an afterthought, and few took notice. But then in 1962, Michael Harrington published *The Other America*, a powerful expose of persistent poverty in the United States that jolted the Kennedy liberals. The poor in this country, wrote Harrington, were now largely invisible. Their presence was masked by the rugged terrain of Appalachia or tucked away out of sight of mid-century Americans who traveled by car or plane. They were also removed from middle-class concern by a mistaken belief that existing social welfare programs took good care of them. Within a short time of the publication of Harrington's book another component would be added to the problem of impacted poverty: white flight from the cities, eroding their economic base and leaving an impoverished black inner city.

In the 1960s the customary American indifference toward the poor gave way for a time to the persuasion that all problems are to be confronted and vanquished. Liberals were addressing the issue of poverty in the confident spirit of the Kennedy era, convinced that with enough dedication the country could reduce or eliminate want, as it could hurl a spaceship into the sky. Public discussion began to center on poverty as the product not of bad people but chiefly of environmental conditions. Radicals soon were blaming "the system," by which they meant not only raw, unvarnished capitalism but the liberal institutions designed to moderate its effects. Meanwhile, however, the very definition of poverty was becoming more complex.

At the turn of the century, poverty as sheer economic deprivation had been a very clear matter. It was depicted in the farmland stories of Hamlin Garland, the urban novels of Theodore Dreiser and Stephen Crane. If your clothes were ragged, if you lived in a shack or a heatless room with a leaky roof, if you did not have enough food to keep from being hungry, you were poor. You were also poor if, like a farmer at the mercy of the weather and the market, you were in danger of slipping into that state of need. Even then poverty was identified as having a cultural component as well, but assessments of it varied widely. The poor were lazy; or they were victims, men driven to drink by the hopelessness of their lot, women driven to prostitution; or the poor embodied the simple virtues of humility, piety, patient suffering; or they were sullen malcontents; or at heart they were sturdy revolutionaries. The Great Depression, especially in its Farm Security Administration photographs of southern sharecroppers, added stark images: a wooden shack papered inside with newspapers; careworn faces etched in the hard lines of black-and-white photos; a woman resolute and statuesque in a sunbonnet, her hands on a plow. Differing vices or virtues, customs, states of mind have been presumed as attendants to poverty. But until recently poverty itself was simple in definition: it consisted of basic physical need.

That remains the essential description even today. But with time the awareness has grown that poverty has a social and psychological side. At least one feature of poverty has faded, as the well-to-do have learned to dress down and stylish mass-produced clothing has become available to the poor. The disappearance of tattered clothing, once the uniform of poverty, was among the reasons Harrington offered for the invisibility of the poor. Then the time of civil rights militancy riveted the nation's attention on a people for whom material poverty and psychological oppression had become inseparable. School integration had as one of its purposes to provide black children with access to a fair share of state funding. Laws against job discrimination quite obviously confronted want. While integration itself perhaps has as its most immediate beneficiary the black middle class, the accompanying attack on racism was an assault at once on economic want and on the culture of poverty. In other times it had been assumed throughout much of the world that the poor were in the majority. Now the very fact of being an impoverished minority became recognizable as contributing to the psychology of poverty. Liberals, then, were coming to associate poverty with a social, mental, and cultural condition—with crime-ridden streets, with unemployment that saps the will of the victims, with dropouts from school, with exclusion from the politics and economics and culture of the dominant sectors of society.

Beginning in the late fifties and early sixties the policymakers and the aware public began to talk specifically of a culture of poverty. According to Oscar Lewis's 1961 study of a Mexican-American family, *Children of Sanchez*, the poor lived for the present and had little capacity for deferred gratification. They had small regard for existing institutions and were often in trouble with the law. Their sexual unions were irregular: serial marriage was the norm and often ended in divorce and desertion. The poor shared few interests with others outside their families and could not be rallied for social or political causes. This culture, moreover, was lasting, passed along from parents to children, and it relegated each successive generation to the same dismal trap. Some people on the left would denounce the concept of a culture of poverty for blaming the victim rather than society. But many experts found it a useful clue to the direction that poverty's cure must take. It was not enough just to end discrimination or even to provide retraining. Lifting people from poverty required providing confidence and ambition.

By the 1960s few Americans starved, though many were ill-nourished out of ignorance or neglect. Was poverty, then, becoming of secondary importance? Not if the psychology and the social milieu of poverty were the horror that liberals and even conservatives said they were. Much of the culture of American poverty was behavioral, and still is: drugs, violent crime, disappearing fathers, abusive parents. Does that mean that poor individuals and families are responsible for their condition, and the rest of the country is free to tell them to straighten up? That would amount to believing that a twelve-year-old child in a drug-decayed neighborhood could will her surroundings into becoming a middle-class suburbia, if only she would tense her moral resolve more tightly. The individual is trapped within the collectivity: conservatives should know that as well as liberals. Some individuals, of course, manage to escape from their collectivity; but liberals know that as well as conservatives. In any event, the revelations of Michael Harrington and the attempts at amelioration by the liberal administrations of the sixties had now fixed poverty in the consciences of a sufficient number of citizens to ensure that it would be the subject of continuing public argument. And defining poverty by its cultural content made the discussion very much a part of the 1960s, when even political talk, often the most superficial form of discourse, was forced to address questions about the national character and its ills.

The liberal Democratic administrations of the 1960s attacked poverty along a wide front. The Democrats had a constituency among the poor. They were also heirs of the New Deal with its commitment to rescuing the destitute and reducing the extremes of wealth and income. Liberal Democrats, moreover, as at least cautious champions of the civil rights movement were specifically concerned about poverty among blacks as a product of their nation's racist past.

Some scholars believe that President Lyndon Johnson's War on Poverty had roots in the urge among liberal federal bureaucrats to test new social science principles and techniques and to implement their long frustrated vision of a just society. Daniel Moynihan, one of their number while remaining something of an outsider, would later insist that the War on Poverty was "preeminently the conception of the liberal, policy oriented intellectuals, especially those who gathered in Washington, and, in a significant sense, came to power in the early 1960s under the Presidency of John F. Kennedy." Somewhat later, Robert Lampman, another initiator of the War on Poverty, declared: "It was an elite group inside the Kennedy administration that started talking about this, and I think they saw it as an attempt to follow in some logical way in the spirit of the Social Security Act and the [Full] Employment Act of 1946."

The conviction that poverty is not only wrong but remediable soared during the Kennedy and Johnson years, lodged in part in the buoyant state of the economy. Kennedy came to office just as the economy was recovering from the last of three recessions of the previous few years. To provide a further boost he would propose a substantial cut in personal and corporate income taxes. It passed in 1964, after his death, and by mid-decade the economy began its ascent into the stratosphere. During the rest of the sixties economic growth, at first without inflation, forced employment rates to historic peacetime levels. Never had Americans felt so prosperous, so confident, and so generous. Money for the poor need not be at the expense of the middle class; it could come out of rising productivity and rising revenues.

Yet even before running for President, Kennedy had already been supporting Medicare, manpower training, extension of public assistance, and federal aid to education. In August 1960, he praised social security for making a "war on poverty." Three times his inaugural address referred to poverty. In 1962 he announced the daring resolve to end poverty. Government, he declared, "must contribute to the attack on dependency, delinquency, family breakdown, illegitimacy, ill health, and disability. It must reduce the incidence of these problems, prevent their occurrence and recurrence, and strengthen and protect the vulnerable in a highly competitive world."

The New Frontiersmen, coats off and sleeves rolled up, would rid the country of a poverty that had continued only in the absence of resolve to abolish it. They could also look for the help of the social sciences with which liberals felt much at home as had Progressive Era intellectuals before them: precise working tools for determined architects of economic justice. Kennedy's small, experimental poverty programs included projects for the redevelopment of blighted neighborhoods, the acceleration of public works in poor regions, the retraining and rehabilitation of the unemployed, the stimulation of youth employment to fight juvenile delinquency, and the eradication of illiteracy. His Manpower Development Act of 1963, a response to the threat of automation, in providing employment training had a cultural implication, insofar as the pride that comes with the attainment of skills can liberate the trainees from the psychology of poverty. Later studies indicated that the legislation permanently increased annual earnings for females by $300 to $600, males enjoying slightly smaller benefits.

The actual War on Poverty, as a general assault rather than a piecemeal attack on specific ills, was a Kennedy initiative. JFK read Harrington's disturbing book, or at least a *New Yorker* review of it by Dwight Macdonald, and was impressed. In December 1962, in a year-end review of economic conditions, he exclaimed to Walter Heller, chairman of the Council of Economic Advisers: "Now look! I want to go beyond the things that have already been accomplished. Give me the facts and figures on the things we still have to do. For example, what about the poverty problem in the United States?"

In early 1963 Heller sent the President a memo on the subject. Setting $3,000 a year per family as the lowest figure above the poverty line, it concluded that since 1956 overall economic growth had reduced poverty only two percentage points. Soon after, the President asked Heller's staff to prepare "a practical Kennedy anti-poverty program." This was to be incorporated in the President's 1964 Economic Report. Kennedy never lived to make his Report, but his successor carried on his work.

Lyndon Johnson's father, Sam Ealy Johnson, had been a member of the Texas state legislature, where he supported populist causes. The new President's own social awareness probably had its origins in a youth spent in the remote Texas Hill country where he saw poverty firsthand. He encountered another face of poverty in 1928 when, as a college student, he briefly instructed poor Mexican-American students in a small country school in the town of Cotulla. Johnson began his political career in the shadow of Franklin Roosevelt and the New Deal and embraced its liberal philosophy. FDR became his patron and appointed him Texas state director of the New Deal's National Youth Administration. The post brought with it patronage, influence, and close association with state politicians. In it Johnson distinguished himself from other New Dealers by his concern for blacks. In 1935 LBJ ran successfully for Congress. As a young congressman he voted predominantly with the New Deal administration and made his friends among the circle of liberal New Deal bureaucrats and officeholders in Georgetown.

But Johnson was pulled two ways. The exhaustion of progressive energies during World War II left Texas in a conservative frame of mind, to which Johnson quickly adapted. The aircraft industry, along with oil and natural gas companies, appreciated his ability to secure favors and protection from the federal government. In 1947 Johnson voted to override President Truman's veto of the mildly antilabor Taft-Hartley Act. The next year he won a close election to the Senate.

In the 1950s Johnson gave nominal support to southern segregationists, but he was not a man they could rely on. In 1953 his mastery of politics, along with his ideological blandness, helped him become Senate Democratic leader. After working closely with the White House during

Eisenhower's first presidential term, Johnson later came to sense a change in the public mood. His affinity for liberal social programs gradually became stronger until in the mid-1960s it was the dominant element in his politics.

The presidential primary and election campaigns of 1960 marked the last appearance of Johnson as a chiefly regional figure. Undeterred by a major heart attack suffered in 1955, he wanted the presidency and declared his candidacy. John Kennedy, after defeating him at the 1960 convention, shrewdly picked him for vice-presidential running mate, in part to offset the unpopularity that Kennedy's Roman Catholicism brought him in the South. The Texan crisscrossed his native state and the entire region, preaching loyalty to the party in his best southern drawl. His folksy campaign helped the Democrats hold most of the South, yielding votes essential for Kennedy's victory.

Johnson's acceptance of the vice presidency—a quiet, sedate job compared with the majority leader's work in the Senate—puzzled many of his colleagues. The reason for his decision probably lay in its proximity to the presidency. Johnson, of course, brought his activist temperament to his new office and led the Kennedy administration on civil rights. More than any other major figure, he spoke out vigorously for the movement, and he headed the President's Committee on Equal Employment.

Within days of his abrupt elevation to the presidency Johnson had signed aboard his predecessor's campaign against poverty. Heller told Johnson about Kennedy's antipoverty initiatives and asked whether he wanted the work to go forward. "I'm interested," LBJ told his chief economic adviser. "I'm sympathetic. Go ahead. Give it the highest priority. Push ahead full tilt." A month later in Texas, at the President's ranch on the Pedernales River, Heller told him about the proposal for a modest pilot program in a few cities to try out various antipoverty strategies. Johnson quickly objected. He wanted to make his mark before the election, less than a year away, and this feeble plan had no excitement. The program would have to be "big and bold and hit the nation with real impact." Get a poverty program for every community that wanted one. The President soon told the media people at his ranch that he intended to mount a major campaign against poverty in the coming congressional session.

Johnson launched the antipoverty program with his usual hyperbole. "This administration today, here and now, declares unconditional war on poverty in America," he proclaimed in January 1964 in his first State of the Union address. The struggle would not be easy, but "we shall not rest until that war is won." It would be waged "in city slums and small towns, in sharecropper shacks and in migrant labor camps, on Indian reservations, among whites as well as Negroes, among the young as well as the aged, in the boom towns and in the depressed areas." Its weapons would be "better schools, better health, and better homes, and better training, and better job opportunities to help more Americans, especially young Americans, escape from squalor and misery and unemployment."

The program was not a welfare plan. LBJ never liked a dole and never endorsed a guaranteed income. He considered the War on Poverty a "handup," not a "handout." "What you have and what you own," Johnson told the United States Chamber of Commerce, are "not secure when there are men that are idle . . . and young people adrift in the streets." The unskilled, the untrained, the ignorant would be provided with the tools to become self-sufficient. They would be converted from welfare cases to self-employed, self-respecting individuals.

This principle was incorporated into the Economic Opportunity Act of 1964. As passed in August, the bill authorized a billion dollars, only about half fresh appropriations, for a clutch of programs to retrain, re-tool, and reinvigorate the poor. The program was to be headed by a poverty czar responsible to the President. Johnson quickly chose Sargent Shriver, an energetic, likeable Kennedy clan son-in-law, to head the Office of Economic Opportunity.

Title I of the new legislation was the Job Corps, establishing centers where poor youths, male and female, could learn both basic and advanced skills. It also included provision for a Neighborhood Youth Corps and a college work-study program. Title II was the Community Action Program, an innovative attempt to nurture active community through "maximum feasible participation" of local residents in the conception and implementing of programs to train and educate the poor. Other Titles included provisions for rural loans, small business development centers, a work experience program, and Volunteers in Service to America (VISTA), a sort of domestic Peace Corps. Beyond those specified in the bill itself, Shriver and his staff concocted programs to soak up unused antipoverty funds or to put flesh on the bare bones of the law. Among these, Legal Services was intended to provide the poor with the same access to legal help that other Americans enjoyed, and Head Start was a preschool enrichment program designed to overcome the cultural and educational handicaps of poor children.

Community action, for which Robert Kennedy served as a major advocate, was one of the more controversial programs Shriver administered. The idea behind it was to avoid projects conceived in Washington with minutely detailed specifications. Instead, federal funds would flow to local community action agencies to fund programs established by local citizens. By this process incipient communities would be converted into real ones, and local people, beaten down by the culture of poverty, would gain confidence and begin to function as competent people.

But maximum feasible participation was difficult to implement. The community action system bypassed the mayors and the city councils, many of them Democratic; and they protested losing power and money. The Johnson administration could not easily ignore their complaints. It was also hard to assure that the local people were really the poor. Despite efforts to promote true representation by local elections, many community action agencies fell under the domination of self-serving hustlers. Finally, there were the radical activists who saw the poverty program as an opportunity to raise the political consciousness of the poor and turn it to demanding fundamental social change. In places like Syracuse, San Francisco, and New York's Harlem, the agencies were taken over by militants who sought to supply radical principles learned in the civil rights movement or from gadflies like Saul Alinsky, the skilled community organizer. Worse was the hiring by HARYOU in New York City of black nationalist youth, which if it taught anything was a lesson in how to hustle. But while establishment figures were accusing OEO locals of revolution, radicals were accusing participants of selling out to the government.

The first community action agencies began to operate soon after the November 1964 presidential landslide that elected Johnson in his own right to the presidency and gave the Democrats unprecedented majorities in Congress. But by the late summer of 1965 the program, though not without its successes, had aroused the ire of local officials, the mainstream press, and a large chunk of the middle-class public.

The Job Corps too came under attack. The scheme was admirable in concept. Exemplifying in the most direct way the idea of a handup, it offered job training rather than the transfers of funds to the poor that would keep them dependent. On the pattern of the New Deal's Civilian Conservation Corps, the new agency gathered young people into camps. It trained them not only in job skills but also in reading and writing. But difficulties soon arose. The program took in some young blacks with criminal records and some racist white southerners. Many of the recruits were school dropouts who could not find jobs. Inevitably, the Corps camps were plagued by rowdyism, alcohol, drugs, crime, and sex scandals. Some radicals complained that removing slum youths from their environment was a scheme to deny the validity of their culture and make them more like middle-class Americans.

In later years evaluations of the success of the Job Corps, measured by improvements in employment and wages of its beneficiaries, showed disappointing results. Added to this were the complaints of residents in the neighborhoods of Job Corps camps and the relatively high cost of the program per trainee. Together these eroded the program's support.

Most Americans would not approve of undeserving poor adults. But they had a warm spot for small children and perhaps especially black children. Sargent Shriver was aware of this feeling. After the turmoil of community action and the Job Corps during the fall and winter of 1964–65, moreover, the poverty program needed a success. Inspired by both opportunity and need, in the early spring Shriver came up with a sweeping, nationwide preschool program for poor four-year-olds to last through the summer.

By late August 1965 Head Start was widely judged a success. During the summer over half a million children in twenty-five hundred communities, from the rural South to the nation's largest cities, were enrolled in Head Start programs. Many were run by local volunteers through community civic groups. The projects were housed in schools, churches, stores, apartments, civic centers, even abandoned sheds. Their teachers used imaginative methods to broaden the lives of their small clients. One Washington, D.C., Head Start teacher took her pupils to a suburban Grand Union supermarket. Few of them, she discovered, had ever seen an eggplant, a cauliflower, or an avocado. Other teachers took their charges to gas stations, zoos, and working farms. For many children the attention seemed to count the most.

By the end of its eight weeks, Head Start stood out from most of the other War on Poverty programs. In August 1965 Johnson announced that it would become a full, one-year permanent program for 350,000 poor three-year-olds and up. What had started as an experiment had been "battle-tested" and "proved worthy," he announced. Hope had "entered the lives of more than a half-million youngsters who needed it most."

Johnson's optimism and self-congratulation came too soon. No one doubted that Head Start had improved the health of the children, sprinkled money liberally in poor communities, and helped local people by employing them as teaching aides, cooks, and cleaning personnel. But judgments of its larger efficacy differed. The public, and some of the experts, nonetheless believe the program beneficial, and it has continued to our own day, though under attack by conservatives.

The War on Poverty extended beyond the programs authorized by the Economic Opportunity Act or conceived by Shriver and his staff. An antipoverty component was incorporated into many measures that made up Lyndon Johnson's Great Society.

One major new law with important antipoverty features was the Elementary and Secondary Education Act of 1965. This measure is usually treated as the breakthrough in the long campaign for a general law giving federal aid to education. In fact, the law focused on the poor. Under its terms federal money would go primarily to school districts with a large proportion of children whose family income fell below $2,000 a year. One reason was the need to overcome resistance by the teachers' National Education Association and various liberal and Protestant groups to federal contributions to Roman Catholic parochial schools. Neither side in the bitter battle over federal aid to education could afford to seem indifferent to the fate of poor children.

Yet as a mechanism to improve the quality of education in the ghettos and the nation's depressed rural backwaters, the education act was not a notable success. There was too little money, and inevitably it was spread too thin. It was also misspent. Little of it went into innovative programs; much was used to reduce the school-tax burden of local householders.

Medicare, most effective of Great Society programs, came of an idea that Franklin Roosevelt had considered for inclusion in his 1935 Social Security Act and Harry Truman had introduced again after World War II. For years, federal health insurance schemes were victim to the organized opposition of the nation's physicians. Appealing to the public's sentimental attachment to the family doctor, the American Medical Association labeled every such plan a form of "socialized medicine" that would destroy the precious relationship between doctor and patient. Proposals by Kennedy to provide hospital coverage for retirees under the Social Security system went down to defeat under the same barrage.

The 1964 Democratic landslide worked a revolution. Johnson's liberal congressional majorities swamped the opposition. Even the conservative Wilbur Mills, the powerful head of the House Ways and Means Committee, could read the election returns. Abandoning his opposition, Mills not only endorsed the Kennedy Medicare proposal but added to its hospitalization provision a section to include payment of retirees' doctor bills. Mills also augmented the package with a measure to create a joint federal and state program called Medicaid to pay the health bills of the poor. Recognizing that the medical profession would have to be placated, the bill's sponsors made concessions. Doctors would receive customary fees rather than amounts specified or negotiated with the government. In-hospital specialists such as anesthesiologists, pathologists, and radiologists were to be paid separately rather than through the hospital as in the past. Both provisions assured that medical costs, already rising, would sharply accelerate.

Still, the bill was a breakthrough for the nation's health. Men and women who despite health problems had seldom seen doctors now flocked to clinics and physicians' offices. Many old people, once faced with financial catastrophe when they became sick, could now avoid indigence. The nation's overall health undoubtedly improved, though one price was soaring costs for the country as a whole.

It is common to think of Great Society programs as primarily devoted to helping the poor. But many cut across class lines and benefited the educated middle class as well. Medicare aided solvent as well as poor retirees. The various higher education laws, providing loans and scholarships for college students, helped hard-pressed middle-class parents with children seeking bachelor degrees. The wide range of consumer protection measures—clean air, pure water, and product safety acts—were for the good of the affluent as well as the impoverished. Through the National Endowments for the Arts and the Humanities, the Corporation for Public Broadcasting, and funding of the Kennedy Center in Washington, the Johnson administration sought to encourage the arts and intelligent discourse. These cultural subsidies were of course not labeled "middle class." Their sponsors claimed that they would give the masses access to the cultural flowering of civilization. Spreading dance, theater, classical music, and other cultural products across the American landscape, they undoubtedly reduced the cultural hegemony of the big cities, especially New York, but the chief beneficiaries were the educated.

Another project of the administration, the Housing Act of 1968, was an instance of the alliance taking shape at the time between liberalism and various sectors of American business. The act provided funds for housing construction. Although it fostered a degree of scandal—the building industry had long been among the most corrupt elements of American businesses—it financed the construction of over a million new dwellings. Only about 13 percent of homeowners and 43 percent of renters benefiting from the program were among the poor as defined by the Kennedy yardstick, an annual income of $3,000 for a family of four. And buildings abandoned in the inner cities deteriorated still further, crime sites ripe for drug dealing. But a number of poor people, besides those who took over residences abandoned by the middle class, got better housing by way of the Johnson law until it expired in 1973.

Johnson's State of the Union message for January 1966 embodied the farthest reach of the presidency into the substance of civil rights. Johnson urged that it be made a federal crime to interfere with the exercise of rights in voting, education, housing, employment, jury service, and travel, and proposed that discrimination in the sale or rental of housing be made illegal.

After the early struggles for integration of the schools and for an end to segregation in its other more visible forms, the fight for integrated housing was the most controversial expression yet of the civil rights movement. It attacked prejudice more ingrained than any that the government had confronted since the desegregation of the schools. It would mean not merely integration in the transient encounters of strangers in buses or restaurants but a substantial mixing of populations and the opening of areas formerly monopolized by whites. The campaign for open housing was therefore perhaps the largest project to restructure society in the interests of social justice. It was also the most difficult.

Demonstrations over the issue could not have the same meaning as in, say, the case of a sit-in at a lunch counter, in which the symbolic act and the practical object merged: a black demonstrator seated in a white dining room made integration an immediate reality. No such simple action could integrate a residential neighborhood: that required money, negotiations, contracts, law continuously administered. Bold and right, housing legislation along with other strategies would be necessary to open up territories that whites had heretofore possessed for their exclusive use. But whereas petty customs ordaining separate public accommodations vanished almost as soon as they were challenged, an assault on basic residential patterns stirred deep white racial fears and animosity that did not promise to end anywhere near so easily.

To attack segregated housing, Martin Luther King in 1966 concentrated on Chicago, where CORE had unsuccessfully challenged white control of the schools. This city had suffered in the 1940s some of the worst racial violence in this century. In the Chicago freedom movement of 1966, King led open-housing marches, lived among the urban poor, and mounted a campaign far more difficult than that in Montgomery or Selma.

Chicago had a rigid pattern of residential and therefore educational discrimination that had 90 percent of black students in all-black classes. Black children, confined in neighborhoods and schools where almost no whites were to be seen, were sometimes found to believe that theirs was the nation's majority race. Under Mayor Richard J. Daley's aegis there was no explicit Jim Crow legislation. Yet black schools were overcrowded while hundreds of white classrooms remained empty. Rather than bus black students out, the city shipped mobile classrooms in. The government changed zoning boundaries at its convenience to keep blacks in shifting neighborhoods from entering white schools. It is probable that Daley was not among the worst of white politicos in his racial feelings, but in Chicago the problem went deeper than his will and resources could reach. Further complicating matters was a sharp social division between the black underclass and well-to-do blacks, some of whom constituted the majority of slumlords in the black ghettos.

As King addressed six hundred marchers who were protesting neighborhood segregation in Chicago's Marquette Park, police struggled to control four thousand whites, some waving Confederate flags or wearing Nazi insignia. "I think the people from Mississippi ought to come to Chicago to learn how to hate," King said to the crowd of whites. King announced a march to nearby Cicero, where eleven thousand blacks worked by day while the residential composition was lily-white. White mobs in the South were rabble; in Chicago, white families who saw themselves as defending their neighborhoods turned themselves into rabble. In other neighborhoods, rabble changed its color and became young black street gangs.

Rather than risk racial war between Chicago's blacks and staunchly Democratic ethnic groups, Daley made a show of capitulating and vowed to use every means to promote fair housing. The need was astonishing: in the Gage Park–Chicago Lawn area, for example, which was 90 percent Roman Catholic, reportedly two blacks lived among 28,244 residents. The demonstration in Cicero went on without King and with some two hundred CORE marchers under the protection of two thousand National Guardsmen.

As soon as King left town, the Daley administration neglected most of its promises to desegregate schools and force nondiscrimination in the sale of housing. Blacks in Chicago did get some good patronage jobs, and Daley built some swimming pools in the ghettos, perhaps sensing that the changes the poor wanted must be specific, limited, and material. The mayor won reelection in 1967 with a 73 percent margin and 80 percent of the black vote; thereafter the campaigns for open housing and integrated schools both collapsed. King remarked that Daley was "no bigot," but "fighting him was like fighting a pillow." Yet in time Illinois law was to forbid discrimination in housing, and in 1983—after many whites and successful blacks had moved to the suburbs, leaving the south and west side ghettos in worse shape than ever—Chicago elected a black mayor.

It was ominous for the future of the liberal Democratic coalition that so much of the conflict over housing was in the North, where middle-class and ethnic blue-collar beneficiaries of the New Deal and its successors had to choose between their loyalty to the party of FDR and their racial sentiments. The vicious response to King's march was one sign; the congressional elections of 1966 were another. A Republican gain of forty-seven seats in the House was, to be sure, within the range of a predictable rebound after the big Democratic victory of 1964. But racial messages were detectable in Republican victories in Michigan, Illinois, and particularly California, where Ronald Reagan defeated the incumbent liberal governor, a fair housing law decisively lost, and an open occupancy law was repealed by a margin of two to one. California voters, just a few days before the riots in the Watts section of Los Angeles, also inserted a provision into the state's constitution prohibiting the introduction of similar open housing legislation thereafter.

Yet in 1968 Johnson got through Congress a ban on discrimination in the financing, selling, and rental of what amounted to 40 percent of the country's housing. He did so with the support of Senate minority leader Everett Dirksen, who in aiding the civil rights legislation of 1964 had already shown a willingness to include racial justice within his generally conservative outlook.

Today the Great Society is often remembered for bloated programs, mismanagement, and in the end political failure. Yet for whatever reasons—an expanding economy, government largesse, or some combination—the median income for poor families increased; for blacks it went from $5,921 in 1964 to $8,074 in 1969.

In designing and implementing housing legislation, the simplest and on the whole most believable solution was to stick with the awareness that poverty at bottom is physical deprivation, absolute or relative, its more elusive cultural characteristics being dependent on the very practical fact of want. The answer, then, is to shift to the needy, on some continuing institutional basis, a portion of the nation's wealth, either through economic growth or redistribution. The last, however, is a strategy most invasive of what substantial numbers of Americans regard as sacrosanct: the rights of private property. Yet the distributionist solution had one of its most straightforward presentations in a proposal put forward in 1965 by Daniel Patrick Moynihan, then an assistant secretary of labor and a social critic known for fusing conservative with liberal perceptions.

"The United States," Moynihan observed, "is the only industrial democracy in the world without a system of automatic income supplements for people living with their children. It is the simplest and possibly the most effective of all social-welfare arrangements, not least because its administration involves no judgments as to whether or not the recipients are worthy and entitled to assistance." The specific superiority of such an allowance to AFDC was that families with a father in the home would not be penalized, so the system would not itself break up families. The expenditure, as Moynihan explained it, would fulfill the promise of the civil rights movement, advancing legal equality to "equality as a fact and as a result." Moynihan's idea of a guaranteed family allowance was soon to win favor among many conservatives. The free-market economist Milton Friedman and Richard Nixon's later Republican administration championed much the same concept under the rubric of the "negative income tax."

That concept would have extended to the recipients of family assistance the same principle that governs the present graduated income tax: that government policy must make it advantageous to the individual to seek a job paying a higher wage or salary. The more a taxpayer earns, the higher the tax payment climbs, but the tax goes up less than the income. Under the negative income tax in its varying proposed forms, a family having no income at all was to receive a subsistence grant based on the size of the household. A family that then found a job at low pay would be subject to an income tax. But the tax and the grant would be so calibrated with wage earnings as to make the employment financially worth the surrender of free time. Each passage from wage to higher wage was to bring an increase in the tax or a decrease in the grant, but not so much as to prevent the change in work from providing a rise in net income, consisting of wage and grant after taxes. At a certain level in salary or wages, the family would pass out of the program and into the regular taxpayer system: again, to its advantage, for the greater earnings would more than make up for the loss of the program's benefits.

The plan could claim at least some legitimate roots in the liberal New Deal heritage. But the New Deal had broken with the traditional American unwillingness directly to transfer one person's wealth to another, while Johnson insisted that the Great Society programs would be paid for out of expanding revenues. Franklin Roosevelt's programs, however, were in order to extend and diversify membership in the institutions of small, substantial private property. Unemployment and old-age insurance, for instance, defined the individual as a worker establishing a work record and on that basis entitled under specific circumstances to specific funds from the government, much as an employee receives a salary from a company. New and Fair Deal government loans for home ownership spoke to an American tradition and longing for this most substantial kind of property. The negative income tax, like social security, would define the individual as an essentially productive participant in the nation's life. The program was specifically designed to attack not only material need but the culture of poverty, substituting for the degrading institutions of welfare a graduated income presented as an entitlement. Even a family out of work and obtaining its entire income from the government would be part of a system that identified all its members as workers and taxpayers, actual or potential.

It is almost certainly for that reason that in its typical presentation the program even at its lower levels was to consist of taxes and compensating grants. Mathematical simplicity might have dictated a system of grants alone, the grant shrinking as the wage rose, but shrinking less than the increase in work income. That is what the formulas combining taxes and grants amounted to. But imposing a tax, so the program designers may have reasoned, brings a social and psychological gain, defining the individual as a contributing member of society. The negative income tax thereby accords its recipients the same dignity that the rest of the population feels entitled to. Medicaid and food stamps have provided sufficient transfers of resources to lessen poverty defined as physical need; what they have not lessened is the degradation that goes with poverty as a condition of dependency or handouts. The negative income tax along with universal health insurance would go far toward eliminating that stigma. The negative income tax is well within the tradition of social democracy, and the failure of liberals to embrace it as quickly as conservatives indicates a larger unwillingness on the part of recent liberalism to shape its programs to the measure of its New Deal past. The negative income tax has never been adopted on a large scale. It remains an attractive alternative to a miserable welfare system that wastes money on administrative costs as well as encouraging fraud, and it offers one model for incorporating marginalized classes into the larger society. For the case against dependency in welfare, conservatives and liberals alike can look to one of the nation's great social democrats (though himself a Hudson Valley patrician). "Continued dependence upon relief," said Roosevelt in 1935, "induces a spiritual and moral disintegration fundamentally destructive to the national fiber. To dole out relief in this way is to administer a narcotic, a subtle destroyer of the human spirit."

Liberals, conservatives, and most leftists can agree that poverty is self-perpetuating from generation to generation: that parents without education, for example, cannot themselves pass education on to their children; that an upbringing in misery discourages any trust in the promise of success, and therefore any submission to the demands, of formal schooling. Self-respect in American culture is both cause and effect of certain habits in education, work, and social conduct; take away either the self-respect or the habits, and the other will wither.

The Johnson era in effect posed this question: if the cycle is to be broken from within, which must be addressed first, the absence of pride or the impoverished schooling and the destructive patterns of behavior? A danger here is that liberals in their laudable wish to eliminate the self-contempt of the impoverished will virtually endorse the culture of the ghetto at its worst. Do ghetto children speak black English, in monosyllabic thoughts at that? Then let black English prevail in ghetto schools and do not try to teach them Dickens and Shakespeare: so say liberals of the most deferential sort. Simply tell the kid hanging out on the streetcorner that whatever he is doing is all right, and he will feel better, and feeling better will lead to . . . well, not middle-class conduct—we don't want to imply that the middle classes do anything better than the poor—but to some kind of improvement in his lot. Tell black or Hispanic teenagers that all their problems are the fault of racism, and not one is their own: see then how they act. Or don't even worry about how they act. Their conduct is exempt from whatever fault-finding the privileged classes might presume to venture. Some social-work theorists now refuse to distinguish between the deserving and the undeserving poor, but ordinary people do, including working-class poor. And so would a liberal who adheres to the best implications of the New Deal.

From 1955 to 1990 the likelihood of a robber's robbing successfully rose threefold. And while over the same period the prison population grew steadily, the numbers convicted were only half as likely to go there. Prison sentences, not frequently given, were rarely long, which probably accounts for the sharp turn toward mandatory sentencing in the 1990s. The conservative theorist James Q. Wilson has argued sensibly enough that crime increases when its benefits sufficiently outweigh the risks. Because crime is easier, drugs have become easier to support. Crime in turn is a component of the cultural impoverishment of poor neighborhoods, contribution both to self-contempt and, among young criminals, to an aggressive false pride. The cycle continues, with liberal help if conservatives are to be believed.

That easy praise and the denial of responsibility have become characteristic of American society is a truth that conservatives have proved not only in their arguments but by their own conduct. Republicans in the 1980s have oozed rhetoric flattering to the public and promoted among the middle classes a self-pitying outrage at being taxed. So if it is liberals who coddle, then who in this country are the conservatives?

Moynihan places much blame on the urban ghetto schools, where illiterate students are graduated, while once-dedicated teachers have given up in the face of local control and parental pressures to make a lie out of the educational system. When most students did not hand in homework, teachers stopped assigning it and took the maximum number of days off that their unions had won for them. Conservatives who wish to bolster their case can observe that during the sixties sanctions such as in-school discipline, suspension, holding back students who do not perform, and expulsion all nearly died at the hands of liberal courts, aggressive parents, and tired teachers. Meanwhile, under Title VI of the 1964 Civil Rights Act, school systems exasperated with unruly students could be compelled to put up with them. And under *Gault v. Arizona* (1967) schools had to offer due process for suspension. For these reasons and others, a student who refused learning was probably much freer to do so in 1970 than in 1960.

Whoever the critic, and whatever may have been the level of enthusiasm for study among American children in the past, for much of the school population, white, black, or Hispanic, there is little studying. Minority students who do work hard in school, moreover, may deprive others of an excuse for failing and find themselves accused of "acting white." Yet it is perhaps asking a good deal of such students to expect them to defer leisure, when the evidence of the past is scant that American society, by and large, will reward goal-seeking work on the part of minorities.

One classically capitalist enterprise in ghetto neighborhoods today does reward the deferral of leisure. Young blacks and Hispanics may succeed beautifully at the crack cocaine trade. They push their product, they are adept at making money, and they face danger as did Italian or Jewish gangsters of the 1920s. In another incarnation they would have been the white newsboys of an earlier time: smart, disciplined, sacrificing short-term pleasure for the sake of future rewards. But crack brings immediate pleasure to the customers, who see no gain in not going for it. So sellers and buyers both act in consonance with an ethos of hustle and self-grati-fication that also moves readers of *Fortune*. Meanwhile the market-economy media sparkle with plush advertisements and scenes of affluence that make a virtue of acquisition, and adolescent drug-sellers prove their devotion to the American dream.

From the New Left came an attack on the liberal welfare state that made conservative objections sound like quibbles. Especially in the angri-est days of Vietnam, many radicals were unwilling to believe any good of the government, or of the liberals who had brought the escalation of the war and now were divided between continued supporters and madden-ingly temperate opponents. The welfare state, as its enemies on the left saw it, was a form of pacification, imperialism at home at a time of impe-rialist venture in Southeast Asia. A welfare check, in effect, equates to economic aid for a Vietnamese village; a housing project, to a fortified hamlet; city police, to the marines.

Much of this was based on a special perception that the New Left had of the poor. Instructed particularly by black radicals, some New Leftists defined black Americans as a nationality entitled to separate control of its own destiny. That meant that the white United States, as an imperial power, in its bestowal of goods on its subject peoples could not be cred-ited with any good motives. At best it was surrendering, undoubtedly out of bad motives, a portion of what it had earlier stolen in the form of slave or peon labor. Along with this notion went one more concept of the cul-ture of poverty, which with some variation the New Left has shared with many other advocates of the cause of the poor. The poor, so the idea goes, are not degraded and broken by oppression: it has ennobled them, given them a hard, mature wisdom unavailable to the sheltered white middle classes.

To say that poverty was being romanticized here by Americans who could afford to romanticize it is to say the obvious, and yet not altogether justly. Surely many whites, in the days of Mississippi's Freedom Summer, had been rightly impressed by examples of courage in the presence of great danger that were foreign to their blanched suburban neighbor-hoods. And if their family background and college education had given the northern volunteers anything, it was a capacity for self-critical com-parison. Still, this like any other celebration of the poor raises the ques-tion, If oppression and poverty forge superior virtues, why eliminate pov-erty and oppression?

All this said, the left might have had much to contribute to the discussion of welfare. Liberals and conservatives could agree, though each rarely heard the other agreeing, that welfare is a demeaning, unhappy present necessity, the desired objective being to bring its temporary clients fully into the broader economy and society. What neither would do was confront the economic class structure in itself or the continuing existence of the ghetto. The relatively comfortable classes in this country, of course, are not going to accept the idea that their superiority of station is unjust. No politician with any sense of survival would suggest such a thing. But one luxury the left possesses in being at the margins rather than the center of American politics and culture is that of being free to speak straightforwardly: to say that redistribution is not mere compassion but simple equity. The left, then, might have attacked the very premises of the discussion of welfare, and without any sentimentality about the deathless nobility of the poor.

Neither the radical left nor proponents of the Great Society offered such a challenge. What, with all its faults, the Johnson administration did was respond to social evils with a large vision and, incidentally, provide some insurance against unrest in this country. Perhaps as the Vietnam War increasingly raided the public treasury, not much more could have been done than to experiment tentatively with various models of alleviating poverty. The poverty programs of Johnson and Kennedy did at least that; they amounted to a great deal in precedent. The budget for food stamps, for instance, rose from under a billion dollars in the sixties to around $30 billion by 1995. The War on Poverty was a failure, say conservatives: declared but never fought, bloated with bureaucracy, infested with special interests. But in the case of an indeterminate number of Americans who because of it had a ticket out of poverty, it was no failure.

The liberal attack on poverty constituted the most ambitious of the national Democratic party's domestic programs during the 1960s. It was a larger undertaking than the abolition of institutional racism, which for all its emotional force has been less embedded in American society than was, and remains, the maldistribution of wealth and power. That such maldistribution characterizes perhaps every nation in the world, and over much of the globe is far worse, makes even more notable the attempt of the Great Society to address it. The effort failed in practice; it also failed to win for Democratic liberalism the political hegemony that, from the time of the New Deal, has time and again been within or just beyond its grasp. The reason lies partly within the limits imposed by American political realities, and partly within the destruction that liberalism wrought upon itself.

The absence of any clear vision of an achievable and reasonably democratic future may turn out to be the major way in which the movements of the sixties differed from the New Deal. In the 1930s when a rough majority of the people were recognizable as the sufferers, politics could define the problem as broadly as the nation itself. The poor wished to cease being poor; the middle classes wanted relief from economic instability; Americans in general wanted the country to get back to work. The Social Security Act of 1935 defined the New Deal as a nation providing for itself. The political folk culture of the New Deal celebrated the land and the farms and cities its cooperative people had wrought upon it. Out of that time came programs and a spirit as close to economic and social democracy as the United States has ever attained. The Roosevelt years manifested one terrible sin of omission: the failure even to consider racism much less to confront it. But the victories of the civil rights movement could have been grafted onto the strong and enduring stock of New Deal programs. The fading of that movement before it attacked the problem of the northern ghettos, and the decision to treat the black community as separate, privileged, and in fact condescended to, severed liberalism from the heritage that had been its distinctive contribution and its greatest political strength.

 **The Liberals' War in Vietnam**

> The stupidest dumb thing we ever got into.
> *(Senator Barry Goldwater)*
>
> We were wrong, terribly wrong.
> *(Robert McNamara, 1995)*

THE CIVIL RIGHTS movement was the unfolding of an idea. So was the black power movement that followed it. And so were the liberal and then the white radical responses to the racial revolution. To relate the history of the civil rights movement is to describe ideas translated into historical events.

The conflict in Vietnam was also an unfolding of ideas. On the one side were the nationalism and communism that drove Hanoi and the South Vietnamese insurgents: on the other the principles, the commitments, and the hesitations that governed the American liberals who took the nation into Vietnam. But the leading American idea, the belief that communism must be stopped whenever and wherever it threatened to spread, itself gripped the mind of policymakers with the force not of a chosen conviction but of a deterministic force. And in Vietnam, events took over, made ideas their captive and vehicle, and in time rendered concepts irrelevant, until the peace forces in the United States came fully to articulate their own ideas in a diverse and widespread movement.

The American engagement in the Cold War, its terms set by the liberal administration of Harry S Truman, carried over into the years of Dwight D. Eisenhower, who was somewhere near the liberal pole of the Republican party. Those terms indicated, though they did not dictate, that the United States should as a matter of course defend South Vietnam with economic and military aid. But the fact of that aid, quite apart from the idea that inspired it, made it likely that Eisenhower's successor, John F. Kennedy, would continue to support South Vietnam. He did, and with a considerable further involvement, and that in turn led ultimately to a full-scale military commitment in the administration of Lyndon B. Johnson. Events, reflecting to be sure the mechanistic Cold War conviction that the United States must resist communism wherever it appeared, had taken on their own preordained momentum. And once the nation was fully engaged militarily in Vietnam, the war rendered obsolete the ideas that had given rise to it.

The story of the American entanglement in Indochina is a saga of liberal internationalism. The escalation of the fighting there was the product of nearly twenty years of the liberals' Cold War. It was at the same time abhorrent to the liberal strategy of wearing down communism through the slow and emotionally unfulfilling processes of international politics, economics, and diplomacy along with selective military confrontations—processes that in the 1980s, against the predictions of right-wingers, would prove themselves. Liberals went into Indochina on an understanding of communism as a brutal system to be resisted when resistance was feasible. Yet they stayed there, and increased their involvement, at a time when they knew that communism was not a monolith stretching from the Baltic Sea to the Pacific, from Siberia to Hanoi, but a diffuse doctrine strongly modified in practice by local conditions.

Liberal internationalism has been analogous in nature to liberalism at home. Liberals in this century have respected the technical and scientific virtues—their clarity, the opposition they pose to self-indulgence and wishful thinking—and see them as a model for thought and conduct. This colder component of liberalism has attended its warmer impulse, the active pursuit of the New Deal as a powerhouse of technocrats in search of humane public policy. So the Truman administration was acting in accord with liberalism in combining, with the Marshall Plan for the reconstruction of Western Europe, the finely executed Berlin airlift compounded of firmness and maneuver in the face of Soviet provocation.

While many conservatives immediately after the Second World War preferred isolation, liberals elected for steady encounters with communism. Their first decision was to confront the Soviet Union in Europe; then their defense of South Korea, under the sanction of the United Nations, marked their determination to face militant communism throughout the globe. A similar steadiness guided liberals when conservatives wanted something more emotionally gratifying. During the earlier years of the Cold War when liberals for reasons both benevolent and strategic called for large expenditures on foreign aid, the wish among conservatives was for a tight wallet. Liberalism, then, spoke for values so exactly balanced that it seemed perpetually in need of explanation.

Basic to an understanding of how and why a liberal administration moved the country to full engagement in Vietnam is the ingrained liberal habit of combining action and restraint that allowed neither retreat nor decisive engagement. To retreat would have meant abandoning the logic of the Cold War that had been at the very core of liberal internationalism, while to advance too quickly would have signified abandoning liberal prudence. Liberals had to temporize; and so—cautiously, reasonably, firmly—they temporized the nation right into the Vietnam War. Balance, restraint, nerves steady against either withdrawal or emotionally satisfying overreaction: these were the evident concerns animating the liberal mind in its disagreements with conservatism at home and its collisions with communism abroad. Yet in the end, the Cold War persuasion that was so much of liberal making led its adherents into a trap much like the ideological constriction that was the curse of communism itself.

Liberals, like conservatives, started from a reasonable assumption: that doctrinaire communists were aiming to banish alternate political and social schemes from every spot on the globe they could reach. The policy of containment for which the Democrat George Frost Kennan was an early spokesman intended to resist the expansionist impulses of Moscow's empire. At the same time, liberal cold warriors grew to know with some part of their minds that political and national conditions varied from region to region. This reality would in fact prevent Moscow or any other communist capital from maintaining control over local revolutions and achieving its one-world hegemony, no matter how much it wished to do so. Still, the larger aims attributed to Moscow and later to communist China so preoccupied cold warriors that they believed themselves committed to contain whatever looked like the enemy at every possible point of advance. This meant in practice that anticommunists felt obliged to press upon as much of the globe as possible their own one-world system. Liberals did want progressive regimes abroad, practicing forms of social democracy and instituting at least some redistribution of wealth. But a government or movement that appeared to cross the line between reformist and leftist might be perceived as dangerous. And so liberals as much as conservatives accepted repressive regimes in Portugal, the Dominican Republic, and elsewhere, eyes fixed on enemies to their left. In 1954, Washington, under the mildly liberal Republican presidency of Eisenhower, engineered the overthrow of a populist regime in Guatemala, and eleven years later Lyndon Johnson sent American troops to the Dominican Republic to keep the socialist leader Juan Bosch from governing.

The goals of liberal foreign policy dictated that diplomacy, politics, public opinion, and the opinion of leaders keep strictly within the terms of the Cold War. The imperatives of containing communism led the government secretly to fund private education and journalistic activities so that they would promulgate the right ideas. Containment led Americans to become hostile, sometimes actively so, to foreign nations that wished to stay aloof from the bipolar politics and alliances of the Cold War. The policy of containing communism, then, had the effect of containing freedom, including the intellectual freedom of the cold warriors themselves. They put blinders on themselves, refusing to confront the world in all its complexity and ambiguity. It was a mode of thinking that all but programmed our entry into Vietnam.

During the middle and late nineteenth century, the small country of Vietnam, along with Laos and Cambodia constituting Indochina, had fallen under French control. Some Vietnamese embraced and welcomed French rule and culture. Others resisted. The patriot Ho Chi Minh, living in Paris, was at once a cultural Francophile—he worked for a time in the French chef Escoffier's pastry kitchen—and, by the early 1920s, an opponent of French imperialism in Vietnam, finding communism an appropriate vehicle for Vietnamese national aspirations. By the early 1940s, operating from headquarters near the Cambodian border, Ho concentrated on expanding his Vietminh forces into a broad nationalist coalition. The immediate enemy was the occupying Japanese forces, who controlled a nominal French administration.

For a brief period at the end of the Second World War, Ho was at the head of a coalition that had some claim to be the government of all of Vietnam. Eager for American support, he paraphrased for his own manifesto of independence for his people some passages from the American Declaration of Independence. He suggested that Vietnam would be rich ground for American enterprise, and offered the United States a naval base at Camranh Bay. The American government, for its part, was hoping in those early days at the close of the war that the French would not return to Vietnam, or that if they did they would ultimately give the region genuine self-government. But Washington had no wish to antagonize France, no clear plan for preventing the reabsorption of Vietnam into the French empire, and perhaps no strong feelings either way. Before long the French did regain shaky control of Vietnam, in association with a puppet emperor operating under a facade of national independence. Ho's forces began a protracted struggle against the French. After the fall of China to the communists in 1949, President Truman, who regarded France as a main component of NATO, began heavily to subsidize a hopeless conventional war in the jungles of Vietnam. This, along with the Korean War that began in 1950, marked an important point in the passage of the Cold War from a defense of Western Europe to a confrontation throughout the globe with communism, and any movement perceived as allied to communism.

Toward the end of a decisive siege by Ho's followers, the Vietminh, of the remote French and anticommunist Vietnamese outpost of Dienbienphu in 1954, the chairman of the American joint chiefs of staff along with the French commander pleaded for a last-ditch American air strike in support of the outpost's defenders. But the Eisenhower administration refused. After Dienbienphu fell, an ongoing conference in Geneva temporarily divided Vietnam at the seventeenth parallel in preparation for internationally supervised elections, scheduled to take place in two years. Ho became head of the northern sector of the country. The United States did not sign the Geneva accords, but acknowledged its authority.

Secretary of State John Foster Dulles hurriedly supervised the creation of the Southeast Asia Treaty Organization (SEATO) with the intention of keeping as much of Indochina as possible within the anticommunist orbit. Since, however, neutral countries like India were unwilling to join and a binding mutual defense pact was lacking, SEATO counted for little. But the Eisenhower administration continued American support for the conflict by sending South Vietnam billions of dollars in aid, and it was instrumental in sabotaging the nationwide elections scheduled for 1956, which Ho Chi Minh would almost certainly have won. Ngo Dinh Diem, a conservative nationalist leader largely sponsored by the United States, kept power in South Vietnam. Dulles assumed in the case of Vietnam, as it was then customary to assume, that resisting the spread of communism had to be the prime consideration. China, Dulles believed, would not have fallen to the communists in 1949 if the United States had sufficiently supported Chiang Kai-shek's Nationalist forces.

This kind of thinking was part of the domino theory, which envisaged the fall to communism of one Asian country after another like a line of dominoes balanced on their edges unless the West propped up the first chip. Eisenhower and Dulles both publicly embraced this thinking, which made further thought unnecessary. And during the Red-baiting years, Asian specialists who might have steered the country away from the domino theory toward a more sophisticated policy—at least one assigning the dominoes unequal significance—were fired from the Department of State.

The man on whom the administration relied in South Vietnam was a rigid and uncompromising Roman Catholic in a largely Buddhist country. Ngo Dinh Diem had no broad base of popular support, and the actions that he took to consolidate his own power only alienated large sectors of the population. He ended centuries-old local control in the villages, placing in power men loyal to him. His administration opposed the redistribution of land. Newspapers critical of the regime were shut down, and unfriendly foreign journalists were expelled. Diem's government enforced its rule by imprisonment, torture, and killings. One of Saigon's schemes, to establish strategic hamlets in which the government would relocate peasants to insulate them from the insurgents, uprooted lives in the countryside and increased hostility to the regime. The indigenous South Vietnamese communists, who in time came under North Vietnamese direction, meanwhile roamed freely across much of the countryside. By the end of 1960 these insurgents had organized themselves as the National Liberation Front, soon acquiring the name Vietcong, for Vietnamese communists. South Vietnam had a wretched and unpopular regime, but unlike North Vietnam's, it tolerated at least a modicum of dissent. However grave the faults of Diem's rule, it made some sense to liberals at the time to support a state in which we might have a nurturing role: a government permitting some freedom offered hope that it could open itself to more.

During John Kennedy's presidency, events did not quite overtake ideas. The aid already extended to Diem created, in the logic of such matters, its own momentum for continuing to supply more aid. The Cold War argument for stopping communism wherever it threatened to expand, moreover, came naturally to Kennedy liberals. Kennedy was aware, however, of the dangers of creeping expansion. As early as November 15, 1961, in a National Security Council meeting, Kennedy was expressing doubts about military commitments to South Vietnam. According to his defense secretary, he thought the situation there "ambiguous," unlike that in Korea. But he was undeniably frightened by the specter of losing a battle to what many Americans saw as Asian communism and a virulent Red China; such an outcome could only strengthen the Republican right. His later comment on sending group after group of military advisers to South Vietnam could serve as a commentary on the whole logic of continuing American involvement there. It was, he said, "like taking a drink. The effect wears off, and you have to have another." Kennedy's moderation was observable in other foreign policy venues as well. He had enough sense of restraint not to send air reinforcement to the ill-planned exile invasion of Cuba at the Bay of Pigs in April 1961. Later he settled with Nikita Khrushchev for a neutral government in Laos rather than use force to back an anticommunist contender for power. Yet by the end of his presidency the militancy that was one component of liberal foreign policy had won out. In abeyance was the liberal feeling for contingency, limits, and the distinctiveness of each separate part of the world. Kennedy sent sixteen thousand American noncombatant advisers to aid Diem's military, and lent South Vietnam helicopters and artillery along with fighter planes and bombers. In what turned out to be a prelude to greater horrors later, planes in which Americans flew with South Vietnamese dropped herbicides and napalm. Kennedy himself had taken that drink he spoke of; he might have defined it as just a sip.

That the Cold War mentality would eventually predominate in Vietnam over the caution that often tempered it had for liberals a certain logic. The situation seemed designed for the kind of limited guerrilla combat that Kennedy, his secretary of defense Robert McNamara, and his chairman of the joint chiefs, General Maxwell Taylor, had been preparing for. What these liberals envisioned was a counterinsurgency operation conducted by elite American units sophisticated both in the intricacies of guerrilla warfare and in the needs of the peasantry. The strategic hamlets that Saigon used merely to isolate the peasants from the Vietcong Kennedy liberals envisaged as communities in which democratic reform would flourish. That concept they could not put into effect against the indifference of the South Vietnamese government. But the American presence, in effect, was supposed to bring the fusion of expert knowledge and democratic progressivism that had characterized domestic liberalism at least since the New Deal.

With new ordinance Diem managed to stave off collapse. Then, in June 1963, the yellow-robed Buddhist monk Thich Quang Duc burned himself to death in downtown Saigon—the first of several self-immolations in Vietnam and the United States. Diem's ultra-Catholic sister-in-law, Madame Nhu, said she had "clapped gaily" at the Buddhist "barbecues," and offered to supply gasoline and matches for more. When on a subsequent visit to the United States she appeared at Fordham and Georgetown Universities, she received heavy applause. The anticommunism of the Roman Catholic church had a largely unexamined role in bringing the United States into the Vietnam War. As true believers themselves, as Paul Conkin has written, "and thus as totalitarian as any version of Marxism, [Catholics] posed their truth against alien error."

With the greatest irony, of course, such prominent Catholic lay figures as Robert Kennedy and Eugene McCarthy, not to mention the Berrigan brother priests, became leaders of the antiwar movement.

In the United States, critics of involvement began to emerge. Among them were the liberal senators Mike Mansfield from Montana, a former professor of Far Eastern history, and Frank Church of Idaho. Together they sponsored with thirty-two colleagues a resolution arguing that American aid to Diem was unconscionable. The resolution did not pass the Senate, but it served to increase concern about the course of events in South Vietnam. When Diem stepped up his repressive campaign against the Buddhists, leading members of the Kennedy administration decided that the South Vietnamese leader was dividing the country and would injure the war effort. Washington hinted that a coup would be acceptable. The military overthrew Diem, who along with his politically powerful brother Ngo Dinh Nhu was assassinated, to the consternation of the Kennedys.

In 1964 Republicans, in the presidential candidacy of Barry Goldwater, espoused a simplistic conservatism. Referring to the fighting in Vietnam, Goldwater himself openly speculated about whether atomic weaponry might yield a quick victory. During the campaign, Richard Nixon called for an air war against North Vietnam and parts of Laos under communist control. That Goldwater declined in popularity as he championed increased American military involvement in Vietnam should have made a point to Johnson. But the President, accustomed to serious

right-wing challengers in Texas, chose to believe the competing inter-
pretation that if he escalated the war he would preempt his opponent. In
July the administration sent five thousand more military personnel to
Vietnam.

On August 2 and 3, American forces operating in the Gulf of Tonkin
off the coast of North Vietnam engaged in skirmishes with communist
vessels insignificant in size; the exact nature of the clashes has remained
unclear to this day. On August 4, during a campaign in which the Republicans were portraying Johnson as insufficiently belligerent, the President
announced that the United States was retaliating. American air strikes are
estimated to have damaged or destroyed several North Vietnamese sea-
craft and an oil storage site. Johnson was eager to get a congressional
mandate that would permit him to take whatever action events might
suggest. He got his mandate. The Senate by a vote of eighty-eight to two,
and the House without a dissent, gave Johnson authority to take action
he deemed fit in Vietnam. The Tonkin Gulf Resolution thereby established the complicity of both liberals and conservatives in advancing the
war. One of the two dissenters, Senator Wayne Morse of Oregon, warned
that the resolution would prove a "historic mistake."

Two weeks before election day, Johnson seemed to pull back, saying,
"We are not about to send American boys nine or ten thousand miles
away from home to do what Asian boys ought to be doing for themselves." The remark recalls his hero Franklin Roosevelt's promise during
the 1940 presidential campaign not to send American sons to foreign
wars. LBJ's most famous television commercial of the campaign showed
a little girl plucking the petals of a daisy against the backdrop of a nuclear
countdown. The implication was that Goldwater's rashness could trigger
a nuclear war. The Tonkin Gulf Resolution and this commercial define
the conflicting criteria for which foreign-policy liberalism spoke. The war
was about to rip it apart.

Following his triumphal election in November 1964, Johnson plunged
into Vietnam. In a quantum leap of hostilities in response to the near
collapse of South Vietnam, he began systematic bombing of North Vietnam in February 1965—a policy of "sustained reprisal" called Rolling
Thunder—and that July dispatched fifty thousand more American
troops. Vietnam was now fully an American war. The President, perhaps
wishing not to let matters fall into the hands of still more hawkish officials, insisted that he would keep tight control: "They can't even bomb an
outhouse without my approval," he is said to have claimed. The *New
York Times* and the liberal establishment in general quickly fell in behind
the President, submerging doubts expressed previously. Labor unions,
always staunch partisans of the Cold War, gave strong support.

The United States had cast its lot with South Vietnam's raffish putative leader Nguyen Cao Ky, customarily attired in air force suit and purple scarf, carrying an ivory-handled pistol on his hip. "People ask me who my heroes are," Ky observed. "I have only one hero—Hitler. . . . We need four or five Hitlers in Vietnam." By early 1966 the United States had two hundred thousand troops to which the Cold War and the accumulation of involvements in Vietnam had committed it.

Costing $20 million daily, the bombing of North Vietnam failed to stem the infiltration of troops or supplies from the North. South Vietnam's own armed forces were largely ineffectual. Soon the United States had spent enough to pave South Vietnam with concrete.

Johnson's war policies enjoyed the support of a cadre of liberals whose collective progressive political credentials and years of service at progressive academic institutions were impressive. Secretary of State Dean Rusk had joined the NAACP. The National Security adviser McGeorge Bundy had been dean of the Harvard Faculty of Arts and Sciences; the tenacious White House hawk Walt Rostow, a professor of economics at the Massachusetts Institute of Technology. Robert McNamara, when an instructor at the Harvard Business School, had been one of two faculty members to favor Franklin Roosevelt for reelection in 1940. The very sparkle of their achievements, their intimacy with the world of intellect, inspired a misplaced confidence in academic and statistical ways of understanding problems. "North Vietnam will never beat us," McNamara observed. "They can't even make ice cubes."

It was second nature among these liberals to assume that the struggle in Vietnam was simply one part of the global confrontation with communism. Liberals were also trapped within their own belief in expertise. In that confrontation the technical and military experts would surely find a way to reshape South Vietnam and defeat the communists. Together, morality and the cold calculations of technocracy were supposed to guide the enterprise. If the United States did not protect South Vietnam, Rusk explained, "our guarantees with regard to Berlin would lose their credibility." More specifically Washington believed that China was the communist power for which the Vietnamese communists were surrogates. As William Bundy, the assistant secretary of state for Far Eastern affairs, claimed, "It takes no vivid imagination to visualize what Peking would do in Malaysia, Singapore, and Burma if Hanoi were to succeed in Vietnam." Rusk in March 1966 observed that the war aim was to ensure that a Maoist China some day would move toward peaceful coexistence with the West: a liberal twist there—right-wingers could not abide the very thought of peaceful coexistence with a communist nation. Adlai Stevenson, the ambassador to the United Nations, could sound like the most convulsed Cold War liberal of all: an "arrogant, aggressive, resourceful and resolute" China might lead the forces of world revolution.

The war to prevent China from dominating Asia was meanwhile taking its own course, which made a mockery of liberal rationales for the conflict. Whatever the moral shortcomings of the communists, and they were large, they were nearly buried from sight beneath the flare and pounding of American bombs. Air Force B-52s dropped on suspect villages cluster bombs designed to kill or maim everyone within range. White phosphorus and inextinguishable napalm—jellied gasoline, or Dow Chemical's infamous "Incinderjell," in the consumer-minded jargon of the Pentagon—fastened to human skin and seared the body (an unrepentant Dow in a later time would furnish chemical weapons to Iraq). American planes sprayed thousands of acres of the Vietnamese countryside with poisonous defoliants to make it easier to observe guerrillas, with the result that many farmers were forced off their now polluted land into urban slums. In each mission transport planes carried half-ton loads of the defoliants to annihilate two to three hundred acres of rice or jungle; the quantity of timber destroyed would have been enough to supply the country's need until the end of the century. Another kind of American plane carried electronically operated rapid-fire machine guns that pumped three thousand bullets a minute into the ground, pinpointing their targets—supposedly Vietcong cooking fires but actually anybody's—by infrared photography. Lighter aircraft sighted Vietnamese in fields or on roads and swooped down to kill them as suspicious people moving outside of "pacified" villages. A technocratic war was wrecking Vietnam, pock-marking much of the pristine jungle with craters and burned-out patches. It was also wrecking American credibility worldwide and sending peasants in substantial numbers over to the Vietcong. Meanwhile, the massive American support of South Vietnam was keeping that country dependent on the United States while the war made sense only insofar as Saigon's regime could become independent and self-sustaining.

Nor was the bombing of the North especially effective on its own terms. North Vietnam was able to disperse its people and resources, relocate its infiltration routes into the South, and build up a system of defenses against air attack. If railroads and highways were attacked, people could resort to bicycles and feet. And the bombing, which was supposed to break the morale of the North Vietnamese, actually strengthened it.

Much of the world focused on the pointless devastation wrought by American technology. But while bombings visibly dominated the fighting, Americans and Saigon's troops needed cold nerves for day-to-day ground operations, made especially difficult by the knowledge that on patrol the very earth beneath their feet was the enemy, hiding booby traps that with any step might bring maiming or death. And if American bombs killed civilians in dreadful numbers, the Vietnamese communists did their best with the technology at their disposal, murdering a quarter million South Vietnamese, including mayors, teachers, and health workers.

The air raids and much of the war's lethal work were carried out in full view of news reporters and television cameras, for there was no organized censorship, and the American authorities lacked the will to mobilize public sentiment and suppress dissent. In World War I the Wilson administration, ancestral as it was to later foreign-policy liberalism, had mounted a massive campaign of propaganda and repression; but this was one policy that liberals did not turn into a legacy.

In 1967 the administration brought General William Westmoreland back from South Vietnam to rally the home front; but efforts of that kind were almost innocent in their modesty and ineffectuality. Not until late in Lyndon Johnson's presidency did the administration take significant action against antiwar groups. It was the Central Intelligence Agency that first kept extensive files on them, and subsequently Johnson assigned a thousand FBI agents to monitor the left. If an upsurge of repressive superpatriotism threatened, it was not from the liberal managers of the war, who might more likely be its targets. The "right wing of the Republican party," Daniel Ellsberg has observed, had "tattooed on the skins of politicians and bureaucrats alike some vivid impressions of what could happen to a liberal administration that chanced to be in office the day a red flag rose over Saigon."

The government's hesitancy about orchestrating public passions and suppressing dissent owed something to a general liberal distaste for such acts. During the Vietnam period the memory of the fifties, when leftists and even liberals had been Red-baited, was still sharp. Administration supporters, moreover, lacked any clear and convincing theme to mobilize public sentiment. They employed the rhetoric of the Cold War. But that language—fresh in earlier days when the focus had been on the Soviet Union itself, or on East Germany, or on the role of China in Korea and when the confrontation had demanded the steady deployment of a nation's will—did not offer a satisfactory vocabulary for the Vietnam War. By now that vocabulary was hollow, self-conscious, and repetitive.

Freedom of the press, and relatively open access to the war zones, made information about the conflict widely accessible to the public. In January 1967 the New Left magazine *Ramparts* published color photographs of Vietnamese children maimed and scarred by napalm. That same year Jonathan Schell wrote in the *New Yorker* about the pacification of the village of Ben Suc, where policy had forced evacuation and the razing of what was left behind. By 1968 some seven hundred correspondents were reporting on the war, and many were finding plenty of stories unfavorable to the United States. Journalists enjoyed easy access to hospitals to look for napalm victims. During the Republican presidency of Richard Nixon, the American massacre of villagers at My Lai in March 1968 was to become public knowledge.

The war as the press reported it had a major effect on public sensibilities. Yet even while the consciences of many Americans must have smarted from the barrage of information, the war in its very brutality also spoke to the underside of human nature. Exaggerated enemy body counts were reported on the evening news like sports scores. Press coverage unfortunately declined in the later years of the war, the period when Laos and Cambodia became involved in a major way, bombing operations increased, and three million people were refugees.

In the last analysis, public opinion was influenced most deeply by American war casualties. But the defining event for the antiwar cause was the Tet offensive of 1968.

Beginning in late January during the Vietnamese New Year's celebration, some seventy thousand Vietcong assaulted over a hundred southern cities and towns. A tiny squad of Vietcong even temporarily took over part of the United States embassy compound in Saigon, and many cities, notably Hue in the north, came under enemy control for days. Communists in Hue slaughtered some three thousand civilians. Communist forces also continued their siege of an outpost at Khesanh manned by American marines and South Vietnamese, an effort begun before Tet and perhaps intended to draw attention and resources away from the regions where communists were about to launch their major attack. Khesanh held, and the communists, who sustained great casualties from American firepower, finally withdrew. Then, in June, the Americans themselves abandoned the post that they had earlier described as vital. The whole event remains a commentary on the stubborn obtuseness of the military mind as the leadership of both sides embodied it. The mindless butchery on the battlefields of World War I had taught the world nothing.

What made the Tet offensive particularly devastating to American public opinion was that it followed closely on a series of optimistic reports of progress in the war. For months the Pentagon, the State Department, and the White House had been claiming that the position of Saigon and the United States in Vietnam was improving and that an end to the war was in sight. Tet thereby weakened the credibility of Johnson's administration and ripped at what remained of Johnson's coalition.

After Tet, more businessmen and conservative isolationist Republicans joined radicals, liberals, and young people in opposing the war, and frank opposition became respectable and widespread on major news programs. "We are mired in stalemate and must negotiate," observed the avuncular CBS Evening News anchor Walter Cronkite on February 27 after returning from a trip to Vietnam. Cronkite here followed the journalistic injunction to keep it simple. Though he did describe the Tet battles as an American military victory, he and his colleagues embedded Tet in the public mind as an American setback, and did so, moreover, at the beginning of a presidential election year. *Life*, *Time*, and *Newsweek*, and even the conservative *Wall Street Journal*, called for a change of course in Vietnam.

In reality, during Tet the communists sustained enormous losses and a tactical defeat. General Giap had anticipated a propaganda victory in the United States and got it, but his hopes for a popular uprising in South Vietnam's cities went unrealized. The American public never came fully to recognize the strategic failure of the Tet offensive, and for good reason: the result was at least impressive enough to give the lie to the administration's optimism, to shatter its indulgent hope of an early successful conclusion to the war. While Tet might technically be called a turning point in the war, at least two or three more years of steady fighting would have been necessary for American success.

For Americans who cared only for American casualties and American success, then, Tet proved decisive. But long before Tet, major opposition to the war had grown within a portion of the public disturbed about the fate of both Americans and Vietnamese, about what the war was doing to Vietnamese society, and about the underlying reasons for its being fought. At the center of this antipathy to the liberals' war were the liberal college campuses.

Some evidence indicates that it was outside rather than within the nation's universities that the main opposition to the war was to be found. The working class, often thought to be possessed by mindless patriotism, was disproportionately drafted. Blue-collar families had reason to dislike a war in which their sons were less likely than sons of the affluent to have the protection of student deferments. That inequity, opposed especially by liberal Democratic senator Edward Kennedy of Massachusetts, was to remain until the Nixon administration, when legislation abolished student deferments and installed a system of draft by lottery.

Yet all along college students had been the chief antiwar activists. The relative confidence among the well-to-do and the educated that the world is changeable and improvable convinced college youth that an evil war could be stopped. With the perspicacity to recognize the immorality of the conflict and a willingness to endure police harassment and in many cases the horror of parents and the outrage of friends, antiwar students picketed military recruiters, organized demonstrations, and in a few instances gave up American citizenship until pardoned by President Jimmy Carter in 1977. Other students protested as a lark: it was all much more interesting than spring final examinations. Unimpressed with what activists had accomplished incrementally in weakening popular support for the war, some opponents ended up as enraged revolutionaries—the Bernardine Dohrns and the Kathy Boudins who in the Weather Underground and other tiny radical groups resorted to imitative terrorism.

Most students who took to the streets probably did not have to worry about being drafted. Perhaps a majority were not subject to conscription: women, men exempt for physical or other reasons, students who for some time after the buildup of 1965 enjoyed deferments that they could continue from year to year, a scattering who were above draft age or perhaps had already done their peacetime military service, and, of course, antiwar Vietnam veterans. Besides, students governed by a dread of conscription might be reluctant to engage in activities that could draw the attention of their local selective service boards. Some registrants publicly and illegally burned their draft cards. Others sent them back to the selective service system, an action that, far from freeing the young rebel from the draft, invited conscription, along with criminal prosecution when he refused induction.

Opponents of the Vietnam war could trace back to religious pacifists of colonial times an American antiwar tradition. In 1917, at the time of United States entry into World War I, socially activist Quakers formed the American Friends Service Committee. That war was an event of such meaninglessly dedicated destruction as to spawn a revulsion against the organized lunacy of war itself. After the end of World War II internationalists organized the United World Federalists, urging global law and a worldwide peace. Part of the same antiwar mode was the Committee for a Sane Nuclear Policy (SANE), organized during the 1950s in face of the threat of nuclear war. SANE was a moderate liberal critic of the liberal establishment's failure adequately to safeguard against that nightmare.

An entirely different strain of antiwar thinking was both incipient and manifest among the Beats. Jack Kerouac was to defend the war in Vietnam. But within the Beat subculture grew a perception of the larger nation as an organized, repressive, and lethal madness, and against it the liberating essence of poetry, jazz, and the road. That way of thinking prepared the way for the later countercultural repudiation of the war. And in Allen Ginsberg, alienation and politics came together as they had among other Beats who were active in the 1950s and early sixties. The movement against the war in Vietnam would bring further into the mainstream the celebration of mad sanity.

The more immediate predecessor to the resistance to the war was, of course, the civil rights movement. At the 1964 memorial service for Michael Schwerner, James Chaney, and Andrew Goodman in Philadelphia, Mississippi, one speaker explicitly compared the use of force against Asians to the violence against blacks in the South. When Secretary of

Defense McNamara visited Mississippi and called the state's racist but prowar senator John Stennis a man "of very genuine greatness," rights workers immediately picketed him. By the mid-sixties the rights movement was stymied by the economic realities of the black urban ghetto. As the search for racial justice at home became more tangled, the killing in Vietnam began to press its immediate claim for redress. And the early civil rights movement offered, for those opponents of the war who had the self-discipline for it, an appropriate tactic: nonviolent civil disobedience. Nonviolence was a symbolic opposite to war as well as to the violence of segregation, and a means of witness against the conventional wisdom about the inevitability of force and retaliation. Such principled disobedience made a statement about all the behavior that amounted to passive complicity in racism and war.

Prominent in the nonviolent wing of resistance to the war were the religious groups that civil rights actions had awakened to the political uses of protest. Clergy and Laity Concerned was an antiwar organization that lasted beyond the Vietnam days, engaging in other peace and justice issues. The Berrigan brothers, Daniel and Philip, both Catholic priests, along with others whose opposition to war was founded in religion, became in word and deed eloquent practitioners of civil disobedience against the Vietnam conflict. On May 17, 1968, they and seven companions raided a selective service office in Catonsville, Maryland, burning draft records in the files. The preceding October 27, Philip with three other resisters had poured animal blood on draft records in Baltimore. Other acts of resistance against selective service offices would take place. In subsequent years Daniel Berrigan has made a point of condemning violence on the part of the revolutionary left, from that of Latin American radicals to the totalitarianism of victorious Hanoi. Other activists, among them the folksinger Joan Baez, have similarly adhered to a spirituality that does not confuse repression with liberation.

In nonviolent civil disobedience, as in campus radicalism and in the Beat subculture, Cold War liberals were confronted with ideas not far distant from a part of the liberal mind. While militant in action against communism, liberals remained suspicious of the verbal militancy of the right. Their preference was for a dry rhetoric of purpose and reason and strategy, a political equivalent to the vocabulary of the science and technology in which liberals put their trust. That was not the language of nonviolence that the Berrigans spoke. But the renunciation of the satisfactions of violence had enough in common with the liberal temper to suggest that here as in so much else, the history of the 1960s is the history of the breaking apart of the liberal mentality. Liberals had customarily defended the right of principled dissent, even when they did not approve the cause. Now that dissent had turned against the liberals' war.

Visible opposition to the war had begun almost immediately after Johnson's escalation of it in early 1965. At an antiwar teach-in on March 24 at the University of Michigan, the school of some of the founders of Students for a Democratic Society, students and faculty gathered to hear arguments against the war and to deepen their sense of belonging to a community in opposition. The administration's spokesman McGeorge Bundy, occupied with foreign policy business, canceled his appearance, but another defender of the war stood in for him. Other teach-ins followed quickly afterward at Columbia and the University of Wisconsin and, with twenty thousand participants in a thirty-six-hour marathon, at Berkeley in May. There Robert Parris Moses, in one of his last public appearances before retreating to Tanzania, argued that the war was the policy of an unrepresentative bureaucratic elite. That same month in the nation's capital a teach-in drew an audience of five thousand from around the country, with some defenders of the government's position allowed to present their case. The teach-ins gave the antiwar movement forward thrust and expertise. The quickness with which the tactic spread across the country reflected the presence of a growing public culture evoked by modern media.

In April 1965, an antiwar demonstration of about twenty-five thousand people took place in Washington, D.C., under the sponsorship of SDS. In a departure from tradition, SDS had invited all interested groups to participate, not excluding communists. Some leftists of the old anticommunist persuasion, including Irving Howe and the young Michael Harrington, found it contradictory to include the supporters of a totalitarian ideology. Both by inviting communists and by rejecting the idea of a monolithic communist enemy, SDS was going against the basic rationale of the war.

Now television was carrying images of massed protesters, and the Johnson administration began to respond to them. In that same month of April 1965 the President announced at Johns Hopkins that he was willing to talk with anyone about ending the war, and was prepared to inaugurate for the development of the Mekong River valley a $1 billion program like that of the Tennessee Valley Authority.

Also that spring, the White House Festival of the Arts became the scene of a war protest inspired by the poet Robert Lowell, who had returned a ringingly negative response to the invitation. Others did attend but used the occasion to lambaste the President, sign petitions, read from descriptions of wartime devastation, and otherwise violate liberal ideas, including Johnson's, of what constituted good manners.

In August, marking the twentieth anniversary of the dropping of atomic bombs on Japan, peace groups once again demonstrated in Washington; some 350 protesters were arrested. Thousands marched in demonstrations on the West Coast. In the East, draft card burnings took place despite a law recently passed making the act a crime punishable by five years in jail. Three opponents of the war burned themselves to death, one on the steps of the Pentagon, another at the United Nations, another in Detroit. On a cold, windy day in late November some thirty thousand marchers surrounded the White House: a smaller number of supporters of the war had turned out in New York City on October 30. The Bread and Puppet Theater staged a Christmas week pageant against the war featuring a napalmed, bloody Jesus doll.

During 1966 war protests proliferated. The range of opposition was widening. In major magazine articles two prominent retired generals, James M. Gavin and Matthew Ridgway, expressing concern about the overtaxing of the military, endorsed a policy of establishing protected enclaves within South Vietnam. George Kennan, an early architect of the Cold War, told the Senate Foreign Relations Committee that to imagine an aggressive China was to misread history. In the Senate, J. William Fulbright made his Foreign Relations Committee a platform for antiwar opinions. George McGovern became outspoken in opposition. Eugene McCarthy began to voice his detached, ironic skepticism. Robert Kennedy for a time even proposed negotiations directly with the Vietcong. That fall a number of peace candidates ran for office. It was not a good autumn for administration loyalists. Antagonism toward Democratic domestic policy accounted for a gain in 1966 of forty-seven House seats by the Republicans, a greater increase than is usual in midterm elections for a party out of power.

Johnson's modest attempts at what in another time and administration might have been political repression (he denounced "nervous Nellies") had little effect: the heart and conscience of the administration were not in it. Prowar zealotry did bring the bombing of the communist W.E.B. Du Bois Clubs in San Francisco and Berkeley. As photographers recorded the scene for the evening news, high school toughs in Boston beat up young antiwar demonstrators while police looked on. But such incidents suggested emotions far to the right of prowar liberalism. The left largely avoided violence, but SDS members accosted Robert McNamara in Harvard Square, rocking his car until he got out and answered some questions. Some Harvard professors compared this incident to street fascism in Europe; others saw it as merely an impolite means of conveying a message the administration was not interested in considering.

In a speech at Riverside Church in Manhattan on April 4, 1967, Martin Luther King explained why the cause of civil rights was inextricably bound up with opposition to the war. New groups joined the opposition. The National Coordinating Committee to End the War in Vietnam worked on the formidable task of uniting radicals. Every public discovery of misdoing fueled antiwar sentiment. The disclosure by *Ramparts* in 1967 that the CIA had provided funds to the National Student Organization to influence its actions was the first of a number of such revelations. The American Friends Service Committee, the National Council of Churches, the anticommunist magazine *Encounter*—all, in fact, had received disguised government subsidies in the interest of fostering a national Cold War groupthink.

On April 15, 1967, war opponents marched again throughout the country, this time organized by the Mobilization to End the War in Vietnam, or the Mobe. In Sheep Meadow in Manhattan's Central Park, between one and two hundred thousand gathered in wind and rain to protest the war. Martin Luther King marched side by side with Stokely Carmichael from the park toward the United Nations. Steel construction rods were dropped on paraders from a partially finished building along Park Avenue; high-rise apartment windows opened, and eggs and shouts of derision plummeted from the sky. At the United Nations, King urged college students—a thousand had come in buses from Cornell University alone—to spend a Freedom Summer working against the war. In San Francisco, marchers overflowed from the sixty-five thousand seats in Kezar Stadium into Golden Gate Park. The count in other major cities made this easily the largest demonstration of its kind in American history.

Dean Rusk responded: "I am concerned . . . that the authorities in Hanoi may misunderstand this sort of thing." American troops, General William Westmoreland observed, "are dismayed, and so am I, by recent unpatriotic acts here at home. Regrettably, I see signs of success in that world arena which [the enemy] cannot match on the battlefield. He does not understand that American democracy is founded on debate, and he sees every protest as evidence of crumbling morale and diminishing resolve." A "Loyalty Day Parade" two weeks after Sheep Meadow drew only seventy-five hundred participants. On May 13, twenty thousand union members marched in opposition to the war.

The Pentagon would levitate some three hundred feet in the air, take on an orange glow, and vibrate, ridding itself of the demon of war: that is what Jerry Rubin promised for Washington, D.C., on the weekend of October 21. He got it wrong. Despite the exorcism performed by the Diggers and the rock group the Fugs—"Out, demon, out!"—the demon would continue to possess the Pentagon. But the levitational chanting of the more festive fringe of the antiwar movement combined with the earnest protests of the marchers, some hundred thousand in all. Thirty-five thousand crossed the Arlington Memorial Bridge to enter the north parking lot of the Pentagon. Most returned to the city, but for about thirty-two hours a few thousand occupied the plaza and steps of the Pentagon itself. Three thousand soldiers and marshals were on duty: for the first time since the Bonus Army march of 1932 a military force had been called up to guard the capital area. Some beat senseless numbers of plaza demonstrators, including women. Many resisted, taunting or spitting at soldiers, who replied with tear gas; other demonstrators put flowers in the barrels of the soldiers' weapons. After midnight on Sunday the remaining demonstrators on the steps of the Pentagon were arrested: a total of 647 went to jail. On NBC news, David Brinkley, a self-described snob in those days, called the march "a coarse, vulgar episode by people who seemed more interested in exhibitionistic displays than [in] any redress of grievances." Lady Bird Johnson complained of the refuse left by the militants. If it is true that the press, as right-wingers believe, has been liberal, liberalism more than once revealed in news reports its genteel disapproval of uncombed emotions.

One form of war resistance was to burn draft cards or return them to the selective service system. On October 15, 1965, David Miller became the first to burn his after Congress made it a federal crime. He was sentenced to thirty months in prison. On April 15, 1967, defiance of the draft received special public visibility. In Sheep Meadow, between 150 and 200 cards were burned. The Resistance, a movement directed against the draft whose chief organizers were David Harris and some fellow students at Stanford, instigated a week of antidraft actions in October of that year; it took place in several cities. Young men turned their cards over to the selective service system, prepared to accept the legal consequences. At a service held in Boston's Arlington Street Unitarian Church, over two hundred handed in their cards while more than fifty burned them at a candle. One especially prominent draft resister was the boxer Muhammad Ali (formerly Cassius Clay), now a Black Muslim, who was stripped of his heavyweight championship and sentenced to five years in jail for refusing induction. Because of his pacifist religious beliefs, courts overturned his conviction and he was not made to serve his sentence. Rejection of the draft added to a popular perception of antiwar activists as unpatriotic, and the Daughters of the American Revolution denied to the protest singer Joan Baez the use of their Constitution Hall in Washington.

Groups such as Vietnam Summer, the Resistance, and Negotiations Now! lent diversity and strength to the antiwar movement. A Beverly Hills group called Another Mother for Peace sent the White House a message in a child's script, "for peddie saecks give peace talks." By late 1967, antiwar sentiment had invaded the administration itself. A number of leading officials left the White House: George Ball, Bill Moyers, and even Secretary of Defense McNamara, whose loss of faith in the war deeply disturbed the President. In 1995 McNamara would release his memoirs. This book is an honest testimony to his conflicted feelings during his participation in a conflict that even while he believed in it increasingly horrified him in its futility of carnage. The passions, sympathetic or angry, with which commentators received his tortured reflections speak of the continuing hold of Vietnam on the American conscience. In the case of the *New York Times*, which delivered a particularly blistering attack on McNamara, the question might better be that of why it for so long invoked notions of Vietnam as a vital national interest.

By 1968 important new elements were joining the ranks of the disillusioned. Business, much of it having assumed a partial and tentative membership in the liberal coalition, began to fear the inflation caused by the war. An antiwar group composed of Wall Street business executives, including Marriner Eccles, chair of the Federal Reserve Board under Presidents Roosevelt and Truman, took out an ad in the *New York Times* opposing the war on grounds it termed practical.

One antiwar activist, Sheila Ryan, attacked Eccles for owning mining operations that might conceivably benefit from the war's end: evidently since he was not openly on the side of Hanoi and the National Liberation Front he had to be on Johnson's. Ms. Ryan and some other members of the New Left had come to believe that only mass violence by urban guerrillas would end the evil sway of United States imperialism. Appearing to dislike Eccles and such liberals as Arthur Schlesinger more ardently than they did Johnson, they took as their hero the Argentine-Cuban revolutionary Ernesto "Che" Guevara.

On Labor Day weekend, 1967, the New Politics Conference met in Chicago to plan election tactics for the next year. Left-liberal in its origins, the convention wanted "ordinary people" to take part in politics: housewives would make foreign policy, blacks choose sheriffs. Vietnamese would decide their own destiny. To that extent, the New Politics Convention appeared to advocate nothing more than the perfecting of democratic institutions. But there was much more. A caucus of two or three hundred blacks out of about two thousand delegates demanded and got approval, without debate or qualification, of a list of statements to which whites were supposed to submit out of faith, or guilt, or revolutionary solidarity; seeking their reasoned assent was beside the point. White delegates agreed to give the black caucus half of the convention's votes. The reporter June Greenlief would remember "whites masquerading as either poor or black, blacks . . . as arrogant whites, conservatives pretending to be communists . . . , and liberals pretending not to be there at all." Still, for all the silliness of such portions of American dissent, they did reveal a recognition that Vietnam was a war and a perception that liberals, if they got out of it, would take forever doing so.

The year 1968 was the time when it became absolutely clear, if it had not been so already, that the war was now dictating its own terms, making irrelevant the will of the administration that only three years before had attempted to impose that will on Vietnam. On the battlefield, Tet ambushed the American government and military. Within American society, forces unleashed by the civil rights and other social movements but intensified by opposition to the war were discarding conventions of behavior that Americans had taken as permanently given. And Vietnam was tearing up the political consensus in foreign policy and domestic reform that had given power to the liberals for more than a generation.

During a hearing of the Senate Foreign Relations Committee in August of the previous year, Minnesota's fifty-one-year-old Senator Eugene McCarthy, six feet tall, handsome, gray-haired, not easily ruffled, had lost his composure. Testifying before the Committee, Attorney General Nicholas Katzenbach was discussing the issue of presidential power in foreign affairs. "Things happen too fast now," he said, "for a President to be able to consult the Senate before starting a war." McCarthy angrily objected that such extension of presidential authority left the Senate, along with the rest of the American people, with no tangible role in foreign relations.

A good Roman Catholic, of German and Irish background, McCarthy had been so serious about his religion as once to take monastic vows. He had debated Senator Joe McCarthy in 1952. His speech in support of Adlai Stevenson at the Democratic Convention of 1960 was famous: "Do not reject this man who made us proud to be called Democrats." His proposal in 1965 of an investigation of the CIA put him among the earliest of liberals to question the conduct of the Cold War. He had chiseled unsparingly at Dean Rusk's warnings about a billion Chinese armed with nuclear weapons, dismissing them as the "ancient fear of the yellow peril." Though not politically effective in conventional terms, McCarthy lent the antiwar movement a badly needed dignity and reserve: "I am prepared to be your candidate." It was the liberal inclination toward self-containment that prevailed in him as against liberalism's more activist impulses, and so his anger during the Senate hearing was all the more forceful an indicator of his growing conflict with the administration.

In 1968, long before New Hampshire's snow and frozen ground gave way to spring, McCarthy ran in its March 12 Democratic primary against Lyndon Johnson. The President's name was not officially on the ballot, but a write-in campaign and a set of Johnson electors made him a real candidate. A corps of enthusiastic college students, some two thousand traveling from Eastern schools to New Hampshire every weekend, carried the McCarthy message throughout the Granite State as long underwear flapped frozen on the wash lines. The students' presence signified the distinction between the Johnson and the McCarthy strain of liberalism. Aware that the least appearance of New Leftist scruffiness among them could injure the cause, they were careful to be well-groomed: men with long hair stayed in the organizing offices. The young political army canvassed every single New Hampshire Democrat three times. The state's Democratic governor and senator supported the President with television appeals to hardcore patriotic sentiment. "A vote for McCarthy is a vote for Hanoi," the governor proclaimed, and he warned that the communists were watching the primary. But even hawkish Democrats liked McCarthy, who probably meant for them as for opponents of the war an unfavorable judgment of the conflict's progress. On March 12, McCarthy won more electors than Johnson and 42 percent of the popular vote, not far behind the president's write-in total of 49 percent. The gap between the two candidates narrowed to 230 votes when the write-in ballots were counted. That an incumbent President could do no better than that in his party's first primary was a disaster for Johnson.

The day after McCarthy's victory, Robert Kennedy told reporters he was reassessing the situation, and just three days later, he announced that he too would oppose the President in coming primaries. The announcement may suggest in part a crude opportunism on Kennedy's part, but he had been seriously considering a candidacy for some weeks. Whatever may have been his secret wishes, it is reasonable to suppose that he believed that McCarthy could not galvanize the nation's minorities, that the Minnesota senator had little charisma except among intellectuals, liberal suburbanites, and the upper middle class. To the thinking of the journalist I. F. Stone, McCarthy's weakness lay precisely in his "wit, charm and grace. . . . He seems to lack heart and guts." Robert Kennedy meanwhile was projecting a grander campaign and national future. "At stake," he said in his announcement speech, "is not simply the leadership of our party, and even our own country, it is our right to the moral leadership of this planet." Even in calling for a retreat of sorts from his country's overextended adventure, this Kennedy was possessed of a Wilsonian vision of American mission and greatness. And that signifies the difference in tone between the two men, who were not far apart in actual policy. Kennedy exuded energy, hope, the opportunity for fundamental change; McCarthy embodied skepticism. His plan for scaling down the war was moderate (and probably no different from what Kennedy would have done): stop the bombing, pull back into enclaves, try to negotiate peace. In contrast to Kennedy, who as President would surely have emulated or even surpassed his older brother in radiating purpose and determination, McCarthy wished to have presidential power curtailed. His views represented one of the many ways in which certain kinds of liberalism and some varieties of conservatism could intersect.

For Lyndon Johnson, Kennedy's decision, coupled with McCarthy's showing in New Hampshire, demonstrated clearly what lay ahead. Polling done in preparation for the Indiana primary, moreover, indicated that

Johnson's support among Democrats there was at only 35 percent. On March 31, just two days before the Wisconsin primary, the President went on television and made one of the most startling speeches in the history of American presidential politics. He began by announcing that the time had come to limit the American engagement in the war. Henceforth, he would refrain from increasing American troop strength in Vietnam and would also cut back the bombing of the North. There followed a pronouncement even more astonishing. The times were wrong for partisanship, he declared, and he would not seek reelection in November. Vietnam had torn the presidency from Johnson; and it would soon take the White House from the Democrats.

Johnson's sudden withdrawal, though long under consideration for reasons of health, was a triumph of the antiwar movement. It also indicated, in refutation of the claims of disaffected radicals, that some change was possible within the normal workings of the system. That it did not bring an early end to the war is attributable to circumstances that were gravely to injure the political effectiveness of the Democratic party in the coming months. If Johnson's speech, however sincere, and subsequent events had persuaded the left wing of the peace movement to unify instead of deliberately splintering the antiwar effort, it could have made for a completely different history of the late sixties and beyond. And that, in turn, might have encouraged liberals and the left to a more unified politics in the future.

Yet Johnson's withdrawal also deprived the peace candidates of an easy target. McCarthy later reported feeling as if he had been tracking a tiger through long jungle grass: all of a sudden he rolls over and he's stuffed. But the beast grew another head: Vice President Hubert Humphrey became the administration's handpicked candidate.

By April McCarthy's presidential race had become oddly desultory. He and his staff sometimes did not even get around to opening the mail. He spent parts of many days writing poetry, and retired for a short time to a Benedictine monastery when he should have been spending every moment on the campaign. His candidacy seemed now to be more a protest movement than a serious try for the presidency. Kennedy thought McCarthy lazy, snobbish, and ineffectual; McCarthy considered Kennedy too secular and a bit of a demagogue. They differed in constituencies, these two northern Roman Catholic Democrats. Kennedy spoke for the fragments of the old New Deal coalition. McCarthy's following drew heavily from educated suburbanites and college campuses. The suburbs gave him a primary victory in Oregon—the only political defeat Robert Kennedy ever suffered—while Kennedy won in Indiana and South Dakota. McCarthy's seeming indifference later that summer to the Soviet invasion of Czechoslovakia during the Prague Spring defined his limits.

The Democratic primaries made clear that while McCarthy's air of intellect and cold virtue had its attractions for a portion of the educated classes, he was incapable of generating a broader political insurgency. In California, Kennedy went into the ghettos and barrios, where mobs of Mexicans and blacks would tear at his shirt and press around him. Kennedy, in fact, would have had only an outside chance of gaining the nomination, for the Democratic Convention, along with the nominating process in many states, was under the control of establishment Democrats, most of whom were wary of him. On June 4, the very evening of his narrow win in California, he was assassinated, and the peace movement was deprived of its most promising candidate for November.

For some time the Mobe and the Yippies had been contemplating a Festival of Life to confront the warmakers at the Democratic Festival of Death in Chicago that August. In planning street theater for the city, Jerry Rubin teamed up with Abbie Hoffman. Advocating the use by radicals of mass communications to influence public opinion against the war, they envisioned that antiwar fervor and rock bands might bring a hundred thousand people to Chicago's Grant Park.

By the standards of earlier protests, not many people actually showed up in Chicago. Eugene McCarthy asked young people not to come, warning of possible violence. The folksinger Phil Ochs was there. Ed Sanders, publisher of *Fuck You: A Magazine of the Arts*, brought the Fugs, but most other rock bands backed out. The mythic enemy, embodied in LBJ, did not even attend the convention. Only a few thousand demonstrators came. The Yippies lightened the moment, supporting full unemployment and protesting the crime of pay toilets; their last demand was blank so you could fill in whatever you wished. But after Yippies jested about adding LSD to the water supply (five tons would have done the trick), Mayor Daley placed guards around the city's pumping stations and filtration plants. The small contingent of demonstrators alarmed the old-fashioned politicos. Police worried about mortar shelling, poisoned food, Yippie girls luring delegates. The national guard joined the Chicago police in fencing in the demonstrators and clubbing many of them senseless. The city used huge street-cleaning vehicles to spray demonstrators with tear gas.

Inside the convention hall raged a battle of social politics in which matters of drugs and hair length vied with Depression-nurtured loyalty to the Democratic party. Many working-class Democrats had already begun drifting to the Republicans, repelled by the administration's racial policies and enjoying an economic well-being, provided by Democrats, that turns voters into Republicans. When from the convention podium Senator Abraham Ribicoff of Connecticut denounced the "Gestapo tactics" on the streets of Chicago, Mayor Daley, in front of the television cameras—some eighty-nine million Americans were watching—

addressed to Ribicoff a commentary easily discernible by simple lip reading: "Fuck you, you Jew son of a bitch. You lousy motherfucker, go home." Humphrey won the nomination by a margin of two to one and, in a gesture typical of his artless enthusiasm, kissed his wife's image on a TV screen in his room. That night the police raided some McCarthy student suites in the convention hotel because a few had dropped objects on them from the windows, and some of McCarthy's young supporters were beaten bloody.

Humphrey was a politician solidly within the New Deal tradition. His tastes were outwardly simple: once in a fine Paris restaurant he tried to order a hamburger. He lived politics: it was said that he knew his Senate colleagues better than his family. It was consistent with his party's social democratic side that he also had a cold warrior's past. He had worked to give the CIA a billion dollars to expand its activities and sponsored the Communist Control Act of 1954 outlawing the Communist party of the United States, offering an amendment to allow the setting up of detention camps for communists in times of national emergency. He informed students at the University of Pittsburgh that only the Vietcong committed atrocities. He told the AFL-CIO that Americans who called for peace in Vietnam were like the people who had let Hitler roll his tanks across the Lowlands. If South Vietnam was corrupt, he said, so were many American cities—a favorite observation of Vietnam's Ky.

In 1968 any sensible Republican candidate had a good chance to win. The Republicans never had a strong antiwar candidate. Michigan's personable governor George Romney had made at one point the admission, honest and reasonable but devastating to his campaign, that the army and diplomats had "brainwashed" him while he was in Vietnam on a fact-finding mission. Nelson Rockefeller, a liberal Republican, avoided the campaign until April 30, 1968, which was too late—although he gave it the good old Rockefeller try by spending over $5 million on a last minute media blitz. Ronald Reagan also was touted as a candidate. Rockefeller and Reagan hoped together to pull enough votes away from Nixon to throw the nomination into doubt, but Nixon had forged a powerful coalition with southern conservatives and won on the convention's first ballot.

Though he came to be favored by conservatives and identified with them, Nixon never fitted clearly and permanently in either wing of his party. His conduct in the hearings of the House Un-American Activities Committee, investigating the communist associations of Alger Hiss, bespoke more concern for personal rights than was typical for Red-hunters. In 1950 he defeated Helen Gahagan Douglas in a race for the Senate, Red-baiting her with campaign literature referring to her as the pink lady, "pink" being a term at the time implying a state somewhat short of Red (her lieutenants reached about the same level when they called Nixon anti-Semitic). But as Eisenhower's Vice President, Nixon was on the liberal side of such thinking about civil rights as went on within establishment politics. In 1968 he presented himself not as a peace candidate but as the contender who at least had a plan for ending the war. He won a victory against Humphrey, who had been gaining support as he increasingly stressed the search for peace. Had the New Left supported Humphrey, he might have been the victor. George Wallace, the candidate of the populist right, came in third. He represented sectors of the populace's blue-collar classes that had been a reliable partner in the Democratic New Deal and Fair Deal coalitions, and his showing added evidence that his party was losing its hold on that component of the electorate. Without the presence of Wallace, Nixon's popular victory would doubtless have been larger.

Peace talks meanwhile had actually been taking place in Paris since May 10, 1968, for not only Washington but Hanoi was interested in negotiating an end to the war—or at least American participation in it. Nixon continued the Paris conference. But in the summer of 1969 he and Henry Kissinger, his national security adviser and later secretary of state, became dissatisfied with the pace of negotiations and decided on an ultimatum to Hanoi threatening massive assaults on North Vietnam. In the spring of 1970 the President oversaw an American and South Vietnamese invasion of Cambodia, where from protected bases the communists had been able to launch operations in Vietnam. The reaction to this attack brought some of the most widespread protests against the war, one result of which was the killing of four students at Kent State University in Ohio by state guardsmen called in to halt student turmoil and of two students by local police at Jackson State in Mississippi. Another was the journey of a group of Harvard University professors to Washington in order to tell Henry Kissinger that the Cambodian "incursion" was destroying the Cold War consensus.

———————

Despite the demonstrations, Nixon carried on with a policy that involved both military action and negotiation, in itself a logical enough combination but in the case of Vietnam reflective of an American engagement that had lost any clear sense of definable, achievable goals. For a time, much of the attention was on making sure Hanoi would return captured American airmen, a repatriation that could reasonably be expected as an outcome of any peace settlement. Toward the end of the war, the administration conducted particularly heavy bombings of North Vietnam. But at last on January 23, 1973, a peace settlement was signed, temporarily allowing communist and anticommunist forces each to continue occupying whatever South Vietnamese territory they then held. Within a few months, all but a few American troops had been withdrawn from Vietnam. The war had cost the United States fifty-eight thousand lives; Vietnamese deaths numbered some two million.

Two years after a settlement that was supposed to preserve an intact South Vietnam, Saigon fell to the communists, an utter defeat for American policy. The communist victory brought the remainder of Vietnam into the hands of a regime both oppressive and plagued with corruption, and innumerable inhabitants fled from it by sea: the boat people, whom the West treated with scant generosity. Laos too came under communist control, and Cambodia fell to a rulership, that of the Khmer Rouge, so vicious that when Vietnam went to war with it, driving it from power, Hanoi actually looked like a liberator. But no further dominoes fell. A major argument for the war against the communists in Vietnam had been that in triumph they would be agents of Chinese communist expansion. But a border war between Vietnam and her huge neighbor made clear that Vietnam, far from being a cat's paw of China, was its potential antagonist for the foreseeable future.

So concluded the involvement of the American military in Southeast Asia, during the presidency of Richard M. Nixon, a politician conservative in style and mean in manners but in policy modestly progressive. That involvement had amounted to the extension into Southeast Asia of a worldwide anticommunist engagement crafted primarily by liberals. Against the war was arrayed a spectrum of groups and opinions, the most visible being the mutually hostile quaternity of old left, New Left, disaffected liberals, and counterculture. Among these, the New Left could count as antecedents the traditional left and elements of liberalism, while the counterculture had some grounding in liberal ideas of artistic and expressive freedom. Nor was there, within the antiwar movement, any one perception of the communist forces. Some activists championed their cause. Others, out of the same humane considerations that set them against the war, detested the ruthlessness of the communists in the field and their repressiveness in power. The American pacifist academician Staughton Lynd refused to participate in a mock war crimes tribunal organized by the British philosopher Bertrand Russell to condemn American wrongs in Vietnam: Lynd noted the failure of the tribunal to try the communists as well as the United States.

Radicalism here as well as abroad has had a compulsion to splinter. In the Vietnam conflict liberalism, too, splintered, turning hesitant and then at contraries, facing its own alienated self in a new political left and a cultural rebellion.

In the American phase of the long anticolonialist conflict in Vietnam, Laos, and Cambodia that is one of the epochal stories of the century, war was ultimately, as it always is, an affair not of leaders but of common people: in this case the foot soldiers in the jungle, on all sides of the fighting, and at home in neighborhoods and campuses. A small percentage of Americans, including many college students, by wearing down the nation's middling classes contributed to reversing the administration's unsuccessful war policies. They, along with antiwar leaders in Congress, ensured that truth was nursed back to health. It was a vital and expanding band of truthtellers who, along with the costs of the war itself, instilled among politicians since then a fear of foreign entanglements. After Vietnam, the United States took to aiming only at easy targets, Grenada and Libya, Panama and Iraq. That represented a certain cheapening of the national character as the country learned to pride itself on triumphs that made no demands on the bulk of its people.

15. President Johnson rounds up a steer on a visit to his Texas ranch, 1964. Photograph courtesy of AP/Wide World Photos.

16. First Buddhist monk to protest the South Vietnam government by setting himself afire. Photograph courtesy of AP/World Wide Photos.

17. Mario Savio speaking to sit-in students at Berkeley in 1964. Photograph courtesy of UPI/Bettmann.

18. Students locked in Sproul Hall, Berkeley, by campus police after a day-long sit-in protest. Photograph courtesy UPI/Bettmann.

19. Robert Parris Moses explains a point to a student volunteer for Freedom Summer. Photograph by Steve Shapiro, courtesy of Black Star.

20. Mark Rudd speaking at Columbia University in 1968. Photograph courtesy of UPI/Bettmann.

21. *(Top left)* Stokely Carmichael. Photograph by Doug Wilson, courtesy of Black Star.

22. *(Top right)* George Wallace. Photograph by Richard Howard.

23. 1970 demonstration against the Vietnam War on the Ellipse in rear of the White House. Photograph courtesy of UPI/Bettmann.

24. God Bless America. Hardhats March, New York City, 1970. Photograph by
Charles Gatewood, courtesy of Magnum Photos.

25. U.S. astronauts Virgil I. Grissom, Edward H. White, and Roger B. Chaffee (left to right), just ten days before they perished in an Apollo project training session. Photograph courtesy of AP/ Wide World Photos.

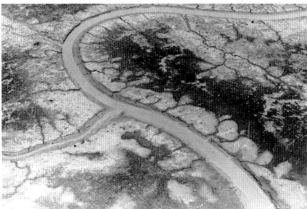

26. An aerial view of a defoliated mangrove forest in Vietnam in 1970, the result of chemical herbicides used by the U.S. Photograph courtesy of UPI/ Bettmann.

27. Presidential candidate Senator Eugene McCarthy greets students in Tallahassee, Florida, 1968. Photograph courtesy of UPI/Bettmann.

28. Mayor Richard J. Daley responds to Senator Abraham Ribicoff, Chicago Democratic Convention, 1968. Photograph courtesy of AP/Wide World Photos.

29. *Easy Rider*.
Photograph
courtesy of UPI/
Bettmann.

30. Woodstock,
1969. Photograph
by Ken Heyman.

Epilogue _____

AT HOME the Vietnam war contributed to the breaking up of Democratic liberalism, which has never recovered. It completed the destruction of Lyndon Johnson's presidency, a political fall that halted a Democratic surge begun with Kennedy or just before. It strained the economy, making more difficult the implementing of a domestic program that was sure anyway to antagonize taxpayers for its costliness and working-class whites for its attempts to open up jobs and housing to blacks. Though the conflict was a liberals' war, it produced among liberals and activists to their left an antiwar movement that antagonized much of the population. And prominent among other rebellions intensified in that war-maddened time were legitimate aspirants to political power that in their manner of presentation has made liberalism seem ever since a clamor of demands for special treatment in recompense for past victimization. Thereby an era promising in its beginnings and heroic in its ambitions ended by programming liberalism into a long decline.

The unsuccessful 1964 campaign of the Republican senator Barry Goldwater, often seen as a premature forerunner of the increasingly triumphant conservative politics of more recent days, had faced a Democratic party still capable of embracing a multiplicity of interests out of the New Deal coalition, and acting as the party of an effective majority. The summer of Goldwater was also Freedom Summer, the last moment of integrationist nonviolence, to be followed that fall by stirrings of the later-named black power movement. The inability of black and white liberalism and the white left clearly to distance themselves from the shriller and more separatist implications of that phenomenon were to have ill consequences for the Democratic party. Even in the 1990s, black politicians would be courting, and liberals tolerating their courtship, of black racists and anti-Semites. The Gulf of Tonkin, in August of the Goldwater candidacy, was meanwhile preparing the Democrats for disaster—not to mention disaster for the Vietnamese—even at about the time that a Democratic television political spot suggested that in a Goldwater presidency nuclear weapons would fall on little girls.

Richard Nixon's candidacy in 1968 benefited from student and black power excesses of a kind nearly absent in the year of Goldwater's try. Humphrey was as much as Nixon an enemy of the increasingly strident New Left, and perhaps got more hostility from that quarter than did his Republican foe. But the public anger at the conduct of black militants and student radicals went against the Democrats, who suffered as well from

public hostility even to responsible civil rights efforts and the peace movement. At the same time, many advocates of peace and racial justice who
ought to have seen that their better if weakened hopes lay with the Democrats petulantly refused to put their energies behind Humphrey. George
Wallace, the Alabama governor who ran as candidate of the right-wing
American party, drew votes both from working-class Democrats that
otherwise would have gone to Humphrey and from a fringe of conservatism that Nixon would have captured.

The campaign of 1968 presaged more than that of four years earlier
the course of American politics. Still, it had strongly distinctive and
clearly momentary characteristics. The war made for immediate frustrations in the Democratic party. The Republican candidate, possessing a
predisposition for political moderating of differences, was not prepared
to make a full ideological assault on Humphrey's liberalism. And the incumbent Vice President had so identified himself with Lyndon Johnson's
war policy as to have little discernible political profile of his own: his New
Deal credentials now had little visibility or meaning. Philosophical
choices within the public bore on the elections, but almost in spite of the
candidates.

In 1972, the Democrats fixed upon themselves a new and lasting profile. In the Miami Beach convention, liberals conditioned by the sixties
ousted their opponents of an older New Deal stripe and granted special
representation in future conventions to distinct groups: blacks, women,
gays and lesbians, Hispanics. Among Iowa delegates there were no
farmers. Among delegates from New York only three represented labor
while nine were gay liberationists. And in Illinois the party excluded all
Mayor Daley's delegates from Chicago, instead including a Jesse Jackson
contingent that did not represent the state's white urban ethnics. In itself,
a politics by interest groups was perfectly common to both parties, and
especially to the Democratic, which by skillful temporizing had once
managed to hold the white South while welcoming into the New Deal
whatever blacks possessed the vote. But in that past, the party presented
particular needs and interests as no more than provisional distinctions
within a common republic. Union members, farmers, the urban middle
class were definable as workers and citizens who happened to differ in
what they made or transported. After 1972, however, a portion of liberalism seemed determined to stamp on each of the groups it favored a permanent, separate identity by gender, sexual preference, ethnicity, or race.

It was also from this time onward that some radical feminists would be
defining men by characteristics, genetic or socially induced, that should
promise at best an armed neutrality between the sexes. The tone of radical
feminism being that also of much of black militancy, Democratic liberalism was inviting a public image of itself as the champion of complainants

demanding a right to outrage and privilege for their indelibly distinctive selves. Women and blacks do add up to a substantial majority. But what if you are uninterested in the political primacy of such things? In time, the victim game fostered the most annoying of presumptive victims, the white male, whose discovery of the uses of anger and self-pity has both wounded the Democratic party and further demeaned political discourse.

In 1972 the Democratic party candidate George McGovern became associated with the character of the party convention. Nixon, on the other hand, was perceived both as the more staunchly patriotic of the contenders, the better friend to the military, and as steering the Vietnam war to an early settlement. His victory was assured.

Had it not been for the burglary of Democratic headquarters in Washington's Watergate apartment complex and Nixon's subsequent cover-up, Republican possession of the White House might have continued for some time. When Congress appeared on the verge of constitutional proceedings against him, he resigned, and his party suffered. Nixon's successor, the plain and straightforward Vice President Gerald Ford, could not manage the public presence to lift his party above its temporary slump, and he lost the next election, in 1976, to Jimmy Carter.

As President, Carter embodied something different both from conservatism and from what liberalism had become. An adherent to civil rights on the model of an earlier generation of southern liberals, he did not especially represent his party's new ways with women and minorities. The militantly Islamic Iranian seizure of American hostages in Tehran after the United States admitted the ousted Shah of Iran for medical treatment put Carter's country to a humiliation and his presidency to an embarrassment that he could not remedy. An attempted military rescue ended in failure. Between Carter, who had censured self-indulgence, and a Republican candidate who reassured the white middle classes that government would make fewer demands upon them, affluent whites had little trouble deciding where their ballots should go. With the triumph of Ronald Reagan, conservatism was well on its way to ascendancy in American politics.

Movements that during the sixties had battled courageously now remain in the Democratic party only as echoes of themselves, unable either to muster sufficient votes for a practical majority or to compose themselves into a larger body politic. Illustrative is the anxiety of black and white liberals at the Supreme Court's invalidation of congressional districts gerrymandered to create black constituencies. The task of working with other citizens for a socially and economically democratic alternative to Republicanism, as the recombining of black with white voters would require, gets little support from the left. The uprisings of the 1960s, capable of evoking pride, bravery, social innovation, and at times a crystalline moral clarity, could not evoke, as had the New Deal, any sense of a wider community. The Republicans now do, though it is in great part a community disdainful of whatever social obligations liberalism still dares, timidly, to propose.

Somewhere, in real space or nostalgic imagination, a post-office mural is crowded with images that belong to the WPA political art of the Depression thirties. Against splashes of sky blue and prairie brown, in a landscape placing wigwam and log cabin side by side with hard-angled skyscraper, a black freedman tills his own plot of southern land. A pioneer woman steers a rugged plow. A mustachioed immigrant steps off the boat from Ellis Island. A scholar turns a page; a scientist adjusts the focus of a microscope. A factory laborer with muscles bunched pours molten steel. At a time when the New Deal was reconstructing the nation, the muralist captured an old and enduring vision within American political culture: the idea of a commonwealth at work.

The limitless abundance of the American continent, its surfaces open to be wrought and rewrought by the brain and sinew of its restless people, had long nourished the idea of a workers' republic. Jeffersonians and their successors imagined a future of virtuous farmers and craftsmen sustained by a perennial westward-moving opportunity. The antislavery movement envisioned at once a republic of liberty and a republic of work, of free farmers cultivating the western lands the slaveocracy had wished to capture for itself.

As the country's population grew denser, populists and socialists each offered an American version of a laborers' and farmers' commonwealth. So did the Wobblies, that most American of outlaw radical movements, in their enlistment of western migrant workers who drifted from wheat field to lumber camp. By the turn of the twentieth century, Americans had long since embarked on their special romance with machine technology, with the material abundance it promised and the mental exactness it required. But the land remained to define the American enterprise; and in the poetry of Carl Sandburg, the clean geometries of Chicago spring out of the prairie as though the land in its immensity had hurled them up into the midwestern sky. Meanwhile the American labor movement, both craft and industrial unions, aimed to give the nation's urban workers identity and dignity to go with a union card, uniting though not collectivizing them. An electrician who had done his part in the construction of a huge midwestern office building would often go past the edifice, tasting a craftsman's satisfaction as he contemplated the giant structure into which he had molded a bit of himself.

The political culture that is distilled in literature, visual art, and the most articulate kinds of political statement is not, of course, the same thing as the practical politics of interest groups, favor swapping, and elections. In the 1930s, when the Depression, along with its liberal and radical progeny, made for an especially rich imagery of democracy, the New Deal loosely gathered to itself a multiplicity of interests as self-seeking as is customary in politics. While photography was presenting in sharp, hard lines the poverty-etched faces of southern sharecroppers, the New Deal was favoring largely the big landowners. And though industrial unions reached deeper into the ranks of unskilled labor than craft unions had previously done, the migrants and domestics, the blacks and the Hispanics who toiled in the shadows of American society were by and large left outside. Still, the grainy photography of croppers and union militants, the Depression-era poetry with its Whitmanesque chanting of the place and river names scattered across the continent, the angry political rhetoric demanding a restoration of the American promise of labor and justice bestowed a defining tone on the politics of the Roosevelt years.

The political ethos of a republic at work survived into World War II. More than survived: in very American fashion, popular culture defined the war as a job to get done. The presidency of the scrappy, folksy Harry Truman sustained not only the substance but something of the rhetorical flavor of New Deal politics. Subsequently, John Kennedy's New Frontier revised but did not diminish the popular traditions on which New Deal politics had drawn. Once American workers, a small minority of them in fact, could have taken as their symbol the American ax, famed for its sleek line and its wastefulness, or the heavy plow that broke the prairie; and the greatest of nineteenth-century Presidents was known as a rail-splitter. Now a new generation had a President whose crisp, slightly harsh New England accent seemed exactly appropriate to a cooler age of electronics and cybernetics.

Then, just at the time when the veteran New Deal loyalist Lyndon Johnson was attempting to build the Great Society, the idea of a workers' commonwealth faltered. The groups that sought their advantage in the Great Society or feasted on the energies of those politically restless times learned to define themselves not as aspirants for the labor force but by their racial, ethnic, or sexual identity.

In the politics of the 1960s and early seventies, and especially against the background of Vietnam, almost any cause could command a serious hearing. New Leftists often proclaimed and acted upon an uncompromising conscience, requiring of themselves immeasurable anger against whatever might at any moment be defined as belonging to the structure of oppression. The practice of a relentless conscience, the public acting out of unabashedly moral convictions, was in its way an admirable venture beyond the modest conventions of the normal politics of personal and group self-interest. But it brought radicalism to one of the contradictions that became its growing plight. It is this: that from the exaltation of every spasm of the moral self it is but a step to the celebration of every twitch of the hedonistic self.

Black separatism, encouraging the deep exploration of the black experience, and feminism, in its practice of consciousness raising, both of them legitimate introspective enterprises, were yet consonant with this preoccupation with every nuance of the private psyche. The fervent politics of the New Left came out to be culturally consistent with the fad of self-cultivation in the politically tepid times that followed the sixties. More than any specifically political fact, these inward-turnings marked the temporary vanishing of the cultural mind that had fashioned the popular political manners of the New Deal. What it portended, in effect, was that the ideal of a commonwealth at work was now to give way, at least for a time, to a culture and politics of consumption.

Consumption was most notably victorious in the Republican administrations of Ronald Reagan and George Bush that supposedly aimed to restore traditional American virtues. Republican conservatives scarcely bothered to define those virtues; they had something to do with saluting the flag, ridiculing environmentalists, supporting militarism, and hating the income tax. You need only celebrate your American self and prosperity and the industrial might that surrounds you; then you can lead the life of a consumer. Whatever remained of the work ethic amounted to no more than the protection of the affluence of the affluent; don't tax my dollars to relieve my neighbor's poverty.

In these lost American years, foreign policy especially became a field of consumption. We were, it seemed, in a relentless struggle with an implacable enemy. But the public did not need to be taxed or otherwise inconvenienced in order to sustain the struggle. The thing for Americans to do was enjoy the fight, as spectators pretending to be participants. In the invasion of the Caribbean island of Grenada, consumption reached its apogee. In front of its television sets, the public was invited to consume the training and skill of the invading troops, consume the event and the island, consume its own flattered self-image. Then, when communism collapsed of its own spent and sodden ideology, Americans were enticed to congratulate themselves over the victory. For decades, under both Democratic and Republican administrations, they along with very many other peoples had in fact borne the tasks and responsibilities, at times on the battlefield, of the confrontation with communism. But all that the Republicans of the last years of the Cold War asked them to do was endorse a foreign policy, free of domestic demands, that found reason for tolerating paramilitary abduction and torture in rightist anticommunist regimes abroad.

The separatist portion of the left has not had the opportunity for so carnival an engorgement of spectacle and wealth. Consumption in its case has taken a subtler form—the consumption of self-awareness; that is what it has often encouraged: the narcissistic contemplation of a group and personal selfhood, the stroking of the victim role.

The point is not that the new cultural, gender, and racial studies have no substance. Analyzing social structure or personal psychology as an expression of gender is no less fruitful than, say, examining either as a function of economics. The folkways of a particular ethnicity invite close and endless exploration. Thinking them to be the fixed and inviolable heritage of some particular folk, to be sure, is a sentimental falsehood. The Panthers themselves recognized this when they insisted that black Americans live within a distinctively black American culture, not that of the African continent. But a culture or ethnicity can more properly be understood as an ongoing work, having its continuity as does a language and changing, again like language, as its crafters from one generation to another shape its materials of art and custom and spoken dialect. In that form it is not only desirable but inevitable. To attempt to attack it in the name of some abstract unitary Humanity—and such concepts have emerged in recent Western history—requires the attacker to use a particular language, and language itself is the richest, most idiomatic of the works of a culture. No human being is a disembodied consciousness. Becoming acquainted with the layers of cultural acquisition within your psyche is to become better acquainted with yourself. To study these within the people of another ethnicity is to begin to discover who an individual within it is. Nor are programs in gender, ethnicity, or race necessarily at fault for having ideological motives. Advocacy has an ancient place in teaching: Socrates is not thought the worse of for it.

It is the specific set of assumptions behind the recent proliferation of ethnic and gender programs that threatens their promise. The liberal belief that identity comes of self-discovery and self-making is now giving way to a notion that your identity is assigned from the beginning, its treasury of merits and its entitlements assured to you if your sex, race, or ethnic group has been historically oppressed. And the ideal of a commonwealth of work and cooperation, in which personal self-making finds a social enactment, vanishes into the liberal and radical past. This is perhaps the first major occasion in which the left has examined power relations with no serious and publicly promoted scheme for democratically changing them. Why should they be changed, if eliminating them would eliminate the satisfying consciousness of their existence? It is a mark of recent ideology that in the triad race-class-gender, the smallest attention goes to class: the one category among them that describes a diversity of disempowered people and suggests a way to the widest social equality.

At least one policy of the Democratic administration of the 1990s indicated that liberalism might have been able to welcome these newly assertive interests in a way that would retain its own integrity. The unsuccessful effort to end questions about sexual preference in military recruitment signified that enlistees were now to be defined by their ability to drive a truck or read a radar screen, their capacity for work. Contrast that with the gay militant practice of outing, which demands that individuals take their public identity from sexual preference: again, consumption of self-image.

Possibly in a better time the ideals of the New Deal can enjoy a return, and the American vision of a working commonwealth can once again enter politics. That will mean that it has survived not only the hegemony of the Republican years but the self-absorbed ideologies of a left that has forgotten its past.

Bibliography

This bibliography is meant to be inclusive not of the 1960s but of only the particular content and themes of this book. Important and controversial topics may receive more detailed treatment. The organization reflects to some extent that of the book but also the chronology of the decade itself.

Civil Rights and Black Power

Oral Histories and Chronologies

To recall some of the images and words that played at the moral temperament of the nation during the civil rights movement, see the video series *Eyes on the Prize, I and II: History of the American Civil Rights Movement* (Boston: Henry Hampton and Blackside, 1986). Journalist Juan Williams is the author of a crisply written companion volume to the series, *Eyes on the Prize: America's Civil Rights Years, 1954–1965* (New York: Viking, 1987). Howell Raines has compiled a collection of oral histories in *My Soul Is Rested: Movement Days in the Deep South Remembered* (New York: G. P. Putnam's Sons, 1977). Oral histories present special opportunities for understanding the personal dimensions of the movement; they also create some problems. Kim Lacy Rogers discusses the promise and difficulties of using interviews and personal recollections in "Oral History and the History of the Civil Rights Movement," *Journal of American History* 75 (1988): 567–76.

It is always necessary to get events in their proper sequence and locale. Here Alton Hornsby, Jr., ed., *Chronology of African-American History: Significant Events and People from 1619 to the Present* (Detroit: Gale Research, 1991), is indispensable. Charles D. Lowery and John F. Marszalek, eds., *Encyclopedia of African-American Civil Rights: From Emancipation to the Present* (Westport, Conn.: Greenwood Press, 1992), is a useful reference for identifying important individuals, organizations, and occasions in civil rights and black power history. Also see Paul T. Murray, *The Civil Rights Movement: References and Resources* (New York: G. K. Hall, 1993), and Augustina Herod and Charles C. Herod, eds., *Afro-American Nationalist Literature* (New York: Garland, 1986).

General Studies

Among the best of the general studies of the civil rights era are Taylor Branch, *Parting the Waters: America in the King Years, 1954–63* (New York: Simon and Schuster, 1988); Robert Weisbrot, *Freedom Bound: A History of America's Civil Rights Movement* (New York: Norton, 1990); Harvard Sitkoff, *The Struggle for Black Equality, 1954–1992*, rev. ed. (New York: Hill and Wang, 1993); Aldon D. Morris, *The Origins of the Civil Rights Movement: Black Communities Organizing for Change* (New York: Free Press, 1984); and Fred Powledge, *Free at Last? The Civil Rights Movement and the People Who Made It* (Boston: Little, Brown,

1991). Other works that take a wide look at civil rights activities include Sean Dennis Cashman, *African-Americans and the Quest for Civil Rights, 1900–1990* (New York: New York University Press, 1991); Thomas R. Brooks, *Walls Come Tumbling Down: A History of the Civil Rights Movement, 1940–1970* (Engle-wood Cliffs, N.J.: Prentice-Hall, 1974); Manning Marable, *Race, Reform, and Rebellion: The Second Reconstruction in Black America, 1945–1982*, 2d ed. (Jackson: University Press of Mississippi, 1991); and Vincent Harding, *The Other American Revolution* (Los Angeles: UCLA Center for Afro-American Studies, 1980). Rhoda Lois Blumberg, *Civil Rights: The 1960s Freedom Struggle*, 2d ed. (Boston: Twayne, 1991), looks at the critical decade in the history of the move-ment. John Egerton, *Speak Now against the Day: The Generation before the Civil Rights Movement in the South* (New York: Knopf, 1994), is an important study.

There are also several fine collections of essays: David J. Garrow, ed., *We Shall Overcome: The Civil Rights Movement in the United States in the 1950s and 1960s*, 3 vols. (Brooklyn: Carlson Publishing, 1989); Charles Eagles, ed., *The Civil Rights Movement in America: Essays* (Jackson: University of Mississippi Press, 1986); Armstead Robinson and Patricia Sullivan, eds., *New Directions in Civil Rights Studies* (Charlottesville: University of Virginia Press, 1991); and Her-bert Hill and James E. Jones, Jr., eds., *Race in America: The Struggle for Equality* (Madison: University of Wisconsin Press, 1993). James F. Findlay, *Church People in the Struggle: The National Council of Churches and the Black Freedom Move-ment, 1950–1970* (New York: Oxford University Press, 1993), describes the vital role of religion in stimulating the movement, organizing its activities, and staffing its ranks. The culture of the freedom movement along with some of its images is captured in Guy and Candie Carawan, eds., *Freedom Is a Constant Struggle: Songs of the Freedom Movement with Documentary Photographs* (New York: Oak Publications, 1968). An important study by Richard H. King, *Civil Rights and the Idea of Freedom* (New York: Oxford University Press, 1992), offers an intellectual history of the civil rights era that focuses on the different and con-tested ways in which the idea of "freedom" was invested with meaning. Also see King's recent essay, "The Role of Intellectual History in the Histories of the Civil Rights Movement," in Melvyn Stokes and Rick Halpern, eds., *Race and Class in the American South since 1890* (Providence: Berg, 1994). The cultural historian Scott A. Sandage, "A Marble House Divided: The Lincoln Memorial, the Civil Rights Movement, and the Politics of Memory, 1939–1963," *Journal of Ameri-can History* 80 (June 1993): 135–67, examines the symbolic importance of the Lincoln Memorial, the site of more than one hundred civil rights demonstrations between 1939 and 1963.

Biographies and Autobiographies

Paula F. Pfeffer, *A. Philip Randolph, Pioneer of the Civil Rights Movement* (Baton Rouge: Louisiana State University Press, 1990), assesses the life and think-ing of the man who founded the Brotherhood of Sleeping Car Porters and Maids in 1925 and organized the 1941 March on Washington Movement to achieve fair hiring practices in government. Another excellent biography of Randolph is Wil-liam H. Harris, *Keeping the Faith: A. Philip Randolph, Milton P. Webster, and the Brotherhood of Sleeping Car Porters* (New York: Oxford University Press,

1982). Roy Wilkins, who succeeded W.E.B. Du Bois in 1934 as editor of the *Crisis* and was executive director of the National Association for the Advancement of Colored People (NAACP) from 1955 until he retired in 1977, recalls campaigning for rights in a work written with the assistance of Tom Mathews, *Standing Fast: The Autobiography of Roy Wilkins* (New York: Viking, 1982). In two books, *Freedom—When?* (New York: Random House, 1965) and *Lay Bare the Heart: An Autobiography of the Civil Rights Movement* (New York: Arbor House, 1986), James Farmer recounts some of the history of the Congress of Racial Equality (CORE), which he helped organize in 1942, and of the Freedom Ride project he initiated in 1961. The lawyer and minister Floyd B. McKissick, *Three-Fifths of a Man* (New York: Macmillan, 1969), succeeded Farmer as national director of CORE in 1961 and as an advocate of black power urged the organization to assume a more aggressive posture.

Whitney Young, Jr., head of the moderate research-oriented National Urban League, in *To Be Equal* (New York: McGraw-Hill, 1964), tells the story of his participation in an organization that believed it necessary to arm the movement with the sorry statistics of the social and economic consequences of racial discrimination. See, too, Nancy J. Weiss, *Whitney M. Young, Jr., and the Struggle for Civil Rights* (Princeton: Princeton University Press, 1989). Roger Wilkins, *A Man's Life: An Autobiography* (New York: Simon and Schuster, 1982), offers the unique perspective of a black attorney working in Lyndon Johnson's Justice Department at the time of the passage of the major civil rights laws. Ralph David Abernathy, *And the Walls Came Tumbling Down: An Autobiography* (New York: Harper and Row, 1989), is the recollection of the friend and associate who succeeded Martin Luther King, Jr., as president of the Southern Christian Leadership Conference (SCLC). Brian Urquhart, *Ralph Bunche: An American Life* (New York: Norton, 1993), covers Bunche's civil rights activity.

Others who recall the movement days include Pat Watters, *Down to Now: Reflections on the Southern Civil Rights Movement* (New York: Pantheon, 1971), and Danny Lyon, *Memories of the Southern Civil Rights Movement* (Chapel Hill: University of North Carolina Press for the Center of Documentary Studies, Duke University, 1992), a collection of photographs and commentary by the author, who was the staff photographer for the Student Nonviolent Coordinating Committee (SNCC). Drawing upon his personal experiences, especially his religious upbringing, James Baldwin made the case in *The Fire Next Time* (New York: Dial Press, 1963) of the need for African Americans to draw strength from their suffering and warned white Americans to attend to the complaints of blacks or suffer the consequences. David Leeming chronicles Baldwin's life and thought in *James Baldwin: A Biography* (New York: Knopf, 1994). Kenneth Robert Janken, *Rayford W. Logan and the Dilemma of the African-American Intellectual* (Amherst: University of Massachusetts Press, 1993), is a fascinating study of the brilliant but mercurial black intellectual and radical activist (1897–1982), who had an uncomfortable relationship with the leadership of the movement but who pioneered the use of voter registration drives in the 1930s and 1940s.

In the pursuit of racial justice, however, no voice was stronger and no one more influential than Dr. Martin Luther King, Jr. Not surprisingly, there is a large body of scholarship concerned with Dr. King only some of the most recent and best of which is sampled here. The historian Clayborne Carson has organized a bibliography of materials dealing with King, *A Guide to Research on Martin Luther King, Jr., and the Modern Black Freedom Struggle* (Stanford: Stanford University Libraries, 1989). Carson is also the general editor of *The Papers of Martin Luther King, Jr.* (Berkeley and Los Angeles: University of California Press). Two volumes have appeared: vol. 1, *Called to Serve, January 1929–June 1951* (1992), ed. Clayborne Carson, Ralph E. Luker, Penny A. Russell, and Louis R. Harlan; and vol. 2, *Rediscovering Precious Values, July–November 1955* (1994), ed. Clayborne Carson, Ralph E. Luker, Penny A. Russell, and Peter Holloran. King's views on nonviolence are available in his own words in *Stride toward Freedom: The Montgomery Story* (New York: Harper, 1958). *Strength to Love* (1963; rev. ed., New York: Viking, 1982) is a collection of King's sermons. Biographies, in addition to that by Taylor Branch, include Stephen B. Oates, *Let the Trumpet Sound: The Life of Martin Luther King, Jr.* (New York: Harper and Row, 1982), and David Levering Lewis, *King: A Critical Biography* (New York: Praeger, 1970). John J. Anshoro, *Martin Luther King, Jr.: The Making of a Mind* (Maryknoll, N.Y.: Orbis Books, 1982), describes the origins and development of many of King's ideas. Ira G. Zepp, Jr., *The Social Vision of Martin Luther King, Jr.* (Brooklyn: Carlson Publishing, 1989), also looks at the philosophical roots of King's thinking. James A. Colaiaco, *Martin Luther King, Jr.: Apostle of Militant Nonviolence* (New York: St. Martin's Press, 1993), considers the way King employed the strategy of nonviolent direct action in various campaigns. Two important collections of essays are David J. Garrow, ed., *Martin Luther King, Jr.: Civil Rights Leader, Theologian, and Orator*, 3 vols. (Brooklyn: Carlson Publishing, 1989), and Peter J. Albert and Ronald Hoffman, eds., *We Shall Overcome: Martin Luther King, Jr., and the Black Freedom Struggle* (New York: Pantheon, 1990). Another recent collection of essays is Brian Ward and Tony Badger, eds., *The Making of Martin Luther King and the Civil Rights Movement* (New York: New York University Press, 1995). Keith D. Miller, *Voice of Deliverance: The Language of Martin Luther King, Jr., and Its Sources* (New York: Free Press, 1992), examines the roots of King's oratory. Similarly, the essays in Carolyn Calloway-Thomas and John Louis Lucaites, eds., *Martin Luther King, Jr., and the Sermonic Power of Public Discourse* (Tuscaloosa: University of Alabama Press, 1993), study elements of rhetoric and communication. And Richard Lentz, *Symbols, the News Magazines, and Martin Luther King* (Baton Rouge: Louisiana State University Press, 1990), looks at King as the symbol of the civil rights movement as presented in the media, especially the news magazines *Time, Newsweek*, and *U.S. News and World Report*.

Desegregation

For background on segregationist customs and policies one work remains unsurpassed: C. Vann Woodward, *The Strange Career of Jim Crow*, 3d ed. (New York: Oxford University Press, 1974). W. Fitzhugh Brundage, *Lynching in the New South: Georgia and Virginia, 1880–1930* (Urbana: University of Illinois Press, 1993), describes the ruthlessness with which the codes of racial etiquette were enforced in the South. The ways in which matters of race overrode considerations of justice, especially in cases involving white women, are discussed in three recent studies: James Goodman, *Stories of Scottsboro* (New York: Pantheon, 1994); Eric W. Rise, *The Martinsville Seven: Race, Rape, and Capital Punishment* (Charlottesville: University Press of Virginia, 1995); and Richard B. Sherman, *The Case of Odell Waller and Virginia Justice, 1940–1942* (Knoxville: University of Tennessee Press, 1992).

School desegregation began with the May 17, 1954, Supreme Court decision in *Oliver Brown v. Board of Education of Topeka, Kansas*, sometimes referred to as *Brown I*, which reversed the long-standing doctrine, established by the *Plessy* decision of 1896 that allowed separate educational facilities for the races, by declaring that "in the field of public education the doctrine of 'Separate but equal' has no place." *Brown II*, decided in 1955 and viewed by many as a step back from the aggressively egalitarian position of *Brown I*, held that federal judges would determine the pace of integration as local conditions warranted. Joseph Tussman, ed., *The Supreme Court on Racial Discrimination* (New York: Oxford University Press, 1963), gives the full texts of Supreme Court decisions dealing with matters of race. The best history of the *Brown* case is Richard Kluger, *Simple Justice: The History of Brown v. Board of Education and Black America's Struggle for Equality* (New York: Knopf, 1975). Paul A. Wilson, *Time to Lose: Representing Kansas in Brown v. Board of Education* (Lawrence: University Press of Kansas, 1995), is the memoirs of the young attorney general who argued for Kansas in the Brown case. The legal scholar Mark V. Tushnet analyzes the work of the NAACP's Legal Defense and Educational Fund lawyers in challenging the *Plessy* principle in *The NAACP's Legal Strategy against Segregated Education, 1925–1950* (Chapel Hill: University of North Carolina Press, 1987). See also Tushnet's *Making Civil Rights Law: Thurgood Marshall and the Supreme Court, 1936–1961* (New York: Oxford University Press, 1994). Michael J. Klarman in "How Brown Changed Race Relations: The Backlash Thesis," *Journal of American History* 81 (June 1994): 81–118, makes the argument that the decision indirectly contributed to the civil rights movement by crystallizing southern opposition to racial change and instigating a sequence of events that would lead more and more Americans to view white southern racial intolerance with horror. J. Harvie Wilkinson, III, *From Brown to Bakke: The Supreme Court and School Integration, 1954–1978* (New York: Oxford University Press, 1979), carries the story of the Court and desegregation forward through the 1970s and its decisions in the 1978 case of the *University of California Regents v. Bakke*, a case in which the issue of "reverse discrimination" was raised and affirmative action programs for minorities and minority quotas were challenged. Local studies of the response to *Brown* include Robert C. Smith, *They Closed Their Schools: Prince Edward County, Virginia, 1951–1964* (Chapel Hill: University of North Carolina Press, 1965), and Robert A. Pratt, *The Color of Their Skin: Education and Race in Richmond, Virginia, 1954–89* (Charlottesville: University Press of Virginia, 1992). David S. Cecelski, *Along Freedom Road: Hyde County, North Carolina, and the Fate of Black Schools in the South* (Chapel Hill: University of North Carolina Press, 1994). I. A. Newby, *Challenge to the Court: Social Scientists and the Defense of Segregation, 1954–1966* (Baton Rouge: Louisiana State University Press, 1969), discusses the quarrel surrounding the use of sociological evidence in the desegregation cases. Most scholars who have written about *Brown* have been supportive; Raymond Wolters, *The Burden of Brown: Thirty Years of School Desegregation* (Knoxville: University of Tennessee Press, 1984), is more critical.

School integration was fiercely resisted by many white southerners, and just as tenaciously pursued by many black southerners and their white allies. Daisy Bates, an official of the local chapter of the NAACP, recalls the desegregation crisis at Little Rock, Arkansas, in *The Long Shadow of Little Rock: A Memoir* (1962; reprint, Fayetteville: University of Arkansas Press, 1987). Also see Tony Freyer, *The Little Rock Crisis: A Constitutional Interpretation* (Westport, Conn.: Greenwood Press, 1984). Frye Gaillard, *The Dream Long Deferred* (Chapel Hill: University of North Carolina Press, 1988), gives an account of school busing in Charlotte, North Carolina, the first city to use busing for school desegregation. And Ronald P. Formisano, *Boston against Busing: Race, Class, and Ethnicity in the 1960s and 1970s* (Chapel Hill: University of North Carolina Press, 1991), discusses the racial divisiveness that resulted from busing in a northern city. And desegregation of the South's universities is a topic for James Meredith, who in 1962 was the first black to gain admission to the University of Mississippi, *Three Years in Mississippi* (Bloomington: Indiana University Press, 1966); Russell H. Barrett, *Integration at Ole Miss* (Chicago: Quadrangle Books, 1965); the television newswoman Charlayne Hunter-Gault, who as Charlayne Hunter integrated the University of Georgia in January 1961, *In My Place* (New York: Farrar, Straus and Giroux, 1992); and E. Culpepper Clark, *The Schoolhouse Door: Segregation's Last Stand at the University of Alabama* (New York: Oxford University Press, 1993).

On the boycott of public transportation in Montgomery, Alabama, that began when rights activist Rosa Parks refused to move to the back of the bus, see David J. Garrow, ed., *The Montgomery Bus Boycott and the Women Who Started It: The Memoir of Jo Ann Gibson Robinson* (Knoxville: University of Tennessee Press, 1987), and the essays in *The Walking City: The Montgomery Bus Boycott, 1955–1956* (Brooklyn: Carlson Publishing, 1989), also edited by Garrow. And see Roberta H. Wright, *The Birth of the Montgomery Bus Boycott* (Southfield, Miss.: Charro Books, 1995). William Chafe, *Civilities and Civil Rights: Greensboro, North Carolina, and the Black Struggle for Freedom* (New York: Oxford University Press, 1980), is a local history of the civil rights movement focusing on the city that on February 1, 1960, was the site of the famous sit-in demonstration at the Woolworth lunch counter. The sit-in campaign spread rapidly to other southern cities: Merrill Proudfoot, *Diary of a Sit-In* (Chapel Hill: University of North Carolina Press, 1962), examines the efforts to desegregate the restaurants and lunch rooms of Knoxville, Tennessee; the essays in David J. Garrow, ed., *Atlanta, Georgia, 1960–1961: Sit-Ins and Student Activism* (Brooklyn: Carlson Publishing, 1989), look at the events in one of the South's major cities. For a sociologist's assessment of the sit-ins, see Martin Oppenheimer, *The Sit-In Movement of 1960* (Brooklyn: Carlson Publishing, 1989). James H. Laue, *Direct Action and Desegregation, 1960–1962* (Brooklyn: Carlson Publishing, 1989), also takes a sociological approach to the tactics of the desegregationists. Two works by rights workers provide firsthand accounts of the sit-ins and freedom rides: Diane Nash, "Inside the Sit-Ins and Freedom Rides," in Matthew Agman, ed., *The New Negro* (Notre Dame, Ind.: Fides Publishers, 1962), and James Peck,

Freedom Ride (New York: Simon and Schuster, 1962). Diane Nash was one of the founders of the Nashville Student Movement, a group that conducted a number of successful nonviolent demonstrations in Nashville, Tennessee, in the early 1960s. James Peck was an official with CORE. Also Catherine A. Barnes, *Journey from Jim Crow: The Desegregation of Southern Transit* (New York: Columbia University Press, 1983).

Civil Rights Organizations

Though there is no comprehensive treatment of the NAACP, some older works are very informative. See especially Charles Kellogg Flint, *NAACP: A History of the National Association for the Advancement of Colored People* (Baltimore: Johns Hopkins University Press, 1967), and Barbara Joyce Ross, *J. E. Spingarn and the Rise of the NAACP, 1911–1939* (New York: Atheneum, 1972). Genna Rae McNeil, *Groundwork: Charles Hamilton Houston and the Struggle for Civil Rights* (Philadelphia: University of Pennsylvania Press, 1983), and Gilbert Ware, *William Hastie: Grace under Pressure* (New York: Oxford University Press, 1984), look at men who served as legal counsel for the NAACP. Robert L. Zangrando, *The NAACP Crusade against Lynching, 1909–1950* (Philadelphia: Temple University Press, 1980), deals with the issue that was the chief concern of the NAACP, its effort to publicize racial problems, before the desegregation campaign. Jack Greenberg's recent book, *Crusaders in the Courts: How a Dedicated Band of Laywers Fought for the Civil Rights Revolution* (New York: Basic Books, 1994), describes the work of the black and white lawyers who staffed the NAACP Legal Defense and Educational Fund. The history of CORE, which was formed in 1942 out of the membership of the Fellowship of Reconciliation, a pacifist group, is documented in a thoroughly researched work by August Meier and Elliot Rudwick, *CORE: A Study in the Civil Rights Movement, 1942–1968* (New York: Oxford University Press, 1975). The story of the Southern Christian Leadership Conference is told in David J. Garrow, *Bearing the Cross: Martin Luther King, Jr. and the Southern Christian Leadership Conference* (New York: William Morrow, 1986); Thomas R. Peake, *Keeping the Dream Alive: A History of the Southern Christian Leadership Conference from King to the 1980s* (New York: P. Lang, 1967); and Adam Fairclough, *"To Redeem the Soul of America": The Southern Christian Leadership Conference and Martin Luther King, Jr.* (Athens: University of Georgia Press, 1987).

Among the civil rights organizations that appeared in the wake of the *Brown* decision, the small Student Nonviolent Coordinating Committee is perhaps the most interesting, largely because of the changes in tone and activity the group underwent over the course of its history but also owing to the many arresting personalities, women and men, it attracted to its causes. There are several good studies of SNCC, the best of which is Clayborne Carson, *In Struggle: SNCC and the Black Awakening of the 1960s* (Cambridge, Mass.: Harvard University Press, 1981). Also consult Emily Stoper, *The Student Nonviolent Coordinating Committee: The Growth of Radicalism in a Civil Rights Organization* (Brooklyn: Carlson Publishing, 1989); Howard Zinn, *SNCC: The New Abolitionists*, 2d ed. (Boston: Beacon, 1965); and Clayborne Carson, ed., *"The Student Voice," 1960–1965: Periodical of the Student Nonviolent Coordinating Committee* (Westport,

Conn.: Greenwood Press, 1990). Cleveland Sellers with Robert Terrell, *The River of No Return: The Autobiography of a Black Militant and the Life and Death of SNCC* (New York: William Morrow, 1973), and James Forman, *The Making of Black Revolutionaries: A Personal Account* (New York: Macmillan, 1972), are works by members of SNCC, one of whom, James Forman, served as executive secretary of the organization for five years, 1961–66.

Many of the men and women who emerged as leaders, among them James Bevel, Rosa Parks, and several SNCC activists, trained at the Highlander Folk School in Monteagle, Tennessee. Founded in 1932 by Myles Horton and Don West, Highlander taught a philosophy of community empowerment and employed training methods aimed at assisting community representatives to organize on behalf of their own interests. The voter education programs and Freedom Schools established by SNCC owed much to the inspiration of Highlander. The school's history is told in three works: Frank Adams with Myles Horton, *Unearthing Seeds of Fire: The Idea of Highlander* (Winston-Salem, N.C.: John F. Blair, 1975); Aimee Isgrig Horton, *The Highlander Folk School: A History of Its Major Programs, 1932–1961* (Brooklyn: Carlson Publishing, 1989); and John M. Glen, *Highlander: No Ordinary School, 1932–1962* (Lexington: University of Kentucky Press, 1988). Irwin Klibaner, *Conscience of a Troubled South: The Southern Conference Educational Fund, 1946–1966* (Brooklyn: Carlson Publishing, 1989), is a stimulating study that endeavors to connect the civil rights movement with earlier radical organizations. Sudarshan Kapur, *Raising Up a Prophet: The African-American Encounter with Gandhi* (Boston: Beacon, 1992), is an intellectual history that looks at the ways various civil rights leaders and groups understood and used the theories of nonviolence and direct action of Mohandas K. Gandhi. In a chapter entitled "Mohandas, Malcolm, and Martin," Dennis Dalton, *Mahatma Gandhi: Nonviolent Power in Action* (New York: Columbia University Press, 1993), compares how Gandhi, Malcolm X, and Martin Luther King, Jr., understood the philosophy of nonviolence and employed its methods.

Mississippi

Nowhere was the struggle for the soul of America more bitterly contested than in Mississippi. For background on the conditions of black life in the state, see Neil R. McMillen, *Dark Journey: Black Mississippians in the Age of Jim Crow* (Urbana: University of Illinois Press, 1989); James W. Silver, *Mississippi: The Closed Society*, 2d ed. (New York: Harcourt, Brace and World, 1966); and Stephen J. Whitfield, *A Death in the Delta: The Story of Emmett Till* (New York: Free Press, 1988). The murder of the fourteen-year-old Till on August 24, 1955, for wolf-whistling at a white woman and touching her, and the subsequent acquittal of his killers, brought attention to the special viciousness of Mississippi racism. See also Clenora Hudson-Weems, *Emmett Till: The Sacrificial Lamb of the Civil Rights Movement* (Troy, Mich.: Bedford Publishers, 1994). The important voter registration campaign waged by SNCC and other groups, and the famous Freedom Summer of 1964 that aimed at building the populist Mississippi Freedom Democratic Party, are discussed in several works. See Anne Moody's poignant recollections of movement days in the Deep South in *Coming of Age in Mississippi* (New York: Dell, 1968). Recent studies of the rights struggle in Mississippi include the exhaustive John Dittmer, *Local People: The Struggle for Civil Rights in Mississippi* (Urbana: University of Illinois Press, 1994); Nicolaus Mills, *Like a Holy Crusade: Mississippi 1964—The Turning of the Civil Rights Movement in America* (Chicago: Ivan Dee, 1992); and Charles M. Payne, *I've Got the Light of Freedom: The Organizing Tradition and the Mississippi Freedom Struggle* (Berkeley and Los Angeles: University of California Press, 1995). Also see Len Holt, *The Summer that Didn't End* (New York: William Morrow, 1965); William McCord, *Mississippi: The Long Hot Summer* (New York: Norton, 1965); Sally Belfrage, *Freedom Summer* (Charlottesville: University Press of Virginia and Curtis Brown, Ltd., 1965); and Doug McAdam, *Freedom Summer* (New York: Oxford University Press, 1988). Mary Aiken Rothschild, *A Case of Black and White: Northern Volunteers and the Southern Freedom Summer, 1964–1965* (Westport, Conn.: Greenwood Press, 1982), discusses the relations between the almost one thousand college students, most of them white, who went south during Freedom Summer and the black rights workers and Mississippians they worked alongside in 1964–65. Elizabeth Sutherland Martinez, ed., *Letters from Mississippi* (New York: McGraw-Hill, 1965), has collected some of the writings of those young freedom fighters who communicated their experiences. John R. Salter, Jr., *Jackson, Mississippi: An American Chronicle of Struggle and Schism* (Hicksville, N.Y.: Exposition Press, 1979), recalls rights activity, and some of the tensions and divisions among black activists, in the Mississippi city with the largest concentration of black residents. Salter was an associate of Medgar W. Evers, one of the most influential voices in the Jackson movement, who was assassinated on June 11, 1963. For the story of Byron de la Beckwith, who was convicted of murdering Evers, see Adam Nossiter, *Of Long Memory: Mississippi and the Murder of Medgar Evers* (Reading, Mass.: Addison-Wesley, 1994). The violence of southern racism is further explored in two works dealing with the murder of three Freedom Summer volunteers in Philadelphia, Mississippi, in June 1964: William Bradford Huie, *Three Lives for Mississippi* (New York: New American Library, 1968; originally published, New York: WCC Books, 1965), and Seth Cagin and Philip Dray, *We Are Not Afraid: The Story of Goodman, Schwerner, and Chaney and the Civil Rights Campaign in Mississippi* (New York: Macmillan, 1988). The journalist Calvin Trilling in "State Secrets," *New Yorker*, May 29, 1995, 54–64, discusses the activities of the secret Mississippi State Sovereignty Commission, which was established by the state legislature in 1956 and spent much of its time spying on those in the movement. Some of Robert Parris Moses' views are available in Bob Moses, "Mississippi: 1961–1962," *Liberation* 14 (January 1970): 7–17, and Eric Burner, *And Gently He Shall Lead Them: Robert Parris Moses and Civil Rights in Mississippi* (New York: New York University Press, 1994), which provides a good appreciation of the texture of his thought.

Other Campaigns

The freedom struggle in Selma, Alabama, is recalled in Amelia Boynton Robinson, *Bridge across Jordan: The Story of the Civil Rights Struggle in Selma*, 2d ed. (Washington: Schiller Institute, 1991). Also see J. L. Chestnut, Jr., and Julie Cass, *Black in Selma: The Uncommon Life of J. L. Chestnut, Jr.* (New York: Farrar, Straus and Giroux, 1990), and David J. Garrow, *Protest at Selma: Martin Luther*

King, Jr., and the Voting Rights Act of 1965 (New Haven: Yale University Press, 1978). Stephen L. Longenecker, *Selma's Peacemaker: Ralph Smeltzer and Civil Rights Mediation* (Philadelphia: Temple University Press, 1987), analyzes the response of southern white moderates to the political and economic challenges of the campaign for racial equity. Along similar lines, Hollinger F. Barnard, ed., *Outside the Magic Circle: The Autobiography of Virginia Foster Durr* (Tuscaloosa: University of Alabama Press, 1985), describes the role of progressive southern whites in some of the black civil liberties campaigns. The essays in David J. Garrow, ed., *Birmingham, Alabama, 1956–1963: The Black Struggle for Civil Rights* (Brooklyn: Carlson Publishing, 1989), deal with events in a southern city in which the response of many whites to black demonstrations was especially brutal. Paul Good, *The Trouble I've Seen: White Journalist, Black Movement* (Washington: Howard University Press, 1974), describes how one newspaperman covered the events in the South. Robert J. Norrell, *Reaping the Whirlwind: The Civil Rights Movement in Tuskegee* (New York: Knopf, 1985), deals with protests in another Alabama city, home of Booker T. Washington's Tuskegee Institute. In 1968 the civil rights movement turned its attention to Memphis, Tennessee, and the strike there of black garbage workers. The Memphis campaign is examined in Michael K. Honey, *Southern Labor and Black Civil Rights: Organizing Memphis Workers* (Champaign: University of Illinois Press, 1993), and Joan Turner Beifuss, *At the River I Stand: Memphis, the 1968 Strike, and Martin Luther King* (Brooklyn: Carlson Publishing, 1989). Alan Draper, *Conflict of Interests: Organized Labor and the Civil Rights Movement in the South, 1954–1968* (Ithaca: ILR Press, 1994), examines the often uneasy relationship between white unions and black workers. Three works deal with the resistance and frustration Dr. King and the movement encountered in its first major effort, the Chicago Campaign, 1965–66, to desegregate to a northern city: Alan B. Anderson and George W. Pickering, *Confronting the Color Line: The Broken Promise of the Civil Rights Movement in Chicago* (Athens: University of Georgia Press, 1986); James R. Ralph, Jr., *Northern Protest: Martin Luther King, Jr., Chicago, and the Civil Rights Movement* (Cambridge, Mass.: Harvard University Press, 1993); and the essays in David J. Garrow, ed., *Chicago 1966 Open-Housing Marches, Summit Negotiations and Operation Breadbasket* (Brooklyn: Carlson Publishing, 1989).

    In the years before the *Brown* decision civil rights advocates had been partially successful in altering the regulations affecting blacks in the military. Two works discuss the setting for the integration of the armed forces: Morris J. MacGregor and Bernard C. Nalty, eds., *Blacks in the United States Armed Forces: Basic Documents*, 13 vols. (Wilmington: Scholarly Resources, 1977), and Richard Dalfiume, *Desegregation of the U.S. Armed Forces: Fighting on Two Fronts, 1939–53* (Columbia: University of Missouri Press, 1969).

Presidential Policies

The relationship between the civil rights campaigners and American Presidents often has been richly rewarding for both sides; and at the same time has proven a source of dissatisfaction to both parties. On blacks and presidential politics in the era of Franklin D. Roosevelt, see Harvard Sitkoff, *A New Deal for Blacks: The*

Emergence of Civil Rights as a National Issue, The Depression Decade (New York: Oxford University Press, 1978). William C. Berman, *The Politics of Civil Rights in the Truman Administration* (Columbus: Ohio State University Press, 1970), is very critical of Truman and his handling of civil rights issues; Donald R. McCoy and Richard T. Reuten, *Quest and Response: Minority Rights and the Truman Administration* (Lawrence: University Press of Kansas, 1973), describe the Truman presidency and its politics more sympathetically. In 1946 Truman appointed a biracial committee of prominent Americans to investigate race relations in the United States. The President's panel issued its report the following year: President's Committee on Civil Rights, *To Secure these Rights: The Report of the President's Committee on Civil Rights* (Washington: U.S. Government Printing Office, 1947). The presidential politics and programs of the 1950s are the subject of Robert Fredrick Burk, *The Eisenhower Administration and Black Civil Rights* (Knoxville: University of Tennessee Press, 1984).

Civil Rights Legislation

The legislative history of the civil rights movement and the processes whereby it reshaped public policy are explored in Charles Whalen and Barbara Whalen, *The Long Debate: A Legislative History of the 1964 Civil Rights Act* (New York: New American Library, 1985). Stephen C. Halpern, *On the Limits of the Law: The Ironic Legacy of Title VI of the 1964 Civil Rights Act* (Baltimore: Johns Hopkins University Press, 1995). Benjamin Muse, *Ten Years of Prelude: The Story of Integration since the Supreme Court's 1954 Decision* (New York: Viking, 1964); and Hugh Davis Graham, *The Civil Rights Era: Origins and Development of a National Policy, 1960–1965* (New York: Oxford University Press, 1990). Donald G. Nieman, *Promises to Keep, African-Americans and the Constitutional Order, 1776 to the Present* (New York: Oxford University Press, 1991), looks at the relationship between blacks struggling for equal rights and the courts. The journalist Nicholas Lemann, in an excellent and moving book, *The Promised Land: The Black Migration and How It Changed America* (New York: Knopf, 1991), studies the migration of five million southern African Americans into the northern cities that began in the 1940s and continued until the 1960s.

The South

The history of the black struggle for political recognition is also, like so much of African American life, a history of the South and southern politics and the interaction between black and white Southerners within the political arena. Works on these themes include Earl Black and Merle Black, *Politics and Society in the South* (Cambridge, Mass.: Harvard University Press, 1987); Numan V. Bartley and Hugh D. Graham, *Southern Politics and the Second Reconstruction* (Baltimore: Johns Hopkins University Press, 1975); Earl Black, *Southern Governors and Civil Rights: Racial Segregation as a Campaign Issue in the Second Reconstruction* (Cambridge, Mass.: Harvard University Press, 1976); and Pat Watters and Reese Cleghorn, *Climbing Jacob's Ladder: The Arrival of Negroes in Southern Politics* (New York: Harcourt, Brace and World, 1967). Stephan Lesher, *George Wallace: American Populist* (Reading, Mass.: Addison-Wesley, 1994), is a biography of the politician and one-time presidential candidate. David Goldfield, *Black, White, and Southern: Race Relations and Southern Culture 1940 to the Present* (Baton Rouge: Louisiana State University Press, 1990), identifies the common elements in the culture of southern blacks and whites.

African American Political Participation

The drive for political recognition and voting rights ushered in the age of a distinctive African American political culture. Three works by Steven F. Lawson assess the impact of African American voting rights on regional and national politics: *Black Ballots: Voting Rights in the South, 1944–1969* (New York: Columbia University Press, 1976); *In Pursuit of Power, Southern Blacks and Electoral Politics, 1965–1982* (New York: Columbia University Press, 1985); and *Running for Freedom: Civil Rights and Black Politics in America since 1941* (New York: McGraw-Hill, 1991). Also see the collection of essays edited by Chandler Davidson and Bernard Grofman, *Quiet Revolution in the South: The Impact of the Voting Rights Act, 1965–1990* (Princeton: Princeton University Press, 1994). Frank Parker, *Black Votes Count: Political Empowerment in Mississippi after 1965* (Chapel Hill: University of North Carolina Press, 1990), assesses the impact of the 1965 Voting Rights Act on one Deep South state. James W. Button, *Blacks and Social Change: Impact of the Civil Rights Movement in Southern Communities*, 2d ed. (Princeton: Princeton University Press, 1993), measures the consequences of black participation on the political life of six Florida cities. Doug McAdam, *Political Process and the Development of Black Insurgency, 1930–1970* (Chicago: University of Chicago Press, 1982), gives a long history of the black campaign to seize political responsibility. Denton L. Watson, *Lion in the Lobby: Clarence Mitchell, Jr.'s Struggle for the Passage of Civil Rights Laws* (New York: William Morrow, 1990), is a biography of the NAACP's chief lobbyist, and the story of the most visible, powerful, and flamboyant elected black official in the nation before the 1960s is told in Neil Hickey and Ed Edwin, *Adam Clayton Powell and the Politics of Race* (New York: Fleet Publishing, 1965), and Charles V. Hamilton, *Adam Clay Powell, Jr.: The Political Biography of an American Dilemma* (New York: Atheneum, 1991).

White Resistance

As broad and insistent as was the movement for black equal rights, so too was the reaction and resistance of whites to that movement. For general studies of the white opposition, see Michal R. Belknap, *Federal Law and Southern Order: Racial Violence and Constitutional Conflict in the Post-Brown South* (Athens: University of Georgia Press, 1987); Jack Bloom, *Class, Race, and the Civil Rights Movement: The Political Economy of Southern Racism* (Bloomington: Indiana University Press, 1987); and Herbert Shapiro, *White Violence and Black Response: From Reconstruction to Montgomery* (Amherst: University of Massachusetts Press, 1988). The southern white campaign against desegregation was centered in the well-organized institution of the Citizens' Council, which at least publicly professed nonviolence and the policy of massive resistance. The origins and implementation of the policy and the work of the various citizens' leagues is discussed in Numan V. Bartley, *The Rise of Massive Resistance: Race and Politics in the South during the 1950's* (Baton Rouge: Louisiana State University Press,

1969); Neil R. McMillen, *The Citizens' Council: Organized Resistance to the Second Reconstruction, 1954–1964* (Urbana: University of Illinois Press, 1971); and Francis M. Wilhoit, *The Politics of Massive Resistance* (New York: Braziller, 1973). Studies of Virginia include Benjamin Muse, *Virginia's Massive Resistance* (Bloomington: Indiana University Press, 1961), and Robbins L. Gates, *The Making of Massive Resistance: Virginia's Politics of Public School Desegregation, 1954–56* (Chapel Hill: University of North Carolina Press, 1964. The journalist James Jackson Kilpatrick, now a news commentator of national reputation but during the heady days of the civil rights campaign editor of the prosegregation *Richmond News Leader*, defended massive resistance, advocated state interposition against federal law, and argued for the advantages of keeping the races separate in *The Southern Case for School Segregation* (New York: Crowell-Collier Press, 1962). Three studies examine federal interference with the black freedom movement and the effort by the FBI to identify some black leaders with radical or communist organizations: David J. Garrow, *The FBI and Martin Luther King Jr.* (New York: Norton, 1981; and New York: Penguin, 1983); Kenneth O'Reilly, *"Racial Matters": The FBI's Secret File on Black America, 1960–1972* (New York: Free Press, 1989); and Clayborne Carson, *Malcolm X: The FBI File* (New York: Carroll and Graf Publishers, 1991). Elizabeth Jacoway and David R. Colburn in *Southern Businessmen and Desegregation* (Baton Rouge: Louisiana State University Press, 1982) discuss an important and little acknowledged group of southerners who mediated between their white clients and customers who supported segregation and black southerners, also clients and customers, determined to bring segregation to an end.

The role played by southern white moderates and liberals in civil rights activities has only recently begun to receive serious attention. Harry S. Ashmore, *Civil Rights and Wrongs: A Memoir of Race and Politics, 1941–1994* (New York: Pantheon, 1994), offers the recollections of a southern newspaperman who espoused racial reform. David Chappell, *Inside Agitators: White Southerners in the Civil Rights Movement* (Baltimore: Johns Hopkins University Press, 1994), argues that whites were essential to the success of the movement.

Women in the Civil Rights Movement

Works analyzing the participation and influence of women in the civil rights movement—in addition to books already mentioned earlier here—include two reference collections edited by Darlene Clark Hine, *Black Women in American History: The Twentieth Century*, 4 vols. (Brooklyn: Carlson Publishing, 1990), and *Black Women in America: An Historical Encyclopedia*, 2 vols. (Brooklyn: Carlson Publishing, 1993); Jessie Carney Smith, ed., *Notable Black American Women* (Detroit: Gale Research, 1992); and the collection of scholarly essays in Vicki L. Crawford, Jacqueline Rouse, and Barbara Woods, ed., *Women in the Civil Rights Movement: Trailblazers and Torchbearers* (Brooklyn: Carlson Publishing, 1990), vol. 16 of Darlene Clark Hine, ed., *Black Women in the United States*. Also see Rhoda Lois Blumberg, "Rediscovering Women Leaders of the Civil Rights Movement," in Jeannine Swift, ed., *Dream and Reality: The Modern Black Struggle for Freedom and Equality* (Westport, Conn.: Greenwood Press, 1991), and Paula Giddings, *When and Where I Enter: The Impact of Black*

Women on Race and Sex in America (New York: William Morrow, 1984). Sara Evans, *Personal Politics: The Roots of Women's Liberation in the Civil Rights Movement and the New Left* (New York: Knopf, 1979), argues that the women's liberation movement developed out of the experience of white female activists in the civil rights organizations, especially membership in SNCC, where they came in touch with strong black women in local communities throughout the deep South. And Pearl Cleage, *Deals with the Devil, and Other Reasons to Riot* (New York: Ballantine Books, 1993), is a new work certain to provoke debate as an activist black woman reflects on the struggle for black freedom.

Some of the women of the civil rights era have told their stories, or they have had their lives examined in some carefully wrought biographies. Mrs. Fannie Lou Hamer, one of the founding members of the Mississippi Freedom Democratic Party, talks of her part in the freedom movement in *To Praise Our Bridges: An Autobiography of Mrs. Fanny [sic] Lou Hamer* (Jackson, Miss.: KIPCO, 1967), reprinted as Fannie Lou Hamer, "To Praise Our Bridges," in *Mississippi Writers: Reflections on Childhood and Youth*, ed. Dorothy Abbott (Jackson: University Press of Mississippi, 1986). Kay Mills, *This Little Light of Mine: The Life of Fannie Lou Hamer* (New York: Dutton, 1993), is an excellent history of the life and times of the endearing Mrs. Hamer. A complete biography of Ella Baker has yet to appear, but two essays deal with her life and thought: Ellen Cantarow and Susan Gushee O'Malley, "Ella Baker: Organizing for Civil Rights," in Ellen Cantarow with Susan Gushee O'Malley and Sharon Hartman Strom, *Moving the Mountain: Women Working for Social Change* (Old Westbury, N.Y.: Feminist Press, 1980), and Charles Payne, "Ella Baker and Models of Social Change," *Signs* 14 (1989): 885–99. Rosa Parks describes the event that led to the Montgomery bus boycott and her life of rights activism in *Rosa Parks: My Story* (New York: Dial Books, 1992), with Jim Haskins. Two books, Septima Poinsette Clark with LeGette Blythe, *Echo in My Soul* (New York: Dutton, 1962), and Septima Poinsette Clark with Cynthia Stokes Brown, *Ready from Within: Septima Clark and the Civil Rights Movement* (1986; reprint, Trenton, N.J.: Africa World Press, 1990), describe the work of Clark, one of the founders of the Highlander program and an organizer of Southern "citizenship schools" that aimed at qualifying blacks to register to vote. Mary King, *Freedom Song: A Personal Story of the 1960s Civil Rights Movement* (New York: William Morrow, 1987), is a chronicle of SNCC's movement from reform to revolution by a SNCC staffer.

Black Power

"Black Power" could be used to describe any number of attitudes and philosophies—from an angrily antiwhite insistence on black separatism or nationalism to the more peaceable encouragements to African Americans to be more aware of their heritage and to cultivate a greater appreciation of their culture. General studies of Black Power, all sympathetic, include William L. Van Deburg, *New Day in Babylon: The Black Power Movement and American Culture, 1965–1975* (Chicago: University of Chicago Press, 1992); Herbert Haines, *Black Radicals and the Civil Rights Mainstream, 1954–1970* (Knoxville: University of Tennessee Press, 1988); and E. U. Essien-Udom, *Black Nationalism: A Search for an Identity in America* (Chicago: University of Chicago Press, 1962). Julius Lester, *Look*

Out, Whitey! Black Power's Gon' Get Your Mama (New York: Dial Press, 1968), provides an example of the literature and rhetoric of Black Power by an author who both supported the Black Power movement and could be among its harshest critics. Stokely Carmichael's views are available in two of his essays, "Toward Black Liberation," *Massachusetts Review* 7 (Autumn 1966): 639–51, and "What We Want," *New York Review of Books*, September 26, 1966, and in a tamer book with co-author Charles V. Hamilton, *Black Power: The Politics of Liberation in America* (New York: Random House, 1967).

Though Carmichael was the first to popularize the phrase "Black Power," the individual who came to symbolize that movement, to be inseparably identified with black militancy in the minds of blacks and whites, is Malcolm X. Interest in Malcolm recently has been revitalized by a feature film directed by Spike Lee, *Malcolm X* (screenplay by James Baldwin, Arnold Perl, and Spike Lee). Two essays assess the historical reliability and the influence of Spike Lee's movie: Nell Irvin Painter, "Malcolm X across the Genres," *American Historical Review* 98 (April 1993): 432–39, and Gerald Horne, "'Myth' and the Making of 'Malcolm X,'" *American Historical Review* 98 (April 1993): 440–50. There is a bibliography of secondary sources on Malcolm X: Timothy V. Johnson, *Malcolm X: A Comprehensive Annotated Bibliography* (New York: Garland, 1986). The complex and controversial Malcolm X relates his personal history and his views in Malcolm X, *The Autobiography of Malcolm X* (1965; reprint, New York: Ballantine Books, 1992), with the assistance of Alex Haley; George Breitman, ed., *Malcolm X Speaks: Selected Speeches and Statements* (New York: Merit Publishers, 1965); George Breitman, ed., *By Any Means Necessary: Speeches, Interviews, and a Letter by Malcolm X* (New York: Pathfinder, 1970); and Bruce Perry, ed., *Malcolm X: The Last Speeches* (New York: Pathfinder, 1989). Malcolm X's relationship with Elijah Muhammad's Lost-Found Nation of Islam (Black Muslims), from which he resigned in 1964, is discussed in C. Eric Lincoln, *The Black Muslims in America*, 2d ed. (Boston: Beacon, 1973). Biographies include Bruce Perry, *Malcolm: The Life of a Man Who Changed Black America* (Barrytown, N.Y.: Station Hill Press, 1991), and Peter Goldman, *The Death and Life of Malcolm X*, 2d ed. (Urbana: University of Illinois Press, 1979). Joe Wood, ed., *Malcolm X: In Our Own Image* (New York: St. Martin's Press, 1992), and James Gwynne, ed., *Malcolm X—Justice Seeker* (New York: Steppingstones Press, 1993), contain scholarly essays. James H. Cone, *Martin and Malcolm and America: A Dream or a Nightmare* (Maryknoll, N.Y.: Orbis Books, 1991), compares the religious thought and philosophy of Malcolm X with that of Martin Luther King, Jr. See also George Breitman, *The Last Year of Malcolm X: The Evolution of a Revolutionary* (n.p., 1967). The journalist Karl Evanzz, *The Judas Factor: The Plot to Kill Malcolm X* (Emoryville, Calif.: distributed by Publishers Group West, 1992), investigates the assassination of Malcolm.

The Black Panthers

If Malcolm X was the individual most closely associated with Black Power in the public mind, the Black Panthers, organized in Oakland, California, in October 1966, was the group identified with black radicalism, violence, and revolutionary politics. Many of the organizers of the Panther party have provided written records of their activities and beliefs: Bobby Seale, *Seize the Time: The Story of the Black Panther Party and Huey P. Newton* (New York: Random House, 1970); Bobby Seale, *A Lonely Rage: The Autobiography of Bobby Seale*, with a foreword by James Baldwin (New York: Times Books, 1978); Huey Newton with J. Herman Blake, *Revolutionary Suicide* (New York: Harcourt, Brace and Jovanovich, 1973); H. Rap Brown, *Die, Nigger, Die!* (New York: Dial Press, 1969); Eldridge Cleaver, *Soul on Ice* (New York: McGraw-Hill, 1968); and David Hilliard and Lewis Cole, *This Side of Glory: The Autobiography of David Hilliard and the Story of the Black Panther Party* (Boston: Little, Brown, 1993). Earl Anthony describes his time as a member of the Panthers in *Picking Up the Gun: A Report on the Black Panthers* (New York: Dial Press, 1970). A pathbreaking book by a black journalist who looks askance at the Panthers is Hugh Pearson, *Shadow of the Panther: Huey Newton and the Price of Black Power in America* (Reading, Mass.: Addison-Wesley, 1994). Also see G. Louis Heath, *Off the Pigs! The History and Literature of the Black Panther Party* (Metuchen, N.J.: Scarecrow Press, 1976); John Hulett, *The Black Panther Party* (New York: Merit Publishers, 1966); and Gene Marine, *The Black Panthers* (New York: New American Library, 1969). Three works describe the place of women in the black revolutionary movement: Angela Davis, *Angela Davis: An Autobiography* (1974; reprint, New York: International Press, 1988); J. A. Parker, *Angela Davis: The Making of a Revolutionary* (New Rochelle, N.Y.: Arlington House, 1973); and Elaine Brown, *A Taste of Power: A Black Woman's Story* (New York: Pantheon, 1992). The essays in Clyde Taylor, ed., *Vietnam and Black America: An Anthology of Protest and Resistance* (Garden City, N.Y.: Anchor Press, 1973), assess the influence of the civil rights crusade and the Black Power movement on other forms of social protest.

Urban Riots

Works that examine the ghetto riots and their consequences include Fred R. Harris and Tom Wicker, eds., *The Kerner Report: The 1968 Report of the National Advisory Commission on Civil Disorders* (New York: Pantheon, 1988); Sidney Fine, *Violence in the Model City: The Cavanaugh Administration, Race Relations and the Detroit Riot of 1967* (Ann Arbor: University of Michigan Press, 1989); Tom Hayden, *Rebellion in Newark: Official Violence and Ghetto Response* (New York: Random House, 1967); James W. Button, *Black Violence: Political Impact of the 1960s Riots* (Princeton: Princeton University Press, 1978); Paul Bullock, ed., *Watts: The Aftermath by the People of Watts* (New York: Grove Press, 1969); and the forthcoming Gerald Horne, *Fire This Time: The Watts Uprising and the Meaning of the 1960s*.

The 1950s

Among works that assess the development of the United States in the postwar decades, with some special attention to the fifties, John Patrick Diggins's *The Proud Decades: America in War and Peace, 1941–1960* (New York: Norton, 1988) is recent and sound. Also see William L. O'Neill, *American High: The Years of Confidence, 1945–1960* (New York: Free Press, 1986), which captures the extraordinary optimism of the postwar years. In *Another Chance: Postwar America, 1945–1968* (Philadelphia: Temple University Press, 1981), James B. Gilbert assesses postwar social and cultural change, and Frederick F. Siegel, *The Troubled Journey: From Pearl Harbor to Ronald Reagan* (New York: Hill and Wang, 1984), concentrates on presidential policies with good coverage of the Eisenhower years. For an analysis of the baby boomers—people born between 1946 and 1964—see Landon Y. Jones, *Great Expectations: America and the Baby Boom Generation* (New York: Coward, McCann and Geoghegan, 1980).

The journalist David Halberstam's *The Fifties* (New York: Villard Books, 1993) is an engaging overview of the decade. Paul Carter, *Another Part of the Fifties* (New York: Columbia University Press, 1983), looks at politics and culture in a pleasantly idiosyncratic way. See J. Ronald Oakley's *God's Country: America in the Fifties* (New York: Dembner Books, 1986); Jeffrey Hart, *When the Going Was Good: American Life in the Fifties* (New York, Crown, 1982); and Stephen J. Whitfield's artful and balanced *The Culture of the Cold War* (Baltimore: Johns Hopkins University Press, 1991). Richard H. Pells, *The Liberal Mind in a Conservative Age: American Intellectuals in the 1940s and 1950s*, 2d ed. (Middletown, Conn.: Wesleyan University, 1989), examines American thought. Richard M. Fried, *Nightmare in Red: The McCarthy Era in Perspective* (New York: Oxford University Press, 1990), is an overview of the postwar anticommunist campaign. In *Previous Convictions: A Journey through the 1950s* (New Brunswick, N.J.: Rutgers University Press, 1995), Nora Sayre writes about some of the artists whom the government investigated as subversives.

W. T. Lhamon, Jr., *Deliberate Speed: The Origins of a Cultural Style in the American 1950s* (Washington: Smithsonian Institution Press, 1990), examines the art and popular culture of the 1950s. During the fifties the automobile was instrumental in reorganizing American space; it also changed social customs and became an important symbolic means through which many Americans expressed their claims to social status while others demonstrated their rebelliousness. See Martin Wachs and Margaret Crawford, eds., *The Car and the City: The Automobile, the Built Environment, and Daily Urban Life* (Ann Arbor: University of Michigan Press, 1992). The transformation in the physical and social landscape of the United States in the fifties is the subject of Kenneth T. Jackson, *Crabgrass Frontier: The Suburbanization of the United States* (New York: Oxford University Press, 1985).

Sex, gender roles, and family life were changing swiftly in the fifties. Notions of that decade as an age of sexual self-control and abstinence, for example, were challenged just as the decade began with the publication of the Kinsey Reports, *Sexual Behavior in the Human Male* (1948) and *Sexual Behavior in the Human Female* (1953), which claimed that most American males were sexually active by the time they were teenagers and that half the nation's females had engaged in sexual relations before marriage. Wardell B. Pomeroy, *Dr. Kinsey and the Institute for Sex Research* (New Haven: Yale University Press, 1982), is a study of the man who pioneered in the modern study of human sexuality. Benita Eisler, *Private Lives: Men and Women of the Fifties* (New York: Franklin Watts, 1986), discusses sexuality and gender roles. Joanne J. Meyerowitz, ed., *Not June Cleaver: Women and Gender in Postwar America, 1945–1960* (Philadelphia:

Temple University Press, 1994), examines the condition of women. Betty Friedan's classic *The Feminine Mystique* (New York: Norton, 1963) is a critical assessment of roles assigned to middle-class American white women in the postwar years; it became a stimulus to the women's liberation movement of the later 1960s. On the not overly blissful American family of the fifties, see Stephanie Cootz, *The Way We Never Were: American Families and the Nostalgia Trap* (New York: Basic Books, 1992). Elaine Tyler May's *Homeward Bound: American Families in the Cold War Era* (New York: Basic Books, 1988) also examines gender assignments during the period. On youth and the response to the teenage culture, see James Gilbert, *A Cycle of Outrage: America's Reaction to the Juvenile Delinquent in the 1950s* (New York: Oxford University Press, 1986).

Of all the forms of entertainment available to Americans in the fifties, television most dominated popular tastes, shaping expectations and dissolving some long-held illusions. Erik Barnouw, *Tube of Plenty: The Evolution of Television*, rev. ed. (New York: Oxford University Press, 1982), is a good general introduction to the history of television. Karal Ann Marling, *As Seen on TV: The Visual Culture of Everyday Life in the 1950s* (Cambridge, Mass.: Harvard University Press, 1994), is a recent assessment of the medium and its influence. The decade's television scandals provided critics with the opportunity to announce again what so many others had announced in the past: the end of American innocence. See Kent Anderson, *Television Fraud: The History and Implications of the Quiz Show Scandals* (Westport, Conn.: Greenwood Press, 1978), and Joseph Stone and Tim Yohn, *Prime Time and Misdemeanors: Investigating the 1950s TV Quiz Scandal—A D.A.'s Account* (New Brunswick, N.J.: Rutgers University Press, 1992).

William Darby, *Necessary American Fictions: Popular Literature of the 1950s* (Bowling Green: Bowling Green State University Popular Press, 1987), looks at American reading habits. Tastes in cinema and the politics of moviemaking during the era are discussed in *The Films of the Fifties: The American State of Mind* (New York: William Morrow, 1975); Nora Sayre, *Running Time: Films of the Cold War* (New York: Dial Press, 1982); Peter Thomas Doherty, *Teenagers and Teenpics: The Juvenilization of American Movies in the 1950s* (Boston: Unwin Hyman, 1988); and Peter Bisskind's *How Hollywood Taught Us to Stop Worrying and Love the Fifties* (New York: Pantheon, 1983).

Two firsthand accounts of the era are William H. Whyte, *The Organization Man* (New York: Simon and Schuster, 1956), and David Riesman, in collaboration with Reuel Denney and Nathan Glazer, *The Lonely Crowd: A Study of the Changing American Character* (New Haven: Yale University Press, 1950). The prosperity of the times has explication in John Kenneth Galbraith, *The Affluent Society*, 4th ed. (Boston: Houghton Mifflin, 1984), and David M. Potter, *People of Plenty: Economic Abundance and the American Character* (Chicago: University of Chicago Press, 1954). Vance Packard's *The Hidden Persuaders* (New York: McKay, 1957) gently cautioned against the dangers of consumerism; see also Packard's *The Status Seekers* (New York: McKay, 1959). Daniel Bell's *The End of Ideology: On the Exhaustion of Political Ideas in the Fifties*, rev. ed. (New York: Free Press, 1965), applauded the decade as free from the moralizing and emotionalism that made ideology so dangerous. In describing American society as consensual the historian Louis Hartz, in *The Liberal Tradition in America: An Interpretation of American Political Thought since the Revolution* (New York: Harcourt, Brace and World, 1955), supported the view of the United States as free from ideological and class conflict. The influential sociologist C. Wright Mills in *The Power Elite* (New York: Oxford University Press, 1956) and *White Collar: The American Middle Classes* (New York: Oxford University Press, 1951), described a stratified social order and the increasing concentration of power in the hands of ruling elites.

In Holden Caulfield, the protagonist of J. D. Salinger's *Catcher in the Rye* (New York: Little, Brown, 1951), some young American males in the fifties found a hero who expressed their anger against the excesses of the adult world. Two books of reminiscences by gifted women are Sylvia Plath's autobiographical *The Bell Jar* (New York: Harper and Row, 1971), a story of a sensitive and fragile woman's torturous search for identity; and *Un-American Activities: A Memoir of the Fifties* (New York: Harper Collins, 1994), in which Sally Belfrage—whose parents were active in radical politics—recalls growing up in the 1950s amid pressures to conform and be popular. Wini Breines, *Young, White, and Miserable: Growing Up Female in the Fifties* (Boston: Beacon, 1992), argues that maturing among the gender restrictions of the fifties drove many of the era's women to embrace social activism in the 1960s, giving rise, for example, to the feminist movement. A similar argument is made in Brandon French, *On the Verge of Revolt: Women in American Films of the Fifties* (New York: Frederick Ungar, 1978).

The Beats

Unconventional and unsilent members of the silent generation were those writers and artists, and those who inspired them and copied them, who gathered predominantly in the coffeehouses, the bars, and the jazz clubs of New York's Greenwich Village and the North Beach section of San Francisco: the Beats. The Beats, who prepared the way for the counterculture of the sixties and for current tastes in writing, remain apart from recent movements. The Beat temperament, rooted in the anxieties of the Cold War years, is serious, intellectually edgy, and creative.

The most recent studies of Beat culture are Steven Watson, *The Birth of the Beat Generation, 1944–1960* (New York: Pantheon, 1995), and John Arthur Maynard, *Venice West: The Beat Generation in Southern California* (New Brunswick, N.J.: Rutgers University Press, 1991). Bruce Cook, *The Beat Generation* (New York: Scribner's Sons, 1971), studies the Beats and their influence on the culture of the 1960s; in his last chapter, Cook connects the Woodstock generation to the Beats. The essays in Rick Beard and Leslie Berlowitz, eds., *Greenwich Village: Culture and Counterculture* (New Brunswick, N.J.: Rutgers University Press, 1993), examine the history and culture of the Village, which has nurtured radicals from the early decades of the nineteenth century. Ronald Sukenick, *Down and In: Life in the Underground* (New York: William Morrow, 1987), looks at the Beat subculture as found in the bars of lower Manhattan. What Paris was to American writers and rebels in the twenties, claims Dan Wakefield in a memoir, New York was to another restless generation: *New York in the Fifties* (Boston: Houghton Mifflin/Seymour Lawrence, 1992). Also see Pierre Delattre,

Episodes (St. Paul: Graywolf Press, 1993), which is a memoir of life among the Beats in the San Francisco area. Richard Cándida Smith, *Utopia and Dissent: Art, Poetry, and Politics in California* (Berkeley and Los Angeles: University of California Press, 1995), examines the development of a cultural avant-garde in postwar California.

Roy Carr, Brian Case, and Fred Dellar, in *The Hip: Hipsters, Jazz, and the Beat Generation* (London: Faber and Faber, 1986), look at the important place the jazz culture had among the Beats. Homoeroticism is the subject of Catharine R. Stimpson's "The Beat Generation and the Trials of Homosexual Liberation," in *Homosexuality: Sacrilege, Vision, Politics*, ed. Robert Boyers (Saratoga Springs, N.Y.: Skidmore College, 1983), published as no. 58–59 of *Salmagundi*, pp. 373–92.

What the majority of Americans knew of the Beats in the 1950s it absorbed through popular culture. David Dalton's *James Dean, the Mutant King: A Biography* (New York: St. Martin's Press, 1974) examines the art and influence of the actor. Dean projected a screen persona of the moody, sullen outsider. Both Dean and Elvis Presley conveyed a smoldering sexuality at the same time both threatening and androgynous. Whereas Presley was ultimately embraced as an example of American middle-class values, Dean's early death fixed him in time as the screen's archetypal nonconformist. On Presley, see Peter Guralnick, *Last Train to Memphis: The Rise of Elvis Presley* (Boston: Little, Brown, 1994). A recent and very thorough biography of Dean is Val Holley's *James Dean: The Biography* (New York: St. Martin's Press, 1995). Marlon Brando in a series of performances in the fifties, chief among them *The Wild One* (1953), portrayed a rebelliousness and iconoclasm like Dean's. The most recent biography of Brando is Richard Schickel, *Brando: A Life in Our Times* (New York: Atheneum, 1991). Graham McCann, *Rebel Males: Clift, Brando, and Dean* (New Brunswick, N.J.: Rutgers University Press, 1993), is an important recent study that puts Montgomery Clift among the actors who fashioned for the movies a new kind of character, uncertain and distressed.

No actress of the fifties portrayed the same kind of emotional complexity and sullen behavior as Clift or Brando. Nonetheless, Marilyn Monroe was able to convey in many of her films a vulnerability and confusion, a sense of optimism and despair, that suggests a Beat sensibility. Biographies of her, with analysis of her work, are Fred L. Guiles, *Norma Jean: The Life of Marilyn Monroe* (New York: Paragon House, 1993); Graham McCann, *Marilyn Monroe: The Body in the Library* (New Brunswick, N.J.: Rutgers University Press, 1988); and Anthony Summers, *Goddess: The Secret Lives of Marilyn Monroe* (New York: NAL/Dutton, 1986). S. Paige Baty's *American Monroe: The Making of a Body Politic* (Berkeley and Los Angeles: University of California Press, 1995) is a compelling look at the various interpretations of Marilyn.

In the mid-1990s has come a renaissance in interest in the Beats and their world. On November 9, 1995, the Whitney Museum of American Art in New York City opened an exhibition, "Beat Culture and the New America: 1950–1965," that displays in art and artifacts of the Beat generation its creative energy. On May 17–22, 1994, New York University sponsored a Beat conference, "The Beat Generation: Legacy and Celebration," attended by many surviving artists of the Beat bohemia and students of Beat literature and culture. The conference has documentation in a video series by Mitch Corber, *The Beat Generation* (New York: Thin Air Video, 1994).

Beat Writing

Morgen Hickey, *The Bohemian Register: An Annotated Bibliography of the Beat Literary Movement* (Metuchen, N.J.: Scarecrow Press, 1990), is an excellent source for works by and about Beat authors. Ann Charters, ed., *The Beats: Literary Bohemians in Postwar America*, vol. 16, 2 parts, *Dictionary of Literary Biography* (Detroit: Gale Research Company, 1983), is a standard source.

Dozens of small magazines appeared in the fifties and sixties to publish avant garde literature (see the list compiled by George F. Butterick, "Periodicals of the Beat Generation," in Charters, ed. *The Beats* [1983]: 651–58). *Evergreen Review* 1–17, nos. 1–97 (1957–73), was edited by Bernard Scott and Daniel Wolf. An extensive selection of Beat writing is available in Barney Rosset, ed., *Evergreen Review Reader, 1957–1967: A Ten-Year Anthology* (New York: Grove Press, 1968). Two books edited by Arthur Knight and Kit Knight, *Kerouac and the Beats: A Primary Sourcebook* (New York: Paragon House, 1988) and *The Beat Vision: A Primary Sourcebook* (New York: Paragon House, 1987), include interviews with Beat writers along with some of their letters and critical essays about Beat writing and culture. Many of the pieces in the two books are culled from the journal *unspeakable visions of the individual* (February 1971 to date), ed. Arthur Winfield Knight, Glee Knight, and Kit Knight, which is devoted to publishing and commenting on the writings of Beat authors.

Beat journalist Seymour Krim, who pioneered a style of personal reporting that in the sixties became the New Journalism, in 1960 brought together a representative sampling of significant Beat essays, *The Beats: A Gold Medal Anthology* (Greenwich, Conn.: Gold Medal Books, Fawcett Publications). Park Honan, ed., *The Beats: An Anthology of "Beat" Writing* (New York: Dent, 1987), offers poetry and prose of the principal Beat authors along with commentary. Fred W. McDarrah, comp., *Kerouac and Friends: A Beat Generation Album* (New York: William Morrow, 1985), is a series of articles and essays written by the major Beat writers at the height of the movement. David Kherdian, *Six Poets of the San Francisco Renaissance: Portraits and Checklists* (Fresno, Calif.: Giligia Press, 1967), profiles the poetry of Lawrence Ferlinghetti, Gary Snyder, Philip Whalen, David Meltzer, Michael McClure, and Brother Antoninus (William Everson). Anne Waldman, ed., *The Beat Book: Poems and Fiction of the Beat Generation* (Boston: Shambhala, 1995), is a recently published collection of Beat literature by a poet coming to maturity in the sixties, whose work has been influenced by the Beats. Waldman directs the Jack Kerouac School of Disembodied Poetics at Naropa Institute, Boulder, Colorado, which carries on Beat traditions. See Brian Docherty, ed., *The Beat Generation Writers* (Boulder, Colo.: Westview Press, 1995). Lawrence Ferlinghetti, ed., *City Lights Anthology* (San Francisco: City Lights Books, 1974), is a selection of Beat works edited by one of their number. Gene Feldman and Max Gartenberg, eds., *The Beat Generation and the Angry Young Men*, rev. ed. (1958; reprint, Secaucus, N.J.: Citadel Press, 1984), presents American and English radical literature in the 1950s along with critical commentary. Asiatic philosophy and religion had an important influence on a number of Beat writers. Carole Tonkinson, ed., *Big Sky Mind: Buddhism and the Beat Generation* (New York: Riverhead Books, A Tricycle Book, 1995), is a collection of Beat writings demonstrating that influence.

Carlos Baker's *Ernest Hemingway: A Life Story* (1969; reprint, New York: Avon Books, 1980) is a fine biography of the figure some critics look upon as the most important precursor to the moody disillusionment of Beat writers. Lawrence Lipton, *The Holy Barbarians* (Englewood Cliffs, N.J.: Julian Messner, 1959), is an early study of Beat culture by an author familiar with many of its most prominent writers. John Tytell, *Naked Angels: The Lives and Literature of the Beat Generation* (1976; reprint, New York: Grove/Atlantic, 1991), gives background on the history of the Beat generation and is a close examination of Burroughs, Ginsberg, and Kerouac. Other critical and interpretive studies of Beat writing are Gregory Stephenson, *The Daybreak Boys: Essays on the Literature of the Beat Generation* (Carbondale: Southern Illinois University Press, 1990); Lee Bartlett, ed., *The Beats: Essays in Criticism* (Jefferson, N.C.: McFarland, 1981); and Edward Foster Halsey, *Understanding the Beats* (Columbia: University of South Carolina Press, 1992). See also the essays in *The Fifties: Fiction, Poetry, Drama* (Deland, Fla.: Everett/Edwards, 1970), ed. Warren French. A famous demolition essay on the Beats is Norman Podhoretz's "The Know-Nothing Bohemians," *Partisan Review* 25 (Spring 1958): 305–18.

Beat poetry receives special attention in Beat poet Michael McClure's *Scratching the Beat Surface: Essays on New Vision from Blake to Kerouac* (1982; reprint, New York: Viking, 1994); Ekbert Faas, ed., *Towards a New American Poetics, Essays and Interviews: Charles Olson, Robert Duncan, Gary Snyder, Robert Creeley, Robert Bly, Allen Ginsberg* (Santa Barbara: Black Sparrow Press, 1978); and Michael Davidson, *The San Francisco Renaissance: Poetics and Community at Mid-Century* (New York: Cambridge University Press, 1989). See the essays and poetry about the arts by Allen Ginsberg and William Burroughs, among others, in *Astronauts of Inner-Space* (an international collection of avant-garde activity), ed. Jeff Berger (San Francisco: Stolen Paper Review Editions, 1966).

Kerouac, Ginsberg, Burroughs, and Snyder

In Kerouac's most popular book, *On the Road* (New York: Viking, 1957), readers were introduced to the restless ways of the Beat world. *On the Road* remains the handbook for those alienated from middle-class culture, or uneasy with its customs, and is still read widely today. Useful bibliographical guides to works by and about Kerouac are Ann Charters, *A Bibliography of Works by Jack Kerouac (Jean Louis Lebris De Kerouac), 1939–1975*, rev. ed. (New York: Phoenix Bookshop, 1975), and Robert J. Milewski, with the assistance of John Z. Guzlowski and Linda Calendrillo, *Jack Kerouac: An Annotated Bibliography of Secondary Sources, 1944–1979* (Metuchen, N.J.: Scarecrow Press, 1981). Ann Charters recently has assembled and edited a collection of Kerouac's correspondence, *Jack Kerouac: Selected Letters, 1940–1956* (New York: Viking, 1995), and his writings, *The Portable Jack Kerouac* (New York: Viking, 1995). Also see Michael White, comp. and ed., *Safe in Heaven Dead: Interviews with Jack Kerouac* (New York: Hanuman Books, 1990).

Biographies of Kerouac include Ann Charters's sympathetic portrait, *Kerouac: A Biography* (New York: Straight Arrow Press, 1973); Dennis McNally, *Desolate Angel: Jack Kerouac, the Beat Generation, and America* (New York: Random House, 1979); and Gerald Nicosia's *Memory Babe: A Critical Biography of Jack Kerouac* (1983; reprint, with a new preface, Berkeley and Los Angeles: University of California Press, 1994). Barry Gifford and Lawrence Lee, *Jack's Book: An Oral Biography of Jack Kerouac* (1978; reprint, New York: Penguin, 1979), is an unconventional biography that stitches together interviews with people who knew Kerouac. Charles E. Jarvis, *Visions of Kerouac*, 3d ed. (Lowell, Mass.: Ithaca Press, 1994), is good on its subject's early life and stresses Kerouac's rebellious spirit.

Critical studies of Kerouac include Regina Weinreich, *The Spontaneous Poetics of Jack Kerouac: A Study of the Fiction* (Carbondale: Southern Illinois University Press, 1987), a work of intricate analysis that gives some special attention to the influence of jazz on Kerouac's prose. Robert A. Hipkiss, *Jack Kerouac, Prophet of the New Romanticism: A Critical Study of the Published Works of Kerouac and a Comparison of Them to Those of J. D. Salinger, James Purdy, John Knowles, and Ken Kesey* (Lawrence: Regents Press of Kansas, 1976), sets Kerouac's literary themes alongside those of other writers who explored similar issues. James T. Jones, *A Map of "Mexico City Blues": Jack Kerouac as Poet* (Carbondale: Southern Illinois University Press, 1992), examines Kerouac's poetry, and Tim Hunt, *Kerouac's Crooked Road: Development of a Fiction* (Hamden, Conn.: Archon, 1981), offers a close reading of *On the Road*. Bill Kauffman, *America First: Its History, Culture, and Politics* (Amherst, N.Y.: Prometheus Books, 1995), is a study of American nationalism that includes a chapter describing Kerouac's increasing political conservatism. Frederick Feied's *No Pie in the Sky: The Hobo as American Cultural Hero in the Works of Jack London, John Dos Passos, and Jack Kerouac* (New York: Citadel Press, 1964) is a finely argued study of a marginal American social type as a heroic American literary figure.

In counterpoise to the public persona of Kerouac in his massive broad-stroked paragraphs is that of Allen Ginsberg, its gentle, tatterdemalion poet laureate roused occasionally to violent fits of rhetoric. One of Ginsberg's biographers, Barry Miles, has described him as "the poet advocate of the underdog." Often viewed as the work that first brought the Beat literary movement to the public's attention, Ginsberg's *Howl* contains the best-remembered line from the most famous poem of the Beat era: "I saw the best minds of my generation destroyed by madness, starving hysterical naked . . ." (*"Howl" and Other Poems* [San Francisco: City Lights Pocket Bookshop, 1956]). Ginsberg's art and activism are important links between the Beats of the fifties and the countercultural generation of the 1960s. Fine guides to Ginsberg's writings and the critical response to his work are Bill Morgan, *The Works of Allen Ginsberg, 1941–1994: A Descriptive Bibliography* (Westport, Conn.: Greenwood Press, 1995); Michelle P. Kraus, *Allen Ginsberg: An Annotated Bibliography, 1969–1977* (Metuchen, N.J.: Scarecrow Press, 1980); and George Dowden, *A Bibliography of Works by Allen Ginsberg, October 1943 to July 1, 1967* (San Francisco: City Lights Books, 1971). Three published collections of Ginsberg's journals constitute something of an autobiography. *Indian Journals, March 1962–May 1963: Notebooks, Diary, Blank Pages, Writings* (San Francisco: Dave Haselwood Books, 1970), describes his travels through India and the influence of the East on his thought; *Journals: Early Fifties, Early Sixties* (1977; reprint, New York: Grove Press, 1992), ed. Gordon Ball, cover the years 1952–62. *Journals Mid-Fifties, 1954–1958* (New York: Harper Collins, 1995), are edited by Gordon Ball. Add to these the *Collected Poems, 1947–1980* (New York: Harper and Row, 1984), an excellent single-volume compendium of Ginsberg's work. Also see *As Ever: The Collected Correspondence of Allen Ginsberg and Neal Cassady*, ed. Barry Gifford (Berkeley: Creative Arts Book Co., 1977). A collection of Ginsberg's lectures and conversation dealing mostly with the events and issues of the 1960s is *Allen Verbatim: Lectures on Poetry, Politics, and Consciousness*, ed. Gordon Ball (New York: McGraw-Hill, 1974).

The most recent and thorough biography of Ginsberg is Michael Schumacher's *Dharma Lion: A Critical Biography of Allen Ginsberg* (New York: St. Martin's Press, 1992). Barry Miles, *Ginsberg: A Biography* (New York: Simon and Schuster, 1989), is also excellent. Critical readings of Ginsberg's work include the large assemblage of interpretive essays in Lewis Hyde, ed., *On the Poetry of Allen Ginsberg* (Ann Arbor: University of Michigan Press, 1984); Louis Simpson, *A Revolution in Taste: Studies of Dylan Thomas, Allen Ginsberg, Sylvia Plath, and Robert Lowell* (New York: Macmillan, 1978), which offers a tightly written, concise criticism of Ginsberg's poetry; and Paul Portuges, *The Visionary Poetics of Allen Ginsberg* (Santa Barbara: Ross-Erikson Publishers, 1978), which is chiefly a discussion of the influence on Ginsberg of the English poet-mystic William Blake.

Mysticism was important to the work of the Beats. Nowhere is this more evident than in the writings of Gary Snyder, who spent much of the Beat era in the East, mostly in Japan, absorbing the culture of the Orient and found in its philosophies and religions alternatives to Western ideas and beliefs that he transmitted to other Beat writers, especially Ginsberg and Kerouac. Snyder's sensitive writings on nature and the environment inspire the current generation of ecologists. *A Range of Poems* (London: Fulcrum Press, 1966) is a collection of Snyder's poetry that displays his interest in Asian culture, nature, and the customs of American Indians. *Earth House Hold: Technical Notes and Queries to Fellow Dharma Revolutionaries* (New York: New Directions Publishing, 1969) is a series of notes and essays by Snyder on the richness of Eastern religion and Zen Buddhism. Along with *The Real Work: Interviews and Talks, 1964–1979*, ed. William Scott McLean (New York: New Directions, 1980), these works offer a good sampling of Snyder's poetry and philosophy. Bob Steuding, *Gary Snyder* (Boston: Twayne, 1976), is a good brief introduction to Snyder's life and major writings. Tim Dean's biography, *Gary Snyder and the American Unconscious: Inhabiting the Ground* (New York: St. Martin's Press, 1991), is more extensive. Patrick D. Murphy, ed., *Critical Essays on Gary Snyder* (Boston: G. Hall, 1990), is a collection of scholarly assessments of Snyder's poetry. James I. McKlintock, *Nature's Kindred Spirits: Aldo Leopold, Joseph Wood Krutch, Edward Abbey, Annie Dillard, and Gary Snyder* (Madison: University of Wisconsin Press, 1994), examines authors in whose work nature and the environment have been prominent. See the criticism and interpretation in Paul Sherman, *In Search of the Primitive: Rereading David Antin, Jerome Rothenberg, and Gary Snyder* (Baton Rouge: Louisiana State University Press, 1986). In *The Idea of Wilderness: From Prehistory to the Age of Ecology* (New Haven: Yale University Press, 1991), Max Oelschlaeger includes a chapter entitled "The Idea of Wilderness in the Poetry of Robinson Jeffries and Gary Snyder," pp. 243–80.

The lightness and serenity, the humaneness and delicacy, of Snyder's poetry stands in contrast to the brutality and waywardness of prose and subject in the writings of William S. Burroughs. Burroughs, along with Kerouac and Ginsberg, is generally put at the foundation of the Beat movement. *The Naked Lunch* (New York: Grove Press, 1959) is Burroughs's best-known work. It is unconventional even by the standards of a movement that defined itself by challenging previous literary forms. Its notoriety derives in part from a long and hotly contested effort to free it from court censorship for obscenity. Michael Barry Goodman, *Contemporary Literary Censorship: The Case History of Burroughs' "Naked Lunch"* (Metuchen, N.J.: Scarecrow Press, 1981), follows the litigation surrounding the banning of the book. Excerpts from eight of Burroughs's books, among them *Naked Lunch*, are found in John Calder, *A William Burroughs Reader* (London: Pan Books, 1982). Bibliographical aids to Burroughs's literary output, along with letters, interviews, and information about the critical response to his work, are Michael B. Goodman, with Lemuel B. Coley, *William S. Burroughs: A Reference Guide* (New York: Garland, 1990); Joe Maynard and Barry Miles, comp., *William S. Burroughs, A Bibliography, 1953–73: Unlocking Inspector Lee's Word Hoard* (Charlottesville: published for the Bibliographical Society of the University of Virginia by the University Press of Virginia, 1978); and Michael B. Goodman, *William S. Burroughs: An Annotated Bibliography of His Works and Criticism* (New York: Garland, 1975).

Burroughs's views on a variety of subjects are available in Daniel Odier, *The Job: Interviews with William S. Burroughs*, rev. ed. (New York: Grove Press, 1974); Burroughs's *Letters to Allen Ginsberg, 1953–1957*, rev. ed., ed. Ron Padgett and Anne Waldman (New York: Full Court Press, 1982), collects the correspondence of two giants of the Beat literary rebellion at the height of the movement. Add to these *The Letters of William S. Burroughs: 1945–1959*, ed. Oliver Harris (New York: Viking, 1993), which prints correspondence with other Beats.

Ted Morgan's *Literary Outlaw: The Life and Times of William S. Burroughs* (New York: Henry Holt, 1988), a thorough and imaginative biography based on extensive interviews with the subject. Barry Miles, *William Burroughs, El Hombre Invisible: A Portrait* (New York: Hyperion, 1993), is the most recent biography of Burroughs. Jennie Skerl, *William S. Burroughs* (Boston: Twayne, 1985) and *William S. Burroughs at the Front: Critical Reception, 1959–1989* (Carbondale: Southern Illinois University Press, 1991), are also useful. Robin Lydenberg emphasizes Burroughs's radical experimental use of language and his destruction of conventions in *Word Cultures: Radical Theory and Practice in William S. Burroughs' Fiction* (Urbana: University of Illinois Press, 1987). It is a matter of some consternation that this personification of drug abuse has lived well into his eighties; when a graduate student asked if she could stop and visit him at

Lawrence, Kansas, in her bus full of undergraduates, Burroughs replied that it would be impossible since he was not a roadside attraction.

Other Beat Writers

The principal members of the Beat generation were often the inspiration for many other writers of the movement. The poet Lawrence Ferlinghetti was the founder of City Lights in San Francisco, an early paperback bookstore and a gathering place for most of the major figures of the Beat rebellion. Ferlinghetti's collaboration with Ginsberg in 1956, and the publication of Ginsberg's *Howl* by City Lights Books, marked the beginning of national recognition for the movement, although it was probably Kerouac's *On the Road* that popularized the word *beat*. Bill Morgan, *Lawrence Ferlinghetti: A Comprehensive Bibliography to 1980* (New York: Garland, 1982), is a good guide to the works of this prolific writer. Biographies are Barry Silesky, *Ferlinghetti: The Artist in His Time* (New York: Warner Books, 1990); Larry R. Smith, *Lawrence Ferlinghetti, Poet-at-Large* (Carbondale: Southern Illinois University Press, 1983); and Neeli Cherovski's *Ferlinghetti: A Biography* (Garden City, N.Y.: Doubleday, 1979), which is based on interviews with the poet.

The world Kerouac and Ginsberg and others imagined through their fiction and poetry, Neal Cassady lived. Most notably he is Dean Moriarty in *On the Road*; Cassady also drove the bus that carried Ken Kesey's Merry Pranksters across country and into the first days of the counterculture. A few pieces of Cassady's limited, mostly autobiographical writings are found in Neal Cassady, *The First Third and Other Writings*, rev. ed. (San Francisco: City Lights Books, 1981). His letters are available in Barry Gifford, ed., *As Ever: The Collected Correspondence of Allen Ginsberg and Neal Cassady* (Berkeley: Creative Arts Book Co., 1977), and Neal Cassady, *Grace Beats Karma: Letters from Prison, 1958–1960* (New York: Blast Books, 1993). William Plummer, *The Holy Goof: A Biography of Neal Cassady* (Englewood Cliffs, N.J.: Prentice-Hall, 1981), is a good description of Cassady's life. Ken Babbs's edited collection of essays about Neal Cassady includes an unpublished manuscript by Cassady, in *The Cassady Issue* (Pleasant Hill, Oreg.: SITO, 1981); these materials originally appeared in *Spit in the Ocean*, a magazine occasionally published by Ken Kesey.

Works by or about some other Beat writers or figures prominent among that generation include Aram Saroyan's *Genesis Angels: The Saga of Lew Welch and the Beat Generation* (New York: William Morrow, 1979). Welch co-authored a piece with Kerouac and appeared as a character in Kerouac's *Big Sur*. Kenneth Rexroth, who was uncomfortable at being called the father of the Beat generation, has had some of his essays collected in *The Alternative Society: Essays from the Other World* (New York: Herder and Herder, 1970). See also Rexroth's *An Auto-Biographical Novel* (1966; expanded ed., New York: New Directions, 1991), which describes life in San Francisco's bohemia within the avant garde. Linda Hamalian, *A Life of Kenneth Rexroth* (New York: Norton, 1991), is a recent biography. Lee Bartlett has written a long critical essay, *Kenneth Rexroth* (Boise, Idaho: Boise State University, 1988), Boise State University Western Writers Series no. 84.

Like Neal Cassady, Herbert Huncke is known for the friends he made. Beat mythology has it that Huncke, a sometimes thief and drug addict, passed along to his writer friends the word *beat*, which, in the vocabulary of Huncke's drug world, meant played-out and exhausted. Huncke relates his own story in *Guilty of Everything: The Autobiography of Herbert Huncke* (New York: Paragon House, 1990), an often harrowing look at street-inspired Beat life. Huncke, *The Evening Sun Turned Crimson* (Cherry Valley, N.Y.: Cherry Valley Editions, 1980), is an example of the author's occasionally eloquent prose.

Among the earliest expressions of what later came to be identified as the Beat temperament was Paul Bowles's 1949 novel *Sheltering Sky* (New York: New Directions). Bowles was familiar with a few of the Beat writers and he relates his view of them and their work in *Without Stopping: An Autobiography* (New York: Putnam, 1972). See also Gena Dagel Caponi, *Conversations with Paul Bowles* (Jackson: University Press of Mississippi, 1993). Benefiting from his association with a number of Beat writers, Kerouac and Ginsberg among them, John Clellon Holmes has been among the principal interpreters of their work. In his novel *Go* (New York: Scribner's Sons, 1952), written before there was a Beat movement, he was the first to employ the term *Beat generation* to depict the evolving bohemian subculture of the 1950s. See also Holmes's *The Horn* (New York: Random House, 1958), a novel in which he examines the Beat interest in jazz (reissued as *The Horn: A Novel* [New York: Thunder's Mouth Press, 1988]). Another work that offers a fictionalized account of life among the Beats, in this case in the San Francisco area, is Charles Lymell's *The Last of the Moccasins* (San Francisco: City Lights Books, 1971). Harold Norse, *Beat Hotel* (Calexico, Calif.: Atticus Press, 1983), is a novel, more fact than fiction, about the Beats. Norse was an intimate of many of the Beat writers, especially Burroughs. *Beat Hotel* is a collection of his observations of Beat ideology and life from a location in Paris frequented by many of the important figures in the movement. Also see Norse's *Memoirs of a Bastard Angel* (New York: William Morrow, 1989). Among those who came into touch with the Greenwich Village Beat life in the late fifties was a young black man known then as LeRoi Jones. Later, as Amiri Baraka, Jones became a leading voice and activist for social and political justice for African Americans. Imamu Amiri Baraka, *The Autobiography of LeRoi Jones/Amiri Baraka* (New York: Freundlich Books, 1984), offers the view of an African American on Beat culture. See William J. Harris, *The Poetry and Politics of Amiri Baraka: The Jazz Aesthetic* (Columbia: University of Missouri Press, 1985).

Another important figure attracted to Greenwich Village early in 1961, to its clubs and bars, was Bob Dylan, the poet-musician whose lyrics displayed a Beat aesthetic and dealt with Beat issues. Perhaps no single artist had a greater influence on the activist generation of the sixties than Dylan. See Clinton Heylin, *Bob Dylan, Behind the Shades: A Biography* (New York: Summit Books, 1993). Ed Sanders, *Tales of Beatnik Glory* (1975; reprint, New York: Carol Publishing Group, 1990), describes in the language of the era the music and poetry along with the arts community of Manhattan in the late fifties and early sixties. Sanders and Beat writer Tuli Kupferberg, who along with Sanders was a founder of the anarchist rock band the Fugs, used their poetry and music as the means of social and political protest. They are transitional figures between the Beat culture of the 1950s and that of the young rebels and activists of the 1960s

No modern American literary movement made greater use of poetry to announce its presence than the Beat movement. All its major figures were poets, if not principally then occasionally. Never before the Beat era, it seemed, had so much attention been accorded to what the American reading public was used to looking upon as an arcane medium.

Some artists in addition to the writers already cited employed the Beat sensibility in their poetry. Known as the Beat Friar, William Everson was a one-time member of the Dominican Order where he took the name Brother Antoninus. Lee Bartlett's *Benchmark and Blaze: The Emergence of William Everson* (Metuchen, N.J.: Scarecrow Press, 1979) is an edited collection of essays by various scholars, and *William Everson: The Life of Brother Antoninus* (New York: New Directions, 1988) is a biography. An important precursor to the Beats is Kenneth Patchen, whose writing one admiring critic called "antiliterature." His antiwar poetry and poetry of social protest inspired, among others, Allen Ginsberg. Two works ease the way to an understanding of Patchen and his writings: Larry R. Smith, *Kenneth Patchen* (Boston: Twayne, 1978), and Raymond Nelson, *Kenneth Patchen and American Mysticism* (Chapel Hill: University of North Carolina Press, 1984). A more restrained poetic taste is found in the work of Frank O'Hara, a principal of the "New York School" of poetry and a curator of New York City's Museum of Modern Art. Alan Feldman, *Frank O'Hara* (Boston: Twayne), is an introduction to O'Hara's life and poetry, and Marjorie Perloff's *Frank O'Hara: Poet among Painters* (New York: Braziller, 1977) is a critical study. Gregory Corso's poetry is known for its intensely personal style. Ginsberg and Kerouac had developed their hipster vocabulary as part of their art; Corso knew it firsthand from growing up in the alleys and basements of New York and from a stay in jail. A strong critical study of Corso's poetry is Gregory Stephenson, *Exiled Angel: A Study of the Work of Gregory Corso* (Sudbury, Mass.: Water Row Press, 1989). The works of Alan Watts, a specialist in Eastern religions and thought, had begun to appear in the late 1930s. Widely read throughout the Beat community, they were a rich source of learning for the many Beat writers, among them Gary Snyder, fascinated by Buddhism and other Eastern beliefs. Watts's *This Is It and Other Essays on Zen and Spiritual Experience* (1960; reprint, New York: Vintage, 1973) includes the influential 1959 piece "Beat Zen, Square Zen and Zen."

By most accounts the Beat movement was overwhelmingly misogynist, its writers and representative figures often preoccupied with exploring male bonding (the misogyny of the Beats carries over into many of the movements of the 1960s). There is a need for a feminist examination of women's roles in Beat writing, but it would probably be a depressing work. Diane di Prima is certainly one the most visible female figures among the Beats and one of their most important poets. *Memoirs of a Beatnik* (1969; reprint, San Francisco: Last Gasp of San Francisco, 1988) is her description of the Beat life, with a frank emphasis on sex and her own sexual adventurousness, and her participation in the Beat movement, mostly in New York. Joyce Johnson's *Minor Characters: A Young Woman's Coming-of-Age in the Beat Orbit of Jack Kerouac* (New York: Anchor, 1994), previously published as *Minor Characters* (Boston: Houghton Mifflin, 1983), offers another rare opportunity to listen to a woman talk of coming to maturity in the late fifties in the company of the Beats. For a short time, she was Kerouac's lover. In *Off the Road: My Years with Cassady, Kerouac, and Ginsberg* (New York: William Morrow, 1990), Carolyn Cassady reminisces about some prominent Beats: she was married to Neal Cassady from 1948 to 1962. *Baby Driver* (New York: Holt, Rhinehart, and Winston, 1981) is the autobiography of Jan Kerouac, Jack's daughter. Although estranged from her father, who for many years denied that she was his child, Jan Kerouac describes experiences and views of her own that very much resemble those of her father. Bonnie Bremser's *Troia: Mexican Memoirs* (New York: Croton Press, 1969), reissued as *For Love of Ray* (London: London Magazine Editions, 1971), is an unconventional woman's account, told in a raw and unapologetic tone, of an unconventional life with poet Ray Bremser, a Cassady-like character. Lenore Kandel is among the better-known women poets of the Beat era. The poetry of *The Love Book* (San Francisco: Stolen Paper Editions, 1966), her best-known work, is characterized by its open depiction of sexual situations. Like Burroughs's *Naked Lunch*, *The Love Book* was condemned as obscene, and a court case ensued. Joanna Kinnison McClure, along with her husband Michael McClure, were part of the San Francisco poetry scene during the Beat era and her work shows the characteristic Beat themes and the influence of some of its best-known figures. See, for example, *Wolf Eyes* (San Francisco: Bearthm Press, 1974).

The Beats and the Counterculture

The Beat era is commonly located in the middle and late 1950s. Of course it is by no means that clear when the movement came to life or when it passed out of existence. Uncertain as well is when the Beat culture with its peculiar social and political concerns gave way to the counterculture and a somewhat different set of issues and activities. Some of the prominent social commentators of the Beat generation were visible in the movements of the 1960s, among them Ginsberg and Ed Sanders. But though continuing much of the Beat sensibility, the counterculture was more political even in its deliberate withdrawal from much of politics, and less introspectively concerned with moods, sounds, energy, and words.

Ken Kesey is a bridge. He is definable as among the last of the Beats or the first of the counterculture rebels. *One Flew over the Cuckoo's Nest* (New York: Viking, 1962), Kesey's best-known book, rejects the controlling institutions of modern life in a way that could please either movement. Works about Kesey include Stephen L. Tanner, *Ken Kesey* (Boston: Twayne, 1983); Barry H. Leeds, *Ken Kesey* (New York: R. Ungar, 1981); and M. Gilbert Porter, *The Art of Grit: Ken Kesey's Fiction* (Columbia: University of Missouri Press, 1982).

A work that looks at some of the connections between the Beats and the movements of protest in the 1960s is the essay by Paul S. George and Jerold M. Starr, "Beat Politics: New Left and Hippie Beginnings in the Postwar Counterculture," in *Cultural Politics: Radical Movements in Modern History*, ed. Jerold M. Starr (New York: Praeger, 1985), pp. 189–233. Emmett Grogan, *Rinolevio: A Life Played for Keeps* (Boston: Little, Brown, 1972), is the autobiography, mixing fiction with fact, of the founder of the Diggers. On the Youth International Party, see David Lewis Stein, *Living the Revolution: The Yippies in Chicago* (Indianapolis: Bobbs-Merrill, 1969), and Joseph R. Urgo, *Novel Frames: Literature as Guide to Race, Sex, and History in American Culture* (Jackson: University Press of Mississippi, 1991), especially chapter 6, "The Yippies' Overthrow: What Everybody Knows in America," pp. 189–221.

Bibliographies of the 1960s

Rebecca Jackson, *The 1960s: An Annotated Bibliography of Social and Political Movements in the United States* (Westport, Conn.: Greenwood Press, 1992), makes no claim to being comprehensive but provides brief descriptions of more than thirteen hundred books on the political and social history of the United States from 1960 through the early 1970s. Mari Jo Buhle, Paul Buhle, and Harvey J. Kaye, eds., *The American Radical* (New York: Routledge, 1994), contains useful essays on American leftists who influenced the radicalism of the 1960s or participated in the various campaigns of the era. Mari Jo Buhle, Paul Buhle, and Dan Georgakas, *Encyclopedia of the American Left* (Champaign: University of Illinois Press, 1992), and Bernard K. Johnpoll and Harvey Klehr, eds., *Biographical Dictionary of the American Left* (Westport, Conn.: Greenwood Press, 1986), also provides information on radicals and many of their organizations. David DeLeon, ed., *Leaders from the 1960s: A Biographical Sourcebook of American Activism* (Westport, Conn.: Greenwood Press, 1994), centers on radical activity in the sixties. An important guide to the student revolution is Kenneth Keniston, Mary-Kay Duffield, and Sharon Martinek, *Radicals and Militants: An Annotated Bibliography of Empirical Research on Campus Unrest* (Lexington, Mass.: Lexington Books, 1973).

Among historiographical essays on the sixties, see Maurice Isserman, "The Not-so-Dark and Bloody Ground: New Works on the 1960s," *American Historical Review* 94 (October 1989): 990–1010; Jon Wiener, "The New Left as History," *Radical History Review* 42 (1988): 173–88; and two articles by Winifred Breines, "Whose New Left?" *Journal of American History* 75 (September 1988): 528–45, and "The Sixties Again," *Theory and Society* 14 (1985): 511–23. The three commentators were all active on the left during the sixties. Alan Brinkley, "Dreams of the Sixties," *New York Review of Books* 34 (October 22, 1987): 10–16, is a critical review of some studies of the radicalism of the sixties by a historian generally sympathetic to the left.

General Works on the 1960s

Recent studies include David Farber, *The Age of Great Dreams: America in the 1960s* (New York: Hill and Wang, 1994); David Chalmers, *And the Crooked Places Made Straight: The Struggle for Social Change in the 1960s* (Baltimore: Johns Hopkins University Press, 1991); Edward P. Morgan, *The Sixties Experience: Hard Lessons about Modern America* (Philadelphia: Temple University Press, 1991); Douglas Knight, *Streets of Dreams: The Nature and Legacy of the 1960s* (Durham, N.C.: Duke University Press, 1989); David Steigerwald, *The Sixties and the End of Modern America* (New York: St. Martin's Press, 1995); and John Morton Blum, *Years of Discord, 1961–1974* (New York: Norton, 1991).

Terry Anderson, *The Movement and the Sixties: Protest in America from Greensboro to Wounded Knee* (New York: Oxford University Press, 1995), is a study of forms of dissent. Also concerned with protest is Meta Mendel-Reyes, *Reclaiming Democracy: The Sixties in Politics and Memory* (New York: Routledge, 1995). One of the earliest studies of the 1960s is David Burner, Robert Marcus, and Thomas West, *A Giant's Strength: America in the Sixties* (New York: Holt, Rinehart and Winston, 1971). Another early treatment of the decade is William L. O'Neill, *Coming Apart: An Informal History of America in the 1960's* (Chicago: Quadrangle, 1971). Allen Matusow's *The Unraveling of America: A History of Liberalism in the 1960s* (New York: Harper and Row, 1984) pursues relentlessly the failings of modern liberalism. Politics is also the subject of Godfrey Hodgson's important *America in Our Time* (New York: Random House, 1976), a history of the sixties from Kennedy to Nixon. Ronald Berman, *America in the Sixties: An Intellectual History* (New York: Free Press, 1968), examines the sources of the radicalism of the era and offers a conservative critique of the era. Milton Viorst's *Fire in the Streets: America in the 1960s* (New York: Simon and Schuster, 1979) is a sympathetic history of that radicalism.

Good anthologies about the sixties include James Haskins and Kathleen Benson, *The 60s Reader* (New York: Viking, 1988); Stewart Burns, *Social Movements of the 1960s: Searching for Democracy* (Boston: Twayne, 1990); and Jane Stern and Michael Stern, *Sixties People* (New York: Knopf, 1990). In *Living Legacy: How 1964 Changed America* (Lanham, Md.: University Press of America, 1994), Joseph J. Mangano puts together a series of essays on the events of a single significant year during the 1960s. David Farber, ed., *The Sixties: From Memory to History* (Chapel Hill: University of North Carolina Press, 1994), is a recent collection with a central theme. Barbara L. Tischler, ed., *Sights on the Sixties* (New Brunswick, N.J.: Rutgers University Press, 1992), is very sympathetic to the radical culture. Sohnya Sayres, Anders Stephanson, Stanley Aronowitz, and Frederic Jameson, eds., *The 60s without Apology* (Minneapolis: University of Minneapolis Press, 1984), as the title implies, assembles essays mostly unqualified in their defense of the social movements of the decade. See also Jo Freeman, ed., *Social Movements of the Sixties and Seventies* (New York: Longman, 1983).

Joan Morrison and Robert K. Morrison, eds., *From Camelot to Kent State: The Sixties in the Words of Those Who Lived It* (New York: Times Books, 1987), interviews many prominent leaders and activists of the decade. Judith Clavir Albert and Stewart Albert, eds., *The Sixties Papers: Documents of a Rebellious Decade* (New York: Praeger, 1984), includes many statements and declarations. Mitchell Goodman, ed., *The Movement toward a New America: The Beginning of a Long Revolution, (a Collage), a What?* (Philadelphia: Pilgrim Press, 1970), also brings together documents from the era along with photos and other memorabilia. *Sixties Going on Seventies*, rev. ed. (New Brunswick, N.J.: Rutgers University Press, 1995), is a compilation of the journalist Nora Sayre's essays, written during the late sixties and early seventies. See Alexander Bloom and Winifred Breines, eds., *Takin' It to the Streets: A Sixties Reader* (New York: Oxford University Press, 1995).

Campus Protest

Calvin B. T. Lee, *The Campus Scene, 1900–1970* (New York: McKay, 1970), and Helen Lefkowitz Horowitz, *Campus Life: Undergraduate Cultures from the End of the Eighteenth Century to the Present* (New York: Knopf, 1987), provide good background. David L. Westby, *The Clouded Vision: The Student Movement in the United States in the 1960s* (Lewisburg, Pa.: Bucknell University Press, 1976), narrows the study. In *The Multiversity: A Personal Report on What Happens to Today's Students at American Universities* (New York: Holt, Rinehart and Winston, 1966), Nicholas von Hoffman lays much of the responsibility for student unrest to the cold impersonality of the mega-university. In a famous essay, "The Student as Nigger," Jerry Farber also describes indifference to the young. Nathan Glazer, a sociologist at Berkeley during the 1960s, reflects on the times in *Remembering the Answers: Essays on the American Student Revolt* (New York: Basic Books, 1970). Seymour Martin Lipset, Glazer's more liberal colleague in the Berkeley sociology department, gives his views on student activism and its consequences in *Rebellion in the University* (Chicago: University of Chicago Press, 1971). Richard Flacks, *Youth and Social Change* (Chicago: Markham, 1971), reflects the student side.

Essays dealing with the youth movement are collected in Paul D. Knott, comp., *Student Activism* (Dubuque, Iowa: W. C. Brown, 1971), and Philip G. Altbach and Robert S. Laufer, eds., *The New Pilgrims: Youth Protest in Transition* (New York: McKay, 1972). Michael Brown, ed., *The Politics and Anti-Politics of the Young* (Beverly Hills: Glencoe Press, 1969), is a compilation of readings. In three major works Kenneth Keniston applauded the radical young: *The Uncommitted: Alienated Youth in American Society* (New York: Harcourt, Brace and World, 1965); *Young Radicals: Notes on Committed Youth* (New York: Harcourt, Brace and World, 1968); and *Youth and Dissent: The Rise of a New Opposition* (New York: Harcourt, Brace, Jovanovich, 1971). See also Morton Levitt and Ben Rubenstein, eds., *Youth and Social Change* (Detroit: published for the American Orthopsychiatric Association by Wayne State University Press, 1972).

Among those unfriendly to the youth movement are to be counted Lewis Feuer, *The Conflict of Generations: The Character and Significance of Student Movements* (New York: Basic Books, 1969), which, using Freudian analysis, claims that student movements are organized and populated by psychically dysfunctional opponents of the established culture. Daniel Yankelovich undertakes a statistical and analytical survey of the shifting values of youth from the late sixties into the seventies: *The Changing Values on Campus and Political and Personal Attitudes of Today's College Students* (New York: Washington Square Press, 1972); *The New Morality: A Profile of American Youth in the 70's* (New York: McGraw-Hill, 1974); and *New Rules: Searching for Self-Fulfillment in a World Turned Upside Down* (New York: Random House, 1981). Allan Bloom, *The Closing of the American Mind: How Higher Education Has Failed Democracy and Impoverished the Souls of Today's Students* (New York: Simon and Schuster, 1987), is an indictment of the student radicals for disrupting traditional functioning of the university. In *Confrontation: The Student Rebellion and the Universities* (New York: Basic Books, 1968), Daniel Bell and Irving Kristol have compiled and edited a collection of generally neoconservative essays on campus unrest.

A pair of volumes by Immanuel Wallerstein and Paul Starr, eds., *The University Crisis Reader: The Liberal University under Attack* (New York: Random House, 1971) and *The University Crisis Reader: Confrontation and Counterattack* (New York: Random House, 1971), collect documents on the nature of the modern university. Also see Wallerstein's *University in Turmoil: The Politics of Change* (New York: Atheneum, 1969).

Berkeley

Clark Kerr's *Uses of the University* (Cambridge, Mass.: Harvard University Press, 1963) is the place to begin on Berkeley. The most complete history of the student movement at Berkeley is W. J. Rorabaugh, *Berkeley at War: The 1960s* (New York: Oxford University Press, 1989). A more narrowly focused study is David Lance Goines, *The Free Speech Movement: Coming of Age in the 1960s* (Berkeley: Ten Speed Press, 1993). Max Heirich's volumes are useful: *The Beginning: Berkeley, 1964* (New York: Columbia University Press, 1968), and *The Spiral of Conflict: Berkeley, 1964* (New York: Columbia University Press, 1971). Hal Draper, *Berkeley: The New Student Revolt* (New York: Grove Press, 1965), contains the observations by a member of the library staff sympathetic to the students. Tom Farber, *Tales for the Son of My Unborn Child, Berkeley, 1966–1969* (New York: Dutton, 1971), profiles members of the Berkeley community and participants in the various demonstrations. Early assessments of the events at Berkeley can also be found in Seymour Martin Lipset and Sheldon Wolin, eds., *The Berkeley Student Revolt: Facts and Interpretations* (Garden City, N.Y.: Anchor, 1965), and Christopher G. Katope and Paul G. Zolbrod, eds., *Beyond Berkeley: A Sourcebook on Student Values* (New York: Harper and Row, 1966). Alan Copeland and Nikki Arai, eds., *People's Park* (New York: Ballantine Books, 1969), documents in photographs the creation of the park, its dismantling, and the riots that followed.

Columbia

A somewhat dispassionate, official version of events, known as the Cox Commission Report for the Commission's chief officer, Archibald Cox, is available as Fact Finding Commission on Columbia Disturbances, *Crisis at Columbia: Report of the Fact-Finding Commission Appointed to Investigate the Disturbances at Columbia University in April and May 1968* (New York: Vintage, 1968). Now a lawyer and journalist, James S. Kunen was a student at Columbia in the late sixties and describes his transformation from an observer of campus unrest to radical protest in *The Strawberry Statement: Notes of a College Revolutionary* (New York: Random House, 1969; reprint, Brandywine Press, 1994). Jerry L. Avorn et al., *Up Against the Ivy Wall: A History of the Columbia Crisis* (New York: Atheneum, 1968), is a collection of interviews conducted by the staff of the *Columbia Daily Spectator.* Mark Rudd's essay "Columbia—Notes on the Spring Rebellion," in Carl Oglesby, ed., *The New Left Reader* (New York: Grove Press, 1969), is the view of a principal instigator of the uprisings. Roger Kahn, *The Battle for Morningside Heights: Why Students Rebel* (New York: William Morrow, 1970), and Joanne Grant, ed., *Confrontation on Campus: The Columbia Pattern for the New Protest* (New York: New American Library, Signet, 1969), add to the story.

Other Campuses

Conflict elsewhere receives attention in David Grossvogel and Cushing Strout, *Divided We Stand: Reflections on the Crisis at Cornell* (Garden City, N.Y.: Doubleday, 1971), and Lawrence F. Eichel et al., *The Harvard Strike* (Boston: Houghton Mifflin, 1970). Student strikes at San Francisco State College are the subject of William H. Orrick, Jr., *Shut It Down! A College in Crisis: San Francisco State College, October 1968–April 1969, A Report to the National Commission on the Causes and Prevention of Violence* (Washington: U.S. Government Printing Office, 1969)—the product of an official government investigation—and *An End to Silence: The San Francisco State College Student Movement in the '60s* (Indianapolis: Bobbs-Merrill, 1971), whose authors, William Barlow and Peter Shapiro, were participants. In *The Year of the Monkey: Revolt on Campus, 1968–69* (New York: McGraw-Hill, 1982), William J. McGill, who was the university chancellor, describes the unrest at the University of California–San Diego campus and the influence the Berkeley uprisings had on the San Diego students and administration. Julian Foster and Durward Long, eds., *Protest! Student Activism in America* (New York: William Morrow, 1970), describes student demonstrations at a number of schools, among them Indiana University, Princeton, and Howard.

The New Left

For documents, see Teodori Massimo, ed., *The New Left: A Documentary History* (Indianapolis: Bobbs-Merrill, 1969); Mitchell Cohen and Dennis Hale, eds., *The New Student Left: An Anthology* (Boston: Beacon, 1966); Paul Jacobs and Saul Landau, *The New Radicals: A Report with Documents* (New York: Random House, 1966). Essays by New Left theorists and activists are gathered in Arthur Lothstein, comp., *"All we are saying . . .": The Philosophy of the New Left* (New York: Putnam, 1970), and Priscilla Long, comp., *The New Left: A Collection of Essays* (Boston: P. Sargent, 1969). *The New Left Reader* (New York: Grove Press, 1969), Carl Oglesby, ed., is an assortment of New Left writings by foreign and American authors. Dick Cluster, ed., *They Should Have Served That Cup of Coffee: Seven Radicals Remember the 60s* (Boston: South End Press, 1979), is a forum for activists to review their participation in protest movements.

A well-written account is Irwin Unger and Debi Unger, *The Movement: A History of the American New Left, 1959–1972* (1974; reprint, Lanham, Md.: University Press of America, 1988). See George Vickers, *The Formation of the New Left: The Early Years* (Lexington, Mass.: Lexington Books, D.C. Heath, 1975); Edward J. Bacciocco, *The New Left in America: Reform to Revolution, 1956 to 1970* (Stanford: Hoover Institution Press, 1974); and Michal Friedman, *The New Left of the Sixties* (Berkeley: Independent Socialist Press, 1972). Van Grosse, *Where the Boys Are: Cuba, Cold War America, and the Making of the New Left* (New York: Verso, 1993), locates the origins of the New Left in the years 1956–60 and the popularity among liberals and radicals of Fidel Castro and the Cuban revolution. Stanley Rothman and S. Robert Lichter, *Roots of Radicalism: Jews, Christians and the New Left* (New York: Oxford University Press, 1982), studies the psychological origins of the radical personality type and the role of Jews in radical movements. The influence of older radical activities and reform movements on the New Left is treated in Maurice Isserman, *If I Had a Hammer . . . The Death of the Old Left and the Birth of the New Left* (1987; reprint, Urbana: University of Illinois Press, 1993), and Peter B. Levy, *The New Left and Labor in the 1960s* (Champaign: University of Illinois Press, 1994). See the standard Wini

Breines, *Community and Organization in the New Left, 1962–1968: The Great Refusal*, new ed. (1982; reprint, New Brunswick, N.J.: Rutgers University Press, 1989).

Jack Newfield's *A Prophetic Minority: The American New Left* (New York: New American Library, 1966), is an early, optimistic account of the New Left. *Democracy From the Heart: Spiritual Values, Decentralism, and Democratic Idealism in the Movement of the 1960s* (Eugene, Oreg.: Communitas Press, 1991), is by another activist of the decade, Gregory Nevala Calvert. Excellent descriptions of the radical left in the sixties have come from the historian James Miller and the Berkeley sociologist Todd Gitlin, both of whom were participants in SDS in the sixties. Miller's *"Democracy Is in the Streets": From Port Huron to the Siege of Chicago* (New York: Simon and Schuster, 1987) centers on the evolution in the thinking of a handful of the early leaders of SDS, chiefly Tom Hayden, and the development of the idea of participatory democracy. Todd Gitlin's *The Whole World Is Watching: Mass Media in the Making and Unmaking of the New Left* (Berkeley and Los Angeles: University of California Press, 1980) studies the critical relation between the media and SDS. See also Gitlin's *The Sixties: Years of Hope, Days of Rage* (New York: Bantam Books, 1988) and Alexander Cockburn and Robin Blackburn, *Student Power: Problems, Diagnosis, Action* (Baltimore: Penguin, in association with New Left Review, 1969). R. David Myers, ed., *Toward a History of the New Left: Essays from within the Movement* (Brooklyn: Carlson Publishing, 1989), collects articles dealing with the New Left by leaders and theoreticians of the movement. Other essays by activists or about the New Left can be found in Matthew F. Stolz, comp., *Politics of the New Left* (Beverly Hills: Glencoe Press, 1971), and Alan M. Wald, *Writing from the Left: New Essays on Radical Culture and Politics* (New York: Verso, 1994). Paul Buhle, ed., *History and the New Left: Madison, Wisconsin, 1950–1970* (Philadelphia: Temple University Press, 1989), is a collection of pieces by a number of scholars, mostly historians, many of whom studied or worked at a campus known for its radical temper.

Social and Economic Issues

Christopher Bone, *The Disinherited Children: A Study of the New Left and the Generation Gap* (Cambridge, Mass.: Schenkman Publishing Company, distributed by Halsted Press, 1977), describes concerns that triggered the radicalism of the young. Cyril Levitt, *Children of Privilege: Student Revolt in the Sixties* (Toronto: University of Toronto Press, 1984), is a class analysis of the student left in three countries—the United States, Canada, and West Germany. Stephen Goode, *Affluent Revolutionaries: A Portrait of the New Left* (New York: Franklin Watts, 1974), also looks at the social and economic origins of the young radicals. B. Bruce-Briggs, ed., *The New Class?* (New Brunswick, N.J.: Transaction Books, 1979), is a collection of essays, mostly critical assessments by neoconservatives, describing the emergence in the sixties of a New Class, a well-educated, prosperous, professional class that gave support to various radical activities. Ayn Rand, *The New Left: The Anti-Industrial Revolution*, 2d rev. ed. (New York: New American Library, 1975), is a libertarian critique of the left and the student movement.

Books that summarize some of the ideas associated with the New Left include

Lyman Tower Sargent, *New Left Thought: An Introduction* (Homewood, Ill.: Dorsey Press, 1972); James L. Woods, *New Left Ideology: Its Dimensions and Development* (Beverly Hills: Sage, 1975); and Assar Lindbeck, *The Political Economy of the New Left: An Outsider's View*, 2d ed. (New York: Harper and Row, 1977). A sense of how the government responded to the activities of the American left is conveyed in Allan C. Brownfeld, comp., *The New Left: Memorandum* (Washington: U.S. Government Printing Office, 1969). Robert A. Goldwin, ed., *How Democratic Is America? Responses to the New Left Challenge* (Chicago: Rand McNally, 1971), provides looks at how some of the nation's intellectuals and academics replied to the new American radicalism.

Intellectual Sources

Andrew Jamison and Ron Eyerman, *Seeds of the Sixties* (Berkeley and Los Angeles: University of California Press, 1994), is a series of intellectual biographies of those whose work influenced the 1960s. In *Thinkers of the New Left* (Harlow, United Kingdom: Longman, 1985), the philosopher Roger Scruton discusses the ideologues and theorists of the New Left. Two intellectuals, the sociologist C. Wright Mills and philosopher Herbert Marcuse, stand out for the extraordinary impact of their work on the New Left, the student movement, and the counterculture. Together Mills and Marcuse described modern society as a technological and bureaucratic monster that deprived the individual of meaningful work and a complete emotional and erotic life. Mills's principal writings are *The Power Elite* (New York: Oxford University Press, 1956); *The Sociological Imagination* (New York: Oxford University Press, 1959); and *White Collar: The American Middle Classes* (New York: Oxford University Press, 1951). Also see Mills, *Power, Politics, and People: The Collected Essays of C. Wright Mills* (New York: Oxford University Press, 1963). Two full-length biographies of Mills are Irving Louis Horowitz, *C. Wright Mills: An American Utopian* (New York: Free Press, 1983), and Rick Tilman, *C. Wright Mills: A Native Radical and His American Intellectual Roots* (University Park: Pennsylvania State University Press, 1984). Marcuse's chief contribution to the sixties was his stimulating *One-Dimensional Man: Studies in the Ideology of Advanced Industrial Society* (Boston: Beacon, 1964). John Bokina and Timothy J. Lukes, eds., *Marcuse: From the New Left to the Next Left* (Lawrence: University Press of Kansas, 1994), measures the influence of Marcuse's ideas. Peter Clecak, *Radical Paradoxes: Dilemmas of the American Left, 1945–1970* (New York: Harper Torchbooks, 1973), is an intellectual history of the postwar left that includes discussion of the work of both Mills and Marcuse.

Tom Hayden's own account is *Reunion: A Memoir* (New York: Random House, 1988). John H. Bunzel, *New Force on the Left: Tom Hayden and the Campaign against Corporate America* (Stanford: Hoover Institution Press, Stanford University, 1983), is an unsympathetic portrait. In two volumes of autobiography, *More Power than We Know: The People's Movement toward Democracy* (Garden City, N.Y.: Doubleday, 1975) and *From Yale to Jail: The Life Story of a Moral Dissenter* (New York: Pantheon, 1993), Dave Dellinger describes his views. In two books, *The Other America: Poverty in the United States* (New York: Macmillan, 1962) and *Toward a Democratic Left: A Radical Program for a New Majority* (New York: Macmillan, 1972), Michael Harrington depicts the harsh social and economic consequences of competition in the United States and offers his outline of an alternative, more cooperative American society. Also see Harrington's *The Long Distance Runner: An Autobiography* (New York: Henry Holt, 1988). Sanford D. Horwitt, *Let Them Call Me Rebel: Saul Alinsky—His Life and Legacy* (New York: Knopf, 1989), is the history of the community activist.

Women and the New Left

The women's liberation movement is not a topic of this book because it is barely a phenomenon of the 1960s either chronologically or as discussed herein. Sara Evans, *Personal Politics: The Roots of Women's Liberation in the Civil Rights Movement and the New Left* (New York: Knopf, 1980), traces the emergence of the new feminism in part to the New Left and the counterculture, whose organizations were dominated by males while their ideas were egalitarian. Alice Echols, *Daring to Be Bad: Radical Feminism in America, 1967–1975* (Minneapolis: University of Minnesota Press, 1989), makes a similar argument and demonstrates that the language of some new feminists could be just as aggressive and uncompromising as that of the male radicals with whom they often battled. See Ellen Willis, *No More Nice Girls: Countercultural Essays* (Hanover, N.H.: Wesleyan University Press, 1992). Sara Evans and Harry C. Boyte, *Free Spaces: The Sources of Democratic Change in America* (New York: Harper and Row, 1986), documents the nastiness women encountered from male associates within the New Left movement but is primarily concerned to locate continuities with left movements of the 1970s and 1980s. Background on the emergence of the new feminism is provided in Jo Freeman, *The Politics of Women's Liberation: A Case Study of an Emerging Social Movement and Its Relation to the Policy Process* (New York: McKay, 1975); Cynthia Harrison, *On Account of Sex: The Politics of Women's Issues, 1945–1968* (Berkeley and Los Angeles: University of California Press, 1988); and Susan M. Hartmann, *From Margin to Mainstream: American Women and Politics since 1960* (Philadelphia: Temple University Press, 1989).

Critical Views

Guenther Lewy, *Peace and Revolution: The Moral Crisis of American Pacifism* (Grand Rapids, Mich.: W. B. Erdmans Publishing Company, 1988), and Peter Collier and David Horowitz, *Destructive Generation: Second Thoughts about the Sixties* (New York: Summit Books, 1989), savage the New Left. John H. Bunzel, ed., *Political Passages: Journeys of Change through Two Decades, 1968–1988* (New York: Free Press, 1988), is a collection of essays by former activists who describe their disillusionment. In the autobiographical *Breaking Ranks: A Political Memoir* (New York: Harper and Row, 1979), Norman Podhoretz describes how his experience with the left in the sixties led him to become one of the organizers of the neoconservative movement.

Other books critical of radicals include Joseph Conlin, *The Troubles: A Jaundiced Glance Back at the Movement of the 1960s* (New York: Franklin Watts, 1982); Ben J. Wattenberg, *The Real America: A Surprising Examination of the State of the Union* (Garden City, N.Y.: Doubleday, 1974); Frank E. Armbruster,

The Forgotten Americans: A Survey of Values, Beliefs, and Concerns of the Majority (New Rochelle, N.Y.: Arlington House, 1972); Lewis H. Gann and Peter Duignan, *The New Left and the Cultural Revolution of the 1960's: A Reevaluation* (Stanford: Hoover Institution on War, Revolution, and Peace, Stanford University, 1995); and Phillip Abbott Luce, *The New Left* (New York: McKay, 1966) and *The New Left Today: America's Trojan Horse* (Washington: Capitol Hill Press, 1971). Two important left critiques of the radicalism of the sixties are Irving Howe, ed., *Beyond the New Left* (New York: McCall, 1970), and Christopher Lasch, *The Culture of Narcissism: American Life in an Age of Diminishing Expectations* (New York: Norton, 1979).

Extremism

Kirkpatrick Sale, *SDS* (New York: Random House, 1973), is a good history of Students for a Democratic Society. G. Louis Heath, *Vandals in the Bomb Factory: The History and Literature of the Students for a Democratic Society* (Metuchen, N.J.: The Scarecrow Press, 1976), is a collection of documents. On violence and the student movement see the documents assembled in *Weatherman* (Berkeley: Ramparts Press, 1970), ed. Harold Jacobs. Also see Richard G. Braungart and Margaret M. Braungart, "From Protest to Terrorism: The Case of SDS and the Weathermen," in Donatella Della Porta, ed., *Social Movements and Violence: Participation in Underground Organizations*, vol. 4 in the *International Social Movement Research* series (Greenwich, Conn.: JAI Press, 1992). Susan Stern, *With the Weathermen: The Personal Journal of a Revolutionary Woman* (New York: Doubleday, 1975), is an insider's account of the organization. In *Diana: The Making of a Terrorist* (Boston: Houghton Mifflin, 1971), Thomas Powers tells the story of another revolutionary woman. Jane Alpert, *Growing Up Underground* (New York: William Morrow, 1981), is the recollection of a radical feminist who went underground in 1969 after helping to set off eight bombs in government and corporate buildings. Tom Bates, *Rads: The 1970 Bombing of the Army Math Research Center at the University of Wisconsin and Its Aftermath* (New York: Harper Collins, 1992), is about the use of violence by antiwar activists.

The Decline of the New Left and the Rise of the New Right

On the decline of the New Left see Michael Kazin's chapter on the New Left, "Power to Which People? The Tragedy of the White New Left," in his *The Populist Persuasion: An American History* (New York: Basic Books, 1995), and Maurice Isserman and Michael Kazin, "The Failure and Success of the New Radicalism," in Steve Fraser and Gary Gerstle, eds., *The Rise and Fall of the New Deal Order, 1930–1980* (Princeton: Princeton University Press, 1989). Earlier studies of the New Left's decay are Nigel Young, *An Infantile Disorder? The Crisis and Decline of the New Left* (Boulder, Colo.: Westview Press, 1977), and Greg Calvert and Carol Neiman, *A Disrupted History: The New Left and the New Capitalism* (New York: Random House, 1971). On the rise of the right see Dan T. Carter, *The Politics of Rage* (New York: Simon and Schuster, 1995); Mary C. Brennan, *Turning Right in the Sixties: The Conservative Capture of the GOP* (Chapel Hill: University of North Carolina Press, 1995); Alan Crawford, *Thunder on the Right: The "New Right" and the Politics of Resentment* (New York: Pantheon,

1980); and two chapters in Kazin's *The Populist Persuasion*, "Stand Up for the Working Man: George Wallace and the Making of a New Right" (pp. 220–42) and "The Conservative Capture: From Nixon to Reagan" (pp. 244–66).

The Counterculture

Theodore Roszak, *The Making of a Counter Culture: Reflections on the Technocratic Society and Its Youthful Opposition* (Garden City, N.Y.: Doubleday, 1969), put a name to the cultural rebellion of the 1960s and celebrated its endeavors. An assessment of Roszak is Thomas R. West's essay "Theodore Roszak," in *Contemporaries in Cultural Criticism*, ed. Hartmut Heuermann and Bernd-Peter Lange (Frankfurt am Main: Peter Lang, 1991), pp. 317–44. Also see Roszak's *Where the Wasteland Ends: Politics and Transcendence in Postindustrial Society* (Garden City, N.Y.: Doubleday, 1972). Early endorsements include William Braden, *The Age of Aquarius: Technology and the Cultural Revolution* (Chicago: Quadrangle Books, 1970), and David Horowitz, Michael Lerner, and Craig Pyes, eds., *Counterculture and Revolution* (New York: Random House, 1972). Joan Didion, *The White Album* (New York: Simon and Schuster, 1979), describes some memorable moments in the era of the counterculture. Paul Perry, Ken Babbs, Michael Schwartz, and Neil Ortenberg, *On the Bus: The Complete Guide to the Legendary Trip of Ken Kesey and the Merry Pranksters and the Birth of the Counterculture* (New York: Thunder's Mouth Press, 1990), describes the famous bus trip of 1964 that, some claim, started the counterculture. *The Further Inquiry* (New York: Viking, 1990) is Ken Kesey's own recollections of the Merry Pranksters and much else. Charles Perry, *The Haight-Ashbury: A History* (New York: Random House, 1984), is a guide to place and times. Two early accounts of the hippies in the Haight-Ashbury are Burton H. Wolfe, *The Hippies* (New York: New American Library, Signet, 1968), and Nicholas von Hoffman, *We Are the People Our Parents Warned Us Against* (Chicago: Quadrangle Books, 1968). A recent account of the hippies is Timothy Miller, *The Hippies and American Values* (Knoxville: University of Tennessee Press, 1991).

Paul Goodman, Norman O. Brown, and Herbert Marcuse, theorists whose work reflected Freudian views and stressed the modern individual's need for erotic fulfillment, were major intellectual influences on the counterculture. Richard King, *The Party of Eros: Radical Social Thought and the Realm of Freedom* (Chapel Hill: University of North Carolina Press, 1972), examines the ideas of these three thinkers and other cultural critics. Norman O. Brown, *Life against Death: The Psychoanalytical Meaning of History* (1958; reprint, New York: Random House, Vintage, 1959), is often credited with sparking the sexual revolution of the 1960s. Paul Goodman's *Growing Up Absurd: Problems of Youth in the Organized System* (New York: Random House, 1960) is a reflection on what it meant to come of age in American society. In two works, *One-Dimensional Man* (1964) and *Eros and Civilization: A Philosophical Inquiry into Freud* (1955; reprint, Boston: Beacon, 1966), Marcuse describes the modern West as stifling the psyche and insists that instincts need liberation. See Peter O. Whitmer, *Aquarius Revisited: Seven Who Created the Sixties Counterculture that Changed America* (New York: Macmillan, 1987).

Abbie Hoffman describes his cultural rebellion in a number of books: *Square*

Dancing in the Ice Age (Boston: South End Press, 1982); *Soon to Be a Major Motion Picture* (New York: G. P. Putnam's Sons, 1980); *Woodstock Nation: A Talk-Rock Album* (New York: Vintage, 1969); and *Revolution for the Hell of It* (New York: Dial Press, 1968). See the biographies Daniel Simon, *Run, Run, Run: The Lives of Abbie Hoffman* (New York: G. P. Putnam's Sons, 1994), and Marty Jezer, *Abbie Hoffman: American Rebel* (New Brunswick, N.J.: Rutgers University Press, 1992). Jerry Rubin's *Do It! Scenarios of the Revolution* (New York: Simon and Schuster, 1970) was something of a handbook for the rebellious young. Also see Rubin's *We Are Everywhere* (New York: Harper and Row, 1971).

Assessments

Milton Yinger's *Countercultures: The Promise and the Peril of a World Turned Upside Down* (New York: Free Press, 1982) is a sociological analysis. Morris Dickstein, *Gates of Eden: American Culture in the Sixties* (1977; reprint, New York: Penguin, 1989), is an important history. Charles Altieri studies poetry in *Enlarging the Temple: New Directions in American Poetry During the 1960's* (Lewisburg, Pa.: Bucknell University Press, 1979). Fernandez Benedict, *In Opposition: Images of American Dissent in the Sixties* (New York: Da Capo Press, 1968), uses photography to reveal activists. Jerome Klinkowitz, *The American 1960s: Imaginative Acts in a Decade of Change* (Ames: Iowa State University Press, 1980), examines some of the literature of the decade. One of the decorative arts is depicted in Joel Lobenthal, *Radical Rags: Fashions of the Sixties* (New York: Abbeville Press, 1990). Changing styles and tastes in cinema are the subject of Ethan Mordden's *Medium Cool: The Movies of the 1960s* (New York: Knopf, 1990).

Susan Sontag's *Against Interpretation, and Other Essays* (New York: Farrar, Straus and Giroux, 1966) was one of the more significant works of cultural criticism produced in the 1960s. Gerald Howard, ed., *The Sixties: The Art, Politics, and Media of Our Most Explosive Decade* (New York: Washington Square Press, 1982), offers further examples of the arts culture of the 1960s. In *Fear and Loathing in Las Vegas: A Savage Journey to the Heart of the American Dream* (New York: Random House, 1971), Hunter S. Thompson, the originator of Gonzo journalism, offers his peculiar take on the sixties and describes his own involvement in the drug culture. Paul Krassner, *How a Satirical Editor Became a Yippie Conspirator in Ten Easy Years* (New York: Putnam, 1971) is about the serendipitous editor of one of the more scandalous journals of satire and cultural and political criticism to appear in the 1960s. And see Lawrence Leamer, *The Paper Revolutionaries: The Rise of the Underground Press* (New York: Simon and Schuster, 1972), and Abe Peck, *Uncovering the Sixties: The Life and Times of the Underground Press* (New York: Pantheon, 1985).

The turn by the young to nontraditional forms of religion is the subject of Steven M. Tipton, *Getting Saved from the Sixties: Moral Meaning in Conversion and Cultural Change* (Berkeley and Los Angeles: University of California Press, 1982), and Robert S. Ellwood, *The Sixties Spiritual Awakening: American Religion Moving from Modern to Postmodern* (New Brunswick, N.J.: Rutgers University Press, 1994). In *Storefront Revolution: Food Co-ops and the Countercul-*

ture (New Brunswick, N.J.: Rutgers University Press, 1994), Craig Cox examines the food co-op movement in Minneapolis/St. Paul.

Other works look at the collapse of the youth movement. Jonathan Eisen, ed., *Altamont: Death of Innocence in the Woodstock Nation* (New York: Avon, 1970), assembles essays that probe the dark side of the counterculture. A. E. Hotchner, *Blown Away: The Rolling Stones and the Death of the Sixties* (New York: Simon and Schuster, 1990), uses the biography of a rock band as a metaphor for the decay of the youth culture.

A number of works of social criticism, written just at the end of the 1960s, look to the long-term consequences of the countercultural rebellion. Philip Slater, *The Pursuit of Loneliness: American Culture at the Breaking Point*, rev. ed. (1970; reprint, Boston: Beacon, 1976), views as essentially beneficial to American society the changes wrought by cultural radicals. Charles Reich, *The Greening of America: How the Youth Revolution is Trying to Make America Livable* (New York: Random House, 1970), celebrates the new spirit. In *The End of the American Era* (New York: Atheneum, 1971), Andrew Hacker is less pleased with the decade's transformations.

Communes

An important feature of the counterculture was experiments in forms of shared experience in communal living. Rosabeth M. Kanter, *Commitment and Community: Communes and Utopias in Sociological Perspective* (Cambridge, Mass.: Harvard University Press, 1972), is a general sociological study of communes.

See Gilbert Zicklin, *Countercultural Communes: A Sociological Perspective* (Westport, Conn.: Greenwood Press, 1983). Stephen Diamond, *What the Trees Said: Life on a New Age Farm* (New York: Delacorte Press, 1971), describes living on a Massachusetts commune. Richard Fairfield, *Communes USA: A Personal Tour* (Baltimore: Penguin, 1972, samples a variety of group living experiments in the sixties. Other studies include Laurence Vesey, *Communal Experience: Anarchist and Mystical Counter-Cultures in America* (New York: Harper and Row, 1973); Bennett M. Berger, *The Survival of a Counterculture: Ideological Work and Everyday Life Among Rural Communards* (Berkeley and Los Angeles: University of California Press, 1981); and John Case and Rosemary C. R. Taylor, eds., *Co-ops, Communes, and Collectives: Experiments in Social Change in the 1960s and 1970s* (New York: Pantheon, 1979).

Rock Music and the Drug Culture

The essays in *The Sounds of Social Change: Studies in Popular Culture* (Chicago: Rand McNally, 1972), ed. R. Serge Denisoff and Richard A. Petersen, examine how music was employed in the sixties to effect social change. On the relation between the rebellious times and its revolutionary music see John Orman, *The Politics of Rock Music* (Chicago: Nelson-Hall, 1985); Herbert London, *Closing the Circle: A Cultural History of the Rock Revolution* (Chicago: Nelson-Hall, 1985); and Jonathan Wiener, *Come Together: John Lennon in His Times* (1984; reprint, Urbana: University of Illinois Press, 1991). Two works that capture the history, and some of the allure, of the psychedelic movement and the drug culture are Martin A. Lee and Bruce Shlain, *Acid Dreams: The CIA, LSD, and the Sixties Rebellion* (New York: Grove Press, 1985), and Jay Stevens, *Storming Heaven: LSD and the American Dream* (New York: Atlantic Monthly Press, 1987).

1968

Stephen Spender, *The Year of the Young Rebels* (New York: Random House, 1969), discusses student movements throughout the world, including the rebellion at Columbia. David Caute, *The Year of the Barricades: A Journey through 1968* (New York: Harper and Row, 1988), also describes New Left activity worldwide. Ronald Fraser, ed., *1968—A Student Generation in Revolt: An International Oral History* (New York: Pantheon, 1988), assesses the European and American student movements through interviews with 175 former activists. Also see Robert V. Daniels, *Year of the Heroic Guerrilla: World Revolution and Counterrevolution in 1968* (New York: Basic Books, 1989), and George Katsiaficas, *The Imagination of the New Left: A Global Analysis of 1968* (Boston: South End Press, 1987). The important changes that occurred in the United States and among various radical groups in 1968 are the topic of Irwin Unger and Debi Unger's comprehensive *Turning Point: 1968* (New York: Scribner's Sons, 1988), and Hans Koning, *Nineteen Sixty-Eight: A Personal Report* (New York: Norton, 1987). David Farber, *Chicago '68* (Chicago: University of Chicago Press, 1988), is an innovative history that re-creates the voices of those who participated in the riots at the Democratic National Convention in August 1968. In *Armies of the Night: History as a Novel, the Novel as History* (New York: New American Library, 1968) and *Miami and the Siege of Chicago: An Informal History of the Republican and Democratic Conventions of 1968* (New York: New American Library, 1968), Norman Mailer helped give shape to a literary style. The significance of 1968 as a critical year is also argued in Charles Kaiser, *1968 in America: Music, Politics, Chaos, Counterculture, and the Shaping of a Generation* (New York: Weidenfeld and Nicolson, 1988).

Aftermath and Legacy

Peter N. Carroll, *It Seemed like Nothing Happened: America in the 1970s* (New Brunswick, N.J.: Rutgers University Press, 1990), originally published as *It Seemed like Nothing Happened: The Tragedy and Promise of America in the 1970s* (New York: Holt, Rinehart, and Winston, 1982), measures the impact of the sixties on the succeeding decade. Barbara Epstein, *Political Protest and Cultural Revolution: Nonviolent Direct Action in the 1970s and 1980s* (Berkeley and Los Angeles: University of California Press, 1991), is a study of styles of dissent in the decades after the 1960s. Lauren Kessler, *After All These Years: Sixties Ideals in a Different World* (New York: Thunder's Mouth Press, 1990), follows the careers of fifty individuals who were activists in the sixties to assess the resilience of their countercultural idealism. Similarly, Jack Whalen and Richard Flacks, *Beyond the Barricades: The Sixties Generation Grows Up* (Philadelphia: Temple University Press, 1990), is a longitudinal study of a group of California student activists. Kirkpatrick Sale, *The Green Revolution: The American Environmental Movement, 1962–1992* (New York: Hill and Wang, 1993), locates the origins of the modern "anthropocentric" environmental movement in the sixties. Warren J.

Belasco, *Appetite for Change: How the Counterculture Took on the Food Industry, 1966–1988* (New York: Pantheon, 1989), shows that the present-day health food craze arose out of the dietary concerns of counterculture dissidents. And in the 1990s concerns over the changes engineered by sixties radicalism have become debates over political correctness and culture wars. See Paul Berman, ed., *Debating P.C.: The Controversy over Political Correctness* (New York: Dell, 1992), and James Davison Hunter, *Culture Wars: The Struggle to Define America* (New York: Basic Books, 1991). *Professors, Politics, and Pop* (New York: Verso, 1991), is a collection of Jon Wiener's frequently acerbic essays dealing with the sixties and its legacy.

John F. Kennedy

James Giglio, *John F. Kennedy: A Bibliography* (New York: Greenwood Press, 1995), is a guide to the literature on John Kennedy that expresses strong opinions. The president has had a fair-minded biographer in Herbert Parmet, whose two volumes were published by Dial Press in 1980 (*Jack: The Struggles of John F. Kennedy*) and 1983 (*JFK: The Presidency of John F. Kennedy*). Parmet yields no ground, for instance, in alleging the Kennedys' plans to kill Castro but at the same time manages to acknowledge their abilities and idealism. Parmet's book does not supplant Arthur Schlesinger's *A Thousand Days* (Boston: Houghton Mifflin, 1965) written with the perspective of a contemporary and witness. A much more recent memoir is Richard N. Goodwin, *Remembering America: A Voice from the Sixties* (Boston: Little, Brown, 1988). The standard work on Kennedy's presidency is James Giglio, *The Presidency of John F. Kennedy* (Lawrence: University Press of Kansas, 1991). Allen Matusow's *The Unravelling of America: A History of Liberalism in the 1960s* (New York: Harper and Row, 1984) is an able book with a special perspective.

An interesting development in the Kennedy literature has been a generation of highly critical revisionist commentary much influenced by the Vietnam War. Its most restrained and complex example is Henry Fairlie, *The Kennedy Promise: The Politics of Expectation* (Garden City, N.Y.: Doubleday, 1973); see also Garry Wills, *The Kennedy Imprisonment: A Meditation on Power* (Boston: Little Brown, 1982), Nancy Gager Clinch, *The Kennedy Neurosis: A Psychological Portrait of an American Dynasty* (New York: Grosset and Dunlap, 1973); Richard J. Walton, *Cold War and Counterrevolution: The Foreign Policy of John F. Kennedy* (Baltimore: Pelican Books, 1972); Bruce Miroff, *Pragmatic Illusions: The Presidential Politics of John F. Kennedy* (New York: McKay, 1976); Thomas G. Paterson's "Bearing the Burden: A Critical Look at JFK's Foreign Policy," *Virginia Quarterly Review* 54 (Spring 1978): 193–212; and I. F. Stone, *In a Time of Torment* (New York: Random House, 1967). A muckraking study is Victory Lasky, *J.F.K.: The Man and the Myth* (1963; reprint, New Rochelle, N.Y.: Arlington House, 1966). Thomas Reeves properly raises the question of presidential character but has a tendency to believe anything he reads about his subject's defects in *A Question of Character: John Kennedy in Image and Reality* (New York: Free Press, 1991).

A less detached body of literature is composed of reminiscences by Kennedy's associates. Perceptive are two admiring books by Theodore Sorensen: *Kennedy*

(New York: Harper and Row, 1965) and *The Kennedy Legacy* (New York: Macmillan, 1973). Also useful are Kenneth P. O'Donnell and David F. Powers with Joe McCarthy, *"Johnny, We Hardly Knew Ye": Memories of John Fitzgerald Kennedy* (Boston: Little, Brown, 1972); Pierre Salinger, *With Kennedy* (Garden City, N.Y.: Doubleday, 1966); Lawrence F. O'Brien, *No Final Victories* (Garden City, N.Y.: Doubleday, 1966); Paul B. Fay, *The Pleasure of His Company* (New York: Harper and Row, 1966); Benjamin Bradlee, *Conversations with Kennedy* (New York: Norton, 1975); Evelyn Lincoln, *My Twelve Years with John F. Kennedy* (New York: McKay, 1965); and Edwin Guthman, *We Band of Brothers* (New York: Harper and Row, 1971).

The abundant literature on Kennedy's prepresidential years is well summarized in Herbert Parmet's *Jack*. Doris Kearns Goodwin, the only scholar to have had access to Joseph and Rose Kennedy's papers, adds important detail in her *The Fitzgeralds and the Kennedys: An American Saga* (New York: Simon and Schuster, 1987). Richard Whalen, *The Founding Father* (New York: New American Library, 1964); David E. Koskoff, *Joseph F. Kennedy* (Englewood Cliffs, N.J.: Prentice-Hall, 1974); and Michael R. Beschloss, *Kennedy and Roosevelt: The Uneasy Alliance* (New York: Norton, 1980) contribute to an understanding of the Kennedy patriarch. Rose Kennedy's reminiscences are entitled *Time to Remember* (Garden City, N.Y.: Doubleday, 1974). An important study of JFK's early years is Joan and Clay Blair, *The Search for JFK* (New York: Berkley Books, 1976).

Each episode of Kennedy's foreign policy has generated considerable attention. On the first excursion see Trumbull Higgins, *The Perfect Failure: Kennedy, Eisenhower, and the CIA at the Bay of Pigs* (New York: Norton, 1987); Peter Weyden, *Bay of Pigs* (New York: Simon and Schuster, 1979); Haynes Johnson, *The Bay of Pigs* (New York: Simon and Schuster, 1964); and the initial section of Irving Janis, *Victims of Groupthink* (Boston: Houghton Mifflin, 1972). Books specifically on Berlin include Honore Marc Catudal, *Kennedy and the Berlin Wall Crisis* (Berlin: Berlin Verlag, 1980); Curtis Cate, *The Ides of August: The Berlin Wall Crisis, 1961* (New York: Evans, 1978); Robert Slusser, *The Berlin Crisis of 1961* (Baltimore: Johns Hopkins University Press, 1971); and Eleanor L. Dulles, *The Wall: A Tragedy in Three Acts* (Columbia: University of South Carolina Press, 1972). A fine monograph on the Kennedy administration's relations with Africa is Richard B. Mahoney, *JFK: Ordeal in Africa* (New York: Oxford University Press, 1983); on Algeria there is Ronald J. Nurse, "Critic of Colonialism: JFK and Algerian Independence," *The Historian* 39 (February 1977): 307–26. Two studies concentrating exclusively on Kennedy and Vietnam are Ralph B. Smith, *An International History of the Vietnam War: The Kennedy Strategy* (New York: St. Martin's Press, 1986), and William J. Rust, *Kennedy in Vietnam* (New York: Scribner's Sons, 1985). See also the early memoir by Roger Hilsman, *To Move a Nation* (Garden City, N.Y.: Doubleday, 1967). David Halberstam, *The Best and the Brightest* (New York: Random House, 1972), remains the classic indictment of Kennedy—and the Halberstam of the Kennedy years. Glenn T. Seaborg has written *Kennedy and the Test-Ban Treaty* (Berkeley and Los Angeles: University of California Press, 1983). Gerard T. Rice's *The Bold Experiment: JFK's Peace Corps* (Notre Dame: University of Notre Dame Press, 1986) is well balanced.

Montague Kern and associates have written *The Kennedy Crises: The Press, the Presidency, and Foreign Policy* (Chapel Hill: University of North Carolina Press, 1983). On the Grand Alliance see Frank Costigliola, "The Failed Design: Kennedy, De Gaulle and the Struggle for Europe," *Diplomatic History* 8 (Summer 1984), 227–51. The Alliance for Progress is covered in Jerome Levinson and Juan de Onis, *The Alliance that Lost Its Way: A Critical Report on the Alliance for Progress* (New York: Quadrangle Books, 1970), and Harvey S. Perloff, *Alliance for Progress: A Social Intervention in the Making* (Baltimore: Johns Hopkins University Press, 1969).

The Cuban missile crisis is a cottage industry in itself. A recent treatment is Nestor T. Carbonell, *And the Russians Stayed: The Sovietization of Cuba* (New York: William Morrow, 1989). A classic study emphasizing bureaucratic issues is Graham Alison, *Essence of Decision* (Boston: Little, Brown, 1971). See David Detzer, *The Brink* (New York: Thomas Y. Crowell, 1979); Herbert Dinerstein, *The Making of a Missile Crisis: October 1962* (Baltimore: Johns Hopkins University Press, 1970); Abram Chayes, *The Cuban Missile Crisis* (New York: Oxford University Press, 1974); and Maurice Halperin, *The Rise and Decline of Fidel Castro: An Essay in Contemporary History* (Berkeley and Los Angeles: University of California Press, 1972). An excellent new biography by Deborah Shapley is *Promises and Power: The Life and Times of Robert McNamara* (Boston: Little, Brown, 1993); McNamara's *In Retrospect: The Tragedy and Lessons of Vietnam* (New York: Times Books, 1995), pictures its subject (literally) as an eagle scout. Warren I. Cohen's *Dean Rusk* (Totowa, N.J.: Cooper Square, 1980) is a good biography. Thomas Paterson, ed., *Kennedy's Quest for Victory: American Foreign Policy, 1961–63* (New York: Oxford University Press, 1989), is a recent anthology of note.

Domestic affairs under Kennedy have received considerable treatment. There is the appreciative Irving Bernstein, *Promises Kept: John F. Kennedy's New Frontier* (New York: Oxford University Press, 1990). On Kennedy and civil rights see Harris Wofford's *Of Kennedy's and Kings* (New York: Farrar, Straus and Giroux, 1980), an account by a participant. Carl Brauer's *John F. Kennedy and the Second Reconstruction* (New York: Columbia University Press, 1977) is thorough. Burke Marshall gives his views of a difficult issue in *Federalism and Civil Rights* (New York: Columbia University Press, 1964). More recent studies include Mark Stern, *Calculating Visions: Kennedy, Johnson, and Civil Rights* (New Brunswick, N.J.: Rutgers University Press, 1992); Steven A Shull, *The President and Civil Rights Policy: Leadership and Change* (New York: Greenwood Press, 1989); Catherine A. Barnes, *A Journey from Jim Crow: The Desegregation of Southern Transit* (New York: Columbia University Press, 1983); and John Walton Cotman, *Birmingham, JFK, and the Civil Rights Act of 1963: Implications for Elite Theory* (New York: P. Long, 1989).

Works considering the tone of the Kennedy presidency include Jim F. Heath, *John F. Kennedy and the Business Community* (Chicago: University of Chicago Press, 1969) and Grant McConnell, *Steel and the Presidency, 1962* (New York: Norton, 1963). See Alan Shank, *Presidential Policy Leadership, Kennedy, and Social Welfare* (Lanham, Md.: University Press of America, 1980). Other works include Edmund S. Ions, ed. *The Politics of John F. Kennedy* (New York: Barnes and Noble, 1967); David Burner and Thomas R. West, *The Torch Is Passed: The Kennedy Brothers and American Liberalism* (New York: Atheneum, 1984); David Burner, *John F. Kennedy and a New Generation* (Boston: Little, Brown, 1988); Lewis Paper, *The Promise and the Performance: The Leadership of John F. Kennedy* (New York: Crown Publishers, 1975); John M. Logsdon, *The Decision to Go to the Moon: Project Apollo and the National Interest* (Cambridge, Mass.: MIT Press, 1970). Older studies of interest are Lawrence H. Fuchs, *John F. Kennedy and American Catholicism* (New York: Meredith Press, 1967); James David Barber, *The Presidential Character: Predicting Performance in the White House* (Englewood Cliffs: N.J.: Prentice-Hall, 1972); and James Mac-Gregor Burns, *John Kennedy: A Political Profile* (New York: Harcourt, Brace, 1960).

Great Society

Did the poverty programs of the Great Society fulfill the promises of the civil rights acts of 1964 and 1965, or create a permanently dependent and demoralized population among the very clientele these projects were designed to serve? Standard works on the Great Society that take a favorable view include John Schwartz, *America's Hidden Success: Twenty Years of Public Policy* (New York: Norton, 1983); Marshall Kaplan and Peggy Cucity, eds., *The Great Society and Its Legacy: Twenty Years of U.S. Social Policy* (Durham, N.C.: Duke University Press, 1986); Edward Zigler and Jeanett Valentine, eds., *Project Head Start: A Legacy of the War on Poverty* (New York: Free Press, 1979); Robert D. Plotnick and Felicity Skidmore, *Progress against Poverty: A Review of the 1964–1974 Decade* (New York: Academic Press, 1975); Robert A. Levine, *The Poor Ye Need Not Have with You: Lessons from the War on Poverty* (Cambridge, Mass.: MIT Press, 1970); Irving Bernstein, *Guns or Butter: The Presidency of Lyndon Johnson* (New York: Oxford University Press, 1996); Henry Aaron, *Politics and the Professors: The Great Society in Perspective* (Washington, D.C.: Brookings Institution, 1978); Stephen Bailey and Edith K. Mosher, *ESEA: The Office of Education Administers a Law* (Syracuse: Syracuse University Press, 1968); Stephen Benedict, ed., *Public Money and the Muse: Essays on Government Funding of the Arts* (New York: Norton, 1991); and Livingston Biddle, *Our Government and the Arts: A Perspective from the Inside* (New York: American Council for the Arts, 1988). The Carnegie Commission on Educational Television, *Public Television: A Program for Action* (New York: Harper and Row, 1967), formed the basis for subsidies for public broadcasting.

An unfriendly treatment of Johnson is Vaughn Bornet, *The Presidency of Lyndon B. Johnson* (Lawrence: University Press of Kansas, 1983). Joseph Califano, *The Triumph and Tragedy of Lyndon Johnson: The White House Years* (New York: Simon and Schuster, 1991), is a fascinating look at LBJ and the Great Society by a man very close to the President. Califano is both admiring and critical. Two influential left social work experts critical of Johnson are Richard Cloward and Frances Fox Piven: see *The Politics of Turmoil: Essays on Poverty, Race, and the Urban Crisis* (New York: Pantheon, 1972); Marvin E. Gettleman and David Mermelstein, eds., *The Great Society Reader: The Failure of American*

Liberalism (New York: Random House, 1967), adopt a similar perspective. The standard conservative critique is Charles Murray, *Losing Ground: American Social Policy, 1950–1980* (New York: Basic Books, 1984). Theodore White, *America in Search of Itself: The Making of the President, 1956–1980* (New York: Harper and Row, 1982), suggests that the antipoverty programs were more expensive than effective. See also *For the Poor: The Story of VISTA, Volunteers in Service to America* (New York: William Morrow, 1969). Robert A. Divine, ed., *Exploring the Johnson Years* (Austin: University of Texas Press, 1981), is a good collection of essays by scholars on many of Johnson's foreign and domestic policies; see the sequel, Robert A. Divine, ed., *The Johnson Years*, vol. 2: *The Environment and Science* (Lawrence: University Press of Kansas, 1987). John C. Donovan, *The Politics of Poverty* (New York: Pegasus, 1967), is a good, brief early review of the enactment of Great Society legislation. Eugene Eidenberg and Roy D. Morey, *An Act of Congress: The Legislative Process and the Making of Education Policy* (New York: Norton, 1969), is an account by political scientists of the enactment of the education acts. Lewis L. Gould, *Lady Bird Johnson and the Environment* (Lawrence: University Press of Kansas, 1988), is about Mrs. Johnson's contribution to highway beautification and similar measures. Hugh Davis Graham, *The Uncertain Triumph: Federal Education Policy in the Kennedy and Johnson Years* (Chapel Hill: University of North Carolina Press, 1984), is at best ambivalent about the federal aid to education measures. Polly Greenberg, *The Devil Has Slippery Shoes: A Biased Biography of the Child Development Group of Mississippi* (London: Macmillan, 1969), is a personal and positive account of a controversial Head Start program in Mississippi during the summer of 1965. For community action programs, see J. David Greenstone and Paul E. Patterson, *Race and Authority in Urban Politics: Community Participation and the War on Poverty* (New York: Russell Sage Foundation, 1973), and Peter Harris and Marvin Rein, *Dilemmas of Social Reform: Poverty and Community Action in the United States* (New York: Atherton Press, 1969). Charles M. Haar, an author and administrator of the Model Cities scheme, recounts its genesis and decline in *Between the Idea and the Reality: A Study in the Origin, Fate, and Legacy of the Model Cities Program* (Boston: Little, Brown, 1975). Michael Harrington's classic *The Other America: Poverty in the United States* (New York: Macmillan, 1963) "rediscovered" poverty in affluent America, pricking the national conscience and jump-starting the War on Poverty. Richard Harris, *A Sacred Trust* (Baltimore: Penguin, 1969), a book disdainful of the American Medical Association, recounts the origins of Medicare and national health insurance.

For other leading books on the Great Society programs see Carle Husemoller Nightingale, *On the Edge: A History of Poor Black Children and Their American Dream* (New York: Basic Books, 1993); and Herbert J. Gans, *The War against the Poor: The Underclass and Antipoverty Policy* (New York: Basic Books, 1995). Douglas S. Massey and Nancy A. Denton, *American Apartheid: Segregation and the Making of the Underclass* (Cambridge, Mass.: Harvard University Press, 1993); Stephen Steinberg, *Turning Back: The Retreat from Racial Justice in American Thought and Policy* (Boston: Beacon, 1995); Seymour E. Harris, *Economics of the Kennedy Years and a Look Ahead*; Robert Haveman, ed., *A Decade of Federal Antipoverty Programs* (New York: Academic Press, 1977); Robert

Haveman, *Poverty Policy and Poverty Research: The Great Society and the Social Sciences* (Madison: University of Wisconsin Press, 1987); Joseph Helfgot, *Professional Reforming: Mobilization for Youth and the Failure of Social Science* (Lexington, Mass.: Lexington Books, 1981); Larry Jackson and William Johnson, *Protest by the Poor: The Welfare Rights Movement in New York City* (Lexington, Mass.: Lexington Books, 1974); Julie Roy Jeffrey, *Education for Children of the Poor: A Study of the Origins and Implementation of the Elementary and Secondary Education Act of 1965* (Columbus: Ohio State University Press, 1978); Daniel Knapp and Kenneth Polk, *Scouting the War on Poverty: Social Reform Politics in the Kennedy Administration* (Lexington, Mass.: Lexington Books, 1971); Ralph M. Kramer, *Participation of the Poor: Comparative Community Case Studies in the War on Poverty* (Englewood Cliffs, N.J.: Prentice-Hall, 1969); Gary Larson, *The Reluctant Patron: The United States Government and the Arts, 1943–1965* (Philadelphia: University of Pennsylvania Press, 1983); Sar Levitan, *The Great Society's Poor Law: A New Approach to Poverty* (Baltimore: Johns Hopkins University Press, 1969); Sar Levitan and Robert Taggart, *The Promise of Greatness* (Cambridge, Mass.: Harvard University Press, 1976); Milbrey McLaughlin, *Evaluation and Reform: The Elementary and Secondary Education Act of 1965, Title I* (Cambridge, Mass.: Ballinger, 1975); Theodore Marmor, *The Politics of Medicare* (Chicago: Aldine, 1970); and Stephen Miller, *Excellence and Equity: The National Endowment for the Humanities* (Lexington: University Press of Kentucky, 1984). Daniel P. Moynihan blasts the community action programs in *Maximum Feasible Misunderstanding: Community Action in the War on Poverty* (New York: Free Press, 1969). A strong concise defense of the Great Society Programs is John E. Schwarz, *America's Hidden Success: A Reassessment of Twenty Years of Public Policy* (New York: Norton, 1983).

Paul Conkin, *Big Daddy from the Pedernales* (Boston: Twayne, 1986), is a relatively brief and largely favorable biography of LBJ emphasizing his paternalism. Eric Goldman, *The Tragedy of Lyndon Johnson* (New York: Knopf, 1969) is a readable account by a man who served as LBJ's cultural adviser and ambassador to the intellectuals. Richard Goodwin, a Johnson speechwriter who helped formulate his Great Society concepts, wrote *Remembering America: A Voice from the Sixties* (Boston: Little, Brown, 1988); Goodwin broke with Johnson over Vietnam and resigned. Lyndon B. Johnson, *The Vantage Point: Perspectives of the Presidency* (New York: Holt, Rinehart and Winston, 1971) is Johnson's own self-congratulatory view of his presidency. Merle Miller, *Lyndon: An Oral Biography* (New York: G. P. Putnam's Sons, 1980) is a review of LBJ's career made up of verbatim interviews of people who knew him and participated in his administration. Alfred Steinberg, *On Sam Johnson's Boy: A Close-Up of the President from Texas* (New York: Macmillan, 1968) is negative at great length. Early reviews of the Johnson domestic programs are James L. Sundquist, ed., *On Fighting Poverty: Perspectives from Experience* (New York: Basic Books, 1969), and *On Politics and Policy: The Eisenhower, Kennedy, and Johnson Years* (Washington: Brookings Institution, 1968). Christopher Weeks analyzes the Job Corps in *Dollars and Dropouts* (Boston: Little, Brown, 1967). A defense of Head Start by a participant is Edward Zigler and Susan Muenchow, *Head Start: The Inside Story of America's Most Successful Educational Experiment* (New York: Basic Books,

1992). Harry McPherson, a fellow Texan, LBJ's counsel, and a frank observer, wrote *A Political Education* (Boston: Little, Brown, 1972). Allen J. Matusow, *The Unravelling of America: A History of Liberalism in the 1960s* (New York: Harper and Row, 1984) examines the Kennedy and Johnson administrations and finds wanting the brand of liberalism they represented. See Philip Meranto, *The Politics of Federal Aid to Education in 1965: A Study in Political Innovation* (Syracuse: Syracuse University Press, 1967); Lawrence O'Brien, chief legislative strategist for Kennedy and Johnson, shows how the laws were passed: *No Final Victories: A Life in Politics from John F. Kennedy to Watergate* (Garden City, N.Y.: Doubleday, 1974). See Emmette S. Redford and Marlon Blisset, *On Organizing the Executive Branch: The Johnson Presidency* (Chicago: University of Chicago Press, 1981); and George Reedy, *Twilight of the Presidency: An Examination of Power and Isolation in the White House* (Cleveland: World Publishing Company, 1970). Robert C. Wood, a former aide and bureaucrat, wrote *Whatever Possessed the President? Academic Experts and Presidential Policy, 1960–1988* (Amherst: University of Massachusetts Press, 1993).

The Vietnam War

Guides and Chronologies

The study of the Indochina wars and the United States in Vietnam might begin with some of the images that had an important place in American policy in Southeast Asia. *Vietnam: A Television History* (Boston: WGBH Educational Foundation, 1983), a documentary of the war, is an account of some thirty years of American engagement in Vietnam beginning soon after the expulsion of the Japanese from the country in 1945. Critics of the series include R. C. Raack, "Caveat Spectator," *OAH Newsletter* 12 (February 1984): 25–28, and Stephen Vlastos, "Television Wars: Representations of the Vietnam War in Television Documentaries," *Radical History Review* 36 (1986): 115–32.

Among guides and reference works are William Conrad Gibbons, *The U.S. Government and the Vietnam War: Legislative Roles and Relationships*, parts 1–4 (Princeton: Princeton University Press, 1986–95); three volumes of bibliography produced for the Center for Armament and Disarmament at California State University, Los Angeles: Milton Leitenberg and Richard Dean Burns, *The Vietnam Conflict: Its Geographical Dimensions, Political Traumas, and Military Developments* (Santa Barbara: ABC-Clio, 1973); Richard Dean Burns and Milton Leitenberg, *The Wars in Vietnam, Cambodia and Laos, 1945–1982: A Bibliographic Guide* (Santa Barbara: ABC-Clio, 1984); and Lester H. Brune and Richard Dean Burns, *America and the Indochina Wars, 1945–1990: A Bibliographical Guide* (Claremont, Calif.: Regina Books, 1992). The Burns bibliographies provide brief descriptions of the sources they list. James S. Olson in *The Vietnam War: Handbook of the Literature and Research* (Westport, Conn.: Greenwood Press, 1993) has assembled a collection of bibliographical essays that provide a more critical assessment of recent works on Vietnam. Marc Jason Gilbert's *The Vietnam War: Teaching Approaches and Resources* (Westport, Conn.: Greenwood Press, 1991) similarly offers a critical treatment of materials. Two sources organized very much alike help sort out the bewildering array of names, events, places, military acronyms, and statistics, among the other details associated with the American involvement in Vietnam: William J. Duiker, *Historical Dictionary of Vietnam* (Metuchen, N.J.: Scarecrow Press, 1989), and James S. Olson, ed., *Dictionary of the Vietnam War* (Westport, Conn.: Greenwood Press, 1988). Other reference guides include D. J. Sagar, *Major Political Events in Indo-China, 1945–1990* (New York: Facts on File, 1991); Louis A. Peake, *The United States in the Vietnam War, 1954–1975: A Selected, Annotated Bibliography* (New York: Garland, 1986); and Michael Cotter, *Vietnam: A Guide to Reference Sources* (Boston: G. K. Hall, 1977).

One of the most extensive collections of materials on Vietnam—including items in French and Vietnamese—is housed at Cornell University. Many of these are listed in Christopher Sugnet, John T. Hickey, and Robert Crispino, *Vietnam War Bibliography: Selected from Cornell University's Echols Collection* (Lexington, Mass.: Lexington Books, D. C. Heath, 1983). The World Bibliographical Series, Robert G. Neville, executive editor, contains two volumes relevant to the study of Indochina and its history: David G. Marr, comp., with the assistance of Kristine Alilunas-Rodgers, *Vietnam* (vol. 147) (Oxford: Clio Press, 1992), and Helen Cordell, comp., *Laos* (vol. 133) (Oxford: Clio Press, 1991). Documents of the American engagement in Southeast Asia are abundant. One is essential: *The Pentagon Papers: The Senator Gavel Edition*, 5 vols. (Boston: Beacon, 1971–72). In *The Pentagon Papers: As Published by the "New York Times"* (New York: Quadrangle Books, 1971), Neil Sheehan and others have assembled a useful selection of documents along with commentary that serve as a good introduction to the papers. Despite its pretentious title, Gareth Porter's *Vietnam: The Definitive Documentation of Human Decisions*, 2 vols. (Stanfordville, N.Y.: Earl M. Coleman Enterprises, 1979), is a valuable selection of documents covering the years from 1941 through 1975 (the documentation in the Pentagon Papers concludes in 1968).

The war in Vietnam has inspired many personal narratives and wartime reminiscences of combatants and noncombatants, supporters of the war and antiwar activists. Most of these are described in Sandra M. Wittman, *Writing about Vietnam: A Bibliography of the Literature of the Vietnam Conflict* (Boston: G. K. Hall, 1989). Interest in the special problems of the Vietnam veterans has created a growing body of literature, much of it reported in Norman M. Camp, Robert H. Stretch, and William C. Marshall, *Stress, Strain, and Vietnam: An Annotated Bibliography of Two Decades of Psychiatric and Social Sciences Literature Reflecting the Effect of the War on the American Soldier* (Westport, Conn.: Greenwood Press, 1988).

General Studies

Among prominent general histories of the war is the journalist Stanley Karnow's *Vietnam: A History*, rev. and updated ed. (New York: Penguin, 1991), which originally appeared in 1983 as the companion volume for the series *Vietnam: A Television History*. Recent broad histories include George C. Herring, *America's Longest War: The United States and Vietnam, 1950–1975*, rev. ed. (New York: Knopf, 1986); William S. Turley, *The Second Indochina War: A Short Political and Military History, 1954–1975* (Boulder, Colo.: Westview Press, 1986); and James S. Olson and Randy Roberts, *Where the Domino Fell, America and Vietnam, 1945 to 1990* (New York: St. Martin's Press, 1991). Marilyn B. Young's *The Vietnam Wars, 1945–1990* (New York: HarperCollins, 1991) is very critical of American policy toward Vietnam, as is journalist Neil Sheehan's Pulitzer Prize–winning *The Bright and Shining Lie: John Paul Vann and America in Vietnam* (New York: Random House, 1988). Gabriel Kolko argues in *Anatomy of a War: Vietnam, the United States, and the Modern Historical Experience* (New York: Pantheon, 1985) that the United States intervention in Southeast Asia was part of its imperial design to establish an American hegemony in the Pacific. One of the earliest works to stress the American misunderstanding of the commitment of the Vietnamese, and especially the communist Vietnamese, to nationalism is Frances Fitzgerald's *Fire in the Lake: The Vietnamese and the Americans in Vietnam* (Boston: Little, Brown, 1972). Ms. Fitzgerald has been criticized for her sympathetic portrait of the Communist National Liberation Front. Revisionist histories that view the American role in Vietnam in a more positive light include Guenter Lewy, *America in Vietnam* (New York: Oxford University Press, 1978), and Timothy J. Lomperis, *The War Everyone Lost—And Won: America's Intervention in Vietnam's Twin Struggles* (Baton Rouge: Louisiana State University Press, 1984).

Vietnamese History

The history and culture of Vietnam are described in Keith Weller Taylor, *The Birth of Vietnam* (Berkeley and Los Angeles: University of California Press, 1983), and Milton E. Osborne, *Southeast Asia: An Introductory History*, 5th ed. (New York: HarperCollins, 1991). Also see Pham Kim Vinh's *The Vietnamese Culture: An Introduction* (Costa Mesa, Calif.: Pham Kim Vinh Research Institute, 1990). A brief overview of the history of Vietnam may be found in John K. Whitmore, *Vietnam, Ho Quy, and the Ming* (New Haven: Yale University Southeast Asian Studies Program, 1985). A recent study of Vietnamese culture and the Vietnamese outlook on the world is Neil L. Jamieson's *Understanding Vietnam* (Berkeley and Los Angeles: University of California Press, 1993). An early series of studies by Joseph Buttinger concentrates on the political life of the Vietnamese: *The Smaller Dragon: A Political History of Vietnam* (New York: Praeger, 1958); *Vietnam: A Dragon Embattled*, 2 vols. (New York: Praeger, 1967); and *Vietnam: A Political History* (New York: Praeger, 1968). Edgar Wickberg's *Historical Interaction of China and Vietnam* (New York: Paragon Book Gallery, 1969) provides a more thorough assessment of the Chinese influence on Vietnam and the Vietnamese response. The religious and ethnic diversity of Vietnam are discussed in Pierro Gheddo's *The Cross and the Bo-Tree: Catholics and Buddhists in Vietnam*, trans. Charles U. Quinn (New York: Sheed and Ward, 1970), and in three anthropological works by Gerald C. Hickey: *Village in Vietnam* (New Haven: Yale University Press, 1967); *Sons of the Mountain: Ethnohistory of the Vietnamese Central Highlands to 1954* (New Haven: Yale University Press, 1982); and *Free in the Forest: Ethnohistory of the Vietnamese Central Highlands, 1954–1976* (New Haven: Yale University Press, 1982).

The story of French colonialism is revealed in David G. Marr, *Vietnam, 1945: The Quest for Power* (Berkeley and Los Angeles: University of California Press,

1995), which argues that 1945 was the most important year in the U.S. involvements; John F. Cady, *The Roots of French Imperialism in Eastern Asia* (Ithaca: Cornell University Press, 1954); Milton E. Osborne, *The French Presence in Cochinchina and Cambodia: Rule and Response, 1859–1905* (Ithaca: Cornell University Press, 1969); and Martin Murray, *The Development of Capitalism in Colonial Indochina, 1870–1940* (Berkeley and Los Angeles: University of California Press, 1980). Background on the Vietnamese independence movement is provided in Mark M. McLeod, *The Vietnamese Response to French Intervention, 1862–1874* (New York: Praeger, 1991); William J. Duiker, *The Rise of Nationalism in Vietnam, 1900–1941* (Ithaca: Cornell University Press, 1975); Troung Buu Lam, *Patterns of Vietnamese Response to Foreign Intervention, 1858–1900* (New Haven: Yale University Press, 1967); and Thomas Hodgkin, *Vietnam: The Revolutionary Path* (New York: St. Martin's Press, 1981). Also see two studies by David Marr, *Vietnamese Anti-Colonialism, 1885–1925* (Berkeley and Los Angeles: University of California Press, 1971), and *Vietnamese Tradition on Trial, 1920–1945* (Berkeley and Los Angeles: University of California Press, 1981).

The Vietnamese Wars

The First Vietnam War, 1946–54, is the subject of the French historian Jacques Dalloz's *The War in Indochina, 1945–1954* (Savage, Md.: Barnes and Noble, 1990) and Ellen J. Hammer's *The Struggle for Indochina, 1940–1955* (Stanford: Stanford University Press, 1966). Also see Donald Lancaster, *The Emancipation of French Indochina* (New York: Octagon Books, 1974). The French journalist Bernard Fall, who covered most of the major events in Vietnam until his death during the Second Vietnam War, was a harsh critic of French policies in Vietnam (later, he was equally severe in his treatment of the American program). In *Street without Joy: Insurgency in Indochina*, 4th ed. (London: Pall Mall Press, 1965), Fall describes French military activities during the war. The military history of the war is also covered in Edgar O'Ballance, *The Indo-China War, 1945–1954: A Study in Guerrilla Warfare* (London: Faber and Faber, 1964). Vo Nguyen Giap's *Unforgettable Days* (Hanoi: Foreign Language Publishing House, 1978) is an account of the war by the commanding general of the Vietminh forces that finally defeated the French.

The decisive battle at Dien Bien Phu is described by Bernard Fall in *Hell in a Very Small Place: The Siege of Dien Bien Phu* (Philadelphia: Lippincott, 1967) and by Jules Roy in *The Battle of Dien Bien Phu*, trans. Robert Baldich (New York: Harper and Row, 1965). Giap gives his view of the confrontation in *Dien Bien Phu* (Hanoi: Foreign Language Publishing House, 1962). The conclusion of the war and the consequences of the fall of France in Indochina are examined in three works: Lawrence Kaplan, Denise Artaud, and Mark R. Rubin, *Dien Bien Phu and the Crisis of Franco-American Relations, 1954–1955* (Washington: Scholarly Resources, 1989); Philippe Devillers and Jean Lacouture, *End of a War: Indochina, 1954* (New York: Praeger, 1969); and Robert F. Randle, *Geneva 1954: The Settlement of the Indochinese War* (Princeton: Princeton University Press, 1969). Edward Rice-Maximin's *Accommodation and Resistance: The French Left, Indochina and the Cold War, 1944–1954* (Westport, Conn.: Greenwood Press, 1986) offers a fresh view of the relation of Western politics after

World War II to activities affecting Indochina. See also John R. Mordell, Jr., *The Undetected Enemy: French and American Miscalculations in Dien Bien Phu, 1953* (College Station: Texas A&M University Press, 1995).

A number of good biographies of Ho Chi Minh exist. See especially Jean Lacouture's *Ho Chi Minh: A Political Biography* (New York: Random House, 1968) and David Halberstam's *Ho* (New York: Random House, 1971). Ho Chi Minh's writings and speeches are available in four volumes of his *Selected Works* (Hanoi: Foreign Language Publishing House, 1962–64) and in his *Prison Diary* (Hanoi: Foreign Language Publishing House, 1967). Edited collections of Ho's works are more readily accessible. See, for example, Bernard B. Fall, ed., *Ho Chi Minh on Revolution: Selected Writings, 1920–1964* (New York: Praeger, 1967), and Jack Woodis, ed., *Ho Chi Minh: Selected Articles and Speeches, 1920–1967* (New York: International Publishers, 1970). On the origins and nature of the communist movement in Vietnam, consult Khanh Huyunh Kim, *Vietnamese Communism, 1925–1945* (Ithaca: Cornell University Press, 1982); William J. Duiker, *The Communist Road to Power in Vietnam* (Boulder, Colo.: Westview Press, 1981); Douglas Pike, *History of Vietnamese Communism, 1925–1976* (Palo Alto, Calif.: Hoover Institution Press, 1978); and Robert F. Turner's sharply disapproving *Vietnamese Communism: Its Origins and Development* (Stanford: Hoover Institution Press, 1975).

American Involvement

These works examine the complex reasons that led to American involvement: Gary R. Hess, *The United States Emergence as a Southeast Asian Power, 1940–1950* (New York: Columbia University, 1987); Andrew J. Rotter, *The Path to Vietnam: Origins of the American Commitment to Southeast Asia* (Ithaca: Cornell University Press, 1987); and Robert M. Blum, *Drawing the Line: The United States and Containment in Southeast Asia, 1945–1949* (New York: Norton, 1982). Studies more critical of American policymakers include George M. Kahin, *Intervention: How America Became Involved in Vietnam* (New York: Knopf, 1986); and Richard J. Barnet, *Roots of War: The Men and Institutions behind U.S. Foreign Policy* (New York: Atheneum, 1971). Sandra C. Taylor, in "Vietnam: In the Beginning," *Reviews in American History* 17 (June 1989): 306–11, surveys the historical literature dealing with the initial phase of the American presence in Southeast Asia from 1941 to 1956. Conflicting views about the role of the United States in Southeast Asia have been assembled in John Norton Moore, ed., *The Vietnam Debate: A Fresh Look at the Arguments* (Lanham, Md.: University Press of America, 1990). Susan Jeffords's *The Remasculinization of America: Gender and the Vietnam War* (Bloomington: Indiana University Press, 1989) offers a feminist perspective on the United States and the Second Indochina War.

Presidential Policies

Essays on the leadership skills and Southeast Asia policies of presidents from Harry S Truman through Gerald R. Ford are collected in David L. Anderson, ed., *Shadow on the White House: Presidents and the Vietnam War, 1945–1975* (Lawrence: University Press of Kansas, 1993). On Roosevelt's thinking two good essays are Gary R. Hess, "Franklin Roosevelt and Indochina," *Journal of American History* 59 (September 1972): 353–68, and Walter LaFeber, "Roosevelt, Churchill and Indochina: 1942–1945," *American Historical Review* 80 (December 1975): 1277–95. Edward R. Drachman's *United States Policy toward Vietnam, 1940–1945* (Rutherford, N.J.: Fairleigh Dickinson University Press, 1970) is also useful on the FDR years. See Robert J. Donovan's two-volume biography of Truman, *Conflict and Crisis: The Presidency of Harry S Truman, 1945–1948* (New York: Norton, 1977) and *Tumultuous Years: The Presidency of Harry S Truman, 1949–1953* (New York: Norton, 1982). Melvyn P. Leffler's *A Preponderance of Power: National Security, the Truman Administration, and the Cold War* (Stanford: Stanford University Press, 1992) discusses the place of Southeast Asia in the Cold War strategies of Truman and his advisers. Also see Lloyd C. Gardner, *Approaching Vietnam: From World War II through Dienbienphu, 1941–1954* (New York: Norton, 1988). David S. McLellan's *Dean Acheson: The State Department Years* (New York: Dodd, Mead, 1976) examines the public life of Dean Acheson, Truman's Secretary of State and one of the principal architects of the Cold War policy of containment. Acheson's memoirs, *Present at the Creation: My Years in the State Department* (New York: Norton, 1969), describe his policies and views for the years 1941 to 1953. Douglas Brinkley's *Dean Acheson: The Cold War Years, 1953–1971* (New Haven: Yale University Press, 1992) assesses Acheson's thinking after 1953.

David L. Anderson's *Trapped by Success: The Eisenhower Administration and Vietnam, 1953–1961* (New York: Columbia University Press, 1991) is an excellent treatment of Eisenhower's Indochina policies. Eisenhower, in two volumes of memoirs—*The White House Years: Mandate for Change, 1953–1956* (Garden City, N.Y.: Doubleday, 1963) and *The White House Years: Waging Peace, 1956–1961* (Garden City, N.Y.: Doubleday, 1965)—gives his own account of his policies. Some of Ike's chief strategists are discussed in H. W. Brands, Jr., *Cold Warriors: Eisenhower's Generation and American Foreign Policy* (New York: Columbia University Press, 1988). Two recent studies of Eisenhower's Secretary of State John Foster Dulles are Frederick Marks III, *Power and Peace: The Diplomacy of John Foster Dulles* (Westport, Conn.: Praeger, 1993), and Richard H. Immerman, ed., *John Foster Dulles and the Diplomacy of the Cold War: A Reappraisal* (Princeton: Princeton University Press, 1989). Works that give special attention to John Kennedy and Vietnam include William J. Rust, *Kennedy in Vietnam: American Foreign Policy, 1960–1963* (New York: Da Capo Press, 1987); R. B. Smith, *An International History of the Vietnam War: The Kennedy Strategy* (New York: St. Martin's Press, 1987); and John M. Newman, *JFK and Vietnam: Deception, Intrigue, and the Struggle for Power* (New York: Warner Books, 1992). In *The Making of a Quagmire: America and Vietnam during the Kennedy Era* (New York: Knopf, 1965), David Halberstam argues that it was a mistake for Kennedy to support the corrupt Diem regime in South Vietnam for as long as he did. Halberstam's *The Best and the Brightest* (New York: Random House, 1972) describes many of the principals who served during the 1960s in the Kennedy and Johnson White Houses. Two important recent biographies are Anne E. Blair, *Lodge in Vietnam: A Patriot Abroad* (New Haven: Yale University Press, 1995), and Randall Bennett Woods, *Fulbright: A Biography* (New York:

Cambridge University Press, 1995). Works by Kennedy advisers include Roger Hilsman, *To Move a Nation: The Politics of Foreign Policy in the Administration of John F. Kennedy* (Garden City, N.Y.: Doubleday, 1967); George W. Ball, *The Past Has Another Pattern: Memoirs* (New York: Norton, 1982); Walt W. Rostow, *The Diffusion of Power, 1957–1972* (New York: Macmillan, 1972); Frederick Nolting, *From Trust to Tragedy: The Political Memoirs of Frederick Nolting, Kennedy's Ambassador to Diem's Vietnam* (New York: Praeger, 1988); and Dean Rusk, *As I Saw It: The Memoirs of Dean Rusk* (New York: Norton, 1990). Warren I. Cohen's *Dean Rusk* (Totowa, N.J.: Cooper Square, 1980) is a more critical assessment of Kennedy's Secretary of State; and the head of JFK's Defense Department is the subject of Henry L. Trewhitt's *McNamara: His Ordeal in the Pentagon* (New York: Harper and Row, 1978).

South Vietnam, 1954–1968

Two biographies of "America's Mandarin" in South Vietnam, Ngo Dinh Diem, are Anthony T. Bouscaren, *The Last of the Mandarins: Diem of Vietnam* (Pittsburgh: Duquesne University Press, 1965), and Denis Warner, *The Last Confucian* (New York: Macmillan, 1963). Ellen J. Hammer's *A Death in November: America in Vietnam, 1963* (New York: Dutton, 1987) discusses the collapse of the Diem regime. Two works that look at the function of the American military during this early period are Ronald H. Spector, *Advice and Support: The Early Years of the United States Army in Vietnam, 1941–1960* (1983; reprint, New York: Free Press, 1985), and Robert H. Whitlow, *U.S. Marines in Vietnam: The Advisory and Combat Assistance Era, 1954–1964* (Washington: U.S. Government Printing Office, 1977). The development and operations of the communist insurgency movement in the South, the National Liberation Front (NLF) or Vietcong as insurgents came to be called, are described and analyzed in two books by Douglas Pike, *Viet Cong: The Organization and Techniques of the National Liberation Front of South Vietnam* (Cambridge, Mass.: MIT Press, 1966) and *The Viet-Cong Strategy of Terror* (Saigon: U.S. Mission, 1970). William Andrews, *The Village War: Vietnamese Communist Revolutionary Activity in Dinh Truong Province, 1960–1964* (Columbia: University of Missouri Press, 1973), and Jeffrey Race, *War Comes to Long An: Revolutionary Conflict in a Vietnamese Province* (Berkeley and Los Angeles: University of California Press, 1972), discuss guerrilla campaigns in the villages and provinces of the South. See also Larry E. Cable, *Conflict of Myths: The Development of American Counterinsurgency Doctrine and the Vietnam War* (New York: New York University Press, 1986), and D. Michael Schafer, *Deadly Paradigms: The Failure of U.S. Counterinsurgency Policy* (Princeton: Princeton University Press, 1987). Also see Andrew R. Krepinevich's *The Army and Vietnam* (Baltimore: Johns Hopkins University Press, 1986). Robert W. Chandler's *War of Ideas: The U.S. Propaganda Campaign in Vietnam* (Boulder, Colo.: Westview Press, 1981) describes the American effort to win the "hearts and minds" of the Vietnamese. And Milton E. Osborne's *Strategic Hamlets in South Vietnam: A Survey and Comparison*, Data Paper 55 (Ithaca: Cornell University, Southeast Asia Program, 1965), is the description of another program aimed at fighting communist influence in the South by relocating peasants in protected villages.

Lyndon Johnson in *The Vantage Point: Perspectives of the Presidency, 1963–1969* (New York: Holt, Rinehart and Winston, 1971) gives his own assessment of his presidency. More detached and critical appraisals include Vaughn Davis Bornet, *The Presidency of Lyndon B. Johnson* (Lawrence: University Press of Kansas, 1984); Doris Kearns, *Lyndon Johnson and the American Dream* (New York: Harper and Row, 1976); Paul K. Conkin, *Big Daddy from the Pedernales: Lyndon Baines Johnson* (Boston: G. K. Hall, 1986); Lloyd C. Gardner, *Pay Any Price: Lyndon Johnson and the Wars for Vietnam* (Chicago: Ivan R. Dee, 1995); and Warren I. Cohen and Nancy Bernkopf Tucker, eds., *Lyndon Johnson Confronts the World: American Foreign Policy, 1963–1968* (New York: Cambridge University Press, 1994). In two volumes of biography, *The Years of Lyndon Johnson: The Path to Power* (New York: Knopf, 1982) and *The Years of Lyndon Johnson: Means of Ascent* (New York: Knopf, 1990), Robert A. Caro describes Johnson in harsh terms. Two works by Larry Berman place special emphasis on Johnson's decision to escalate the war: *Lyndon Johnson's War: The Road to Stalemate* (New York: Norton, 1989) and *Planning a Tragedy: The Americanization of the War in Vietnam* (New York: Norton, 1982). Also see Brian VanDeMark, *Into the Quagmire: Lyndon Johnson and the Escalation of the Vietnam War* (New York: Oxford University Press, 1991). The history of policymaking in the Johnson White House is described in a number of books. See especially David M. Barrett, *Uncertain Warriors: Lyndon Johnson and His Vietnam Advisers* (Lawrence: University Press of Kansas, 1993), and Henry F. Graff, *The Tuesday Cabinet: Deliberation and Decision on Peace and War under Lyndon B. Johnson* (Englewood Cliffs, N.J.: Prentice-Hall, 1970). In 1967 Johnson turned to a group of senior foreign policy experts—which included, among others, Dean Acheson, W. Averell Harriman, and George F. Kennan—to advise him on Vietnam. The work of this senior advisory group is told in Walter Isaacson and Evan Thomas, *The Wise Men: Six Friends and the World They Made* (New York: Simon and Schuster, 1986). Also see the memoirs and studies of Kennedy officials George Ball, Walt Rostow, Dean Rusk, and Robert McNamara—cited in the section on the Kennedy era—all of whom also served Johnson. Clark Clifford, a senior Johnson policy adviser who succeeded McNamara at Defense in 1968, in *Counsel to the President: A Memoir* (New York: Random House, 1991), describes his efforts to convince LBJ not to expand the war. Johnson's deteriorating relationship with the media is analyzed in Kathleen J. Turner's *Lyndon Johnson's Dual War: Vietnam and the Press* (Chicago: University of Chicago Press, 1985). On the accuracy and fairness of the media's coverage of the war in general, see Daniel Hallin, *The "Uncensored War": The Media and Vietnam* (New York: Oxford University Press, 1986), and William M. Hammond, *Public Affairs: The Military and the Media, 1962–1968* (Washington: U.S. Government Printing Office, 1990). On Johnson's decision not to seek reelection in 1968, there is Herbert Y. Schandler's *The Unmaking of a President: Lyndon Johnson and Vietnam* (Princeton: Princeton University Press, 1968).

Military Strategy

The United States military strategy in Vietnam remains a source of lively debate. The belief that American forces were hindered at home finds voice in Wilbur H. Morrison, *Vietnam: The Winnable War* (New York: Hippocrene Books, 1990);

U.S. Grant Sharp, *Strategy for Defeat: Vietnam in Retrospect* (Novato, Calif.: Presidio Press, 1978); and Harry G. Summers, Jr., *On Strategy: A Critical Analysis of the Vietnam War* (Novato, Calif.: Presidio Press, 1983). Works that argue that the military should have given more emphasis to counterinsurgency and pacification include Lewis Walt, *Strange War, Strange Strategy: A General's Report on Vietnam* (New York: Funk and Wagnalls, 1970), and William Colby and James McCargar, *Lost Victory: A Firsthand Account of America's Sixteen-Year Involvement in Vietnam* (Chicago: Contemporary Books, 1989). For another view see Eric M. Bergerud, *The Dynamics of Defeat: The Vietnam War in Hau Nghia Province* (Boulder, Colo.: Westview Press, 1990).

Official works surveying American military operations in Vietnam include Shelby L. Stanton's *The Rise and Fall of An American Army: U.S. Ground Forces in Vietnam, 1965–1973* (Novato, Calif.: Presidio Press, 1985) and Jeffrey Clarke, *The U.S. Army in Vietnam: Advice and Support, the Final Years, 1960–1975* (Washington: U.S. Government Printing Office, 1988). Also see Leroy Thomas, *The U.S. Army in Vietnam* (New York: Sterling, 1990). On the role of the Army Special Forces in Vietnam, there is Shelby L. Stanton, *Green Berets at War: U.S. Special Forces in Asia, 1956–1975* (Novato, Calif.: Presidio Press, 1990). Navy operations are discussed in Frank Uhlig, Jr., *Vietnam: The Naval Story* (Annapolis: Naval Institute Press, 1988), and Edward J. Matolda and Oscar P. Fitzgerald, *The United States Navy and the Vietnam Conflict*, 3 vols. (Washington: U.S. Government Printing Office, 1980–88); Marine activity is summarized in Charles R. Anderson, *Vietnam: The Other War* (New York: Warner Books, 1990).

Raphael Littauer and Norman Uphoff, eds., *The Air War in Indochina* (Boston: Beacon, 1972), is a good general account of American air operations in Southeast Asia. Jack Broughton's *Going Downtown: The War against Hanoi and Washington* (New York: Orion Books, 1988) argues that the Air Force could have waged a more effective campaign had it not been for bureaucratic interference from Washington. Important critical appraisals of the air war are James C. Thompson, *Rolling Thunder: Understanding Policy and Program Failure* (Chapel Hill: University of North Carolina Press, 1980); Mark Clodfelter, *The Limits of Air Power: The American Bombing of North Vietnam* (New York: Free Press, 1989); and Earl H. Tilford, Jr., *Crosswinds: The Air Force's Setup in Vietnam* (College Station: Texas A&M University Press, 1993). On the ecological consequences of the bombing and the American use of chemicals and defoliants, see William A. Buckingham, Jr., *Ranch Hand: The U.S. Air Force and Herbicides in Southeast Asia, 1961–1971* (Washington: U.S. Government Printing Office, 1982); John Lewallen, *Ecology of Devastation: Indochina* (Baltimore: Penguin, 1971); Arthur Westing, *The Environmental Aftermath of Warfare in Vietnam* (London: Taylor and Frances, 1982); and the Institute of Medicine, *Veterans and Agent Orange: Health Effects of Herbicides Used in Vietnam* (Washington: National Academy Press, 1994). Two works that argue that it was confidence in its technological superiority that led the United States to trouble in Vietnam are Loren Baritz, *Backfire: A History of How American Culture Led Us into Vietnam and Made Us Fight the Way We Did* (New York: William Morrow, 1985), and James William Gibson, *The Perfect War: Techno-War in Vietnam* (New York: Atlantic Monthly, 1987).

Participants

Oral histories by those who fought in the war include Al Santoli, *Everything We Had: An Oral History of the Vietnam War by Thirty-Three American Soldiers Who Fought It* (New York: Random House, 1981); Mark Baker, *Nam: The Vietnam War in the Words of the Men and Women Who Fought There* (New York: William Morrow, 1981); Harry Maurer, *Strange Ground: Americans in Vietnam, 1945–1975, An Oral History* (New York: Henry Holt, 1989); Otto J. Lehrack, *No Shining Armor: The Marines at War in Vietnam, An Oral History* (Lawrence: University Press of Kansas, 1992); and Eric M. Bergerud, *Red Thunder, Tropic Lightning: The World of a Combat Division in Vietnam* (Boulder, Colo.: Westview Press, 1993). Also see Craig Howes, *Voices of the Vietnam POWs: Witnesses to Their Fight* (New York: Oxford University Press, 1993), and Bernard Edelman, ed., *Dear America: Letters Home from Vietnam* (New York: Norton, 1985). There is a large body of full-length personal accounts by those who served in the military or worked in some other capacity in Vietnam. Three of the better-known are Philip Caputo's *A Rumor of War* (New York: Holt, Rhinehart and Winston, 1977); Ron Kovic's *Born on the Fourth of July* (New York: McGraw-Hill, 1976); and Michael Herr's *Dispatches* (New York: Knopf, 1977).

Minorities and Women

The response of African Americans to the Vietnam experience is analyzed in Robert W. Mullen's *Blacks in Vietnam* (Washington: University Press of America, 1981). Personal narratives of black soldiers in Vietnam are Stanley Goff's and Robert Sanders's *Brothers: Black Soldiers in the Nam* (New York: Berkley Books, 1986) and Wallace Terry's *Bloods: An Oral History of the Vietnam War by Black Veterans* (New York: Random House, 1984). The voices of Hispanic troops are heard in Charley Trujillo, ed., *Soldados: Chicanos in Vietnam* (Albuquerque: Chusma House, 1989). Lloyd B. Lewis's *The Tainted War: Culture and Identity in Vietnam War Narratives* (Westport, Conn.: Greenwood Press, 1985) is a scholar's effort to sort through the themes of this war literature. Christian G. Appy's *Working-Class War: American Combat Soldiers and Vietnam* (Chapel Hill: University of North Carolina Press, 1993) is a recent effort to provide a social and economic portrait of those who fought in the war.

Among the earliest and best of the narratives of American women in Vietnam is Lynda Van Devanter's *Home before Morning: The Story of an Army Nurse in Vietnam* (New York: Beaufort Books, 1983). Oral histories include Dan Freedman, ed., and Jacqueline Rhoads, associate ed., *Nurses in Vietnam: The Forgotten Veterans* (Austin: Texas Monthly Press, 1987); Keith Walker, *A Piece of My Heart: The Stories of Twenty-Six American Women Who Served in Vietnam* (Novato, Calif.: Presidio Press, 1985); and Kathryn Marshall, *In the Combat Zone: An Oral History of American Women in Vietnam* (Boston: Little, Brown, 1987). Elizabeth Norman's *Women at War: The Story of Fifty Military Nurses Who Served in Vietnam* (Philadelphia: University of Pennsylvania Press, 1990) documents the experiences of women who served in Vietnam between 1965 and 1973. *Forever Sad Hearts* (New York: Avon Books, 1982), by Patricia L. Walsh, herself a nurse in Vietnam, is a moving novel of an American woman working in a civilian hospital in Da Nang. For other works dealing with gender issues see Joe P. Dunn, "Women and the Vietnam War: A Bibliographic Review," *Journal of American Culture* 12 (Spring 1989): 79–86.

David Chanoff and Doan Van Toai's *Portrait of the Enemy* (1986) is a collection of interviews with North Vietnamese officials and former members of the Vietcong. Personal histories of Vietcong members are Truong Nhu Tang, with David Chanoff and Doan Van Toai, *A Viet Cong Memoir* (New York: Random House, 1985), and Mrs. Nguyen Thi Dinh, *No Other Road to Take, Memoir of Mrs. Nguyen Thi Dinh*, trans. Mai Elliott (Ithaca: Cornell University Press, 1976). Nguyen Thi Dinh was the NLF's delegate to the Paris peace negotiations. Douglas Pike's *PAVN: People's Army of Vietnam* (Novato, Calif.: Presidio Press, 1986) describes the North Vietnamese army. In *On the Other Side: Twenty-Three Days with the Viet Cong* (New York: Quadrangle Books, 1972), Kate Webb relates what she experienced as a prisoner of the Vietcong. The perspectives of South Vietnamese officials are represented by Bui Diem and David Chanoff, *In the Jaws of History* (New York: Houghton Mifflin, 1987), and Nguyen Cao Ky, *Twenty Years and Twenty Days* (New York: Stein and Day, 1976). Bui Diem was Saigon's ambassador to Washington; the flamboyant Nguyen Cao Ky had served as South Vietnam's president and then longtime vice president. Don Luce and John Sommer have gathered oral histories of the South Vietnamese people in *Vietnam: The Unheard Voices* (Ithaca: Cornell University Press, 1969). A poignant story of the effects of the three Indochina wars on one South Vietnamese woman and her family is Le Ly Hayslip, with Jay Wurts, *When Heaven and Earth Changed Places: A Vietnamese Woman's Journey from War to Peace* (New York: Doubleday, 1990). Jade Ngoc Quang Huynh's *South Wind Changing* (St. Paul: Graywolf Press, 1994) is a refugee's account of beatings and forced labor under the communists after 1975, followed by escape from Vietnam. Also see the recollections gathered from various individuals—officials, veterans, wives of soldiers, and others—in Al Santoli's *To Bear Any Burden: The Vietnam War and Its Aftermath in the Words of Americans and Southeast Asians* (New York: Dutton, 1985).

Later Stages of the War

The principal battles of the Vietnam war took place around the Tet offensive of late January 1968. On the events of Tet there are Dan Oberdorfer, *Tet!* (Garden City, N.Y.: Doubleday, 1971), and James R. Arnold, *Tet Offensive: 1968, the Final Turning Point in Vietnam* (London: Osprey, 1990). Pham Van Son's *Tet 1968: The Communist Offensive that Marked the Beginning of America's Defeat in Vietnam*, 2 vols. (Salisbury, N.C.: Documentary Publications, 1980), is the official South Vietnamese history of Tet by an officer in South Vietnam's army. Also see Ronald H. Spector, *After Tet: The Bloodiest Year in Vietnam* (New York: Free Press, 1992). The fairness of the media in relating the story of Tet to the American public is questioned in Peter Braestrup, *Big Story: How the American Press and Television Reported and Interpreted the Crisis of Tet 1968 in Vietnam and Washington*, 2 vols. (Boulder, Colo.: Westview Press, 1977). Among the better studies of the North Vietnamese siege of the U.S. Marine and South Vietnamese encampment at Khe Sanh are John Prados and Ray W. Stubbe, *Valley of*

Decision: The Siege of Khe Sanh (Boston: Houghton Mifflin Company, 1991), and Robert Pisor, *The End of the Line: The Siege of Khe Sanh* (New York: Norton, 1982). The horror of battle is told in the words of its participants in Eric Hammel's *Khe Sanh: Siege in the Clouds, an Oral History* (New York: Crown, 1989). On Hue, see Keith W. Nolan, *Battle for Hue: Tet, 1968* (Novato, Calif.: Presidio Press, 1983), and Alje Vennema, *The Viet Cong Massacre at Hue* (New York: Vantage Press, 1976). Not long after Hue, on March 16, 1968, American soldiers in Son My, a hamlet of My Lai, executed some three or four hundred civilians. On the incident at My Lai, see Richard Hammer's *One Morning in the War: The Tragedy at Son My* (New York: Coward-McCann, 1970), and two books by investigative journalist Seymour Hersh, *My Lai 4: A Report on the Massacre and Its Aftermath* (New York: Random House, 1970) and *Cover-Up: The Army's Secret Investigation of the Massacre at My Lai 4* (New York: Random House, 1972).

The Antiwar Movement

Surveys of antiwar activity include Thomas Powers, *The War at Home: Vietnam and the American People, 1964–1968* (New York: Grossman, 1973); Nancy Zaroulis and Gerald Sullivan, *Who Spoke Up? American Protest against the War in Vietnam, 1963–1975* (Garden City, N.Y.: Doubleday, 1984); and Charles DeBenedetti and Charles Chatfield, *An American Ordeal: The Antiwar Movement of the Vietnam Era* (Syracuse: Syracuse University Press, 1990). More recent studies are Tom Wells, *The War Within: America's Battle over Vietnam* (Berkeley and Los Angeles: University of California Press, 1994), and Melvin Small and William D. Hoover, eds., *Give Peace a Chance: Exploring the Vietnam Antiwar Movement; Essays from the Charles DeBenedetti Memorial Conference* (Syracuse: Syracuse University Press, 1992). A number of the essays in Barbara L. Tischler, ed., *Sights on the Sixties* (New Brunswick, N.J.: Rutgers University Press, 1992), look at opposition to the war. Kenneth J. Heineman's *Campus Wars: The Peace Movement at American State Universities in the Vietnam Era* (New York: New York University Press, 1993) examines the peace movement on four campuses. Political opposition to the war and the influence of antiwar activity on politics are studied in Melvin Small's *Johnson, Nixon, and the Doves* (New Brunswick, N.J.: Rutgers University Press, 1988) and William C. Berman, *J. William Fulbright and the Vietnam War: The Dissent of a Political Realist* (Kent: Kent State University Press, 1988). African American criticisms of American involvement in Southeast Asia are collected in Clyde Taylor, ed., *Vietnam and Black America: An Anthology of Protest and Resistance* (Garden City, N.Y.: Doubleday-Anchor, 1973). On resistance to the draft, see Sherry Gershon Gottlieb, *Hell No, We Won't Go: Resisting the Draft during the Vietnam War* (New York: Viking, 1991), and David Surrey, *Choice of Conscience: Vietnam Era Military and Draft Resisters in Canada* (New York: Praeger, 1982). Controversial new books on the antiwar movement are Melvin Small, *Covering Dissent: The Media and the Anti-War Movement* (New Brunswick, N.J.: Rutgers University Press, 1995), and Adam Garfinkle, *Telltale Hearts: The Origins and Import of the Vietnam Antiwar Movement* (New York: St. Martin's Press, 1995).

The Last Years

Stephen Ambrose provides commentary on Richard Nixon in a three-volume biography (New York: Simon and Schuster): *Nixon: The Education of a Politician, 1913–1962* (1987); *Nixon: The Triumph of a Politician, 1962–1972* (1989); and *Nixon: Ruin and Triumph of the Presidency* (1992). Nixon's foreign policy is examined in Robert S. Litwack's *Detente and the Nixon Doctrine: American Foreign Policy and the Pursuit of Stability, 1969–1976* (New York: Cambridge University Press, 1984), and C. L. Sulzberger, *The World and Richard Nixon* (New York: Prentice-Hall, 1987). Nixon has described and defended his policies in a number of volumes of memoirs: *RN: The Memoirs of Richard Nixon* (New York: Grosset and Dunlap, 1978); *No More Vietnams* (New York: Arbor House, 1985); and *In the Arena: A Memoir of Victory, Defeat, and Renewal* (New York: Simon and Schuster, 1990). Henry Kissinger, who served both Nixon and Ford as Secretary of State, casts light on the processes by which the United States disengaged itself from Southeast Asia: *The White House Years* (Boston: Little, Brown, 1979) and *Years of Upheaval* (Boston: Little, Brown, 1982). Works critical of Kissinger are Robert D. Schulzinger, *Henry Kissinger: Doctor of Diplomacy* (New York: Columbia University Press, 1989); Roger Morris, *Uncertain Greatness: Henry Kissinger and American Foreign Policy* (New York: Harper and Row, 1977); and Seyom Brown, *The Crisis of Power: An Interpretation of United States Foreign Policy during the Kissinger Years* (New York: Columbia University Press, 1979).

The long road to an armistice and the withdrawal of U.S. troops from Vietnam is the subject of a number of analyses. In *When Governments Collide: Coercion and Diplomacy in the Vietnam Conflict, 1964–1968* (Berkeley and Los Angeles: University of California Press, 1980), Wallace J. Thies assesses Lyndon Johnson's failed efforts to bring Hanoi to a peace settlement. Gareth Porter's *A Peace Denied: The United States, Vietnam, and the Paris Agreement* (Bloomington: Indiana University Press, 1975) provides valuable documentation of the negotiations that led finally to the Paris treaty. Allen E. Goodman's *Lost Peace: America's Search for a Negotiated Settlement of the Vietnam War* (Stanford: Hoover Institution Press, 1978) argues that irreconcilable differences between the United States and the North Vietnamese were the reason the peace settlement failed. Critical of the Nixon peace are Tad Szulc's *The Illusion of Peace: Foreign Policy in the Nixon Years* (New York: Viking, 1978); Stuart A. Herrington, *A Peace with Honor? An American Reports on Vietnam, 1973–1975* (Novato, Calif.: Presidio Press, 1983); and Arnold Isaacs, *Without Honor: Defeat in Vietnam and Cambodia* (Baltimore: Johns Hopkins University Press, 1983).

An overview of relations between Laos and the United States is supplied in Charles A. Stevenson's *The End of Nowhere: American Policy toward Laos since 1954* (Boston: Beacon, 1972) and Norman B. Hannah's *The Key to Failure: Laos and the Vietnam War* (Lanham, Md.: Madison Books, 1987). The CIA's secret war in Laos is the subject of two books by Christopher Robbins, *Air America: The Story of the CIA's Secret Airlines* (New York: Putnam, 1979) and *The Ravens: The Men Who Flew in America's Secret War in Laos* (New York: Crown, 1987), and John Prados's *President's Secret Wars: CIA and Pentagon Covert Opera-*

tions since World War II (New York: William Morrow, 1986). Jane Hamilton-Merritt's recent *Tragic Mountains: The Hmong, the Americans, and the Secret Wars for Laos, 1942–1992* (Bloomington: Indiana University Press, 1993), is very critical of the American treatment of its Laotian allies, the Hmong people. Also see Timothy N. Castle, *At War in the Shadow of Vietnam: U.S. Military Aid to the Royal Lao Government, 1955–1975* (New York: Columbia University Press, 1993). Fred Branfman, ed., *Voices from the Plain of Jars* (New York: Harper and Row, 1972), is a collection of stories of Laotians responding to the U.S. bombings of their country. The 1971 American invasion of Laos is described in Keith W. Nolan, *Into Laos: The Story of Dewey Canyon II, Lam Son 719, Vietnam 1971* (Novato, Calif.: Presidio Press, 1986).

Nowhere were the effects of the Second Indochina War more devastating and brutal than in Cambodia. Marie Alexandrine Martin in *Cambodia: A Shattered Society*, trans. Mark W. McLeod (Berkeley and Los Angeles: University of California Press, 1994), tells the story of Cambodia since the end of World War II. Ben Kiernan's *How Pol Pot Came to Power* (New York: Routledge, 1987) assesses the development of Cambodian communism from the 1930s until 1975 when the Khmer Rouge seized power. The details and implications of America's other war in Cambodia are described in William Shawcross's excellent critical study *Sideshow: Kissinger, Nixon, and the Destruction of Cambodia* (New York: Simon and Schuster, 1979). Also see Keith William Nolan's *Into Cambodia: Spring Campaign, Summer Offensive, 1970* (Novato, Calif.: Presidio Press, 1970). The murderous activities of the fanatical Khmer Rouge, a faction of Cambodian communists, are witnessed in several sources. Among the best is William Shawcross's *The Quality of Mercy: Cambodia, Holocaust, and Modern Conscience* (New York: Simon and Schuster, 1984). Descriptions of the horrors of the Khmer genocide are given in a number of personal stories: James Fenton, *Cambodian Witness: An Autobiography of Someth May* (New York: Random House, 1987); Joan D. Criddle and Teeda Butt Mam, *To Destroy You Is No Loss: The Odyssey of a Cambodian Family* (New York: Atlantic Monthly Press, 1989); and Molyda Szymusiak, *The Stones Cry Out: A Cambodian Childhood, 1975–1980* (New York: Hill and Wang, 1986). The journalist Sydney H. Schanberg tells of the terrifying ordeal he suffered as a captive of the Khmer government in *The Death and Life of Dith Pran* (New York: Penguin, 1980), which became the basis for the 1984 film *The Killing Fields*.

Acknowledgments _____

THE AUTHOR would like to observe that, though their books and articles are not cited directly, this study is based on the hard work of many scholars and journalists. While this procedure allows the narrative and argument to flow without interruption, the debts to other writers are nonetheless extensive.

I am grateful for the criticisms of the individuals who have read parts of the manuscript: Virginia and Jim Bernhard, Mark Buckley, the late Robert Burner, Terry Cooney, Kenneth Dubuque, Tilden Edelstein, David Farber, Jack Garraty, Roland Guyotte, Ellis Hawley, Edwin King, James Kunen, Robert McColley, Forrest McDonald, Robert Marcus, James Olson, David Oshinsky, Randy Roberts, Norman Rosenberg, Mel Rosenthal, Gus Seligmann, Jr., Bernard Semmel, C. Vann Woodward, and Cary Wintz. Special thanks to James Mooney of American University for his perseverance in finding at the Library of Congress a stream of esoteric works on the sixties and for his intelligence in recognizing the meaning and significance of each. Numerous students at the State University of New York at Stony Brook gave helpful advice: Steve Fuchs, Dirk Gerson, Michael Kelly, Craig Markson, Shari Osborn, Ward Regan, and John Stern among them. My intellectual debt to Thomas R. West is sufficiently large to occupy the dedication page, and my thanks and love for my wife, Sandy, are immeasurable. The staff of Princeton University Press, including Brigitta van Rheinberg, Sara Mullen, Lauren Oppenheim, Lauren Lepow, Harriet Hitch, and Frank Mahood, was enormously patient and helpful.

I would also like to express gratitude to the American historians whose work drew me into the profession after I was graduated from college in 1958: my doctoral sponsor, Richard Hofstadter; Arthur S. Link; William Leuchtenburg; Frank Freidel; and Arthur Schlesinger, Jr.

Index

David Burner is a political historian at the State University of New York, Stony Brook. A list of his books appears at the front of this volume.